WHITE CIVILITY:
THE LITERARY PROJECT OF ENGLISH CANADA

DANIEL COLEMAN

White Civility
The Literary Project of English Canada

UNIVERSITY OF TORONTO PRESS
Toronto Buffalo London

© University of Toronto Press Incorporated 2006
Toronto Buffalo London
Printed in Canada

ISBN 13: 978-0-8020-3707-7
ISBN 10: 0-8020-3707-0

Printed on acid-free paper

Library and Archives Canada Cataloguing in Publication

Coleman, Dan, 1961–
  White civility : the literary project of English Canada / Daniel Coleman.

Includes bibliographical references and index.
ISBN-13: 978-0-8020-3707-7
ISBN-10: 0-8020-3707-0

1. Canadian literature (English) – British-Canadian authors – History and
criticism.   2. Canadian literature (English) – White authors – History and
criticism.   3. Race relations in literature.   4. Canadian – Race relations.
I. Title.

PS8191.R33C64 2006   C810.9'8112   C2005-907491-4

University of Toronto Press acknowledges the financial assistance to
its publishing program of the Canada Council for the Arts and the
Ontario Arts Council.

This book has been published with the help of a grant from the Canadian
Federation for the Humanities and Social Sciences, through the Aid to
Scholarly Publications Programme, using funds provided by the Social
Sciences and Humanities Research Council of Canada.

University of Toronto Press acknowledges the financial support for
its publishing activities of the Government of Canada through the
Book Publishing Industry Development Program (BPIDP).

Contents

Illustrations

Acknowledgments

It is a great pleasure and a rare privilege to carry out research. The opportunity to give continuous attention to the topic of study, to read widely, and to gather the details one has learned into a sustained piece of writing is immensely rewarding. While much of this enterprise must be carried out alone, I am very aware of how many people and organizations have contributed to making it feasible for me to undertake this research in the first place. This project has been possible because I have had the good fortune to live and work among people who have seen its importance, have supported me tirelessly, and have offered their criticism, understanding, and fellowship in innumerable ways.

First, I thank Wendy Coleman, whose love and intelligence created the conditions that allowed me to pursue a career in writing and scholarship. I would also like to thank my parents, Murray and Bea Coleman, who taught me by example how reading, prayer, and study were essential for a focused day. I am deeply grateful to lifelong friends such as Gary and Carla Nelson, David Gray, Michael Bucknor, Grant Moore and Dana Antaya-Moore, and Timothy Bascom, who have shown the depth of their friendship through their interest in the work I was doing on this book. And I am very fortunate to work with dynamic and wonderfully generous colleagues at McMaster University whose own writing, research, and social activism have been inspiring. I have looked to them and consulted with them repeatedly throughout the writing of this book. They include Donald Goellnicht, Lorraine York, Michael Ross, Mary O'Connor, Grace Kehler, Imre Szeman, Peter Walmsley, Sarah Brophy, Michael Gauvreau, Gary Warner, and Travis Kroeker.

Colleagues at other universities have contributed significantly to improving this work; these include the two anonymous readers for the Press, who offered crucial criticism, and Janice Fiamengo and Paul Hjartarson, each of whom gave insightful comments on portions of the draft. The staff of the Mills Library at McMaster University have efficiently located materials necessary to this project, and I owe a debt of particular thanks to the Interlibrary Loans staff, including Donna Millard, Greta Culley, Ann Pottier, Valerie Thomas, Laurie Compton, Helen Creedon, and Kathie Fairman. I have had the very great pleasure of working with brilliant graduate students in the Department of English and Cultural Studies at McMaster. They have carried out supplementary research, offered comments, and enlightened me through their own research projects. Kate Higginson, Sabine Milz, Rick Monture, Marc Ouellette, and Melissa Smith were delightfully helpful and extremely thorough research assistants, and I have also had the pleasure of working with Jennifer Blair, John Corr, Elizabeth Jackson, and Agnes Kramer-Hamstra. The members of the Christianity and Theory discussion group offered helpful comments and criticisms on chapter 4; at the time they included Deborah Bowen, Hugh Cook, Dannabang Kuwobong, and Grace Kehler.

Siobhan McMenemy, at the University of Toronto Press, offered perceptive criticisms that produced a shorter, more streamlined manuscript, and Elizabeth Hulse excised errors and coordinated references with her keen editorial eye. The research and writing of this book would not have been possible without a research grant from the Social Sciences and Humanities Research Council of Canada, a junior research grant from the Secretary of State (Multiculturalism), an Arts Research Board grant from McMaster University, and substantial research funding from the Faculty of Humanities at McMaster University in support of my Tier II Canada Research Chair. Once again, I gratefully acknowledge Grandma Tulloch's armchair, whose steady support bore me up under weighty thoughts.

WHITE CIVILITY

1 White Civility: The Literary Project of English Canada

Himani Bannerji's short story 'The Other Family' tells of a South Asian mother in Toronto who asks her little girl over the supper table what she did in school that day. The mother experiences a shock when her daughter gets out the picture she drew in response to her teacher's request that the students draw a picture of their families. '"Listen," said the mother, "this is not your family. I, you and your father are dark-skinned, dark-haired. I don't have a blond wig hidden in my closet, my eyes are black, not blue, and your father's beard is black, not red, do you have a white skin, a button nose with freckles, blue eyes and blond hair tied into a pony tail?"' The little girl replies tellingly: '"I drew it from a book ... all our books have this same picture of the family ... And everyone else drew it too"' (142–3). Bannerji's parable was published during the heights of anti-racist protests in the late 1980s and early 1990s, when Black, Native, and Asian Canadian writers were protesting their continued marginalization in the Canadian arts scene despite the inclusive-sounding directives that had recently been made official in the Multiculturalism Act of 1988. I want to suggest that this story signals a genealogy beyond its specific historical moment, for its outline of how the workings of White normativity shape people's perceptions of themselves, their families, and their relation to social legitimacy highlights two important starting points for my study of the construction of White, English Canadian privilege.[1]

First, it identifies books and the imaginative worlds they present as important means by which the pedagogy of White normativity is purveyed, and second, it demonstrates how the privilege of the norm operates paradoxically as being so obvious that it remains unexamined: it is only by the misfit between the girl's real family and her fantasized one that we (readers and the girl herself) see the artificiality of the blond-haired, blue-eyed family's occupation of the standard position. 'The Other Family' was first published in Linda Hutcheon and Marion Richmond's ground-breaking collection of ethnic and racial minority writing *Other Solitudes*, a title which, like Bannerji's, makes its meaning through contrast, this time through its departure from the bicultural model of Canadian origins made famous in Hugh MacLennan's *Two Solitudes*. In both Bannerji's and Hutcheon and Richmond's titles, 'other' functions, as Bannerji explains in a different context, only by reference to what is understood to be the norm or the standard (*Dark* 111–12). Likewise, multiculturalism itself, as a relatively new way of perceiving the Canadian populace, stands against the conventional way of conceiving nations, which is still largely dominated by the nineteenth-century romantic-nationalist idea that equated each nation with a single culture. 'Multiculturalism,' then, like 'other,' signals difference from a previously assumed standard.

Indeed, many commentators have celebrated the veritable explosion of multicultural or minority writing over the past thirty years in Canada, because they see in it the potential to pluralize what had been a bicultural image of Canada. Christl Verduyn, who has published extensively on this boom in minority writing, exemplifies this common critical move when she writes that

> Canada is being reconstructed through the writing of authors like [Dionne] Brand, [Claire] Harris, and [M. NourbeSe] Philip ... These changes to the framework of Canadian literature, as I encountered it in the 1970s, are 'making a difference,' to play on the title of the most recent anthology of Canadian 'multicultural' literature, a 500-page volume by Smaro Kamboureli (1996) ... This new 'construct' of Canada comprises not just, or even primarily, physical or geographical dimensions but also psychological or emotional dimensions and political passions – as is expressed in the writings of Canadians who identify with ethnic or racial minorities. (109)

In my earlier book *Masculine Migrations*, I myself made use of this logic to describe the way in which Canadian assumptions of normative masculinity are refracted and called into question through the perspectives of immigrant Canadian writers of South Asian and Caribbean descent. The assumptions which I made there and which are illustrated in Verduyn's comment beg the questions that I wish to address in this book: How did this normative concept of (English) Canadianness come to be established in the first place? What are its elements? What is its genealogy? And how might an understanding of the process of its establishment enable twenty-first-century Canadians to anticipate and resist its continuing coercive power?

These questions turned the present study in the direction of literary and cultural history, and over the past eight years I have examined the popular texts, cultural practices, and literary institutions of the past to try to understand how the norm or centre came to be assumed as normative and central. I learned, in brief, that White Canadian culture is obsessed, and organized by its obsession, with the problem of its own civility. As my title, *White Civility: The Literary Project of English Canada,* indicates, my contention is that what has come to be known as English Canada is and has been, as the reference in Bannerji's story to the girl's school books suggests, a project of literary, among other forms of cultural, endeavour and that the central organizing problematic of this endeavour has been the formulation and elaboration of a specific form of whiteness based on a British model of civility.[2] By means of this conflation of whiteness with civility, whiteness has been naturalized as the norm for English Canadian cultural identity.

From my readings of early Canadian fiction, poetry, drama, journalism, and political writing, as well as Canadian social and political history, I have selected four ubiquitous allegorical figures and dedicated a chapter to an intensive study of each one. Chapter 2 examines the figure of the Loyalist brother because the story of the United Empire Loyalists is one of the most commonly cited narratives for explaining why Canada exists as a separate entity from the United States. The Loyalist story of Canadian origins is fascinating, not just because of its adamant insistence upon the Britishness of Canada's founders despite the fact that there were more Germans, Dutch, and Iroquois among the first arrivals from the United States than there were people from the British Isles (see Knowles 16–17), but also because of the remarkable prominence of violence among the British themselves in this oft-repeated narrative of how Canadian civility emerged from a rejection of warmongering and a desire for monarchially administered peace. Chapter 3 studies the figure of the enterprising Scottish orphan not only because the Scots were primary inventers of English Canada through their leading roles in business (the Hudson's Bay and North West Companies, the liquor industry, the Canadian Pacific Railway), in politics (from Sir John A. Macdonald onwards), in religion (the Presbyterian, Highland Catholic, and Baptist churches and later the United Church of Canada), and in

education (nearly every nineteenth-century Canadian university was dominated by Scottish or Scottish-trained faculty, including Dalhousie, Queen's,
McGill, McMaster, and even Toronto after Bishop Strachan – an Anglicized Scot – had to relinquish his grip), but also because Scots, historically, were the primary inventers and promoters of the category of
Britishness that is the conceptual foundation of the Canadian idea of
civility. Chapter 3 shows that the pan-ethnic leeway of Britishness allowed
Scots who were being driven off their lands in Scotland an upward social
mobility in the colonies unavailable back home. As a result, Scottish self-
improvement and enterprise became central principles of Canadian
middle-class concepts of what constitutes civic participation.

The fourth chapter turns to the figure of the muscular Christian, a
specifically Protestant image of socially engaged, upwardly mobile Christianity that fuelled the progressive movements of the early twentieth
century when waves of eastern European immigrants were settling the
recently acquired prairie provinces and when British Canadians therefore questioned how far their pan-ethnic concept of civility could stretch.
Muscular Christianity contributed to the moral purpose that drove a
whole range of socially progressive movements, from church-based social service activism to the women's movement and from labour activism
to the emerging profession of social work. Muscular Christian ideals
simultaneously advocated charitable welcome to 'foreigners' and other
less-fortunate people and, in the very act, represented these others as
beneficiaries, rather than full members, of the civil collective. Chapter 5
extends the discussion of muscular Christianity into a study of the figure
of the maturing colonial son, which allegorizes Canada as a youth that
has recently emerged from its colonial dependency and is now stepping
forth independently onto the international stage. According to this
allegory, the signs of the young nation's maturity were founded upon its
civility, especially its civil treatment of less-fortunate people, whether
world-weary immigrants needing a peaceful new home, even more weary
Aboriginals, who were believed to be fast approaching extinction, or
francophone adopted brothers, who had been abandoned by their French
Catholic fatherland and who needed a way to belong in a new, expanded
British polity.

Together, these allegorical figures – the Loyalist brother, the enterprising Scottish orphan, the muscular Christian, and the maturing colonial son – enable us to trace the ways in which these regularly repeated
literary personifications for the Canadian nation mediated and gradually
reified the privileged, normative status of British whiteness in English

Canada. By reference to these four selected figures, then, this book traces a history for Canada's 'fictive ethnicity,' a term developed by Étienne Balibar to describe the way in which a nation represents the narrative of its diverse peoples' past and future as if they formed a natural community. 'No nation possesses an ethnic base naturally,' writes Balibar, 'but as social formations are nationalized, the populations included within them, divided up among them or dominated by them are ethnicized – that is, represented in the past or in the future *as if* they formed a natural community, possessing of itself an identity of origins, culture, and interests which transcends individuals and social conditions' ('The Nation Form' 224). In order to understand the power of the image that caused the little girl in Bannerji's story to draw her family as White, we need to unravel English Canada's fictive ethnicity; indeed, this historical project is vital not only to a reconsideration of Canada's past but also, as the multicultural context of Bannerji's parable indicates, to the critical reconsideration of multiculturalism that has occupied centre stage in recent debates over Canadian pluralism, citizenship, and race relations.

For many Canadians, multiculturalism represents Canadian progressiveness, not only in comparison to the monocultural nationalisms of other countries but also in comparison to earlier eras of monocultural nationalism in Canada. Indeed, multiculturalism in recent public opinion polls has been selected as the most fundamental and proudly revered feature of Canadian 'identity' (see Mackey, ch. 5). It comes as something of a shock to White English Canadians, then, that the policy which is so widely believed to represent the high achievement of Canadian liberal civility has come under fire from the very people it supposedly protects and includes in the civil sphere. In a 1990 article entitled 'Why Multiculturalism Can't End Racism,' M. NourbeSe Philip, for example, argued that, 'multiculturalism, as we know it, has no answers for the problems of racism, or white supremacy – unless it is combined with a clearly articulated policy of anti-racism, directed at rooting out the effects of racist and white supremacist thinking … And we cannot begin such an eradication by forgetting how [this] brutal aspect of Canadian culture was formed. It is for this reason that an understanding of the ideological lineage of this belief system is so important to any debate on racism and multiculturalism' (185). As Philip's article argues and Bannerji's parable portrays, whatever civil ideals multiculturalism may represent, whiteness still occupies the positions of normalcy and privilege in Canada, and anti-racist activity remains hamstrung until we begin to carry out the historical work that traces its genealogy, or 'the ideological lineage of this belief system,' in an effort to combat the national injunction to forget the brutal elements of our racial history.

In March 2004, Doudou Diène, Special Rapporteur on racism, racial discrimination, and xenophobia to the United Nations Commission on Human Rights, published the report of his visit to Canada during which he had met with federal and provincial government officials, members of the Canadian Race Relations Foundation, and members of Aboriginal and ethnic minority groups across the country. His report concludes that, although Canada has made great progress in combating racism by establishing inclusive and protective legislation such as the Canadian Charter of Rights and Freedoms and the Multiculturalism Act, racism still persists, and Canada has not developed an effective 'intellectual and ethical strategy' for disseminating inclusive and anti-racist values throughout the country. The first objective in formulating this intellectual and ethical strategy, he suggests, would be to develop 'a better understanding of the deep roots of the history, culture, and mentality of racism and discrimination' (24). Like NourbeSe Philip, he suggests that we cannot begin to combat everyday racism in Canada until we unearth, rather than suppress, the history of White supremacy and colonial racism that are fundamental to the establishment of Canada as a nation.[3]

In a seminal article published in 1882, the French scholar Ernest Renan identified the centrality of this forgetfulness to the ideology of the nation when he wrote: 'Forgetting, I would even go so far as to say historical error, is a crucial factor in the creation of a nation, which is why progress in historical studies often constitutes a danger for nationality. Indeed, historical enquiry brings to light deeds of violence which took place at the origin of all political formations, even of those whose consequences have been altogether beneficial. Unity is always effected by means of brutality' (Renan 11; see also Lynette Hunter 16). If Bannerji's parable illustrates the psychological or social violence produced by standardized whiteness, the history of genocide against and cultural decimation of Indigenous people in Canada provides many instances of outright brutality. Both kinds of violence, and a whole range of injustices in between them, must be repeatedly forgotten if White Canadians wish to sit comfortably with their claim to multicultural civility. A major antidote to nationalism's determined disavowal, therefore, comes in a refusal to forget the history of genocide and cultural decimation of Indigenous peoples in Canada that is disavowed by the image of the peaceful settler. Many Canadian anti-racist scholars have recently worked to re-educate themselves and broader Canadian society to the repressed elements of Canada's history of White British supremacy; so mainstream Canadians have been reminded about the extermination of the Aboriginal Beothuks in Newfoundland, the deportation of the French-speaking Acadians from Nova Scotia, the discrimination practised against Black Loyalists and their descendants from 1784 onwards, the head tax upon and eventual exclusion of Chinese immigrants after 1923, the internment of eastern Europeans during the First World War and of Japanese Canadians during the Second World War, the refusal of entry to Jews fleeing Nazi Europe, and the ongoing criminalization of Indigenous and Black Canadians.[4]

Canadians have been reminded of the brutal histories that our fictive ethnicity would disavow, but many of us Canadians may nonetheless be reluctant to give away our pride in Canada's relatively civil racial history in comparison to more dramatically traumatic racial histories and especially our hopes in our civil history's most recent manifestation in the ideal of multiculturalism. We may be troubled by the history of White dominance but still attracted (or distracted) by the ideal of Canadian civility. The question arises: How can we critically examine the reproduction of Canadian whiteness in relation to the real project of its civility? I say the *real project* of its civility as a deliberate alternative to saying the *myth* of its civility. For I am not among those who would trivialize the prodigious effort to create a civil society in Canada by considering it a mere ruse or theatrical trick – as if civility were an easy accomplishment and its failure ready cause for derision and finger-pointing. It would be easy to identify the racism of a completely fraudulent and hypocritical civility. It is much harder and, I believe, more productive in the long term to find ways to analyse the White supremacy embedded in a real project of civility.[5] For it is my contention that civility itself is a positive value that is structurally ambivalent. This is to say that at the same time that civility involves the creation of justice and equality, it simultaneously creates borders to the sphere in which justice and equality are maintained. To note that the borders of civility are maintained by uncivil violence and unfair exclusions is not to deny the degrees of justice and equality that have been achieved within the civil sphere. Rather, it is to insist that these borders have always been, will always be, the sites where new projects of civility are under negotiation. The purpose of looking at how the borders were drawn, challenged, and renegotiated in the past is not only to change from a static to a kinetic model of the civil sphere but also to allow ourselves to be 'read by' the past, to remind ourselves that the margins of our own understandings of civility are often just as violent and exclusive as they were in past generations, though the specific categories for exclusion and their rationalizations may have shifted.

Three general areas of study – feminist-inspired masculinity studies, critical whiteness studies, and Canadian studies of race and racism – have set the groundwork and given me the critical vocabulary to formulate my argument in this book, which is that the central organizing problematic of English Canadian whiteness is a specific form of civility modelled upon the gentlemanly code of Britishness.[6] I call it an organizing problematic because Canadian civility is contradictory and ambivalent, never consistent within itself. Because this very problematic, troubled quality makes it dynamic, it is a project that is able to organize a diverse population around the standardizing ideals of whiteness, masculinity, and Britishness.[7] Since the categories of privilege attempt to secure their privilege by rendering their preferential status as natural and therefore as immutable and irresistible, it is important that we remind ourselves that they are in fact projects. Deeply invested in maintaining, if not increasing, their social status, they are passively dynamic, always engaged in the activities of self-invention, reinvention, self-maintenance, and adaptation, even as they try to avoid observation or detection as anything but fixed.

The meanings of the word 'civility' in the *Oxford English Dictionary* extend from 'a community of citizens collectively,' 'good polity; orderly state,' and 'conformity to the principles of social order' to 'the state of being civilized; freedom from barbarity' and 'polite or liberal education ... good breeding.' Taken together, these various meanings show that the English language's concept of civility combines *the temporal notion* of civilization as progress that was central to the idea of modernity and the colonial mission with *the moral-ethical concept* of a (relatively) peaceful order – that is to say, the orderly regulation between individual liberty and collective equality that has been fundamental to the politics of the modern nation state.[8] In the nineteenth- and early twentieth-century context of my study, the temporal concept of progress and the moral-ethical ideal of orderliness were demonstrated by cultivated, polite behaviour (most commonly modelled on the figure of the bourgeois gentleman), which, in turn, made these concepts fundamental to the production and education of the individual citizen.

For example, at the National Conference on Character Education in Relation to Canadian Citizenship, held in Winnipeg in October 1919, four months after the General Strike and when it was still widely believed the days of rioting and violence had been spurred on by what were commonly called enemy aliens, invited speaker Dr Henry Suzallo, president of the University of Washington, explained to his Canadian listeners that many immigrants were ignorant of how to behave properly under liberal democracy. But they could be taught civilized behaviour, he insisted: 'You can control a man in two ways – by putting a club on one side of his head, or putting an idea inside his head. One is external control and the other is internal control. One is coercive and the other is educative control' (qtd. in Mitchell 17). The advantage of the latter, of course, is that the individual then goes on to govern his or her own behaviour; enemy aliens become citizens when the ideas in their heads make the policeman's club unnecessary. Furthermore, education in civility shepherds people onto the path of progress because it names a future ideal as if it were a present norm. It projects an ideal of social interaction (all members of society should be freely included and accorded equal respect) as something to which individuals should aspire: if you wish to join the egalitarian progressive company, you must be willing to improve yourself, to become worthy of the respect that characterizes the civil group. In this way, civility operates as a mode of internal management: the subjects of the civil order discipline their conduct in order to participate in the civil realm, and they themselves gain or lose legitimacy in an internally striated civil society depending on the degree to which they conform to its ideals.[9]

Combining as it does the temporal notion of progress with the ethical-moral concept of peaceful order, civility purveys the time-space metaphor of the race of civilizations. Departing from previous understandings of race as an eternally fixed and immutable destiny, liberal Canadians of the late nineteenth and early twentieth centuries believed that all people had the potential to be civil, but some societies were farther ahead on the single timeline of civilization, while others were 'backward' or delayed. C.A. Magrath demonstrated this line of thinking in *Canada's Growth and Problems Affecting It* (1909) when he observed that many areas of southeastern Europe had been oppressed for centuries and therefore were 'behind the march of civilization.' Not through their own fault, but as a result of their having been denied familiarity with liberal democratic politics, people from such impoverished backgrounds 'cannot understand the meaning of liberty, which to them is licence, [they] evidently have an intense hatred for the majesty of the law'; as a result, 'we' – English Canadians – must be patient with 'them,' for 'it will take many years under the British constitution with our free institutions to translate

such people into good, intelligent citizens' (qtd. in Howard Palmer 315).
By means of this exemplary time-space metaphor, civility becomes, to
borrow a phrase from Jennifer Henderson, a means by which 'race has
been attached not just to bodies but also to forms of conduct' (18).

A prime instance how civility's time-space image of progress enforces
certain codes for individual conduct can be seen in the way that the idea
of progress itself is deeply informed by a central value of whiteness that
Richard Dyer calls 'spirit' or 'enterprise.' According to Dyer, enterprise
is often presented as the sign of White spirit – that is, to a valuation of
energy, will, discovery, science, progress, the building of nations, the
organization of labour, and especially leadership. 'The idea of leadership,' he writes, 'suggests both a narrative of human progress and the
peculiar quality required to effect it. Thus white people [are understood
naturally to] lead humanity forward because of their temperamental
qualities of leadership: will power, far-sightedness, energy' (31). Of course,
as Imre Szeman has discussed of European modernity in general, this
dense interweaving of White enterprise and civility as progress insists
upon an isochronous temporality (i.e., a single timeline); it does not
consider the possibilities of 'allochrony,' that different civilizations might
operate on different temporal scales of progress, ingress, or regress (191,
193).

European colonial expansion, as Stuart Hall explains in 'The West
and the Rest,' was premised on an isochronous idea of progress. He
observes that colonial-era Europeans tended to believe that 'there was
one path to civilization and social development, and that all societies
could be ranked or placed early or late, lower or higher, on the same
scale' (312). This idea of social evolution, however, introduced
colonialism's troubling ambivalence, for while it confirmed the civility
and modernity of White Europeans by contrast with the stages of primi-
tiveness it posited among Europe's others, it also suggested these others
could be civilized and that, indeed, the signs of European civility would
be best demonstrated when those who were well advanced on the scale
of modernity helped those who were less advanced to ascend the evolutionary ladder.[10] To put it differently, civility became more than something a person or culture simply *had*; it became something that person
or culture *did* – it became a primary instance of what Ruth Frankenberg
in a different context has called a 'white cultural practice' (194). The
idea of civility as a (White) cultural practice not only made it a mode of
internal management and self-definition, because it distinguished the
civil from the uncivil, but it also made it a mode of external manage-

ment, because it gave civil subjects a mandate for managing the circumstances of those perceived as uncivil.

The ambivalence or contradiction of civility, then, can be seen as a central paradox of liberal modernity, for the civil sphere or stage of advancement in which all participants are guaranteed liberty and equality must be protected from those belated or primitive elements or identities, within and without, which may threaten, intentionally or not, that freedom and equality. As a result, the borders of civility must be policed in order to protect this vulnerable civil space of the advanced from those who, in the words of Johannes Fabian, can be denied as coeval, as inhabiting the same time (see Mignolo 35). As Henry Louis Gates Jr, Cornell West, and David Theo Goldberg have shown in their separate studies, in the very period of the Enlightenment, when concepts of democratic rule, egalitarianism, and individual liberty were emerging as social ideals, there also arose the most nefarious and complex system the world has ever seen for classifying and stratifying humans into a hierarchy of racial types. Goldberg summarizes the situation thus: 'So the irony of modernity, the liberal paradox comes down to this: As modernity commits itself progressively to idealized principles of liberty, equality, and fraternity, as it increasingly insists upon the moral irrelevance of race, there is a multiplication of racial identities and the sets of exclusions they prompt and rationalize, enable and sustain ... [T]he more open to difference liberal modernity declares itself, the more dismissive of difference it becomes and the more closed it seeks to make the circle of acceptability' (6–7). Thus modern civility is, paradoxically, a limited or constrained universality that tends to proliferate and striate not only external but also internal differences.[11]

While there are many examples of this paradox of a limited or constrained universality in the history of Canada's project to establish itself as a liberal, modern, and civil nation, such as the immigration policies that attempted to block the entry of Oklahoma Blacks in 1910 and 1911 or that kept Sikhs on the *Komagata Maru* from landing in Vancouver harbour in 1914, the example most fundamental to the constitution of Canadian settler culture is surely the treatment of First Nations people throughout Canadian history. The idea of a bounded civility is clearly evident in the early legislation imposed upon Aboriginal people in Canada, such as the Act for the Gradual Civilization of the Indian Tribes (1857), the Civilization and Enfranchisement Act (1859), and the Indian Act (1876), which collectively viewed Aboriginal people as 'uncivilized human beings whose cultures were decidedly inferior to British culture'

(Satzewich, 'Introduction' 15). Following in the same vein, the residential school system established in the late nineteenth century was based on the racist belief that Aboriginal family and cultural systems were hopelessly 'backward' and therefore culturally bankrupt. Accordingly, the Indian Act between 1880 and 1951 outlawed participation in potlatches, the Sun Dance, and other important Indigenous ceremonies; until 1927 the same act forbade any person to receive money for helping a Native person or group to pursue a legal claim, effectively excluding First Nations people from legal consultation and due process; from 1885 to 1930, the pass law forbade departure from official reserve lands without permission of government-appointed Indian agents (Stasiulis and Jhappan 115); status Indians could not vote in federal elections until 1960; and they were also required to seek permission from the federal government to sell any crops or commodities produced on reserve land. Most of these policies, as Vic Satzewich notes, were 'based on the assumption that Aboriginal people had a child-like nature and needed the help and protection of benevolent government officials who had their best interests at heart' ('Introduction' 15–16).

This view of Indigenous people as delayed in the race of civilizations is clearly schematized in the painting *Civilization and Barbarism* by Canadian artist William George Richardson Hind (1833–89), which makes an allegorical tableau out of the contrast between the dejected figures of the Native people, whose only adornments are blankets (likely gotten from Hudson's Bay Company stores) and who watch passively as a settler rides by smartly in his horse-drawn wagon on a new road that extends in the distance to a snug new settlement of houses and barns (see illus. 1). The Natives are stationary, while progress, in the form of the settler, is clearly passing them by. The concept of civility, therefore, as it evolved under the contradictory impulses of Enlightenment modernity, could rationalize, first, the production of Aboriginal status and, then, its exclusion from the civil sphere, where equality and liberty were 'universally' enjoyed by means of the time-space image of progress, which represented Indigenous people as delayed in the process of civilization, as children or primitives who must be educated before they could be welcomed into the advanced company of the civil.[12]

The timeline of the race of civilizations, however, poses specific problems for settler-invader colonies such as Canada, for the members of these colonies, where expatriate communities from the colonial centres established long-term resident populations, experience the temporal and geographical divisions of the colonial arrangement not just in exter-

1   The race between civilizations becomes a tableau in Canadian artist William George Richardson Hind's painting *Civilization and Barbarism* (c. 1870).

nal political relations (as would commonly be the case in resource-exploitation colonies that did not establish permanent expatriate communities) but also within their own psyches (Lawson 23). The settler-colonist occupies a temporal space between the projected and assumed civility of the metropolitan power and the disavowed and resistant civility of the Indigenous population in the hinterland. Settler colonies are founded on a paradox in that 'they simultaneously resisted and accommodated the authority of an imperialist Europe,' by which process they gained relative economic prosperity and autonomy compared with resource-exploitation colonies (Stasiulis and Youval-Davis, 'Introduction' 4). Alan Lawson reconfigures Immanuel Wallerstein's First-Second-and-Third-Worlds configuration to account for the unique position of settler-invader colonies. Observing that much postcolonial criticism published in Britain and the United States tends to operate upon a First World–Third World binary, he calls attention to 'the Second World of the settler as a place caught between two First Worlds, two origins of authority and authenticity: the originating world of Europe, the imperium, as source of the Second World's principal cultural authority; and that other First World, that of the First Nations, whose authority the settlers not only effaced and replaced but also desired. (This perception is triggered by the very canny insistence of Canadian Native peoples on being called First Nations.) To each of these First Worlds, the settlers are secondary – indeed, supplementary' (29).

The situation of settler-colonial subjectivity sketched by Lawson has several implications for the theory of civility I have outlined above. First, the settler-colonist internalizes the ambivalence of civility in the sense that the settler is both the bearer of the civilizing mission who suffers the paranoia of colonial civility's legitimacy (to echo Homi Bhabha's famous essay 'Sly Civility': maybe the Native hates me, behind his mask of courtesy; maybe the Native will insist that our civility is not civility) and the colonial who fears that he is derided by the metropolitan representative of civility (maybe the metropolitan gentleman despises me, behind his patronizing courtesy).[13] Having internalized civility's ambivalence, the settler-colonist also internalizes imperialism's temporal gap, feeling himself to be caught in the time-space delay between the metropolitan place where civility is made and legislated and the colonial place where it is enacted and enforced. He feels an anxiety of belatedness that he must hurry to catch up, to leap from primitive, colonial incivility to advanced, modern civility. This temporal anxiety is clearly evident in A.J.M. Smith's famous argument in 'Nationalism and Canadian Poetry' that Canadians must abandon their nineteenth-century parochial nationalism and step forward into cosmopolitan modernity.[14] Because of this feeling of belatedness, the settler must construct, by a double process of speedy indigenization and accelerated self-civilization, his priority and superiority to latecomers; that is, by representing himself as already indigenous, the settler claims priority over newer immigrants and, by representing himself as already civilized, he claims superiority to Aboriginals and other non-Whites.[15] Finally, the colonial settler's belatedness is intensified by the delay of writing, for the most legitimate and respectable site of publication is the metropolitan centre, where significance is determined and assessed. The settler may speak in and about the colony, but the written version of his speech will be interpreted in the metropolitan centre (judged in accordance with British constitutional law or with the conventions of British literary taste) for its measure of civility. Thus his speech is required and judged beyond his reach, in a different cultural environment, and only after delay.

That this awareness of distance and belatedness in relation to the metropolitan centres of sophistication was deeply internalized can be seen in the fact that it appears repeatedly in early Canadian literary critics' comments about Canada's belatedness in the race for civility. 'The literature of the world is the foot-prints of human progress' (50), wrote Edward Hartley Dewart in his famous introductory essay to *Selections from Canadian Poets* (1864), the first anthology of Canadian poetry. 'If we cannot point to a past rich with historic names, we have the inspiring spectacle of a great country, in her youthful might, girding herself for a race for an honorable place among the nations of the world' (59). Literary productivity, according to Dewart's allegorical figure, constitutes a foot race between civilizations for the front position in the contest of civility. Modifying this allegory from a foot race to the comparative achievements of youth and adulthood, many nineteenth-century Canadians complained that the conditions for this competition were unfair, for Canada was but a child forced to compete with adults. 'We are also in the anomalous position of being a young race born into the old age of the world,' wrote University of Toronto professor of English Pelham Edgar in 1912. 'All the countries of Europe have passed through the ballad and epic stage of unselfconscious literary production, and we are only vicariously the heirs of all this antecedent activity. They have a mythical as well as an historic past to inspire them, and they possess vast tracts of legends still unexplored which yield ... stores of poetic material' (111). 'Canada was born too late,' critic L. O'Loane lamented in 1890. 'She is the child of old people. She is like the heir to millions: in inheriting the richest literature in the world she is bound in golden fetters ... The masters of English prose and verse have weighted us. We joy in our magnificent possessions, but how shall the sons of giants be equal to or greater than their fathers?' (83). Given the anxious situation wherein the settler-invader needs to legitimize his dispossession of Aboriginals from their lands by reference to the superior civility that he has brought with him, and given that the source of his civility in the metropolitan centre precisely undermined his claim for a mature and established civility in the colonies, on what basis could Canadian civility be conceived? I have already hinted that the answer lay in Britishness – a Britishness, however, that was formulated not in the metropolitan centre but in the colonial peripheries.

'British' and 'Briton' are not, contrary to much popular usage today, synonymous with 'English'; indeed, as Robert Crawford and Linda Colley have shown, 'British' was a term employed by Lowland Scots after the Treaty of Union in 1707 to manufacture a looser cultural identity that would represent them not as junior partners in the larger project of English imperialism but as senior members and equals. Thus Scottish, Welsh, and, later, Irish immigrants in the colonies who would have hated to be called 'English' in their homelands loosened themselves from the restrictions of these old sectional identifications by espousing Britishness (Akenson 395–7; Trumpener 253–4, 300n63). Signs of how Scots led the way in formulating the pan-ethnic notion of Britishness include the Scottish production of the *Encyclopedia Britannica* in the eighteenth century (Crawford 106) and their writing of the popular hymns of the imperial age, including James Thomson's lyrics for 'Rule Britannia'

2   Pan-ethnic Britishness, as celebrated in Alexander Muir's 'The Maple Leaf Forever,' is stretched to include Europeans and Americans in this cartoon from the Liberal election pamphlet *Laurier Does Things*.

(Crawford 49–50) and Alexander Muir's 'The Maple Leaf Forever' (Waterston 28; see illus. 2). Indeed, the opening stanza of the latter song, which served as English Canada's unofficial national anthem until it was nudged aside by 'O Canada!' in the 1960s (but not by legislation until 1980), conveys the image of pan-ethnic Britishness as constitutive of Canadian national identity:

> In days of yore,
> From Britain's shore
> Wolfe the dauntless hero came
> And planted firm Britannia's flag
> On Canada's fair domain.
> Here may it wave,
> Our boast, our pride
> And joined in love together,
> The thistle, shamrock, rose entwined,
> The Maple Leaf Forever.

The popularity of this notion of pan-ethnic British cooperation can be seen in its regular repetition in early Canadian settler writing. Here, for example, is the same notion in Susanna Strickland's (later Moodie's) pre-emigration patriotic poem entitled 'Britannia's Wreath,' published in the *Lady's Magazine* in 1831:

> Freedom's hand the chaplet chose
> Round Britannia's brows to twine;
> Shamrock green and crimson rose
> In the sacred garland shine,
> Whilst her head the thistle rears,
> Surrounded by protecting spears. (qtd. in Ballstadt, 'Secure' 91)

In these popular images of cooperative, pan-ethnic Britishness lies the kernel of the Canadian concept of White civility: 'Britishness' – as a form of government, as a union of formerly hostile peoples, as a civilization – demonstrated that former enemies could set aside their differences and, in a spirit of disinterested objectivity, work cooperatively together in a common enterprise; they could create an orderly society (even a 'race') which provided its members with freedom of conscience and access to economic opportunity regardless of differences of caste and creed. As Governor General Earl Grey told an audience of Canadian schoolchildren in 1909, 'Empire Day ... is the festival on which every British subject should reverently remember that the British Empire stands out before the whole world as the fearless champion of freedom, fair play, and equal rights; that its watchwords are responsibility, duty, sympathy and self-sacrifice; and that a special responsibility rests with you individually to be true to the traditions and to the mission of your race' (qtd. in Francis 66). Because Britishness for these English Canadians represented the most advanced form of political and social life in the world, it was therefore assumed as the civil norm to which non-British Canadians should assimilate. As R.B. Bennett told the House of Commons on 7 June 1928, 'We earnestly and sincerely believe that the civilization which we call the British civilization is the standard by which we must measure our own civilization; we desire to assimilate those whom we bring to this country to that civilization, that standard of living, that regard for morality and law and the institutions of the country and to the ordered and regulated development of the country. That is what we desire, rather than by the introduction of vast and overwhelming numbers of people from other countries to assimilate the British immigrants and the few Canadians who are left to some other civilization' (qtd. in Hjartarson 127–8).

Bennett's speech reminds us that social projects are pitched in rivalry with other projects. The cultural field is never univocal but is a space of contest and competition. Much of the urgency and stridency of English Canadians' formulation of British civility was aimed at alternatives – as in Bennett's case, at the cultural values and traditions that eastern European immigrants brought with them. Other alternatives to the priority of maintaining an essential Britishness in Canada included Goldwin Smith's view that annexation to the United States would provide the only viable future for Canada (see his 'Loyalty') and Henri Bourassa's rejection of British superiority in his campaign for an equal sharing of power between French and English Canadians (see, for example, his 'The French-Canadian in the British Empire'), not to mention the alternatives to Britishness posed by Louis Riel's briefly established mixed-race nation in Manitoba. The threat of the two Métis uprisings in 1870 and 1885 raised the pitch of British advocacy to an especially high level. Canada First member Charles Mair, for example, wrote a letter to the editor of the Toronto *Telegraph* during the first rebellion in which he insisted that 'this country [the North-West Territories] shall be British and not French and shall not be governed by the nominee of either priests or proletarians' (qtd. in Berger, *Sense* 58), and Sir John A. Macdonald stated in 1870 that 'these impulsive half breeds … must be kept down by a strong hand until they are swamped by the influx of settlers' (qtd. in Stasiulis and Jhappan 114).[16]

Because Britishness was believed to represent a unique achievement of liberty and equality while yet retaining a respect for a traditional monarchial (and therefore divinely appointed) order, its proponents insisted that it represented a truer civility than all others, especially that represented by the United States' replacement of a monarchial order with laissez-faire capitalism. For these advocates of a British basis for Canadian society, Britishness constituted the most refined version of an orderly, planned, or 'constrained' society guided by ideals, and it contrasted sharply with an American-style 'free emergence theory' (Day 155), according to which the movements of unrestrained capital set the conditions for social development. This pro-British view is not limited to nineteenth-century Canadians. A famous 1960s example of it appears in George Grant's concept of Canadian Red Toryism: 'In our early expansions,' wrote Grant, 'this conservative nationalism expressed itself in the use of public control in the political and economic spheres … Until recently, Canadians have been much more willing than Americans to use governmental control over economic life to protect the public good against private freedom' (83).[17]

Several instances of Canada's liberal dealings with internal as well as external differences recur in statements by advocates of its British project to demonstrate the virtues of the country's constrained civility; these include lenient treatment of French Canadians after the Conquest,[18] Canada's more humane dealings with Native peoples in comparison to the United States,[19] the early rejection of slavery in John Graves Simcoe's abolition of slavery in the first Upper Canadian legislative council, held in 1793,[20] and Canada's use of civil rather than racist rationalizations for its immigration policies.[21] Commenting on the ongoing tendency among Canadians to refer to these proofs of our own civility (23–8), Eva Mackey argues, 'Pluralism and tolerance have a key place, an institutionalized place, in the cultural politics of national identity in Canada' (2–3). She observes that, rather than suppressing difference and insisting upon a national image of homogeneity, Canadian cultural politics have consistently elaborated Canada's internal pluralism as a sign of its morally enlightened British tolerance, but whereas she uses 'tolerance' for the central term of her analysis, I have chosen 'civility' to emphasize the connection to the Enlightenment discourse of progressive civilization and modernity, as well as to emphasize its dynamic or performative implication. Tolerance is passive, an endurance of difference, whereas civility involves manners and behaviours that must be learned and performed.

J.S. Woodsworth's well-intentioned but now notorious book *Strangers within Our Gates, or Coming Canadians* (1909) provides a concrete instance of the contradictions inherent in the English Canadian project of civility. Despite his remarkable contributions to building a civil society in Canada as a founding member of the Co-operative Commonwealth Federation (CCF) and as an advocate for eastern European immigrants to Winnipeg and the prairies, and despite his public departure in a series of articles in the *Winnipeg Free Press* in 1913 from the ideas he had put forward in 1909 (Christie and Gauvreau 185; Mitchell 10), *Strangers within Our Gates* remains one of the most influential and infamous statements on how Canadians should deal with ethnic and racial pluralism. Based on his experiences as a Methodist minister at All People's Mission church, which ministered to the needs of the large numbers of eastern Europeans who were arriving in Winnipeg under the Laurier government's open-door immigration policy, Woodsworth gathered in his book the latest social science research to provide community service workers with information about the various racial and national groups reaching the nation's immigration ports. Although he declares that English-speaking Canadians must 'divest ourselves of a certain arrogant superiority and exclusiveness, perhaps characteristic of the English race' (240), he follows the predominant thinking of the time, and immigration policy too, in proceeding according to a hierarchy of races organized in descending order from most to least assimilable. The book's chapter list therefore becomes what John Porter, almost sixty years later, would call a vertical mosaic, descending in preference from British, Americans, Scandinavians, Germans, and French to southeastern Europeans, Austria-Hungarians, Balkans, Hebrews, and Italians, before it reaches the cut-off at the White borders of Europe, so that Levantines, Orientals, Negroes, and Indians (both 'Hindus' and Amerindians) are considered incompatible with the national project of building a British-based civility. This descending taxonomy of peoples alerts us to the structural contradiction of civility itself, with its vigilant policing of the borders, even when those borders are being conscientiously expanded and liberalized. It also reminds us of how consistently the borders of Canadian civility have been drawn along those of whiteness.

One feature of Woodsworth's racial taxonomy deserves particular note, however, and this is his devaluation of English immigrants, whom he describes as either from the upper class or the urban poor, in comparison to rural-born, hard-working Celts. Woodsworth echoes the immigration policy of his times, as demonstrated in the recruitment poster in illustration 3, which called especially for British boys to consider farming in Canada. But while he welcomes the Scottish and the Irish readily, he questions the assimilability of the English because, whichever of the two classes they are from, they are less suited to the work of homesteading and tend to be less receptive to their multi-ethnic neighbours. If members of even the most privileged group are not flexible enough to adapt to the high ideals of hospitality, of improving themselves, their properties, and the lives of their neighbours, if they are unwilling to enter enthusiastically and actively into the tasks of welcoming the strangers at the nation's gates and aiding them in the process of Canadianization, then, in the words of a famous pamphlet published in 1909, 'No English Need Apply.'[22]

I understand Woodsworth's devaluation of English immigrants to derive from the larger anxiety in Canadian settler society to address its dependency upon and belatedness in relation to the metropolitan cen-

3   British immigrants remained at the top of Woodsworth's and the government's lists, as this 1920s immigration poster indicates, though the Celts were perceived to be preferable to urban or upper-class English.

tre. Part of the Canadian answer to these problems was to show how the trials of colonial settlement were a kind of crucible that refined the civility inherited from Britain, so that Canadian Britishness became, in fact, superior to British Britishness. One of the major areas of improvement was most consistently registered in terms of class: hard-working labourers rather than the English remittance men of the leisure classes figured as ideal immigrants because they generated their own and the colony's wealth instead of depending upon inheritances and patronage. Woodsworth's preference for Celts and other northern Europeans over Englishmen links class and ethnicity to portray Canada as a place where the gradual ascendancy of the lower classes into the middle classes can go unhindered by an aristocracy and where this process is seen not as grasping opportunism but as a contribution to collective improvement. What has come to be called 'the Northern myth' was central to this figuration of Canada as a testing and improving ground for effete European manhood.[23] According to this myth, the rigours of life in a stern, unaccommodating climate demanded strength of body, character, and mind while it winnowed away laziness, overindulgence, and false social niceties. Canada's placement in the North meant that by a process of social Darwinism, over time its population would shed all over-bred, aristocratic European delicacy as well as repel 'southern' lassitude and hedonism. 'Northern nations always excel southern ones in energy and stamina,' the leading advocate of imperial federation, George Parkin, assured the Canadian Club and the Board of Trade in Saint John, New Brunswick, in 1907, and this 'accounts for their prevailing power' (qtd. in Berger, 'True North' 5).[24]

For early ideologues of the emerging Canadian nation, the country's northern location meant that it would remain the domain of upwardly mobile White people, and its Nordic environment would so strengthen and sharpen them that they would be improved over their British ancestral stock. This environmental Darwinism extended even to the foods that could be grown in the northern plains territory that Canada had recently acquired from the Hudson's Bay Company. In the immigration pamphlet *Manitoba and the North-West of the Dominion* (Toronto, 1871), published the year after Ottawa's purchase of Rupert's Land, Thomas Spence pointed out that wheat, along with beef, produced special qualities in the Anglo-Saxons and Europeans who were these foods' chief consumers. Wheat, he claimed, was 'pre-eminently the food of civilized nations: and perhaps there can be no surer measure of their civilization' than its regular appearance in their diet. Indeed, northern European predominance in world affairs could be explained historically, anatomically, and chemically by the fact that wheat was their basic staple. 'Refinement, fortitude and enterprise,' Spence insisted, 'most distinguish those nations which most consume wheat. Beef-eating and wheat-consuming races, at once dominate and elevate the rice and pork consumers with whom they come into contact' (qtd. in Owram 113). On seeing the huge Canadian National Railways grain elevators at Port Arthur on her first trip into the prairie west, the British Empire's first female magistrate, Emily Murphy, writing as Janey Canuck, reported in 1910 that the elevators 'are chapters which mark the upward steps of our young land in clear, monetary gain, and consequently in knowledge, science, civilisation and all else for which wealth stands' (9). Later in the book, she adds that 'the rulers of the world are they who have the mastership of wheat. It is a big bid Canada is making' (*Janey* 146).

While the northern environment and its products, therefore, were believed to guarantee Canada's eventual surpassing of Great Britain in industry and enterprise, Canadian history was understood to demonstrate a moral-ethical foundation that ensured the nation's superiority was not based on material advantages alone but, more importantly, upon spiritual or ideal principles. This moral-ethical foundation for Canadians' superior civility was argued most commonly by means of the Canadian Loyalist myth. As Carl Berger has shown in *The Sense of Power*, Canadian nationalists of the 1880s and 1890s who campaigned for an imperial federation, which would establish preferential trade between the members of the British Empire in competition with American economic power, led the way in generating a renovated history of the United Empire Loyalists.[25] According to their version of Canadian history, the Loyalists faithfully maintained the essential spirit of Britishness when, out of preference for British orderliness and monarchial rule to American bare-knuckle capitalism, they sacrificed all and fled the United States to make new homes for themselves in what later became Canada. According to such Loyalist mythmakers as William Canniff in *History of the Settlement of Upper Canada* (1872), Canadians had maintained the core of British values, while the British themselves engaged, in violation of their own higher values, in direct trade with the United States. From the mythmakers' perspective, Britain was losing its soul, its higher character, to the amoral ethos of the unrestricted movement of capital, while Canadian Loyalists retained their allegiance to a higher civil order.[26]

Civility in Canada, therefore, was modelled on Britishness, but a Britishness that had been (or would be) purified in North America. By envisioning Canada as a crucible in which overindulged British civility could be smelted and refined, Canadian imperialists imagined that, having proven its strength of purpose through overcoming the adversities of life in the northern frontier, the Canadian character would be able to benefit from Canada's apparently unlimited supply of natural resources in such a way that it would gradually overtake England as the new centre of empire.[27] This is the New World answer to the problem of belatedness: the colonial son will far outstrip the achievements of the European parent. In 'Greater Canada: An Appeal,' Stephen Leacock, noting that Canada's ministers were about to set off for the Colonial Conference in London in 1907, wrote: 'We must realize, and the people of England must realize, the inevitable greatness of Canada.' He goes on to describe the Greater Canada that will soon surpass Great Britain in size, population, and economic clout: the 6 million Canadians of 1907 are as many as the Romans who founded an empire or the Greeks who 'blocked the mountain gates of Europe to the March of Asia.' He predicts the Canadian population will be 'a hundred millions ere yet the century runs out,' and he points to Canada's limitless potential by referring to its enormous capacity to produce hydroelectric power: 'What say you, little puffing steam-fed industry of England, to the industry of Coming Canada. Think you, you can heave your coal hard enough, sweating and grunting with your shovel to keep pace with the snow-fed cataracts of the north?' According to Leacock, the country's greatness is manifest in its sheer size, for the whole German empire, France, England, and Scotland would fit into the two new provinces of Alberta and Saskatchewan and still have room to spare. The time has come, therefore, 'to be done with this *colonial* business, done with it once and forever,' and if Canadians will only just mature from colonial boyhood into cosmopolitan manhood by invigorating their enterprising spirit and dispensing with their small-minded colonial ways and the corrupt, 'sordid traffic of tolerated jobbery' that passes for politics in the colony, they will see that 'imperialism means but the realization of a Greater Canada, the recognition of a wider citizenship.' Accordingly, writes Leacock, 'I, that write these lines, am an Imperialist because I will not be a Colonial,' and it is high time that 'these people of England' be made to see 'that the supreme English Question now is the question of Canada' (4–8).

Even after the expansion into the Canadian prairies failed to attract the huge population that Canadians such as Leacock had anticipated, and after the bid for imperial federation collapsed and the prairie drought and economic catastrophe of the 1930s finally killed the optimistic dream of Canada's developing the economic profile to inherit 'Greater Britain's' empire, an idealist residue of Canadian imperialist aspirations remained current in the concept of Canada's British-derived civility. Hugh MacLennan, for example, envisioned a mission for Canada after the Second World War that would provide a model of civility for the world, a bridge of understanding between war-exhausted and bankrupt Europe and an aggressive, morally unconstrained United States (see *Barometer Rising*). To this day, this image remains current, as Donna Palmateer Pennee and Sherene Razack point out, in the popular image of Canada as a middle power, poised between the superpowers and the poorer nations of the world and therefore perfectly positioned for the role of peacekeeper and arbitrator on the world stage. Even long after the high-water mark of imperialist enthusiasm in Canada waned, therefore, Britishness, because it is central to the idea of civility that emerged in Canada, has remained an important value, and Canadians of all backgrounds, from English remittance men to the Irish refugees they despised, from Scottish railroad executives to the Asian labourers and Black porters who worked on those railways, from southeastern European settlers on the prairies to the First Nations who had been displaced to empty those lands for homesteading, and from Vietnamese 'boat people' to refugees from Serbia and Croatia, have all gained or lost social status on the basis of how well they could approximate this norm of British civility.

The image of Canada's civility, based upon a British model but superior to any British Isles original as well as to its rival in the United States, encountered one of its first challenges in the story of the Loyalists. It did so because the story demanded an account of the moment when the supposed bearers of British civility, the settlers of British North America, went for each other's throats, first in the Revolutionary War and later in the War of 1812. In an 1891 article titled 'Loyalty,' for example, Goldwin Smith expresses bitter regret over the conflict that divided what he calls 'our race' a century ago. He admits there were wrongs on both sides, and he hopes and believes that someday, inevitably, and maybe beyond the course of his life, Canada and the United States will be reunited: 'The unity of the race, and the immense advantages of a settlement which would shut out war from this continent and make it an economical whole, will prevail, I feel convinced over evil memories and the efforts of those who cherish them' (26). Smith's last comment about the people who cherish evil memories is aimed, of course, at those whose understanding of loyalty vehemently opposed his view that Canada would do well to rejoin the former British colonies. For Smith's opponents, the story of the Loyalists must be told and retold to remind Canadians of the great sacrifices that had been made to establish Canada as a separate nation from the United States. For these Loyalists, the idea of annexation was sacrilege; it constituted a forgetting of the traumatic violence that had proven the higher moral and ethical quality of Canadian civility in the first place. In this most obvious sense, then, the Loyalist story demanded that loyal Canadians cherish evil memories not just of their erstwhile British compatriots but of their traumatic and violent origins.

But the injunction to cherish evil memory involves an even more complex process than this sketch indicates. It involves, to borrow terms from Slavoj Žižek, the elaboration of a symbolic history that masks its obscene supplement – what he calls its spectral, fantasmatic history. Žižek's distinction between these two historical modes bears quoting in full:

> One should distinguish between *symbolic history* (the set of explicit mythical narratives and ideologico-ethical prescriptions that constitute the tradition of a community ...) and its obscene Other; the unacknowledgeable *'spectral,' fantasmatic history* that effectively sustains the explicit symbolic tradition, but has to remain foreclosed if it is to be operative ... the spectral fantasmatic history tells the story of a traumatic event that 'continues not to take place,' that cannot be inscribed into the very symbolic space it brought about by its intervention – as Lacan would have put it, the spectral traumatic event 'ne cesse pas de ne pas s'écrire, doesn't stop [or cease] *not* being written [*not* to inscribe itself]' (and, of course, precisely as such, as nonexistent, it continues to persist; that is, its spectral presence continues to haunt the living).
>
> One becomes a full member of a community not by simply identifying with its explicit symbolic tradition, but when one also assumes the spectral dimension that sustains this tradition: the undead ghosts haunt the living, the secret history of traumatic fantasies transmitted 'between the lines', through its lacks and distortions. (64; all quotation marks, italics, and parenthetical insertions in original)

The official symbolic history of Canada is a history of (Loyalist) settlement; according to this way of telling our history, Canada was once a wilderness – wild, uncultivated, largely empty – until Europeans arrived and carved out a society. They fought the overwhelming odds of nature – harsh weather, wild animals, fecund and chaotic vegetation – and won a cultivated, orderly society. They battled not only loneliness, alienation, and factionalism among themselves but also the abandonment and disregard of their European homelands as they built a new home in the New World. The images of carving, fighting, and battling that are repeated motifs in this symbolic settler history are symptoms of the traumatic, spectral history that remains undead in Canadian collective awareness. The representation of Canada's symbolic history by means of the peaceable-seeming term 'settlement' suppresses, even as it depends upon, the violence that was deployed to expunge any claims which First Nations people had to the northern half of this continent. The denial of Indigenous presence in these lands, the disregard of pre-contact history, and the continuing suppression of First Peoples' claims to lands and sovereignty are all signs of the way the spectral, fantasmatic history continues to haunt contemporary Canadian life.

For Canadians, the performance of civility is a way to manage our traumatic history (a complex history usually involving the lower classes, first of Europe and later of Asia, Africa, and the Caribbean, being displaced from their homelands and in turn displacing Indigenous peoples in North America from their traditional lands), and this process means that behind, or within, the optimistic assertions of civility, we often find a different cherishing of evil memories, an elegiac discourse by which Canadians demonstrate their civil sensibilities through mourning the traumatic, but supposedly necessary, losses that were inevitable along the path of progress. The most common version of this melancholic civil remembrance recurs in the ubiquitous myth that Natives were or are a 'vanishing race.' The kind of social Darwinism assumed in the single timeline of the race of civilizations allowed settlers to fantasize that the disappearance of Aboriginal peoples was an inevitability and therefore to mourn this necessary passing of a way of life that was doomed under the unstoppable wheels of progress. Thus Natives make fleeting appearances in verse epics of settlement such as Oliver Goldsmith Jr's *The Rising Village* (1825) or Alexander McLachlan's *The Emigrant* (1861) before they slink off into oblivion without any settler lifting a hand to harm them. Or their doom can be blamed on Americans, as it is in John Richardson's summary statement on the fate of Native peoples at the end of *The Canadian Brothers*: 'With the defeat of the British army, and the death of Tecumseh, perished the last hope of the Indians to sustain themselves as a people against the inroads of their oppressors' (437). The myth of inevitable Indigenous decline enabled narrators of the symbolic history of settlement to blithely assume, as did Emily Murphy in *Janey Canuck in the West* (1910) regarding Aboriginals' future, 'we may give ourselves little uneasiness. This question is solving itself. A few years hence there will be no Indians. They will exist for posterity only in waxwork figures and in a few scant pages of history. However brave and game they may be, there is nothing for them in the end but death' (77).

But such blithe pronouncements, as Žižek reminds us, are never adequate to their own claim. Their spectral, fantasmatic history will not be so easily dispensed with. While settlers such as Catharine Parr Traill or Alexander McLachlan could infamously obliterate the presence of Indigenous people and culture in their complaints that Canada lacked the necessary mythology and history to inspire a local literature, other settlers could write, as John E. Logan did in 1884, 'We have not amalgamated with the native and woven the woof of our refinement of the strong sinuous web of an aboriginal tradition and religion. In our civilized arrogance we swept away that coarser fabric, knowing not that we destroyed that which we would now, as a garment, be proud to wear ... A strain of native blood, though seemingly retarding us at first, might have proved a blessing in the future. But we are here now and they are gone' (116). Here is the regret for what Canadians might have gained, had 'we' – English Canadians – not swept aside the potential to integrate Indigenous traditions with 'our' own, *but* the possibilities for this kind of integration are represented as long past. Natives have disappeared, and now it is too late.

The way in which the fantasmatic historical spectre haunts the present pronouncements of symbolic history is emphasized here by the fact that Logan published these statements during the build-up to the final suppression of the Northwest Rebellion in 1885; even as he was writing regretfully about the lost opportunities of integration with Aboriginal culture, that very culture, or at least a Métis culture which had gone a long way towards such integration, was being suppressed in an action that his statement represents as having already occurred. Logan's intention to remind Canadians that they have failed to see the cultural wealth in Aboriginal traditions is undermined by the racialized concept of time, which equated whiteness with modernity and the administration of industrial development and non-whiteness with pre-modern backwardness and manual labour. The simple sequence of racialized time meant that it was impossible to weave First Nations culture into the progressive narrative of Canadian development: 'we are [always] here now and they are [always] gone.' Civilized Whites, therefore, must cherish evil memories of the necessary losses that have been incurred so that an enterprising, cultivated society could come into full flower.

The remarkable social pathology of this kind of elegiac awareness is

4   The Great Rock of the Aitkow valley (Mistaseni). Photo by O.W. Lillemo of Elbow, SK (c. 1964).

dramatically illustrated in the way that the violence of spectral, fantasmatic history lurks so close to the surface in the symbolic history of the Great Rock of the Aitkow valley in south-central Saskatchewan. In his book about the Qu'Appelle watershed, *River in a Dry Land* (2000), Trevor Herriot tells the story of how on 1 December 1966 a huge erratic at the edge of the rising waters of the artificial Lake Diefenbaker was blasted to smithereens by sixty sticks of dynamite. Thus ended years of debate about what to do with the sacred stone of the Aitkow (see illus. 4). This vast granite boulder, thirty feet long by twenty feet wide and fourteen feet high, had been left by the retreating glaciers of the ice age at a unique place in plains history, for in this valley the Aitkow River strangely used sometimes to run east into the Qu'Appelle watershed and at other times, west and north into the South Saskatchewan River system. This mysterious phenomenon generated the Cree name for the Aitkow: 'The River That Turns.' The close proximity of the two major watersheds, in addition to a natural ford in the South Saskatchewan River, meant that the valley attracted large buffalo herds, thus making the area a haven of ready food, water, and shelter for Indigenous people for thousands of years, even before the Cree came to dominate this area of the Great Plains. The central landmark of this valley was the huge granite erratic unmatched by any stone on or under the ground nearby. Over the centuries, Native peoples had camped near the stone, chipping arrowheads, leaving behind broken pottery, and inserting ceremonial packages in the crevasses of the giant rock.

In the late 1950s the Diefenbaker government in Ottawa and the T.C. Douglas government in Regina finally moved to act upon a proposal that had been bandied about for almost a hundred years: to use the Aitkow valley as the flood plain of a dam on the South Saskatchewan that would provide irrigation and hydroelectricity for the region. Of course, the Great Rock would be submerged. Inspired by anthropologists' concerns that significant sites in First Nations' history would be obliterated under the waters of the reservoir – a University of Saskatchewan anthropologist, Zenon Pohorecky, had found burial grounds, over sixty teepee rings, the sites of Sun Dance lodges, and more than twelve hundred artefacts – the stone was made into the central focus of a popular movement to preserve the environment and its human history. In the resulting 'save-the-rock' campaign, university students went door to door in Saskatoon raising money to save the stone, and public announcements were made over television and radio news. The provincial government announced that it would donate $2,000 to the campaign. One of the campaigners had asked a Cree friend in Saskatoon how to say 'big rock' in Cree, with the result that 'Mistaseni' became the campaigners' name for the stone. Herriot observes, however, that the anthropologists' intention to get the dam redesigned so it would not flood the valley was quickly bypassed. Attention to the rock missed the larger symbolism of the uniqueness of the whole region and was shunted instead into a depressingly hilarious literalism. The rationale for or design of the dam never got much discussion. Instead, campaigners, government memo writers, and newspaper columnists wanted to know how heavy the stone was. How much would it cost to move it? Could a bulldozer budge it, or would it need to be sawn in pieces, carried to dry land and reassembled? What about floating it to safety once the water had risen around it? Or how about wrapping it in concrete and rolling it to higher ground? Might the engineers who had helped to disassemble and reassemble the pyramids threatened by the Aswan Dam in Egypt be consulted on what to do with the Great Rock near Elbow, Saskatchewan?

The Save-the-Rock Committee raised $23,000 to move the stone, but the last estimate put the whole project way out of reach at $200,000. The campaigners quoted Cree chiefs as saying that Mistaseni was sacred to their people, 'like a Christian church,' but it was all to no avail, and the stone was dynamited in December of 1966. The idea was that, since it was too heavy to move, the rock must be broken into transportable bits, some of which could be reassembled into a commemorative cairn. But as it turned out, the ancient granite was hard to work with, so local field-stone, with a piece or two from the Great Rock, was used to build the cairn at Elbow. When Herriot went to visit the Aitkow valley area in 1996, he asked the local historian, a farmer from Elbow, to help him find the cairn. They slid down a wet slope from a golf green on the shores of Lake Diefenbaker to the place where the cairn tipped at an angle on the downslope below the twelfth tee. The farmer explained that the cairn from the 1960s had impeded the view from the tee; so the golf course designers had attached logger's chains to a tractor and dragged it down the slope and out of the way. Now the brass plaques explaining that the cairn memorialized the blasted rock had been removed to two small stone cairns just past the yacht club. Reflecting on the tragicomedy of the whole affair, Herriot writes:

> It seems that eventually, as historical and religious meaning became blurred in the minds of all concerned, the rock began to signify the Indians' [sic] hold on lands that had once been so important to the buffalo hunters, a remnant claim that had somehow escaped the general extinguishing of native title. The tide of white civilization had eddied around the rock, leaving it to the spirits of the past. Now these spirits were becoming meddle-some, getting in the way, complicating what should be simple: if you need electricity and water control, you dam rivers and flood valleys. What really had to be extinguished were the nagging concerns about religious signifi-cance and Indian claims to sacred places. Establish the rock as a common-place icon of little sacred or historical value that even the Indians had forgotten, and this last irksome relic of native title can be shunted aside once and for all. (84–5)

The overkill of the dynamite reminds us of the undead spectre of violence that remains so close to the surface of the official symbolic history of settler civility. The process of memorialization – the absurd series of displacements by which the various cairns ostensibly repre-sented, even as they progressively degraded, whatever significance the stone may have held – reminds us of the contradictions inherent in the concept of civility itself. For civility simultaneously demands that settlers mourn the violence that established their presence in North America and requires that this violence be redeployed to quarantine that uncivil past from the civil present. Civility dynamites *and* memorializes the spectres of the past; it grieves *and* reproduces the ever-vanishing 'Indian.' Thus symbolic histories such as the memorialization of the Aitkow valley stone are instances of the narration of traumatic, spectral events which Žižek says 'continue not to take place' and which Canadians must assume and disavow if they are to be full members of the national community. The losses within Canada's civil ideal, the ruptures of racial and other forms of internal violence that deny the nation's aspiration to become the peaceable kingdom, make up the constitutive losses which settler-citizens are constantly reminded to forget in order to aspire to and belong within White Canadian settler civility. This need to address and account for the losses and traumas of history plunges national aspiration into narrative, the need to cherish the (evil) memories of how 'we' – a fictive ethnicity – came about.

The process of narrating the nation, as Benedict Anderson has famously argued, became possible with the spread of print capitalism after the introduction of the printing press. The sale and distribution of popular texts such as the newspaper and the novel paved the way for the emergence of the modern nation state. For, whereas feudal states cohered by means of dynastic and clan rites of belonging, the modern state required widely dispersed, unrelated people to imagine themselves as part of the same community. Print literacy enabled unrelated groups to read the same narratives and become acquainted with the same information, which provided the collective imagination necessary for national consciousness. This project of literacy-fed, shared imagination, accordingly, is ubiquitous in early Canadian comments about the building a civil society in British North America. David Chisholme, editor of the *Montreal Gazette,* wrote in 1826 that 'it may be safely asserted that native literature is the most desirable and successful instructor of the great bulk of the population of any Country' (8). Thomas D'Arcy McGee concurred in 1858:

> Every country, every nationality, every people, must create and foster a National Literature, if it is their wish to preserve a distinct individuality from other nations. If precautions are not taken to secure this end, the distinctive character and features of a people must disappear; they cannot survive the storms of time and the rude blasts of civil commotion. The popular mind

must be trained and educated according to the physical appearances and social condition of the country; and the people who are so unfortunate as to possess no fountain from which they can procure the elixir of their exist- ence, will soon disappear from the face of the earth, or become merged in some more numerous or more powerful neighbour. (21–2)

Edward Hartley Dewart repeated the theme in his 'Introductory Essay' to *Selections from Canadian Poets* (1864): 'A national literature is an essential element of the formation of national character. It is not merely the record of a country's mental progress: it is the expression of its intellec- tual life, the bond of national unity, and the guide of national energy. It may be fairly questioned, whether the whole range of history presents the spectacle of a people firmly united politically, without the subtle but powerful cement of a patriotic literature' (50).

But we should also note, with Homi Bhabha and Simon During, that the narratives of the nation never speak with just one voice. We should remember that 'Literature knits people together, but it also shows how the knitting was accomplished and at what cost' (Kertzer, *Worrying* 14, also 118). Thus, according to Jonathan Kertzer, 'Literature makes the nation both possible and impossible, imaginable and intolerable. On the one hand, the nation owes its very 'life' to literature, and to all the arts of cultural persuasion ... On the other hand, literature exposes the na- tional life as unjust, and even monstrous, because it has the paradoxical ability to criticize the ideology in which it is immersed and by which it is compromised' (12). Kertzer's language here returns us to the contradic- tory structure of civility and of liberal modernity in general: for civility, in whose service literature is a primary instrument, names justice and equality as its features, and 'in all justice' it must then either acknowl- edge the moments of failure or rationalize the exceptions to this code of universal justice.

By examining popular, 'low culture' literature, we can observe the unstable dynamics between the official symbolic history of the nation and its fantasmatic, repressed histories, because popular writing is usu- ally produced not only by those who securely hold the reins of power but also by those who are lobbying for power. Popular literature allows us to see a contest between representations of the nation that had broad appeal and how these representations jockey for official state adoption. For this reason, I have mined popular texts – poems, heroic epics, formula novels, speeches, and popular journalism – between roughly the 1850s and the 1950s as the central seam to mine in this book. I have situated the project over these approximately one hundred years for several reasons. First, because this period saw the emergence of Canada as an increasingly independent nation with an optimistic national discourse of British Canadian virility and then the undermining of that monocultural discourse with the mass introduction of non-English-speaking labourers before and after the wars, it covers an important series of developments in domestic national narration when certain racial forms such as Britishness and whiteness were formulated as fundamental to the national narrative and these racial forms came to be contested. Secondly, this period predates the major commissions established in the post-war period – the Massey Commission (1949) on arts, letters, and sciences, the Fowler Commission (1955) on radio and television; the O'Leary Commission (1961) on magazine publishing; and the Laurendeau-Dunton Commission (1963) on bilingualism and biculturalism (see Mackey 54ff) – and thus the texts I examine were produced before the development of the officially sponsored and funded system of Canadian cultural production that grew out of the recommendations of these commissions. The authors I study therefore had to appeal to a popular market if they were to be financially successful. As a result, the most influential writers of this period employed popular, formulaic modes of writing that appealed to large, non-elite audiences in order to shape popular views *in advance of* the pedagogies of the state.

In other words, the period under examination constitutes an era in which popular literary forms were common tools in the hands of interested parties, often educated elites or reform-oriented lobby groups, who wished to craft the narratives of the emerging nation to suit their visions. Prominent among these interested parties were the Canada First group of the 1870s as well as the imperial federationists, the first-wave feminists, and social gospel and agrarian reformers of the early decades of the twentieth century. Very often, individual writers belonged simultaneously to several of these interested parties. These conditions of Canadian literary production before the 1950s help us to remember that the symbolic histories that we observe in these early Canadian texts, while operating in the interests of dominant elites, are distinguishable from the official pronouncements of the state. Indeed, many of the texts I examine constitute efforts by powerful elites such as the Canada First group, the imperial federationists, or the United Empire Loyalists to influence official state policies.

A third reason for my choice to locate my study in this period is that Canadian literary culture had not yet undergone the private-public, personal-political split that later became dogma under the modernist turn to the psychological narrative. Before the rise of literary modernism in Canada in the twentieth century, literary texts were overwhelmingly characterized by allegorical or formulaic representation. This tendency is the target of the modernist dismissal of early Canadian writing as hopelessly romanticized and unrealistic. Consider formulaic structures such as gothic, domestic, or sentimental romance, pastoral idyll, or heroic adventure, many of which operate as allegorical bildungsroman, in John Richardson, William Kirby, Rosanna Leprohon, Philippe-Joseph Aubert de Gaspé, Ralph Connor, Nellie McClung, Robert Stead, Thomas Raddall, and Hugh MacLennan. Consistently, these early Canadian writers tend to figure the individual narrative as representative of national narrative, particularly by means of the growing-up story, whereby the youth's process of maturation represents young Canada's emergence onto the international stage of modern nations. These narratives thus regularly present allegorical, representative figures that constitute the statements of a pedagogical discourse which works not very subtly to projectively imagine the utopian collectivity called Canada. The period I have identified for study, then, allows us to observe remarkably overt instances in which popular literature mediated fundamental concepts of Canadianness that have since become reified assumptions of Canadian culture.

In each of the chapters that follow, I have identified one of the four representative figures that recur in popular Canadian narratives of the period – the Loyalist brother, the enterprising Scottish orphan, the (Protestant) muscular Christian, and the maturing colonial son – to examine the ways in which these allegorical figures functioned in these elite groups' projected visions of the emerging nation to inculcate and naturalize the values of British civility that came to define the particular ideals of Canadian whiteness. Of course, these four figures form a list that is far from exhaustive, but a close examination of them and their remarkable reiteration over a hundred years of Canadian literary culture proves a productive way to examine not just the construction but also the fissures in the edifice of what has become known as English Canada, the senior partner of Canada's two White so-called founding nations.

By tracing these cultural forms in the domain of popular literature, I have reasonable confidence that they did in fact have the wide-ranging impact I claim and that they were not simply the assertions of those in power with little claim upon the imaginations of a wider populace. My choices of texts may seem odd to some scholars, since many of these popular texts fell into disregard during the heyday of modernist New Criticism between the 1950s and the 1980s, when the CanLit canon was established. The formulaic structures of these early texts, understood to be derived from outmoded Old World forms that ill-suited the circumstances of the New World, offended the sensibilities of high art–oriented New Critics, particularly because of the tendency in these popular forms towards sentimentality and didacticism.[28] But more recent revaluations of popular culture genres have enabled us to reassess the operations of these forms so that the didactic, pedagogical element of popular literature can be examined for its serious social operations.[29] The career and writings of Ralph Connor, Canada's first best-seller and most widely read author up until the 1930s, when his works largely fell into oblivion, make an excellent case in point. I have regularly returned to Connor throughout the chapters of this book as a kind of touchstone because his works and career so readily illustrate the phenomenon of the popular author who had enormous influence not just upon public opinion but also upon public policy and who held influential positions in public life, even though he never ran for public office. (This profile applies in lesser degree to the careers of other popular writers whose works I examine in this study, including William Kirby, William Wilfred Campbell, Philippe-Joseph Aubert de Gaspé, Thomas Raddall, Emily Murphy, Margaret Murray Robertson, Robert Stead, Frederick Philip Grove, and Hugh MacLennan. Nellie McClung did become a member of the Alberta legislature, but her career otherwise fits this profile.) Connor's career helps to clarify the relations and distinctions between the nation, as imagined by its citizens, and the state, as the set of official institutions which govern that nation; it also helps us to see how popular nation-making narratives are not necessarily the direct productions of the official machinery of the state, while at the same time they mediate the illusory fusion of the nation with the state into the nation state.[30]

If popular authors such as Connor enable us to see how certain cultural producers became privileged purveyors of popular national narratives, the figures they repeatedly produced allow us to observe how popular, formulaic writing tended to anthropomorphize the nation in single allegorical human figures. As Adam Carter and Jonathan Kertzer have separately shown, anthropomorphism functions as a common trope in national narratives because this personifying representation fuses the organic image of romantic nationalism, which figures the nation as a natural growth out of a native soil, with the biographical narrative of the maturation of an individual's (most often a male's) character. 'Personification conveniently assimilates the diversity of historical experience and civil discord into a single figure,' Kertzer writes. 'Then it elevates that figure into a hero in quest of self-fulfillment ... If Canadian history is not an epic, it is at least a Bildungsroman' (*Worrying* 43, 44). Such anthropomorphic tropes for the nation function strategically under the civil ethos of liberal modernity to fuse the codes of personal morality, usually figured as the development of admirable character, with the codes for public citizenship. According to this narrative figuration, a civil nation is composed of citizens of 'good' character. For example, at the National Conference on Character Education in Relation to Canadian Citizenship, which had been organized by the business elite in Winnipeg in 1919, James Aikins, lieutenant-governor of Manitoba, told his listeners that education was centrally about instruction in character, and '"the first business of a nation [was] ... the manufacture of souls of good quality." In short, the social order was secure to the degree that the population was moral' (Mitchell 12). Popular allegory, in statements such as these, functions as a primary form of national pedagogy in its attempts to condense the narratives of private and public, individual and collective life, in such a way as to foster individual govermentality – the assumption by individuals of forms of self-regulation that reiterate the 'natural origins' of the civil sphere that is Canada.

The ideological links between Aikins's desire to educate souls of good quality and Charles Mair's allegory in 'The New Canada' (1875) are not hard to see. 'This new Dominion,' wrote the Canada First group member and vigorous proponent of imperial federation,

> stands, like a youth upon the threshold of his life, clear-eyed, clear-headed, muscular, and strong. Its course is westward. It has traditions and a history of which it may well be proud; but it has a history to make, a national sentiment to embody, and a national idea to carry out. There was a time when there was no fixed principle or national feeling in Canada; when men were Englishmen, Scotchmen, Irishmen, or Frenchmen, and when to be a Canadian was almost to hang the head. But that time has passed away. Young Canada has come to the front, and we are now a nation, with a nation's duties to perform, privileges to maintain, and honour to protect. (151)

Such allegorical figurations of the colonial nation as a youth on the verge of independent manhood are ubiquitous in the late nineteenth and early twentieth centuries. What usually went uncommented upon, however, in the many repetitions of the maturation allegory was the way in which it condensed the fictive ethnicity of Canada's *British* origins in its narrative of national growth.[31]

As Mair's allegory of Canada as a young maturing man illustrates, I mean national allegory to signify an analogical story that is repeatedly incorporated into the nation's self-defining narratives. The allegorical referent is the *pedagogical* ideal, as Homi Bhabha would call it (see 'DissemiNation'), by which national discourse attempts to shape or discipline people's daily and repeated *performances* of citizenship; that is, national allegories teach people what 'Canadian' looks like so they can repetitively act it out themselves.[32] Allegory, then, is a tense rhetorical form because it compresses powerful and often contentiously political ideologies into a dense bundle in its effort to incorporate unassimilated phenomena into the formulations of the familiar and the known.

The tropic structure of allegory, however, with its double-coded, dense bundle of signs, means that its pedagogy is always more complex than the simple, overt 'lessons' it presents at first sight. I want to suggest that, in national allegory, the lesson of the allegory never matches exactly in a tight, one-to-one correspondence the actions or performances of its tropic figures. Perhaps we can measure the gap or distance between the pedagogical and the performative elements in national allegory as the distance between what we might call its official and its suppressed curriculum – Žižek would call these its symbolic and its spectral histories.[33] Charles Mair's allegory of young Canada presents the nation as a vigorous, pan-ethnic youth just launching into independent manhood, but it brings with it the anxious and suppressed curriculum of White enterprise, the assumptions of British superiority, and a huge dose of testosterone. Popular national allegories such as the ones I discuss in this book, then, are this kind of tense pedagogy, meant to inculcate authoritative values yet always destabilized by the non-identity between the values they idealize and the signifying figures that are meant to perform or demonstrate these values. Insofar as allegory's doubleness tends to announce its artificiality in the very moments when it is engaged in naturalizing authority, it undermines its own pedagogy in the moment of performance. It is the aim of this book to read Canada's popular allegories of White British civility backwards from the accretions of naturalness in their present 'forgotten' state so that we can perceive the efforts that went into their construction and recognize them once again for the artificial constructions that they are.

My project to denaturalize the categories of privilege, however, poses difficult questions about the effects of this kind of critical endeavour. For is there not a danger that in describing how norms were created, one inadvertently reaffirms their normative status? How can a description of White privilege avoid reaffirming the privilege accorded to whiteness in Canada? At the very least, does one not re-centre whiteness within critical race studies, confirming once again its pivotal position? And is not my own effort to analyse the contradictory structure of civility inherent in English Canadian whiteness itself not caught up within the justice- and equality-seeking codes of civility? What distinguishes a twenty-first-century project of civility such as mine from nineteenth- or early twentieth-century forms of civility such as the ones I examine and critique? I believe that a critical inhabitation of what I call wry civility can help to address these concerns.

In *A Romantic Education,* the American writer Patricia Hampl writes that 'anyone born after 1945 – was born into an elegy' (175). For Hampl, mourning or the discourse of elegy defines a post-war self-conscious or self-reflexive awareness. She illustrates her periodization of this form of self-reflexivity when she refers to the controversial moment in Henry James's *The American Scene* in which James describes his consternation, upon returning to the United States in 1904, that the country is being overtaken by the hordes of aliens he sees at the Ellis Island immigration centre. Hampl writes: 'James speaks without the reservoir of self-consciousness, the product of diffused guilt, which has become almost predictable luggage among social analysts of our [post-Holocaust] time. He has not yet become a resident of a world that knows that, in time, it has committed atrocities ... James could speak as he did because he harbored no terror of his own power, his own lurking genocidal tendencies. We do. We are terrified of too much attention to the differences among us for fear that our very acuity in matters of racial characteristics will unmask our essential racism' (33).

For the Canadian writers I examine in this study, too, the sorting of people into racial groups was carried out without the looming consciousness of atrocity. They thought of the processes of racialized categorization (for immigration, for social intervention, for national definition) as *civil* acts – very often as recognition, respect, orderly government, and even potential welcome. That these acts were based upon the assumption of British superiority was not as immediately attached, in their minds, to the images of genocide as it is in ours – this despite the fact that a greater devastation had been, and was being, carried out in the Americas under European colonialism than that perpetrated under

Naziism. Olive Dickason reports that the Indigenous population in the Americas has been estimated to have been as high as 112.5 million at the eve of European arrival (as compared to 70 million estimated for Europe), and that up to 93 per cent of this population was decimated within a century as a result of wars of invasion and imported diseases (9). It seems that it took the murder of 6 million 'sometime White' European Jews under the Nazi regime to awaken Euro-Americans to their own capacity for genocide. But the full awareness of this New World genocide – the fact that Australia, New Zealand, or the Canadian and American Midwests have never been burned into public memory as have Dachau or Auschwitz – still remains largely unacknowledged.[34]

If a post-Holocaust notion of civility can be distinguished from that of the late nineteenth and early twentieth centuries, it is distinguishable by the self-reflexivity noted by Hampl. For denizens of the twenty-first century, it seems that the truly civilized person or culture is increasingly the one who not only knows him- or herself generally but knows his or her own capacity for brutality. Paradoxically, we inhabitants of late modernity demonstrate our humanity by manifesting an awareness of our own capacity for inhumanity. For us, civility becomes complex, multi-levelled, even devious; convinced of our own civility in comparison to the past, we tend to demonstrate this subtler conviction by *performing*, even calling attention to, our self-consciousness that we are implicated in the history of racism. If colonials resisted their colonial administrators by means of what Bhabha calls 'sly civility,' early twenty-first-century people resist our own temptation to complacency by means of *wry* civility. Perhaps the most articulate expression of this condition of elegiac, even ironical, White self-consciousness in English Canada is found in Dennis Lee's *Civil Elegies*:

> And what can anyone do in this country, baffled and
> making our penance for ancestors, what did they leave us? Indian-
> swindlers,
> stewards on unclaimed earth and rootless, what does it matter if they, our
> forebears' flesh and bone were often
> good men, good men do not matter to history.
> And what can we do here now, for at last we have no notion
> of what we might have come to be in America, alternative, and how make
> public
> a presence which is not sold out utterly to the modern? utterly? to the
> savage inflictions of what is for real, it pays off, it is only
> accidentally less human? (from Elegy 1, p. 28)

In a famous speech given in 1972 and later printed as 'Cadence, Country, Silence: Writing in Colonial Space,' Lee expressed his conviction that writing which had local authenticity was rediscoverable in an honest assessment of Canada's lost civility and colonial servitude. He explained that after publishing a first version of *Civil Elegies* in 1968, he had four years of writer's block until he read George Grant's *Lament for a Nation*. It was his encounter with Grant's description of Canadian Red Toryism, of the original Loyalists' distrust of American liberalism (as producing unfettered and violent liberty rather than the good), and of Canada's betrayal of its alternative starting ideals and its subsequent submission to the American empire that enabled Lee to see that the words he had available as a poet, living in colonized space, always felt inauthentic and that Grant's lament for a lost ideal was itself a kind of authentic home. 'To find one's tongue-tied sense of civil loss and bafflement given words at last,' Lee writes, 'to hear one's own most inarticulate hunched out loud, because most immediate in the bloodstream – and not prettied up, and in prose like a fastidious groundswell – was to stand erect at last in one's own place' (511). He then revised and republished *Civil Elegies* in 1972.

I call the kind of unflinching reassessment of the losses of English Canadian history that Lee advocates here 'wry civility': 'civil' in the sense outlined throughout this chapter – the contradictory or ambivalent project that purports to provide a public space of equality and liberty for all at the same time as it attempts to protect this freedom and equality from threats within and without – and 'wry' in the sense of being critically self-conscious of this very ambivalence and of the contradictions it involves. For we are a generation, as Richard Day reminds us, who cannot deny that '[a]cts carried out in the name of civilization and culture have caused at least as much death and despair as those deriving their motivation from race, and therefore deserve to be treated with equal caution' (13). Wry in the sense of remaining ironically aware of the pretentiousness of the civility that we nonetheless aspire to, and also of the pretentiousness in trying to be self-aware. For, as Ross Chambers's assessment of the unexaminability of the categories of privilege demonstrates, self-awareness is the eye of the needle through which the camel of privilege can very seldom pass. Wry or self-conscious, too, of the *history* of this contradiction and ambivalence, for critically alert historical study, as Ernest Renan insisted, 'often constitutes a danger for ... nationality' (11).

In the context of nationalism, historical inquiry into the nation as narration produces a wry understanding of the mutually enforcing projects of race and nation. Stuart Hall has famously observed that although race has long been discredited as a reliable system for classifying essential human types, its persistence demonstrates that it is a 'floating signifier,' one which signals a history of discursive productivity and reiteration (*Race*). Awareness of English Canadian whiteness as a floating signifier, as a project with a narrative history, as the anchoring concept that structures Canada's racial hierarchy, produces wry civility. Bhabha claims that to 'study the nation through its narrative address does not merely draw attention to its language and rhetoric; it also attempts to alter the conceptual object itself' ('Introduction' 3). In like manner, critical historical study of the narrative project of English Canadian whiteness, of the allegorical figures which naturalized it as a category and which linked it to the values associated with British civility, enables us to recognize it wryly as a racial project rather than an essential or natural category and, in the process, alters the conceptual object itself.[35]

Wry civility, as a critical positioning, then, must occupy an ambivalence between the gains and the losses of nationalism. On the one hand, the great wars of the early twentieth century, in addition to the ongoing violence of nation states towards internal and external threats, have produced widespread anti-nationalism among social commentators,[36] while, on the other, the independence movements of many former colonies (as well as Black and Québécois nationalisms in North America) have espoused nationalism as a producer of solidarity in the movement towards independence. Furthermore, growing concerns about the rise of multinational corporations under increasingly globalized economic relations have caused some critics to espouse the nation as a local alternative to mass homogenization. Wry civility, then, demands that we heed Simon During's reminder that 'the nation-state is, for better or worse, the political institution which has most efficacy and legitimacy in the world as it is ... To reject nationalism absolutely or to refuse to discriminate between nationalisms is to accede to a way of thought by which intellectuals – especially postcolonial intellectuals – cut themselves off from effective political action' (139). But it also demands that we refuse to forget the suppressed brutalities that are not just part of the nation's past but are also ongoing elements of the structure of civility upon which the nation as an entity is founded. Wry civility must also retain self-consciousness about the myth of progress that often subtends the very activity of historical criticism itself. Kertzer suggests that Canadian historical literary criticism has often been understood to move along a path of 'progress' from 'history, to cultural analysis, to literary criticism' ('Historical' 113). He suggests that even Linda Hutcheon's description of postmodern historiographical metafiction tends to assume this progressive story of Canadian historical-cultural-literary production, even if it is self-consciously ironic about it. The temptation in historical critical endeavour is always to assume that our research allows us to 'see' what was invisible to the people of the past and therefore to assume a progressive relation to them – we have evolved above and beyond them.

Wry civility constitutes an important antidote to this temptation. Dennis Lee's inhabitation of Grant's lament signals an already existing Canadian tradition of self-critical elegiac civility, and it is as an extension of this tradition that I inscribe this book. *White Civility* aims to develop a careful genealogy of the making of English Canadian whiteness as a project that precisely excluded the possibilities of an inclusive peaceable kingdom. It understands that genealogy as continuous with and productive of the situation of the present (rather than quarantining it in the past). Wry civility represents a self-conscious critical positioning, an immersion in our melancholic national history, as well as a critical engagement with the social norms of race, ethnicity, gender, sexuality, and nationalism, so that by reanimating their temporality through historical research, we recognize them not as norms but as pedagogical projects that produce our own governmentality.

2 The Loyalist Brother: Fratricide and Civility in English Canada's Story of Origins

Let me open my discussion of fraternity in Loyalist literature with a primal scene taken from *The Canadian Brothers* (1840), which, together with the earlier *Wacousta* (1832), constitutes Major John Richardson's fictional epic of Canada's formation.[1] This scene from the novel's conclusion occurs during the War of 1812 at its most mythologized battle at Queenston Heights. General Isaac Brock, Canada's Loyalist martyr, lies mortally wounded, and Henry Grantham, his retainer and one of the two Canadian brothers of the novel's title, takes aim at the Kentucky rifleman he thinks shot his venerated commander. No sooner does his bullet strike the rifleman than Henry realizes the man is his brother, Gerald, just returned from Kentucky, where he has been a prisoner of war. 'Who shall tell the horror of the unfortunate young Aid-de-Camp, at recognizing in the supposed enemy his long mourned and much loved Gerald,' remarks Richardson's narrator.

> The musket fell from his hand, and he who had never known sorrow before, save through those most closely linked to his warm affections, was now overwhelmed ... 'Great God, what have I done!' exclaimed the unhappy Henry, throwing himself in a paroxysm of despair upon the body of his bleeding brother. 'Gerald, my own beloved Gerald, is it thus we meet again. Oh! if you would not kill me, tell me that your wound is not mortal. Assure me that I am not a fratricide' (466).

'Assure me that I am not a fratricide' – this disavowing cry, which nonetheless acknowledges that the origin-marking trauma comes 'through those most closely linked with one's warm affections,' echoes through a century of Canadian writers' depictions of the nation's Loyalist beginnings.

Henry's cry constitutes an early instance of a rhetorical trope that contributed significantly to the naturalization of White British masculinity as the assumed norm for Canadian citizenship. Because this trope uses the bond between brothers to represent the unity of the nation, I call it an 'allegory of fraternity' and argue that this allegory, and particularly its menacing corollary of fratricide, functions to manage considerable anxieties at play in the contested field of Loyalist discourse. The allegory of fraternity that recurs throughout Loyalist literature addresses the racial-colonial debacle that occurred when the supposedly civilized White British colonists of North America went for each other's throats in the revolutionary and 1812 wars and tries to assimilate it to the formula story of the nation as a convincingly natural domestic unit. It tries to offer an explanatory story for how these moments of brotherly brutality brought the Canadian nation into being, and it invigilates the filial faith of those who remain within the British American family.

This fraternal allegory is both disturbed and disturbing. It is disturbed because the emerging settler-invader nation needs to present the image of its citizenry as an undivided, peaceable community in order to substantiate the claim of civility that justifies the colonial displacement of the 'barbarous' Indigenous people of North America. The American Revolution and its aftershocks in the War of 1812, as well as the rebellions of 1837–8, undermine this image of a peace-abiding, indivisible White nation in the New World. The allegory of fraternity, then, constitutes a desperate attempt to account for this schism between British colonists and to explain why this brotherly brutality was necessary. But the explanation of this necessity involves a series of disturbing rationalizations. The Loyalist cause must prove its unblemished virtue in comparison to the rebel cause, and so it employs the code of military honour and self-sacrifice to counteract any suspicion of less-admirable motives that the Loyalists may have had, such as the opportunity to secure a land grant or to exact revenge on patriot marauders. This code of honour serves to ennoble the story of original violence by portraying it as the Loyalists' defence of common justice, as demonstrated by their aligning themselves with vulnerable non-Whites. But the homosocial structure of the all-male, all-White world of the brotherhood of officers assumed by this code limits the image of the nation's community to a backward-looking, bachelor society that cannot reproduce itself. This sterility then requires that the women, who have been portrayed as secondary figures throughout the all-male plot of the national allegory of fraternity, are suddenly recruited at its conclusion to project a future beyond the conflict of brothers. This shift is typically achieved in Loyalist narratives by containing fraternity as the story of the nation's past and replacing it with the trope of courtship and marriage as the story of the nation's future. Thus Loyalist literature reminds its readers of what they must eventually forget: the fratricidal disturbance which explains the nation's origin and which forms the central action of the plot in these narratives must be forgotten or sublimated as we turn our attention, late in the story, to the domestic romance of the nation's future.

Henry Grantham's disavowing cry echoes through a century of Canadian writers' depictions of the nation's Loyalist beginnings. The following brief survey indicates the ubiquity and duration of the motif of the struggle between brothers in Loyalist literature, though space limitations will not allow me to comment in detail about each of the texts I mention in the pages that follow. Near the end of William Kirby's epic poem *The U.E.: A Tale of Upper Canada* (1859), the Loyalist patriarch Ranger John raises his tomahawk over the head of his son Hugh, who has been responsible for the deaths of two brothers. The Shawnee chief, Tecumseh, similarly raises his hatchet over his treacherous brother, the Prophet, in Charles Mair's verse drama of 1886, named after the chief who, beside Brock, came to figure as one of Canada's founding martyrs. The paragon of female loyalty in Sarah Curzon's *Laura Secord, the Heroine of 1812: A Drama* (1887) sees a proverbial snake in the Edenic Canadian woods on her way to warn Lieutenant James FitzGibbon of the American attack at Beaver Dams and thinks of it as analogous to a rebel son's treachery to his family. Captain Etherington, in Wilfred Campbell's 1909 novel *The Beautiful Rebel: A Romance of Canada in Eighteen Hundred and Twelve,* retrieves the letter describing his lost paternity from the mortally wounded body of his intended brother-in-law at the Battle of Queenston Heights. A falling-out between friends who were nigh on to brothers back in England makes Thomas Norman a misanthrope in Hiram A. Cody's *The King's Arrow: A Tale of the United Empire Loyalists* (1922) and puts him among the armed rebels who threaten the lives of his erstwhile friend Colonel Sterling and his Loyalist family in what later became New Brunswick. Stephen Ellison, the hero of Jean Norman McIlwraith's significantly titled novel *Kinsmen at War* (1927), has his disgust for what he thinks of as a 'fratricidal conflict' (66) confirmed when he realizes during the Battle of Queenston Heights that the American he has been trying to wrestle over the precipice and into the Niagara Gorge is none other than his brother-in-law, Bill Farnsworth. In Ralph Connor's 1929 novel, *The Runner: A Romance of the Niagaras,* Hubert Brookes, after being banished from his father's house for his republican sympathies, proves his loyalty by sacrificing himself in the battle at Chippewa for the brother he earlier thought had betrayed him in romance. At the end of Maida Parlow French's feminist novel *Boughs Bend Over* (1943), the heroine's Loyalist fiancé, Glen Vulpin, watches with relief as his fratricidal brother, Rad, flees their St Lawrence River settlement, taking his treachery and violence with him.

Finally, the fratricide in Thomas Raddall's *His Majesty's Yankees* (1942) takes place during that other war often cited as the moment of Canada's birth, the American Revolution. Matthew Strang, with his sons Davy and Mark, is preparing to defend their small Nova Scotia town against the predations of privateers from New England. The aged Matthew, no longer steady enough to hold the gun himself, orders Mark to shoot the steersman of the first of the privateers' landing crafts. Mark sees that the steersman is his brother Luke and refuses. So the old man turns to Davy, the novel's protagonist, and orders him to take the rifle. The father tells his son that this is 'a matter between us Strangs' and that it is kill or be killed. 'Now Davy!' he orders. 'Make it sure, my son. We owe that to his mother – and to him' (398–9). With that killing, Raddall's narrator tells us, Nova Scotia declared itself finally for the Crown and against its New England relatives, ensuring that not just the coastal province but all of Canada remained British and did not join the rebel states (403, see also Alan Young 236).[2]

This brief survey registers the echo of Henry Grantham's cry in works written by women as well as men; in Maritimes settings, where historians have concurred that, compared with the Upper Canadian version of the Loyalist myth, military themes did not predominate (Duffy, *Gardens* 6; Barkley 7–8; Ian Stewart 22); in novels written over a century after Richardson first raised the spectre of the Canadian Cain; and equally in texts whether they celebrate or criticize the Loyalist myth. The oft-repeated allegory of fraternity conveys an ideal enforced with a threat. The ideal is, of course, the image of the Canadian colony as a prized member of the British family, but the threat of the prodigal or fratricide puts that family on guard against traitors from within. As its nightmare component, then, the fratricidal undercurrent of the allegory of fraternity constitutes Žižek's spectral, fantasmatic history, which militates against the idealized surface of what he would call the official, symbolic history of Loyalist discourse – that sanitized representation of high-minded men and women whose dedication to the peace and order guaranteed by the British crown and constitution made them relinquish their stateside homes and holdings to take up new lives in the unsettled lands of Nova

Scotia, New Brunswick, and Upper Canada. The genealogy of Britain in America – that favourite discourse of the status-conscious descendants of United Empire Loyalists who wished to insert their ancestors as the progenitors of the Canadian family – carries within it, as Richardson's prophecy predicted, an ur-story of domestic violence.

My examination of Loyalist literature's repeated use of the fraternal allegory is made possible by significant work previously done by historians, who have debated the claims of the Canadian Loyalist myth, and by literary scholars, who have shown how literary works have played key roles in producing and popularizing Loyalist mythology. Uncertainty about how to interpret the story of the Loyalists has generated a veritable industry of historiographical debate. It has done so because of the gap between the widespread view that the Loyalists were foundational to the British ideals out of which Canada was formed and the lack of conclusive evidence about what ideals they actually held. S.J.R. Noel summarizes the problem aptly: 'very little is known of the political beliefs of the loyalist founders of Upper Canada (whose influence is generally acknowledged to have been seminal), in spite of all that has been written about them – in spite of all the ideologies, ancient and modern, that have been variously attributed to them ... And to add to the confusion, what is known can be used, and is used, with about equal plausibility, to support contrary inferences' (4). As Noel and numerous others have pointed out, any certainty about the Loyalists' ideals is undercut by the British government's promise of compensation and land to Loyalist refugees and soldiers (Noel 11; Knowles 20–5). For the fact is that the process of petitioning for these lands meant the generation of myth. To qualify for compensation, one needed a story of loss, exile, or suffering on behalf of the king. It helped if one could represent oneself as having lost rich properties, relatives, and high social status in the flight from the rebel states. The point here is not that such stories were untrue, but that the very process of recording these petitions shaped the narratives that posterity has inherited as documentary evidence of the Loyalist past (Potter-Mackinnon 148–9, 160). And because these narratives were recorded for the purposes of apportioning land grants and compensation, the image of the Loyalists as innocent refugees hounded from their homes and cast upon the king's mercy for protection is inextricably shadowed by the image of Loyalists as those who capitalized on martyr-victim status to gain government patronage.

Thus the malleability of the Loyalist story has itself become legendary in Canadian political history.[3] Indeed, it is one of Canada's most energetically contested mythic discourses. In *Inventing the Loyalists* the historian Norman Knowles, for example, contends that there is no stable 'loyalist tradition' as previous scholars have assumed. He contests Carl Berger's claims for the national influence of the Canadian imperialists in popularizing the Loyalist tradition by showing that their high-flown rhetoric had much less public support than Berger assumes. By examining the debates that divided opposing groups who were involved in organizing the Loyalist centenary celebrations in Toronto, Niagara, and Adolphustown and by placing them alongside the Native and feminist campaigns to establish monuments to Joseph Brant, Laura Secord, and Barbara Heck, Knowles claims there were too many versions of 'loyalism' to settle into anything coherent enough to be called a 'loyalist tradition.' In order to make this point, however, he identifies the traits previous scholars have identified as part of that tradition – 'unfailing devotion to the British Crown and Empire, a strong and pervasive anti-Americanism, suffering and sacrifice endured for the sake of principle, elite social origins, and a conservative social vision' (3) – and then turns to various examples that show these ideals of 'official' loyalism were contested or denied in the 'vernacular' of political and religious debate, feminist activism, First Nations resistance, or just plain indifference from the general public. The ironic point, however, is that Knowles needs to establish the central points of the tradition at the outset of the book in order to point out their inadequacy. The fact that he *can* identify these central points shows that, whatever their accuracy to the lived realities of the Loyalists, they continue to be held widely enough by Canadians to constitute a 'tradition' or myth that even its detractors can identify.[4] My purpose is not so much to expose Loyalist myth as inadequate or inaccurate to the Loyalists' real experiences (see Fellows and Duffy's *Gardens* for this approach), as it is to trace the effects of one of the most common allegorical story forms generated by that myth.[5]

Allegory is a literary trope deeply invested in the management of cultural anxiety or instability. As Deborah Madsen has argued, its very structure of reading the present literal thing in reference to a pre-existent normative code (146) makes it one of society's 'authoritative responses to the trauma of cultural change' (2; see also 109, 135). Allegory, then, is a tense rhetorical form because it compresses powerful and often contentious ideologies into a dense bundle in its effort to incorporate unassimilated phenomena into the formulations of the familiar and the known. Accordingly, the allegory of fratricide cites a soothing ideal of family solidarity to justify the violence against treacherous brothers which made it necessary to establish a separate, British-governed nation north of the thirteen rebel states. It makes virtuous exemplars of the Loyalist heroes who purified the nation's lineage of its treacherous children. But the tropic structure of allegory, with its double-coded, dense bundle of signs, means that its pedagogy is always more complex than its simple, overt 'lesson' would at first suggest.

This fraternal allegory, of which fratricide is the nightmare, unofficially proclaims a backward-looking and static ideal. It is preoccupied with maintaining purity – a concept readily linked to loyalty – and a clear hierarchy in the family, race, and nation. The domestic trope of the family is a common figure for the naturalness of a nation's organization of its people. 'The family trope is important for nationalism,' explains Anne McClintock; 'it offers a "natural" figure for sanctioning national *hierarchy* within a putative organic *unity* of interests' (357). Thus, she says, '[d]espite many nationalists' ideological investment in the idea of popular *unity*, nations have historically amounted to the sanctioned institutionalization of gender *difference*' (353, emphasis in original). For McClintock, the domestic trope inculcates an official curriculum of national unity, even as its unofficial curriculum reinforces the exclusion of women from positions of ultimate power and authority. Jonathan Kertzer goes one step further when he identifies 'purity' as another unofficial element of the domestic trope's curriculum: 'nationalism imposes the homogeneity of family resemblance. Countries are expected to share a domestic language, religion, culture, or race. Any variance from the norm becomes a threat to their integrity. Purity then becomes a prime value, and purity is not a natural state of affairs (nothing in nature is pure) but an ideological imperative, a way of thinking through exclusion' (*Worrying* 9). While the allegory of fraternity explicitly addresses the conflict between loyal and rebel British subjects in America, its unofficial curriculum assumes and promotes an image of the two North American nations as born out of an exclusively White, male conflict.

Richardson, that 'early cartographer of the Canadian imagination' (Hurley, *Borders* 3), gives us the bare bones of the allegory in the tellingly named *Canadian Brothers*. Gerald Grantham's instability of character generates the novel's plot. In the novel's opening action, he abandons his post on the Detroit River when an American boat tries to slip past the British river guard at Fort Amherstburg. His brother Henry is so eager to defend Gerald from the resulting imputations against Gerald's honour that, when he hears one of the British officers say that 'this is the result of entrusting so important a command to a Canadian' (34), he challenges the man to a duel. The issue is Canadian loyalty: can the local colonials be entrusted with His Majesty's defence? The faithful brother believes absolutely in his uncertain brother's honour – this because the good brother is unswervingly loyal, selflessly committed to the collective, and passionately righteous. Gerald starts out matching Henry's virtues, but for one exception: his ambition for personal glory turns into his downfall. He proves himself a hero by capturing the American boat from ambush (the reason why he had abandoned his post), but his unorthodox success proves his undoing. For among his captives is Matilda Montgomerie, an American femme fatale whose beauty mesmerizes Gerald and turns him away from the oath of honour he and his brother had sworn to their father, the king's magistrate and representative of law and order in the colony. During his incarceration as a prisoner of war in Kentucky, he becomes captivated by her sophistries, which are explicitly represented as American. Gerald is compelled by her valuation of individual enterprise over collective well-being, personal retribution over corporate jurisprudence, and sexual passion over temperate fraternity. He learns to dissimulate and eventually ignores the oath of honour he swore to his father by agreeing to become Matilda's personal assassin in a love intrigue. Blind passion for this temptress figure causes Gerald to abandon the gentlemanly codes of British civility and to sink into the ethical morass of American vigilantism.

Gerald Grantham sets the pattern for the prodigal brother throughout Loyalist literature. Again and again in the fraternal allegory, the treacherous brother puts personal, material ambition over natural family loyalty, law and order, and spiritual-communal values. The plot's motivating problem in the Loyalist allegory is usually generated by the prodigal brother's disordered values. The tragic action in Mair's play *Tecumseh* opens with the Prophet's ambitions to supplant his famous brother and take the reigns of power over the alliance of First Nations that Tecumseh has been gathering together (I, i; p. 83). Rad Vulpin's exploitation of the Loyalist villagers, his neighbour's wife, and his own half-brothers drives the plot of French's *Boughs Bend Over*. The Strang brothers' rejection of their father's neutral policy and their departure from the family home in Liverpool stimulates the complicated action of Raddall's *His Majesty's Yankees*. In Kirby's long poem, the story of British emigration and settlement in the Niagara Peninsula rolls placidly through four cantos before Hugh, the fratricide in this work, finally initiates the poem's dramatic action with his shocking declaration that he intends to desert his Loyalist family's farm and go to the United States:

I'm free; and I'll obey no man's command.
To-morrow's sun will see me leave these woods,
For Southern lands, where fortune rolls in floods,
Where daring spirits, men who dare be free,
Defy the laws, and live by mastery;
Free'd from your kingly rule, I there will roam
In golden paths undreamed of here at home. (V, x; p. 75)

As Hugh's speech makes clear, this disordered idea of freedom, according to which individual ambition overwhelms social responsibility, constitutes the seduction of American liberty. It is to this idea of liberty that Kirby assigns the blame for the fratricidal conflicts of 1837. The rebel son is restless, longs to kick over the traces, and seeks personal aggrandizement. By contrast, the loyal son remains faithful to the divinely approved hierarchical order represented by his father, his family, the woman he loves, and the larger social structures that guarantee stability – the Crown, the British constitution, and the law and order they provide.

Indeed, we might interpret this conflict as a struggle between men over degrees of whiteness. Such an interpretation requires an understanding of the links between race, Britishness, and the ideology of enterprise that subtended the values of Canadian nationalists who promoted the British connection. Berger summarizes the beliefs of influential, turn-of-the-century Canadian nationalists and imperial federationists such as George Parkin and George Monro Grant, who held 'that spiritual and not material factors made a nation great.' Such ideologues of the nation-within-the-empire were 'suspicious of wealth as either an index of social status or an object of ambition' and asserted instead that the 'human will, when inspired by ideas, was the real engine of history' (*Sense*, 219, 220). This valuation of the spiritual over the material, of the civilized mind over the self-gratifying body, so graphically portrayed in the opposition between the faithful and the prodigal brothers of the fraternal allegory, plays a key part in the complex interconnection between whiteness and imperialism that Richard Dyer examines in his book *White*. He observes that 'Black people can be reduced (in white culture) to their bodies and thus to race, but white people are something else that is realised in and yet is not reducible to the corporal, or racial ... The white spirit organises white flesh and in turn non-white flesh and other material matters: it has *enterprise*' (14–15). He goes on to say that this ideology of enterprise becomes the sign of White spirit – its energy, will, discovery, science, progress, and particularly its ability to organize collectivities, whether families, labourers, companies, nations, or empires (30–1).[6] Loyalist discourse puts a special emphasis on this high-minded, enterprising spirit. Since both the loyal and the rebel brothers are ostensibly White, this literature leans heavily upon the loyal brother's principled commitment to civic improvement and to the maintenance of law and order to make a contrast with the rebel brother, whose whiteness becomes degraded or sullied when he lets lower impulses overwhelm these ideals.

Throughout Loyalist literature, the degree of the settlers' enterprise – and of their whiteness – can be discerned in the neatness and productivity of their farmsteads (see illus. 5). Even before we meet Jeremiah Desborough in *The Canadian Brothers* and see for ourselves the proofs of his treachery, for example, we know him for a freeloader by the neglected state of his farmlands. The narrator introduces us to Desborough by a kind of ground tour of his neighbourhood in which we learn that, unlike his neighbours' dwellings, which were 'hemmed in by the fruits of prosperous agriculture, he appeared to have paid but little attention to the cultivation of a soil, which in every part was of exceeding fertility. A rude log hut … the imperfect work of lazy labour, was his only habitation' (98). By contrast, we are introduced a few pages later to Simon Gatrie, whose alcoholism is redeemed by his fervent loyalty and even more by the steady good management of his son. This son's hard work has produced 'a snug, well cultivated, property.' This 'neat and commodious farm-house' is surrounded by a productive orchard, fenced pastures, and cultivated fields that produce Indian corn, buckwheat, and tobacco (115). It comes as little surprise that the parasitical Desborough turns out to be an American bootlegger who preys upon the vices rather than supporting the virtues of his British Canadian neighbours. If Canada had reason to be thankful for the war, says Richardson's narrator, it is that it offered a means 'of purging her unrepublican soil of a set of hollow hearted persons' (97). This strong repudiation of a casual attitude to homesteading was central to Loyalist discourse for several important reasons.

First, enterprise in regard to land functioned ideologically to justify Whites' displacement of Natives from the land, and second, it distinguished between good and bad settlers. In Richardson's novel, the US officer Major Montgomerie offers a racialized defence of American policy towards Indigenous people when he suggests that, since Native people are 'incapable of benefiting by the advantages of the soil they inherit, they should learn to yield it with a good grace to those who can'

The shanty in the bush

Fifteen years after settlement

Thirty years after settlement

5   The evolution of a Canadian farm as evidence of progress and civility.

(79). He is repeating the colonial ideology of *terra nullius*, which, as Alan Lawson and others have observed, defines uncultivated land as 'empty' and therefore as in need of European settlement and of progress. According to settler ideology, First Nations people did not practise agriculture (despite Huronian, Iroquoian, and other groups' cultivation of corn, beans, and squash; see Dickason 50–2), and Aboriginal land uses such as hunting, trapping, and gathering left the land an undeveloped wilderness, whereas European agricultural cultivation 'makes' or 'develops' the land. What justifies the White displacement of Native people is enterprise – that passion for organization, civic improvement, and development – invested in the soil.

So improved lands distinguish the settlers from the Indigenous people and justify their replacement. But improved farms also distinguish worthy from unworthy settlers. Not only does the ideology of enterprise guard against the White settler's 'going Native' or becoming a bottom-feeding American parasite (Desborough does both); it also guards against a very different set of parasites – the work-wary would-be oligarchy who fashioned themselves after the decadent and unproductive English aristocracy. The UEL land grants system troubles the high moral tenor of loyalty, as Susanna Moodie's exasperation at her freeloading Yankee neighbours in Upper Canada clearly demonstrates in *Roughing It in the Bush* (1852). Similarly, Ralph Connor's narrator describes the damage done by the UEL cronies of the Family Compact in an early chapter of his romance of the War of 1812, entitled *The Runner*: 'These huge grants of land to government favorites could be selected by the grantees at will, throughout the province. The results were disastrous to the extension of settlement and to the establishment of settlers in their rights and privileges as citizens. These huge areas of land remaining unoccupied, uncultivated, became a hindrance to the settlement of the country. Their owners paid no taxes, assumed no responsibilities for the extension of roads, for the building of schools, mills, and other such conveniences necessary to the wellbeing of the settlers' (33–4). The neighbours of these absent landholders found themselves paying for the development of these essential infrastructures, and then, as John Dunbar Moodie explains in the sections he wrote for Susanna's *Roughing It in the Bush*, once the developments had been made, the absent grant holders would sell their properties through land jobbers at the higher prices demanded for an 'improved' region (182, 390–4). Such injustices, says Sergeant Ross, a loyal half-pay officer in Connor's novel who has himself almost had to give up his own grant of land, threatened to make 'rebels out of loyal men' (48). Thus enterprise, manifested through a cultivated farm-stead, distinguishes the hard-working, thrifty, civic-minded Loyalist set-tler from the opportunistic, hypocritical Loyalist leech. Degraded whiteness – or at least, White treachery – can be found at both ends of the social scale (i.e., among American low-lifes as readily as among Family Compact grandees), and the lack of enterprise sorts these unde-sirables out from the desirable whiteness of the truly loyal settler. Gener-ally, Loyalist discourse posits this higher-order, spiritually enterprising whiteness as British and the lower-order, materially ambitious, and there-fore sullied whiteness as American. But it also associates this enterprise with the hard-working, landowning middle class and not with finance-speculating or aristocratic Britishness.

Precisely because of the need to convey the untarnished virtue of the loyal brother's enterprise, war becomes a problematic necessity for the national myth of Loyalist origins. Ernest Renan observed that a nation's 'Unity is always effected by means of brutality' (11) and that suffering in common has much more unifying power than does joy (19). So we might understand the Loyalist evocations of the three most commonly cited moments of Canada's origin – the Revolutionary War, the War of 1812, and the Rebellions of 1837–8 (Berger, *Sense* 90; Duffy, *Gardens* 11) – as episodes of such commonly shared brutality and suffering. But war is necessary to Loyalist literature for an even more troublingly practical reason: it provides a solution to the embarrassing problem of Loyalist motivations. I am referring, again, to the land-grants system. War shifts attention away from land acquisition and back to high ideals. It provides a crucible in which loyalty can be proven, especially through the mascu-line ideology of honourable self-sacrifice, and it thereby demonstrates that the nation's progenitors were motivated by the collective good and not by personal gain.

Furthermore, wartime settings make the allegory of fraternity appear natural to the Loyalist story of the nation's origin. As Benedict Anderson observes in his introduction to *Imagined Communities*, 'regardless of the actual inequality and exploitation that may prevail in each [community], the nation is always conceived as a deep, horizontal comradeship. Ulti-mately it is this fraternity that makes it possible ... for so many millions of people, not so much to kill, as willingly to die' for their nation (7). Military conflict emphasizes fraternity as an apparently natural trope for society. In a time of civil war, it appears natural to figure warring factions as brothers and the object to be defended as the integrity of the family. Along with its naturalization of fraternity as an ideal, the battlefield constitutes an exceptional moral arena in which a special set of ethical protocols between what Richardson's General Brock calls 'belligerent civilized nations' (88) makes it legal for honourable citizens to kill one another in the service of higher collective values. War instates the highly ritualized protocols of what we might call the officer class or brotherhood of officers. When Davy Strang pulls the trigger under his father's command, he destroys a brother to save not only his family and town but also Nova Scotia and, by extension, Canada. The special conventions of war make him, not a criminal, but a defender of law and order.

Battle, figured as the crucible in which the purity of the nation was smelted, posits the garrison, the homosocial brotherhood of officers, as the arena where the nation was formed. I do not propose here to rehearse the psychology of the inside/outside bifurcation in the garrison mentality, as this work, from Frye ('Conclusion') to McGregor to Hurley and Duffy (*World under Sentence*), has been carefully and convincingly done. Rather, I wish to observe that the wartime dispensation of the officer class shifts loyalty's whiteness from essence to deed. That is, it liberalizes brotherhood from a literal blood kinship to a looser, figurative concept, wherein soldiers of a regiment become brothers-in-arms. Even as the officer code reinforces loyalty's claim to the high principles of spiritualized 'enterprise' through an intensified surveillance of the constancy of the Loyalist's filial faith, it is liberal in the sense that other players, even ones outside the White family, are able to figure as members of or at least as allies in a civil brotherhood. This brotherliness was repeatedly portrayed in the David-and-Jonathan bond between Tecumseh and Brock in Richardson's and Mair's texts, a bond that was a staple of Loyalist depictions, as demonstrated in C.W. Jefferys's early twentieth-century romantic portrait of the two men (illus. 6) and in the references to this bond that recur in Agnes Maule Machar's, McIlwraith's, Connor's, Kirby's, and Campbell's texts. Brock and Tecumseh's brotherly bond arises from their virtuous self-sacrifice on behalf of their respective nations, even though they are not of the same race. The officer brotherhood attaches loyalty to principles rather than racial essence.

Tecumseh, throughout Loyalist literature, is admirable for his maintenance of the codes of the officer brotherhood. His nobility of bearing, clemency to prisoners, military stratagem, enterprise in bringing together the Native alliance, and especially his ability to keep his Native troops from savage acts such as scalping or torturing prisoners receive consistent praise. In fact, as Terry Goldie suggests, this combination of admirable traits makes it more likely that he is a White character – that

6   *Meeting of Brock and Tecumseh, 1812* (c. 1908), by Charles William Jefferys.

is, a fantasy of White imagination – than any fully rounded and autono-
mous Aboriginal person. Goldie's shorthand for Tecumseh-as-White-
fantasy is to say this figure makes the first 'Red Tory' (34). But Mair's
depiction of Tecumseh demonstrates that there are many layers involved
even in the White fantasy of Indigenous figures in Loyalist literature.
Mair deliberately puts Shakespearean diction in Tecumseh's mouth, not
out of unconscious and slavish imitation of British dramatic models, as
some have charged (Filewod 74, Tait 10), but because, as he put it in a
letter to George Dennison on 6 January 1884, he wished to avoid 'the
namby-pamby twaddle of the ordinary novelist when putting language
into the Indian's mouth ... I have been surrounded with Indians for
fifteen years, have been present at the most momentous treaties, and ...
I never yet heard the Indian speak but as a sensible, intelligent man, fully
alive to his interests and conscious of his rights, expressing himself
always in language of remarkable vigour and directness' (qtd. in Shrive
78).

Mair's depiction of Tecumseh's dignified speech drew extremely high
praise from E. Pauline Johnson in her essay 'A Strong Race Opinion: On
the Indian Girl in Modern Fiction' (1892), in which she writes: 'Charles
Mair has enriched Canadian-Indian literature perhaps more than any of
our authors, in his magnificent drama, "Tecumseh." The character of
the grand old chief himself is most powerfully and accurately, drawn' (2–
3). Johnson compliments Mair for refusing to put stereotypical language
in Indians' mouths and adds, 'His drama bears upon every page evidence of long study and life with the people whom he has written of so
carefully, so truthfully' (3). Her only complaint is that he follows stereotypical tradition in allowing Iena, Tecumseh's niece, to die by stopping
the bullet intended for her White lover, Lefroy. This conclusion is
disappointing because Iena is, according to Johnson, 'the one "book"
Indian girl that has Indian life, Indian character, Indian beauty,' and it is
too bad that 'the inevitable doom of death could not be stayed even by
Mair's sensitive Indian-loving pen' (3).

But Mair's depiction of Natives in *Tecumseh* is an even more complex
matter than Johnson's encomiums recognize, for, as he was trying to
complete the play, his old nemesis from Red River, Louis Riel, who had
imprisoned Mair and condemned him to death during the 1870 uprising, was being tried for treason in Regina (Shrive 86). So the nobility of
Tecumseh can be read as a foil for the treachery of Riel, as a demonstration, we might suppose, of how a 'good Indian' should behave.[7] Another
way of interpreting the representation of Tecumseh in Mair's play would

be to read it as the tragic failure of the officer code's liberal inclusion of Indigenous people within the British brotherhood.

In fact, the whole of *Tecumseh* could be read as the tragedy of the Shawnee chief's repeated betrayals by brother officers. The first betrayal comes from the Americans, who have broken their treaty agreements not to cross into the Ohio territories and have continued to expropriate Native lands for White settlers. Tecumseh tries to negotiate with his 'brother,' General Harrison, as he calls him during the council at Vincennes (II, iv; p. 114), but the American general's admission that he himself is his 'nation's servitor; / Gold is the king who overrides the right, / And turns out people from the simple ways' (II, iii; pp. 112–13), makes Tecumseh realize that all treaties with the Long-Knives will be similarly betrayed. The second betrayal, as mentioned above, comes from his literal brother, the Prophet, whom Mair presents as a kind of Edmund to Tecumseh's Edgar: 'My duty to Tecumseh! What are these / Compared with duty here? Where I perceive / A near advantage, there my duty lies' (III, v; p. 132). The Prophet's ambition to replace his brother as leader of the First Nations alliance makes him break the promise he made to Tecumseh to keep the warriors from engaging the Americans while Tecumseh is away, and the poorly organized false start of his attack on Harrison's troops at Tippecanoe causes the destruction of Tecumseh's forces in Ohio and necessitates his flight to Canada and alliance with the British. These two betrayals from 'brother' officers, which are devastating to Tecumseh's cause, tend to bolster the reader's confidence in the rightness of the British cause. But the third betrayal comes from a brother officer within the British army.

Brock's resolution and military acumen in the victory at Fort Detroit gives Tecumseh some confidence that his alliance with the British stands a good chance of sustaining a future for his people. But Brock's death at Queenston Heights and his replacement by the cowardly General Henry Proctor finally betray Tecumseh's hopes. Tecumseh urges his 'brother' Proctor, during the council at Amherstburg, to follow Brock's brave example and face the Americans there. He reminds him that the British promised arms and lands to the Natives after the Revolutionary War, but then they surrendered and betrayed their Native allies. Now the British have repeated the promise, but Proctor's proposed retreat looks like the same betrayal. He demands that, if Proctor retreats, he at least give his warriors the weapons that are due them. When Proctor again refuses, Tecumseh reaches for his hatchet and is barely restrained by the other officers from braining the cowardly general. Later at the fated battle at

Moraviantown, Tecumseh tells Proctor, 'Keep a stout heart, / I pray you, brother' (V, v; p. 189), but despite his promise to stand firm, the perfidious British commander secretly arranges for his carriage to be prepared for immediate flight. Tecumseh, after hearing of Proctor's desertion at the outbreak of the fighting, registers the betrayal in racial terms:

> What matters it
> To those who fled, and left us, if they flee?
> They can join palms, make peace, draw treaties up,
> And son and father, reconciled again,
> Will clap their hands, and glory in their race
> Which hath despoiled our own. (V, vi; p. 192)

The tragedy of Tecumseh, and of the First Nations in North America, according to Mair's play, was the result of Whites' failure to maintain the civil codes modelled in the officers' protocols of brotherhood. And so the dying Tecumseh finally resigns himself to the ideology of the waning race – 'The pale destroyer triumphs! / I see my people flee ... and none to shield or save' (V, vi; p. 196) – an ideology that assigns Natives to the role of predecessors rather than progenitors of the British Canadian nation. The play serves as a melancholic pedagogy, a lesson from the tragedies of Brock and Tecumseh on the importance of restoring the consistency, reliability, and loyalty that good brother officers must maintain for one another if civil society is to survive.

The civility of the officer code is demonstrated not only by the possibility of including non-White brothers in the family but also by the recognition that men on opposite sides of the conflict, as long as they behave honourably, can fraternize with one another and respect one another's differing allegiances. Thus in *The Canadian Brothers*, the American prisoners Major and Matilda Montgomerie are billeted in the home of Colonel D'Egville at Fort Amherstburg, and their safe passage back to Buffalo is guaranteed by General Brock.[8] American officers in Richardson's, Curzon's, Connor's, Campbell's, and Raddall's Loyalist texts are admirable if they demonstrate that they engage in battle out of a consistent sense of duty to their nation, a sincere conviction of the rightness of their nation's principles, and if they play consistently by the rules of a fair fight. Ensign Phil Arnoldi, captured along with the Montgomeries and later revealed as the son and fellow conspirator of the traitor and bootlegger Desborough, is pointedly excluded from the officers' dinner party at the D'Egvilles' because he does not follow this code. At this early point in Richardson's novel, the reader has not yet been given any details about Arnoldi's treachery. Instead, his republican rejection of the hierarchical protocols of the officer code is signified through his brutish language. After Major Montgomerie indicates that he does not know Arnoldi, the ensign says: 'I'll tell you what it is, Mister Major – you may think yourself a devilish fine feller, but I guess as how an officer of the Michigan Militia is just as good and as spry as any blue coat in the United States rig'lars.' The narrator registers the reception of Arnoldi's remark by telling us that an 'ill suppressed titter pervaded the group of British officers – the General alone preserving his *serieux*' (53).

The brotherly officer code is class-stratified, separated from the rank and file not just by military hierarchy but also by education, etiquette, and, most importantly, the maintenance of personal honour. Some months later, Gerald Grantham's expert shelling of Fort Detroit so severely wounds Montgomerie, now back with the American troops after having been traded for a British officer of equal rank, that the major eventually dies of his wounds. But this is the peculiar code of wartime: the moments for violence and armistice are adjudicated by mutually agreed upon and strictly followed codes of military honour.[9] The major admires Gerald's devastating skill, and Gerald returns the compliment through his solicitude over the wounded man. When Desborough, by contrast, breaks these codes by masquerading as a wounded soldier during the evacuation of the infirm from the conquered fort, his cowardly pretence shows he is unworthy of officer-class treatment. This descendant of Wacousta cannot be accorded membership in the officer brotherhood because he does not play by the rules. Like his daughter, Matilda Montgomerie, with whom he shares the role of the novel's primary villain, Desborough does not submit his individual concept of vengeance to the military dispensation, with its particularized codes for the honourable execution of justice. The treacherous Desborough family is shown to be degraded or degenerate in their whiteness. Whiteness, as idealized in the allegory of fraternity, is distinguished by its maintenance of the officers' principled code. This code clearly distinguishes the whiteness of the good British Loyalist from the not-so-whiteness of the practical, no-holds-barred rebel brother.

This enterprising-for-honour officer code becomes, in the allegory of fraternity, the model for British Canadian civility in general. Richardson pits this code explicitly against Matilda Montgomerie's nefarious campaign to sign Gerald on as her personal mercenary. For example, she convincingly challenges his belief that a soldier's killing is different from murder. 'How strange and inconsistent are the prejudices of man,' she exclaims, 'here is a warrior – a spiller of human life by profession ... yet he shudders at the thought of adding one murder more to the many already committed' (410–11). Gerald protests that 'fair and honourable combat' in defence of one's country cannot be called murder; one is 'approved of Heaven and of man,' while the other is condemned of both. Her reply is tellingly anti-monarchial and pragmatic:

> Worldly policy and social interests alone have drawn the distinction, making the one a crime, the other a virtue; but tell me not that an all wise and just God sanctions or approves the slaying of his creatures because they perish, not singly at the will of one man, but in thousands and tens of thousands at the will of another. What is there more sacred in the brawls of Kings and Potentates, that the blood they cause to be shed in torrents for some paltry breach of etiquette, should sit more lightly on their souls than the few solitary drops, spilt by the hand of revenge, on that of him whose existence is writhing under a sense of acutest injury? (411)

This, Richardson's text insists, is where the sophistry of republicanism leads: to the breakdown of civil society to the point where private revenge sounds as readily justifiable as defence of one's nation.

Not only are Matilda's arguments explicitly represented as American (she is regularly called 'the American' throughout the novel), but they are also represented as female. 'Foolish Gerald,' she continues in the above argument, 'why should that seem guilt to you, a man, which to me, a woman, is but justice' (412). Richardson's text prophesies that such feminine sophistries, which rationalize private vengeance as public justice, undermine the possibilities of civil society in the new nations emerging on the frontier. His female seductress embodies a femininity that is a threat or distraction to the coherence of the all-male society of military officers. Matilda tempts Gerald to settle for the individualistic pleasures and priorities of the private life, whereas the fraternal garrison urges him to strive towards the altruistic ideals of public responsibility. Thus the code of the officer brotherhood constitutes the British Canadian nation's guard against the chaos of a society fragmented by the competing desires of self-serving individuals. This is why the ritual of the duel reappears in Richardson's, Campbell's, and Connor's versions of the fraternal allegory: the duel represents the officer class's rules of 'fair play' that regulate violent conflict between civilized men. And in both

Campbell's and Connor's novels, the Loyalist character's virtue is 'proven' by contrast with his opponent's breaking the rules of the duel and showing himself unworthy of the honourable code of the gentleman-officer (Campbell ch. 33; Connor ch. 13).[10]

If the officer code serves as the model for civil society, however, it also inculcates the inexplicit but consistent curriculum of an exclusively masculine society to which women are a distraction if not a menace. Feminist historian Janice Potter-Mackinnon argues that while the disruption of the American Revolution meant that women's roles rose in social significance in the thirteen states, the Loyalist refugee women's sacrifices and substantial contributions to the British cause went undervalued in the masculinist society they encountered on arrival in British North America ('Patriarchy' 3–4). She observes that when their men went off to join the Loyalist forces, the women were often left at the mercy of the patriots. They were regularly imprisoned, molested or terrorized, stripped of their belongings, and transported (if they were fortunate) to Canada, the expenses of passage being met by the sale of their properties. But Potter-Mackinnon notes that when they arrived in the British garrisons of Canada, they encountered a society structured under the aegis of the kind of officers' brotherhood I am describing here. It was a society that assumed fraternity and the hierarchical structures of military rank; and, significantly, it was a society that desperately needed able-bodied men not compromised by loyalties to women and children ('Patriarchy' 18). Thus, while the officer code, a staple of the allegory of fraternity, loosened the essentialist implications of a literal, biological brotherhood and allowed figurative brothers to prove their loyalty to British Canada, this code simultaneously placed added emphasis upon the Britishness of the enterprising-for-virtue kind of whiteness that ought to distinguish Canadians from Americans. Furthermore, it presented a masculinist model of nationhood whose hierarchy relegated women to the margins.

The wartime settings I have been examining cause obvious problems for a nationalist discourse that is intended to convey the Loyalist forefathers as choosers of peace and order over violence. For while the trauma of fratricide must be invoked as constitutive of the nation's origin, it must be contained in the past and not projected into the nation's future. This contradictory imperative finds its rationale in Renan's reminder 'Forgetting, I would even go so far as to say historical error, is a crucial factor in the creation of a nation … [T]he essence of a nation is that all individuals have many things in common, but also that they have forgotten many things' (11). The fraternal allegory's dependence on internecine violence represents the commonly shared memory that Canadians must be reminded to forget. Richardson's exception here proves the rule: his depiction of the trauma of fratricide remains disturbingly compelling long after the gothic romance declined as a dominant genre of Canadian fiction. While the authors I refer to later in this chapter generally attempt to assuage the traumatic memory of fratricide, Richardson does not. Published in 1840, long before post-Confederation nationalists purveyed optimistic romances about the unlimited potentials of the nation within the empire and just a few years after the two rebellions demonstrated how internally riven was the British North America that Richardson had fought to save, *The Canadian Brothers* ends in gloom, with the Canadian Henry Grantham and the American Jeremiah Desborough clasped in mortal combat and falling to their deaths in the Niagara Gorge. For Richardson, the genealogy of the British Whites in America was doomed from the start – a cursed heredity (416) – and it marches inexorably through his two novels to its fated conclusion.[11] His jeremiad of botched origins, by its negative example, calls for a reassertion of the nation's better self – its higher, whiter enterprise.

Accordingly, the nationalists who wrote after Richardson struggled concertedly to turn his gothic tragedy into pastoral or sentimental romance. In fact, it is possible to read most of the early-twentieth-century historical fiction about the revolutionary or 1812 wars as anti-war novels. The contradictions involved in the struggle to acknowledge and disavow war as the agent of the nation's birth are evident in Campbell's preface to *A Beautiful Rebel*, where he writes that Brock's repulsion of American invasion 'made possible the birth and development of a new, young and independent nation, under the British Crown on the northern part of this continent.' But he hastens to add, 'happily, all of the old bitterness has long since passed away, and our Anglo-Celtic brothers in the Republic to the south will be as interested in the struggle of the Canadian people as an element in race-development as the Canadians have been in that of New England, Old New York, Virginia or Louisiana' (6). The rhetoric of racial indivisibility here, central to the allegory of fraternity, serves to underline the authorial desire to repudiate the violence of the nation-forming war that nonetheless orders the action of the entire novel. We can see a similar process of repudiation in McIlwraith's novel when her hero, Stephen Ellison, is frustrated that Lucy Clark, the American woman he loves, 'could not see how wicked was this war between two peoples of one blood, one Lord, one faith, one baptism' (127). And when the war eventually ends and the lovers are finally able to unite,

Lucy's American grandfather chides her patriotism: 'What was the sense of the whole war? Now that we know the terms of the treaty signed at Ghent, Christmas Eve, what have we gained? The United States have spent a hundred million of dollars, and lost thirty thousand men. We have not acquired an inch of territory, nor a right for which we fought ... No, Lucy, I can't say we have much to brag about in this war' (282–3). This tension between the fascinating memory and the deliberate dis-avowal of the nation's birth through war characterizes the productive paradox that animates Loyalist literature.

Perhaps the most telling example of this troubled struggle occurs in William Kirby's verse epic *The U.E.* Two families populate this narrative poem set in the Niagara Peninsula before and during the 1837–8 rebellion; the first is the recently immigrated family of Walwyn, who left England because the taxes levied after the Napoleonic Wars threatened to deprive his sons of their inheritance and who has therefore come to seek 'freedom, peace, and plenty ... / And still rejoice 'neath England's rule benign' (I, xiii; p. 12). The beginning of the poem tells the story of Walwyn, his son Ethwald, and their settlement and quickly gained prosperity in their new woodland home. But once the second family is introduced through its patriarch, Ranger John, the Walwyn story tends to fade into the background of Ranger John's tale of high daring-do (Northey 92; Ken McLean 34). Ranger John is a septuagenarian whose first family were burnt to death in their farmhouse by rebels in the United States. He then joined a group of rangers who scalped and burnt rebels from Carolina to Niagara through the rest of the Revolutionary War. The high point of these years occurred when he caught and scalped the American who had led the rebels that killed his family. Hungry from weeks of pursuit, John ate with relish the loaf of bread soaked in his enemy's blood that he found in the dead man's haversack (IV, xxi; p. 65). Despite Ranger John's subsequent success in establishing a sec-ond family and a thriving farm in Upper Canada, he clearly misses those days of rapine and retribution.

So when the rebellion breaks out, he is more than ready to grasp the notched handle of his old battleaxe and leap to his country's defence. By contrast, Walwyn, the pastoral patriarch, agrees to join up with his sons despite his aversion to war, but he counsels the eager Ranger John to approach the enemy with mercy, for he fears that ''Tis with a sort of joy thou drawst the steel / Upon thy brethren,' who, according to Walwyn, are more dupes than traitors (IX, ix; p. 123). But John will have none of it. If he did not know better, he might even question Walwyn's loyalty.

John's inevitable confrontation with his fratricidal son Hugh, who has become a rebel leader since defecting to the American side, fittingly culminates the poem's trial of loyalty. When the two meet face to face during the fighting at Prescott Mill and Hugh learns he has killed his brother Herman, he throws down his sword and begs his father's forgiveness. The old man refuses: 'Thy father's hand / Never spared a rebel to his king and land' (XII, xxvii; p. 175). The old patriarch lifts his axe, but is spared the slaughter of his son when rifle fire from the rebel side kills Hugh at his feet.

This scene comes from the final canto of the six-thousand-line poem, but although it is clearly the epic's climactic moment, its familial violence cannot be allowed to remain its final statement. When the rebels surrender, Ranger John's youngest son, significantly named Simcoe, rushes to the spot, 'but never knew' we are carefully told, 'The dreadful secret of his brother Hugh' (XII, xxi; p. 176). And so he cannot attach to the hatchet his father bequeaths him the story of his brother's treachery. The story of the prodigal brother and the horror of his fratricide, which have driven the plot that we as readers have followed throughout the poem, must be both alluded to and kept hidden from the younger brother so that the national family's next generation can retain its ostensible innocence. The high drama of the battle now over, the poem closes with an insistence on a pastoral in which Walwyn and Ranger John converse in 'summer shade or by winter's fire' (XII, xxxiv; p. 178):

> Old John sits on his porch, and robins sing
> Amid the apple blossoms, while a ring
> Of children's children cluster round his knee,
> Filled with the spirit of the old U.E.
> Learning to guard, like him, in days of yore
> England's proud Empire, One, for ever more. (XII, xxxv; p. 178)

The struggle to constrain the trauma of fratricide troubles the ostensible quiet of the scene. With the younger generation, we as readers are being reminded to forget that which is essential to our membership in the national family; the poem insists that the story of fratricide is the necessary precursor to the next generation's idyll of innocence. It teaches descendent generations the importance of guarding against treachery from within, even as it keeps them ignorant of the squalid and horrifying details in their story of origins, so that they can retain the kind of innocence that will make the nation into a peaceable kingdom.

War, therefore, is a necessary problem for Loyalist discourse mainly because it removes the suspicion of avarice associated with the Loyalist land-grants system. But the theme of violence complicates the Loyalist myth's idealization of the United Empire refugees as peace-lovers who left the rebel states out of repugnance for mob violence and rule by vendetta. The civil code of the exclusively male brotherhood of officers represents one attempt to justify or at least ennoble that violence, but there is another way in which the makers of Canadian Loyalist literature could fashion a moral high ground for the British Canadians' engagement in battle. They could do so by linking their involvements in war to altruism on behalf of vulnerable non-Whites.

These vulnerable figures in Canadian Loyalist literature are either Blacks or Aboriginals. The Canadian brother in every instance of the fraternal allegory I have encountered is intimate with either Natives or New World Africans, sometimes both, and this intimacy forms a natural alliance against the predations of both rebel treachery and American expansionism.[12] In the case of relations with Blacks, who are usually slaves or runaway slaves, the relationship is meant to expose the hypocrisy of the republican proclamation of liberty for all. The Canadian brother's enlightened attitude towards New World Africans is presented in the allegory as support for the Loyalist claim that true liberty can be found only under the British constitution, as evidenced in Governor Simcoe's legislation to phase out slavery in Upper Canada after 1793. In the case of friendships with Aboriginal people, the strategy follows the pattern of 'indigenization' theorized separately by Terry Goldie and Alan Lawson as essential to the discourse of colonial settlement. Through proximity to Indigenous culture, the settler is represented as having become natural or native to the Canadian landscape; he learns the ways of the land and becomes intimate with its lore, ecology, and inhabitants to such a degree that other characters consider his local knowledge authoritative (Goldie 13, 21, 40; Lawson 26, 28).

Richardson's Grantham brothers are faithfully attended by Sambo, whose name shows that he is more of a type, a place-holder, than a character and whose devotion to their parents makes him the emotional, if not literal, slave of the sons. Cody's Jean Sterling, Campbell's Lydia Bradford, McIlwraith's Laura Secord, and Curzon's Laura Secord also deal humanely, if condescendingly, with their uniformly faithful Black servants and, by so doing, are meant to demonstrate British Canadian enlightenment in contrast to American hypocrisy, exemplified in the institution of slavery. Machar's Lilias Meredith underscores the point, not only by her kindness to the elderly escaped slave Aunt Judy but also by her voiced preference for the abolitionists William Wilberforce, Thomas Clarkson, and Granville Sharp over military or political heroes (74). Richardson's brothers, McIlwraith's Stephen Ellison, French's Glen Vulpin and Peter van Doorn, and Cody's Dane Norwood all derive from their Aboriginal friends and teachers the woodcraft and canoe skills that serve as signs of their fittedness to inherit the Canadian lands. Davy Strang is more than once saved from death by his Micmac (*sic*, rather than Mi'kmaq) companion François; in Machar's *For King and Country*, Major Meredith, having once saved Black Hawk's wife and infant from a rattlesnake, has the favour returned by Black Hawk when he is in a tight spot on Queenston Heights; in Mair's play, Brock and Tecumseh exchange tokens of their mutual respect; and, in Ralph Connor's novel, René LaFlamme's brilliance as a scout in Brock's regiment is traced to his lifelong friendship with Black Hawk of the Six Nations and to his knowledge of a variety of Native languages. In Campbell's *Beautiful Rebel*, Captain Etherington enjoys the wordless solidarity of the mysterious John Brant, son of the famous Mohawk chief. This consistent alignment of the faithful brothers with Black and Indigenous characters links British loyalty to the righting of American injustice against Aboriginals and Black slaves. '[I]f a just weighing were possible,' McIlwraith's Canadian Stephen Ellison tells his Indian-fearing American sweetheart, Lucy Clark, 'we should soon discover that the red man had suffered far more from us than we have from him.' He goes on to list the expropriation of lands, the spread of smallpox, and the degeneration brought on by alcoholism as examples of the evils Whites have perpetrated upon Natives (220). If one of the Canadian brothers mistreats or neglects one of these figures, as Gerald does Sambo in Richardson's novel or Proctor does Tecumseh in Mair's play, it is a telltale sign of the degradation of his moral character. The Black and Indigenous figures that recur in these Loyalist texts are not primarily characters in and for themselves (with the debatable exception of Mair's Tecumseh); rather, they instantiate the ethical differences between the upright and the downfallen White brothers. The alignment of the Loyalist White brother with Native and African characters insists, once again, that his fratricidal violence is motivated by virtuous enterprise – a campaign for justice on behalf of others.

Kirby provides us with the clearest example of how these African and Native characters instantiate the nobility of the White Loyalist's enterprise. One night an escaped slave arrives at Walwyn's door full of the story of his escape across the Niagara River and of the gathering of rebel camps on the other side of the border. Mango – a name to match Richardson's and Machar's 'Sambo,' Cody's 'Mammy,' and the ubiquitous 'Black Hawk' – is amazed at the hospitality he receives from the race who usually tyrannize his kind. He then tells the story of his flight from slavery in Tennessee. After years of faithful service, Mango learned that his master had decided to sell off his family and send his children to Texas and his wife to Georgia. One day soon after, he had the chance to leap from hiding and murder this heartless master, but two things stopped the impulse: first, the commandment not to murder and, second, the recognition of fraternity:

> His sire was mine in sin and shame; twas said
> That my bond-mother, helpless in her fall,
> Bore me a father's slave, a brother's thrall,
> I gazed on his face, and spared his life. (VIII, xxiii; p. 117)

In a statement that might serve as a gloss on the above passage, Machar reminds her readers, in her novel of the War of 1812, *For King and Country*, that 'the war was forced on mainly by the *slave-holding* States' (165), implying that the conflict was really between hypocritical southern ideas of democracy that excluded Africans from personhood and integrous British-northern concepts of civility that guaranteed the rights of all within a hierarchically ordered society.

But there is more in Kirby's story of the escaped slave who refused to murder his brother. Mango has every reason to wreak vengeance on a tyrant who so viciously disavows the natural solidarity of brothers. Yet even he, a slave and therefore a man far removed from the elite officer class, follows a protocol of civil behaviour superior to that of his American master.[13] After refusing to commit fratricide as an act of private justice, he 'seek[s] sweet freedom on Canadian plains' (VIII, xxv; p. 118) and eventually joins the Loyalist militia who will punish treacherous brothers in the legitimate arena of battle. Very often in these narratives, the African or Native figure is used to shame the behaviour of treacherous Whites. Raddall, for example, has the old Maliseet (Raddall spells it 'Malicete') chief Ambroise respond to the British commander's invitation for his people to join the Loyalist side of the conflict by asking, 'How comes it that the Old England and the New England quarrel and come to blows? For the father and the son to fight is terrible' (*Yankees* 160). Later in his valediction against the betrayal of Nova Scotians by the

Boston merchants during the revolution, the narrator says that the New England traders abandoned and then loosed their sea-dog pirates upon their erstwhile family members: 'No wonder our Indians were astonished. Not even a savage would do that' (355). Tecumseh's steadfast dedication to the welfare of his people and his bold desire to engage the Americans in battle contrasts sharply in Mair's play with the self-protecting cowardice of the false brother, General Proctor, at the devastating Battle of Moraviantown. Not even a savage would do that: even slaves and savages reject the incivility that denies family loyalty and attacks from ambush. Though fratricide may constitute a necessary justice in extreme moments, even then it must be carried out, as Mango demonstrates, in the formalized rituals of military contest.

If the Canadian brother's championing of the just causes of Africans and Natives distinguishes Canadian virtue from American greed and perfidy, his indigenization produces an even finer distinction. This is the difference between British Canadian whiteness and English whiteness, and it is a crucial refining distinction that operates within the British officer code I have described above. English parentage is the preferred stock of the national family, but as the Englishman adjusts himself to North American ways, he becomes more vigorous and versatile and therefore the harbinger of the superior new breed being produced in the settler colony. A tension between English-born and Canadian-born members of the officer class shows itself in the aforementioned opening scene of *The Canadian Brothers*, in which the English officers Barclay and Molineux question Gerald's fidelity specifically as a Canadian. Henry exults in his brother's vindication as soon as his unorthodox ambush, a strategy known about and approved by Tecumseh (38), brings the British their first American captives: 'The "Canadian" as he ... had been superciliously termed, would be the first to reap for Britain's sons the fruits of a war in which those latter were not only the most prominent actors, but also the most interested' (40). Whereas the English officers operate by protocol and the obedient performance of one's duties, the Canadian, empowered by Indigenous knowledge of the local topography and liberated from the constraints of how things are done in metropolitan society, acts directly and decisively. The Canadian has learned from his Indigenous friends a practicality that dispenses with the inertia and artificiality of social niceties. His experience of life in the wilderness associates him with the image of the Native child of nature, uncorrupted or sissified by the protocols of urban sophistication that hamstring Europeans.

Consistently throughout Richardson's novel, as well as throughout his many cameo appearances in Loyalist literature, Tecumseh is represented as a frank, 'inartificial son of nature' (26) who is not afraid to tell cowards such as Proctor exactly what he thinks. He speaks 'in plain unvarnished language, what many of the English officers most religiously believed' but were not free to say about their commander (433). Cody's Native-friendly hero, Dane Norwood, likewise is unbound by the niceties of protocol. He explains his failure to salute Major Studholme, the commander of Fort Howe, as the result of his forest upbringing among Maliseets and settlers: 'Where I live we are all equal ... We never bother about such things.' Studholme finds Dane's clear-eyed directness more trustworthy than the obsequious courtesy of characters whose loyalty is less certain (32). The central romance plot of Ralph Connor's *The Runner* posits the indigenized Canadian, René LaFlamme, and the aristocratic fop, Eustace Burton, Lord Glendale, as rivals for the hand of Charlotte, eldest daughter of the Tory Loyalist Colonel Brookes.[14] Again and again, René's courage, his Native-derived knowledge of the land, and his physical dexterity, in addition to his absolute moral integrity, reveal Colonel and Charlotte Brookes's attraction to Eustace's rank and wealth to be misdirected. René's concern for just treatment of Aboriginal people forces him to confront Colonel Brookes with the corruption in the Office of Indian Affairs and Public Lands, even though it may turn Charlotte's father against him (ch. 4 and 5). Ultimately, René's vast superiority to Eustace is demonstrated in a critical moment when, after being wounded by a band of raiders the British have been trying to capture, he still manages to send a message through Charlotte to Lieutenant FitzGibbon that the raiders are in the area and an immediate dispatch of soldiers could capture them. Charlotte is furious when Eustace advises FitzGibbon to seek permission from the general before sending out the pursuit. Eustace's waiting upon protocol aborts the whole mission, allowing the raiders to escape. Then when Charlotte determines to go back to nurse the wounded René, Eustace objects to her going in the middle of the night without a chaperone (405–6). After such episodes throughout the plot have clearly established the buckskin-clad Canadian's superiority to the redcoated English peer, Charlotte asks her father why he ever wanted her to marry the Englishman, and he can only cry, 'God pity me!' (468).

The Canadian brother who is intimate with Native people and lore constitutes a specific refinement in the ideology of whiteness. He manifests the high-spirited enterprise of the British officer class's maintenance of a civil code of fairplay, even, or especially, in the unplayful context of a bloody war. This maintenance of the protocols of civilized warfare restrains him from the barbarisms ascribed to Aboriginals (just as Walwyn restrains Ranger John's bloodlust), as well as from the republican disregard of law and order ascribed to Americans. But the Canadian's indigenization sets him apart from British officers, whose ignorance of practical knowledge makes them indecisive in moments requiring action and whose training in the niceties of Old World etiquette causes them to replace manly integrity with prevarication. Thus the Canadian brother is limned through his association with Native and African characters. These often become 'brothers-in-arms' in the heat of warfare, but ultimately they do not become fully developed characters. Though they begin the narrative as the Canadian brothers' intimates, they are generally expendable by the time the narrative closes. They do not survive as members of the inner fraternity, and so they do not figure as progenitors of the nation. They remain elements of the nation's story of origin but not agents in its future. In this way, fraternal allegory 'whitens' the Loyalist's involvement in warfare by justifying it as altruism on behalf of oppressed non-Whites. Furthermore, the faithful brother's indigenous expertise distinguishes his particularly Canadian virtues of virile action and adaptability from the impractical niceties that impede English officers.

But for all its uses, the fraternal allegory poses a final and irresolvable problem for the national narrative. Fraternity is backward-looking; it is preoccupied with purity (racial, familial, and moral), and it is therefore static. Occupying the homosocial world of bachelors, it has no ability to propagate itself. Henry Grantham's desperate attempt to save his brother from the enticements of Matilda Montgomerie are doomed for more than one reason. Clearly, Matilda poses a threat to Henry's passionate attachment to Gerald; we are told that Henry 'doated upon his brother' (224), for whom he feels 'more than brother's love' (323), and even before Matilda's perfidy is exposed, he feels a dislike for her that is 'impelled by a feeling he was unable to analyze' (224). When Gerald promises (as it turns out, ineffectually) that he will never allow Matilda to persuade him to perform a dishonourable deed, 'Henry offered no other reply than by throwing himself into the arms that were extended to receive him. The embrace of the brothers was long and fervent' (336). One need not interpret this embrace as explicitly homosexual to see that the rivalry Henry feels between himself and Matilda for Gerald's affections constitutes a variation on the classic erotic triangle which Eve Sedgwick has identified as fundamental to the routing of homosocial desire between men through a 'traffic in women' (21–7). Whereas Sedgwick analyses the homoeroticism suppressed in the rivalry *between men* over a woman as a basic convention of fiction, Henry's explicit rivalry *with a woman* for his brother's affection emphasizes the exclusive structure of the male paradigm operating in Richardson's fraternal allegory. As John Moss observes in regard to the complex erotic triangles in *Wacousta*, conventional homophobic morality rules out this exclusive bond between men and demands that it be channelled through hetero-sexual romance ('*Wacousta*,' 471). One could read the tragic ending of *The Canadian Brothers* as the inevitable demise of the sterile, self-consuming paradigm of the officers' garrison.

In this sense, the fraternal allegory has a conceptual shelf life, which is to say that it enables a certain explanatory pedagogy for the nation's violent origins, but it cannot project a future. It can only end with Grantham's and Desborough's bones whitening in the sun in Richardson's Niagara Gorge, with old men reminiscing in Kirby's sexless Arcadia, or with Tecumseh's martyrdom after the treachery of his various brothers. Enter the romantic plot of heterosexual courtship and marriage, which deploys its forward-looking, more inclusive, and reproductive vision via a traffic in women.

The opposition between a filial thralldom to ancestry and future-oriented marriage provides the central debate of Wilfred Campbell's *Beautiful Rebel.* In this novel, Captain Etherington is fresh off the boat with British regulars destined to join General Brock's troops. We soon learn that he is ignorant in two major areas: he does not know why Upper Canadians are discontent under the Family Compact, and he is an orphan who does not know his ancestry. 'Ancestry,' the narrator tells us, 'has ever been a natural pride to the British gentleman, associated as it is with rank, position and personal honor' (34). Etherington falls in love with Lydia Bradford, the beautiful rebel of the novel's title, who soon educates him on the first score. But not until the very end of the novel, when he meets with Colonel Monmouth, his father's estranged brother, does he have the opportunity to learn about his genealogy. Monmouth, however, gives him a Richardsonian warning: ancestry is a curse, and if Etherington persists in discovering his parentage, he will lose every happiness. He counsels the young captain instead to abandon these useless connections to the Old World and marry Lydia Bradford, who can do more for him than ancestry could ever do. 'She has the magic power of youth and love and hope of the New World,' Monmouth tells his nephew, 'to lead you out of the shadow and the mystery, the terrible fate which overhangs so many of those of a certain strain of Old World heredity' (312–13). The novel establishes, therefore, an opposition between the filial founding of identity in sordid family history and romantic adventure. After some careful soul-searching, the young man chooses the latter. It takes a compromise that Kirby's Ranger John would never comprehend, for Etherington and Lydia must admit there were rights and wrongs on both Loyalist and rebel sides, but Etherington believes this is 'the great compromise, on which alone life in this young country can last' (317).

And so reproductive sexuality eventually must replace fraternity if the narrative of the nation is to move from remembrance to progress, from the past to the future. The works that resist or despair of this liberal vision of compromise – Richardson's, Mair's, and Kirby's – run the risk of genealogical doom in which the violence and trauma of fratricide overwhelm any national story that foresees a workable future. Texts that do make the transition – Campbell's, McIlwraith's, Connor's, French's, and Raddall's – disavow, or at least quarantine, the brutal story of origins by turning our attention to the prospect of a new genealogy free of ancient curses. As Henry Grantham suspected, femininity does represent the demise of the primary loyalty of brotherhood. Sentimental romances such as those by Campbell, Cody, McIlwraith, Connor, and French deliberately turn away from an exclusivist interpretation of loyalty, with its emphasis on UEL pedigree, Tory elitism, and strong anti-Americanism, and figure cross-gender courtship and marriage as a reconciliation between opposed factions in the fraternal-familial struggle. These texts tend to rely heavily on the officer code, which holds that honourable patriotism on either side of the conflict can constitute true loyalty. Accordingly, those who prove their virtue on either the loyal or the rebel (or at least reform) side are worthy progenitors of the New World British nation. Marriage between people who behaved honourably on opposite sides of the conflict restores the ideal of the indivisible national family.

A modernist-realist romance such as Raddall's, however, subverts all such claims to high virtue, whether uttered by rebels or by Loyalists. 'Any thief can cry Liberty when there's plunder to be had by it,' proclaims Davy's hardbitten father at the beginning of the novel. 'Any leech can cry Loyalty while there's fat blood to suck' (61). Allegiances shift repeatedly throughout this novel, as do the orientations of loyalty. The rural Nova Scotians of *His Majesty's Yankees* are mostly immigrants from New England, and they resent the opportunistically loyal Halifax merchant elite who huddle around the Assembly to gorge themselves on British government patronage while they reduce political representation for farmers, sailors, and fishermen. Though rural folk such as the novel's central Strang family maintain strong connections to their Pilgrim ancestors in Massachusetts, the war so confuses their allegiances that they find themselves switching from side to side. Early in the novel, the two oldest Strang brothers, Mark and Luke, are press-ganged into His Majesty's fleets. They later escape and join the rebels, as does Davy, the protagonist-narrator. The one Strang brother who joins up with the king's forces, John, turns out to have committed the greatest act of treachery when, as we later learn, he raped his brother's fiancée, Joanna, and thus caused Mark's estrangement from her and raised his ugly suspicion of being cuckolded by his brother Luke.

So the trust and treachery of brothers is at the heart of this novel, too. But the dividing lines between the loyal and the rebel brothers do not hold steady, for after risking their lives with the rebel forces in the under-provisioned attack on Fort Cumberland, Mark and Davy grow disillusioned with empty Yankee talk about freedom, especially when they see the privateering that their Massachusetts brethren inflict upon their coastal villages in Nova Scotia. Davy's final rejection of the rebel cause is paralleled by his eventual espousal of Fear Bingay, who likewise has abandoned any illusions about her Tory family's commitment to the king. The pressure of loyalties comes to a crisis at the end of the novel when Matthew Strang organizes the aforementioned defence of their village against the pirate gang lieutenanted by his son Luke. During this battle, Matthew calls upon Davy to commit the fratricide that Raddall positions as the moment of Nova Scotia's reluctant alignment with the British crown, an alignment he has his narrator predict will eventually produce a self-governing British nation in North America (403). Raddall's story of sullied and shifting loyalties therefore makes the high moral tone of loyalism's White enterprise the object of scathing critique.

Nonetheless, the allegory of fratricide remains prominent even in this critical engagement with the story of Canada's Loyalist origins. And though it shares Richardson's rejection of the simple pedagogy that associates unalloyed virtue with the loyal British Canadian brothers, Raddall's novel does not end like Richardson's in the fulfillment of a terrible curse. Rather, it attempts to suppress that curse. After shooting his brother under his father's orders, Davy wonders 'how long Mother could remain ignorant of a thing the whole town knew. I wonder still. I only know that she never again mentioned Luke's name in my presence, all the days that she lived' (404). The mother never speaks what she most certainly knows. Immediately following this troubling reflection, Davy smothers the trauma of fratricide through a deliberate turn towards the reproductive allegory of heterosexual love. He explains:

> I felt like Cain. In a shuddering spasm of wretchedness I turned to seek Fear [Bingay], instinctively, as a hurt dog seeks the shade. Nothing was more natural. Preachers never understand why love and war go hand in hand, why in time of horror and bloodshed a man should turn to a woman, and not to Heaven, for comfort and release. Heaven is too far and much too bodiless at such a moment; that is why the good God put woman in the world and made her what she is. In her, seeking forgetfulness, a man can find his soul again ... Only she could save me from this black and shaking terror of myself. If I could let my mind fill with the love of her, see only her, feel only her, know only her, if I could surrender myself utterly to her, then the nightmare must remain outside. (404–5)

The woman here represents the site where the brother's nightmare of fratricide is sublimated. Whereas fraternity was once perceived as the natural metaphor for the civil community of the nation, now nothing could be more natural than seeking forgetfulness from the threatening nightmare through the allegory of marriage. Both story forms are explicitly masculinist: whereas the fraternal allegory figures the nation as exclusively male, the romantic allegory figures femininity as the forgiving and reproductive ground in which the masculine nation plants its future seed. Regarding their wedding night in his father's house, the older narrator, Davy, looks back with this concluding statement from the novel's final page:

> The house of the Strangs, which had been full and was now so empty, would be filled with young voices again. There would be sons, as my father prophesied. They would be tall and hard of hand and voice, granting friendship sparingly but giving with it a loyalty unshakeable and ready to fight, suffer, endure anything for the sake of it. They would be a little hard with their women, but passionate in their tender moments, and women would endure the ice for the sake of the fire. But our sons would never give themselves wholly to anything but this rocky homeland on the sea's edge. (409)

This strongly patriarchal allegory figures sex with a woman as the salve of memory, the agent of forgetfulness that enables the terrified hero to imagine a future in his White father's British house beyond the memories he must suppress.[15] Echoing but reorienting Henry Grantham, Davy Strang turns not to a brother but to a female lover when he begs, 'Assure me that I am not a fratricide.'

And so the fratricide that runs through the Loyalist allegory of fraternity calls forth the originating spectral trauma the Canadian nation must be reminded to forget. It is a nervous narration whose official pedagogy explains why and how a White, enterprising British Canadian nation came to be separated from the United States. Its domestic arena locates the sorrow of the nation among those most closely linked to our warm affections. It is a narration that is anxious to assert the unclouded virtue of the Loyalist cause, and so it deploys the rhetoric of military courage and sacrifice to remove any suspicion of the kind of mixed motives that animate degraded White rebels. But the story of the Loyalists' violence must be quarantined almost as soon as it is acknowledged, and so it is civilized and justified through the officer code and an association with altruism on ·behalf of oppressed and vulnerable non-Whites. The homosocial paradigm of the fraternity of officers, however, produces a new impossibility, for its same-sex society cannot reproduce itself, cannot generate a future, without the supplementary presence of femininity. And so the fraternal allegory is forgotten or suppressed through a segue to heterosexual courtship and marriage. Nonetheless, this nervous Loyalist allegory runs consistently, despite substantial perspectival shifts, from Richardson's early tragic vision through Kirby's pastoral idyll and Mair's heroic tragedy, both written during the height of Canadian nation-building, to the sentimental romances by Campbell, McIlwraith, Connor, and others in the tens and twenties and onwards to Raddall's much more cynically modernist version of romance, published in 1942. All the while, its residual, unofficial curriculum naturalizes a consistent image of the Canadian nation's 'true' founders as White, British brothers of the officer class.

3 The Enterprising Scottish Orphan: Inventing the Properties of English Canadian Character

When Sandor Hunyadi, the twelve-year-old protagonist of John Marlyn's novel *Under the Ribs of Death* (1957), asks his Hungarian-born father if they can change 'Hunyadi' to an English-sounding last name, he demonstrates a clear understanding of the link between Englishness and social status in Canada. 'Pa, the only people who count are the English,' the boy explains. 'Their fathers got all the best jobs. They're the only ones nobody ever calls foreigners. Nobody ever makes fun of their names or calls them "bologny-eaters" [*sic*], or laughs at the way they dress or talk ... 'cause when you're English it's the same as bein' Canadian' (17–18). Sandor's equation of the status property of Englishness – that is, the power of English ethnicity to enhance class ascendancy and privilege – with full belonging in Canada identifies one of this country's most powerfully normative ethnocultural pairings. 'English Canada' is as imprecise a cultural designation as that other baggy phrase, 'the rest of Canada,' the loose generalization for everything outside Quebec that recurs in popular political discussion any time tensions mount between Canada's two so-called founding nations. These loose categories, however, have very specific uses. Many scholars and activists have observed the bipolar pathology contained in the binary myth of national origins and especially its disavowal of the First Nations, who preceded the nation's belated French and English 'founders.' This work has been convincingly and powerfully done.[1] Rather than questioning the specious priority claimed by the concept of the two founding nations, therefore, I want to work here towards a denaturalization of the dominant member of that pair, 'English Canada,' through a critical genealogy of its construction. By way of a study of its particular uses for Scottish Canadians, I aim to expose its function, like whiteness in the realm of race and masculinity in the realm of gender, as status property.[2]

There are dimensions of the term 'English' as Sandor uses it in 1913, the year in which Marlyn sets the opening chapters of his novel, that differ from the way it functions in popular Canadian usage today. For Sandor, 'English' serves as shorthand for belonging not just in Canada but, more importantly, in the British Empire. Ten pages after the above scene, Sandor experiences a momentary triumph when he wins a school prize for the essay he has written about Victoria Day. This victory constitutes his revenge over the gang of English boys who regularly beat him up after school, for he has defeated them at their own game and in their own language. But Marlyn emphasizes the tenuous nature of this triumph when he shows that Sandor can gain the accoutrements of English privilege only by desperate and even larcenous measures. Next day the boy attends the Victoria Day parade at the city centre. There he grabs a younger English kid, bloodies his nose, rifles his pockets for ice cream money, and carries off his Union Jack so he can wave it proprietorially when the pipe band marches past (29–31). The swirling kilts of the bagpipe band are an important detail in this scene, for this distinctly Scottish presence in the procession of legitimacy that Sandor thinks of as 'English' (think how the pipers themselves would react to being called 'English'!) shows that this Englishness involves a slippery proximity to the more general term 'British,' and this proximity loosens Englishness away from a strictly national or ethnic concept and disperses it into a looser, elastic category. Sandor's inclusion of the Scottish pipers in the English elite is neither an idiosyncratic error nor a child's misperception. Indeed, my method for scrutinizing the Englishness in 'English Canada' follows Sandor's lead by showing, with reference to five Scottish Canadian novels – John Galt's *Bogle Corbet* (1831), Thomas McCulloch's *The Mephibosheth Stepsure Letters* (1821–3), Margaret Murray Robertson's *Shenac's Work at Home* (1866), Ralph Connor's *The Man from Glengarry* (1901), and Hugh MacLennan's *Barometer Rising* (1941) – how the Scots inserted themselves at the head of the procession in Canada and how, by means of the mediating concept of Britishness, they created the Canadian version of Englishness in their own image.

The term 'British' arose from the need for a pan-ethnic category when the various ethno-national populations of the British Isles united into a larger, single kingdom. The *Oxford English Dictionary* records that although 'Britt,' 'Brett,' or 'Brettisc' appeared in Latin, Old Celtic, Old French, and Old English usages as a geographical reference, the terms 'Britain,' 'British,' and 'Briton' in reference to the region's inhabitants did not come into wide circulation until Henry VIII's and Edward VI's efforts to unite the kingdoms of Scotland and England in the sixteenth century. The concept of Britain became legitimized when James VI of Scotland was proclaimed James I, 'King of Great Britain,' in 1604, but it was not used as a legal category until the Treaty of Union brought Scotland and England into a single kingdom in 1707. As I mentioned in the previous chapter, this genealogy for the term 'Britain' and its reference to an inclusive nation extending across the divides of ethnic, religious, linguistic, and cultural hostility was behind the oft-repeated North American claims of eighteenth-century United Empire Loyalists (often of Dutch, German, or Highlander descent) and nineteenth-century imperial federationists for the superiority of the British constitution and the civility of its administrative models. For Canadians before the advent of multicultural rhetoric in the late 1960s, therefore, 'British' connoted a limited kind of pan-ethnic inclusiveness that had its clearest popular expression in the unofficial anthem 'The Maple Leaf Forever,' with its evocation of British North America as a place where 'The thistle, shamrock, rose entwined' (see illus. 7).

I say it was a 'limited' form of inclusiveness because the perspective of the twenty-first century makes painfully clear the marginalization and denigration of non-British people that Sandor Hunyadi encounters in Marlyn's novel and that are manifested in the relegation of Black and Indigenous characters to minor roles in Canada's founding Loyalist myth, not to mention instances in Canadian racial history such as the *Komagata Maru* incident, the Ukrainian and Japanese internments of the First and Second World Wars, the Chinese Exclusion Act, and the eviction of the traditional leadership from the Six Nations Confederacy Council at gunpoint in 1924.[3] Having witnessed these and many other instances of 'British' as an *exclusive* category, twenty-first-century Canadians cannot think of it and its related term 'English' in the same naive way that Sandor could – we cannot help but see its civility wryly.[4] But for those early Canadian settlers who had been traumatized by the ethnic and national conflicts within the British Isles, who had been dislodged to the colonies in part because of these conflicts, the idea of Britishness represented a remarkable instance of reconciliation and ecumenism between previously bitter enemies.[5] Confederation-era poet and Ottawa civil servant Wilfred Campbell gave this pan-ethnic civility high praise in his own celebration of Sandor's English queen. His poem was entitled 'Victoria (Jubilee Ode, A.D. 1897)':

7   This postage stamp, with two roses, a thistle, and a shamrock circling the crown, was issued in January 1857 by the postal administration in Newfoundland.

> Let all hatreds be forgot,
> All bitterness swept away
> . . . .
> Celt and Scot and Saxon, let us only know,
> A Mighty Queen comes to her own at last. (*Poetical Works* 103)

Because Sandor believes in the liberality of Englishness, he thinks he too can enter its charmed civil circle. He believes a change of name, fluency in the English language, and a few stolen accoutrements will gain him access to the class ascendancy that comes with belonging to the British family. But Marlyn has set Sandor up for a fall. Although Sandor does anglicize his name to Alex Hunter after he grows up and leaves home, and though he does wear the right business suits and visit the hotel restaurants where the men who control money and power in Winnipeg congregate, he never secures a place among them. He has not realized how impervious to outsiders the entwined thistle, shamrock, and rose could be.

Nor has he noticed the slipperiness that haunts the categories of English and British or the tensions this slipperiness produces among those who inhabit these related but not precisely equivalent categories. In *Out of Place: Englishness, Empire, and the Locations of Identity*, Ian Baucom argues that the empire is less 'a place where England exerts control than the place where England loses command of its own narrative of identity' (3). He observes that the traditional idea of citizenship in England was based upon the *ius solis*, or law of the soil, which assumed that whoever resided on English land was English. But the dispersal of England into Great and then Greater Britain – first into the Celtic peripheries of Wales, Scotland, and Ireland and then into the larger empire in Asia, Africa, and North America – troubled the previously 'natural' link of citizenship to residency on British or English soil that had been assumed in the general romantic-nationalist idea that the soul of a people grew out of its long and deep attachment to the spirit of a place. Now the concept met the challenge of empire and the question of which places could qualify as English (Baucom 17, 22). As the signs and accoutre-ments of Englishness became dispersed across the empire – should Bengalis or Barbadians have the same rights as 'true-born Englishmen' if they live on British imperial soil and speak flawless English? – a gap widened between the concepts of English and British that disavowed at the same time as it reinforced a hierarchy of authenticity (6). Ostensibly, Britishness collected all the empire's children into one family, but for the English, Britishness also became the way to preserve the elite distinc-tion of English identity from being dispersed among inauthentic British colonials. Thus Baucom notes that the definition of citizenship gradually shifted in British law from the *ius solis* to the law of blood; the question that established belonging was no longer 'where were you born?' but 'who were your parents?' (13). Eventually, after Canada passed its own citizenship legislation in 1946, London legislators foresaw similar devel-opments emerging in Australia, New Zealand, and India; so they intro-duced the category of the 'British subject' in the British Nationality Bill of 1948, which decreed that all inhabitants of former colonial states, together with as-yet-uncolonized territories, could no longer claim citizenship but instead would be considered 'British subjects.' The redefinition of the relationship between England and its British colonies produced the 'British subject,' a category whose vacuity was made painfully clear when the South Asian 'British subjects' of Uganda unsuccessfully sought asylum in Britain after Idi Amin's eviction order in 1973. Thus, Baucom summarizes, '"British" space was … read as homogenous, interchangeable, everywhere alike, while "English" space remained unique, local, differentiated' (10). By identifying the residents of the former empire who could not prove English descent as British subjects and not citizens, the conservators of England managed 'the neat trick of allowing England to simultaneously avow and disavow its empire' (6).

The parts of Baucom's argument that I have summarized here are set largely in what historians call the 'second empire' of the nineteenth and early twentieth centuries, but in an article on the ethnicity of the English, Robert Young points out that the rivalry between a loose definition of Englishness and a purist definition has a much longer history than this. He outlines two persistent, competing myths about English origins: an Arthurian Celtic myth, which argues for a Britain peopled by Celts whom King Arthur had made into a composite nation along with Saxons and Normans, and a Saxon myth, which argues that the real British arrived with the Saxon invaders in AD 449 and pushed Celtic Britons to the margins that became known as Wales, Ireland, and Scotland. The Celtic myth theorizes a hybrid Englishness, while the Saxon one theorizes separate and fixed racial types. Young and Baucom both quote Daniel Defoe's satiric poem 'The True Born Englishman' (1701) and its depiction of that 'Het'rogenous Thing, An Englishman:/ In eager Rapes, and furious Lust begot, / Betwixt a Painted Britton and a Scot' as an example of the hybrid Celtic myth (Robert Young 130; Baucom 16; italics in the original), while Young cites John Beddoe's prize-winning essay The Races of Men (1885) as an example of the purity myth. For this book, Beddoe carefully collected data on hair and eye colour throughout Britain to prove his racist theory that increased 'nigrescence' had infiltrated England because of the importation of cheap Celtic labour (Young 145). John Fowles's essay 'On Being English but Not British' (1964), with its differentiation between ancient Celtic aggression and primordial English justice, is but a recent example of the kind of fixed-types theory that animated Horace Walpole's scorn in 1773 for the word 'Briton' because it countenanced the presence of barbarous Scots in London's political and cultural elite (Crawford 56).

It is important to recognize that there were good reasons for the conservators of Englishness to fear the looseness of the term 'British.' For, whereas anxious Englishmen may have used Britishness to name an imperial family resemblance from which they then politely distanced themselves, non-English Celts used it to infiltrate that family and its resources. In his discussion of cultural exchange between Britain and her colonies, Donald Akenson debunks the 'conventional picture [of] a "British" culture inherited from the homeland':

> There was no 'British' culture to draw on, but instead, there were several vigorous, distinct, and in many of their details incompatible Anglo-Celtic cultures found in the homeland. Therefore, an integral and absolutely necessary aspect of the development of a sense of [colonial] identity was the creation of a 'British' culture in the new homeland, one that did not in fact exist in the old. The melding of the several Anglo-Celtic cultures to establish a new and synthetic 'British' culture was coterminous with the creation of new national identities. Thus, when one sees Scots, English, Welsh, and Irish accepting in many contexts the term 'British' in Canada, Australia, and New Zealand, one is actually seeing the completion of the first step of their escape from the cultural hegemony of the Old World metropoles. It was then only a short step from being 'British' to being a Canadian, Australian, or a New Zealander. The big step was the first – to cease to be primarily identified with a sectional identity in the Old World. (396–7)

For the Scottish Canadian characters I will be examining in this chapter, their identifications evolve from distinct Scottishness through generalized Britishness to deliberate Canadianness. Furthermore, Sandor Hunyadi's claim that 'when you're English it's the same as bein' Canadian' adds a another dimension to the process of colonial identity formation which Akenson describes here, for it demonstrates how, for outsiders to the fine distinctions of Saxon-Celtic rivalry, Britishness interchanges readily with Englishness. And this interchange occurs even in the speech of those who clearly know more about the fine distinctions than Sandor does. For one thing, the specific Canadian history of the dichotomy between English and French Canadas contributes to a much looser conception of Englishness than either Horace Walpole or John Fowles would approve. For example, two novels of the conquest of Quebec, Philippe-Joseph Aubert de Gaspé's *Les Anciens Canadiens* (1863) and Gilbert Parker's *The Seats of the Mighty* (1896), feature Scottish protagonists whose fathers sided with the Jacobites in the 1745 uprising.

Both novels directly address the shared resentment of the English that constitutes the 'Auld Alliance' between the French and the (Catholic) Scots. Nonetheless, both of these Scottish characters, Lieutenant Archie Cameron of Lochiell and Captain Robert Moray, are consistently referred to as members of the English army, despite the way in which their anti-English cultural positioning constitutes a major component of their depiction as heroic figures in these two Walter Scott–like romances.[6] Their enlistment in the category of Englishness may derive from a linguistic shorthand for the conflict between Britain and France whereby French-speaking characters loosely refer to Cameron or Moray as English, but this proximity between English as a language and English as an ethno-national category demonstrates how the purist idea of Englishness remains ever vulnerable to anyone gifted in learning the English language fluently.

The deliberate construction of British culture in the colonies described by Akenson and the ready interchange between Britishness and Englishness that I am outlining in this chapter can be witnessed in condensed form in the poetry of Alexandar McLachlan, the Scottish-born tailor of Erin, Ontario, who was popularly known as the 'Burns of Canada' at the height of his literary career in the 1860s and 1870s. McLachlan's famous celebration of Canada as a place to escape from the old country's class distinctions in the poem 'Young Canada; or, Jack's as Good's His Master,' gives hearty expression to the anti-aristocratic, anti-English feeling typical among decidedly *British* North Americans:

> I love this land of forest grand,
>   The land where labor's free;
> Let others roam away from home,
>   Be this the land for me!
> Where no one moils and strains and toils
>   That snobs might thrive the faster,
> But all are free as men should be,
>   And Jack's as good's his master! (207).

These bold lines from McLachlan are regularly cited by Canadian critics to illustrate the early Canadian theme of New World emigration as an escape from the oppressions of class stratification in the old country. Another of McLachlan's poems, however, gets much rarer mention, even though it also typifies a common, though opposite, early Canadian desire – the desire, not to escape, but to identify with the larger empire. This poem, 'Britannia,' constitutes a raid on the strongholds of English history, whose spoils McLachlan liberally mixes with famous Scottish treasures in order to demonstrate the riches of combined British culture:

> All hail, my country! hail to thee,
> Thou birthplace of the brave and free,
> Thou ruler of the land and sea,
>   Britannia!
> . . . .
> Oh, nobly hast thou play'd thy part!
> What struggles of the head and heart
> Have gone to make thee what thou art,
>   Britannia!
>
> Great mother of the mighty dead!
> Sir Walter sang and Nelson bled
> To weave a garland for thy head,
>   Britannia!
>
> And Watt, the great magician, wrought,
> And Shakespeare ranged the realms of thought,
> And Newton soar'd, and Cromwell fought,
>   Britannia!
>
> And Milton's high seraphic art,
> And Bacon's learning, Burns's heart,
> Are glories that shall ne'er depart,
>   Britannia!   (32–3)

Here we have the hindsight construction of British cultural history by a liberal mixture of famous English and Scottish figures that makes no distinction between their ethno-national locations. It is as if, for the British North American, Scott's Clyde and Shakespeare's Avon drain the identical heath. And just in case any of McLachlan's *truly* English readers feel threatened by this diffusion of English achievements into the triumphs of a wider British nation, this poem is followed in *Poems and Songs* (1874), as well as in the posthumous *Poetical Works of Alexander McLachlan* (1900), by an obsequious paean of praise entitled 'The Anglo-Saxon':

The Anglo-Saxon leads the van,
   And never lags behind,
For was not he ordain'd to be
   The leader of mankind?
He carries very little sail,
   Makes very little show,
But gains the haven without fail,
   Whatever winds may blow.

. . . .

I love to look upon his face,
   Whate'er be his degree, –
An honor to the human race,
   The king of men is he.   (34–5)

How could a self-respecting Scotsman, the one who insisted that 'Jack's as good's his master,' write such lines? Is this pure irony? Previous critics do not read these lines ironically,[7] and my sense is that they are not so much irony as they are strategy; that is, they are consistent with the larger project of Scots throughout the empire to placate their English rivals with expressions of homage and loyalty that operated as a kind of flux between the categories of Britishness and Englishness, not just to fuse themselves into empire's central alloy but also to recompose the character of that alloy according to their own values. If Jack's as good's his master, why shouldn't his views and objectives carry just as much weight as the erstwhile master's? Indeed, Tom Nairn, the Scottish political historian, considers the Scots so successful at this strategy that he dismisses nationalists' complaints about Scotland's colonization by England. 'Scotland is not a colony, a semi-colony, a pseudo-colony, a near-colony, a neo-colony, or any kind of colony of the English,' he insists. 'She is a junior but (as these things go) highly successful partner in the general business enterprise of Anglo-Scots imperialism' (13). Nairn laments the Scottish complicity in the exploitation and violence of empire, while other commentators have read this success as the victory of the underdog over the favourite.

The claims for Scottish predominance in Canada are many and persistent.[8] As early as the late eighteenth century, a contributor to Thomas O'Leary's collection *Canadian Letters: Description of a Tour thro' the Provinces of Lower and Upper Canada, in the Course of the Years 1792 and '93* observed, 'The persons of greatest weight, in the Canadas, ... are the merchants, or storekeepers. Among these, the gentlemen from Scotland take a decided lead' (qtd. in Trumpener 252), and over a hundred years later Sir Richard Cartwright observed in his *Reminiscences* (1912) that 'Ontario is to a large extent a Scotch colony' (qtd. in MacGillivray 34). John E. Logan, professor of English literature at Acadia University and best known for *Highways of Canadian Literature*, which he co-wrote with Donald French, claimed in 1911 that 'the formative force in Canadian literature, as in Canadian civilization, is the Gaelic (Highland and Irish) genius' (191). Because the 'whole universe is the Gael's church,' Logan claimed, he feels a natural divinity around him at all times, and this predisposes him to poetic invention. The only reason this natural Celtic capacity for poetry (it predominates not just in English Canadian culture because 'the French, too, are Celtic in temperament and psychological genius' [191]) has not placed our literature on 'the upper slopes of Parnassus' is that it has been inhibited by the dour and enervating views of Calvinist theology (193). Nonetheless, for Logan, the 'genius of our poetry is Celtic, and this means that in inspiration it has the finest essence of poetry, whether the craftsmanship of its poets and poetesses is superlative or not' (193).

Perhaps it was with claims such as Logan's in mind that George Bowering quipped in 1977: 'Canadian literature like Canadian history is largely Scottish ... To get into Canadian literature it helps to be ... named Alex or Ian or Malcolm' (qtd. in Trumpener 246). Writing in the same year as Bowering, Clara Thomas agreed: 'There is no other social mythology so pervasive in our literature as that of the Scotch – and perhaps that is true of our histories as well' (367). Accordingly, in his introduction to the collection of essays entitled *The Scottish Tradition in Canada* (1976), the historian Stanford Reid claims that 'the history of Canada is to a certain extent the history of the Scots in Canada' (ix). But Reid seems a touch nervous about the ethnic boosterism of this claim in a volume published by the Secretary of State, Multiculturalism; so he concludes his introduction by saying that he hopes the following essays do not sound 'too much as though the Scots are boasting' (xi). What I find revealing about these statements is the contest they imply but do not overtly state: the reason why these statements of the predominance of Scots in Canada seem feisty is of course because they contest the assumed dominance of the English.[9] John Murray Gibbon makes this contest explicit when he concludes his celebratory 1911 history *The Scots in Canada* by observing that while turn-of-the-century Canadians might see the sense in the title of Basil Stewart's 1909 pamphlet entitled 'No English Need Apply,' 'If any Canadian had the temerity to say, "No Scots need apply," he would not only advertise himself a fool, but he would also probably be lynched' (161). It is this fraught negotiation of the Scots with Englishness and their use of the slippage between Britishness and Englishness to gain social status in Canada that I will trace more specifically below in relation to five Scottish Canadian novels by Galt, McCulloch, Robertson, Connor, and MacLennan.

In all five of the novels under consideration here, and again and again in Scottish Canadian fiction more generally, the Scottish-born or Scottish-descended protagonists are orphans who must struggle on their own to establish themselves on a solid economic foundation before they can become the kind of citizens who can have a leading hand in shaping Canadian society.[10] These orphans inherit no supports and so must make them on their own. Their process of establishment involves self-improvement and the forging of a reputation for good character. Indeed, the central motor of the plot in John Galt's three-volume novel *Bogle Corbet; or, The Emigrants* (1831) is the problem of reputation or character. Set in the turbulent decades at the end of the eighteenth and beginning of the nineteenth centuries, when the Glasgow-based markets in West Indian and North American goods rose and fell with the vicissitudes of the Napoleonic and American wars and when the ongoing shift from an agricultural to a manufacturing-based economy meant an increasingly difficult situation for smaller landowners, Bogle's story is aimed at a readership of the gentry's lower orders who had lost their lands and were trying to retool themselves for commercial life or, equally often, for life in the colonies. In a period when colonial trade represented ever-increasing shares of the overall British economy, reputation became a cardinal requirement for the aspiring merchant. Because colonial investments were made on trust, and because the physical distances of the overseas trade ruled out regular personal inspection, investors had to be able to rely upon the reports and judgments of those who assessed the quality and consistency of goods from across the oceans. Thus a good character became a major component of one's qualification to participate in the world of trade, and its loss precipitated not just a moral but also a commercial disaster.

Galt's emphasis on the importance of character in the world of overseas colonial trade had strong parallels in the author's own experience. By the time he wrote *Bogle Corbet* in 1831, he had already made his fame as the author of over ten Scottish novels, including *Annals of the Parish*. He had served as secretary to the Canada Company and lived for a time in the region of Guelph, where he managed the purchase of Crown lands and then their resale to incoming colonists. Galt had himself experienced the collapse of character and fortune when the company recalled him from Upper Canada after his clashes with powerful members of the Family Compact such as Lieutenant-Governor Sir Peregrine Maitland and Bishop John Strachan undermined the board's confidence in his political dexterity. This failure threw Galt into bankruptcy, and he was put in debtors' prison upon his return to the British Isles in 1829. It was in prison that he began composition of his two North American novels, *Lawrie Todd* and *Bogle Corbet*. His own painful experience of the rise and fall of fortunes and their relation to the rise and fall of character features as a central concern in these novels.

Bogle Corbet is born in Jamaica to Scottish parents who manage a sugar-cane plantation. When they die during his infancy, his Jamaican nurse takes the baby back to Scotland, where his aunt, Mrs Busby, takes over his rearing and education. When he turns fourteen, she chooses two 'curators' from among the village men to help establish the boy in a career. Her choice is determined by her mistake of reputation for character: she chooses the physician, Dr Leach, and the town's richest citizen, Mr Macindoe, not because they will be effective guides for the boy but because they are the 'most respectable' men in the village and, Bogle suspects in hindsight, because she likes their wives (1: 14). The two men differ initially on whether Bogle would benefit best from a classical or a practical education (a distinction I will comment on in more detail in the section below on McCulloch), but the question is resolved by the impetuous Mr Macindoe, who determines that Bogle will be placed in an apprenticeship in the textile industry in Glasgow. Never in the process is Bogle consulted about his own love of science and particularly astronomy. Instead, he learns the textile industry. Despite a brief dalliance with a group of radical weavers, who meet secretly to discuss Jacobin ideas, and despite several shifts in employers, Bogle soon develops a reputation as a promising young man by frequenting the muslin shops and samples rooms where merchants assess the quality and value of fabrics. He reads the newspapers in the coffee shops and so develops a vocabulary and demeanor that gives him the reputation of a reliable, shrewd up-and-comer (1: ch. 9).

Bogle, however, confesses, 'I never was less myself than when engaged in the turmoils of trade, and most applauded for discernment and dexterity as a merchant' (1: 123–4). It is this mistaken reputation, as opposed to proven character, that gets Bogle involved in a business for which he has no real heart or talent. He takes on a partner named Mr

Possy, who brings to the business an inheritance of 7,000 pounds but who has even less talent than Bogle does, and between Possy's over-spending and Bogle's lack of experience, the business falls into bank-ruptcy, despite its early promise and their opening a second office in London. Possy presents himself as the victim and accuses Bogle of playing fast and loose with his inheritance, and rather than respond with counter-accusations of Possy's ineptitude, Bogle agrees to depart for the West Indies, where he hopes to secure what remains of their creditors' investments. But his quiet departure is a public relations mistake, for it is taken to be a confirmation of his guilt, and his reputation for honesty and reliability is ruined. This destruction of his character means that he really has no further hopes of making a good living in Britain.

For a man with a 'ruined' character,[11] emigration offers a chance to re-establish his status in a new environment. After a short and ultimately unsuccessful stint as a London agent for West Indies sugar companies, Bogle departs with his English wife and family from Gravesend on the way to Canada. 'Farewell, my native land!' he cries on board the depart-ing ship. 'England, good night, alas!' (2: 250). *England* – not Scotland, but England. Here is the moment of ethno-national slippage that is central to the movement from the specificity of the British Isles to the larger British Empire. A Glaswegian, born in the West Indies but raised entirely in Scotland, whose trade in colonial commodities has collapsed in Glasgow and London, calls England his native land. Katie Trumpener, in her study of the literatures of Britain's peripheries, calls this slippage 'colonial tilt' and describes it as a 'collective amnesia whereby Scottish (and Irish) settlers misplace in transit their age-old anti-English, anti-British, and anti-imperial hatreds.' She considers this colonial tilt the 'cornerstone and central mystery of empire' (253), but the novel's outward expansion from the Scottish village to Glasgow and then Lon-don and onwards to Jamaica and the London-based West Indies trade, before emigration to Upper Canada, goes some distance towards de-mystifying the process of colonial tilt, insofar as it shows how Bogle's identity is steadily loosened from a primarily Scottish one via his invest-ments in Greater Britain even before he is finally cast forth by circum-stances and a damaged reputation into the further reaches of the empire.

Trumpener reads Bogle as a man disillusioned by his personal busi-ness failure and by his having witnessed first-hand the exploitative as-pects of colonialism when he was in Jamaica. She charts the progress of his demoralization from his early interest in the democratic principles of Jacobinism to his ironic establishment of himself as lord of a squirearchy in Upper Canada (278ff., esp. 282). Bogle's process of disillusionment is undeniable in the novel, and Trumpener is right to read it as a loss of faith in the civility of Britain's commercial empire. But it seems to me that this reading overlooks the important theme of reputation or character and its relation to class status that recurs throughout the novel. Bogle and his family are brought to the extreme measure of emigration, as he puts it, because of 'pecuniary embarrassment' (2: 229), and he reports that his case is common among the déclassé, lower gentry he meets in London, who come to consult him about the possibilities of emigration:

> Money, the want of it, or to get it, is the actuating spring, whatever may be the pretexts of intending emigrants of the middle ranks ... All who consulted me were individuals in impaired, or desperate circumstances, unable to preserve their caste in the social system of this country, wrecked and catching at emigration as the last plank. The lower classes are governed by motives sufficiently manifest; agricultural changes, and the introduction of new machinery, is constantly throwing off swarms of operatives who have no other resource; as their vocation is labour, a shifting of the scene is comparatively of little consequence to them. But it is only amidst the better class of emigrants that the mingled and combined feelings of necessity, interest, and sorrow are found. The cares and fears, the anxieties of enterprise, the wound of the heart, that pains like amputation, and the solitude that waits in the wilderness, are keenest and cruelest among them. (3: 233–4)

This passage does indeed betray, as Trumpener observes, the distance Bogle has travelled from the Jacobinism of his weaver friends during his youth in Glasgow, but it also provides a way to understand his desire to escape a life tied to a system of laissez-faire economics whose players depend on the superficial mystique of their reputation. In his Canadian experiment in founding the village of Stockwell, he tries to establish a more orderly, tightly controlled world, where he, as beneficent master, recognizes and promotes his Highland and Glaswegian serfs on the basis of demonstrated merit and not of urban hearsay.[12] Bogle's system is an unabashed form of feudalism, but he understands it as more truly compassionate and humane than the commerce-driven worlds he had found so distasteful in Glasgow, London, and Jamaica. In the parable he tells his restless Highlanders and Glaswegians when they are tempted to abandon his Canadian emigration scheme in favour of the American republic, just as a bundle of twigs is stronger than any single stick, so the common bond of Britishness makes them stronger than isolated American individuals would be.[13] All they have to do is overcome the ancient grudges between Highlanders and Lowlanders and work as one with the Methodists, Presbyterians, and Catholics in their midst towards the establishment of a new hierarchically ordered society. This time, however, the hierarchy will be constructed on the basis of demonstrated character and actual merit.

Dungowan, a superannuated officer, suggests that Bogle would be better able to motivate 'morality' among the emigrants if he were to establish a series of official ranks after the military model, through which people might rise to higher and higher positions of responsibility and authority (3: ch. xi). The character needed to rise in rank would be judged on the basis of the ideology of improvement. The whole enterprise of establishing the town of Stockwell entails the business of transforming woodlands into a town, farms, roads, mills, churches, and eventually schools. Thus a good character in Stockwell means steadiness, resourcefulness, and a commitment to collective and self-improvement. In short, character means resisting emigrant 'fyke,' Bogle's western Scots term for restlessness (3: 51). Improvement, by contrast, is most readily demonstrated by steady cultivation of the land. One of Bogle's major disappointments during his visit to Jamaica had been the way in which the plantations seemed to be built only for short-term profits and not for long-term habitation (1: 305; 2: 19). This lack of commitment among the plantation owners to long-term improvement has shaken his confidence in the colonial system, with its assumption that Whites were inherently disposed to rule and Blacks to labour (2: 30). Indeed, the building of the Welland Canal in Upper Canada causes him to write that, while waterways and railroads in the old country are seen as merely convenient, 'on this continent they constitute the most efficacious means for spreading colonization. By extending communications through the forest, and by multiplying the means of conveyance, we make atonement for our usurpation of the wide and wild domains of the aborigines' (3: 219).

Here we have a rare glimpse into the pathological core of colonial British/Englishness, for we can see a character make a conscious link between the 'anxiety of enterprise' and its racist underpinnings. For colonists such as Bogle Corbet, Britishness means civility insofar as it represents the reconciliation of previously hostile groups back in the British Isles. Via colonization, Britain can spread this civility to the wilderness hinterlands of its colonies. The civility of this peaceable kingdom is not only expressed but also maintained by cooperative improvement, which makes cultivated properties out of trackless wilderness lands. Improvement compensates for the repressed guilt of having displaced Indigenous people from these lands, who were not candidates for inclusion in the elastic category of Britishness in the first place. This guilt is further diminished by the fact that Native people are presumed extinct in the region of Stockwell, as there are no references to any living Indigenous people in the book. Unimproved land means betrayal of the collective enterprise and is therefore a sign of bad character. Character in Stockwell, as in pioneer ideology more generally, is demonstrated by means of one's relation to property.

In an article in the *Harvard Law Review* entitled 'Whiteness as Property,' the African American legal historian Charyl Harris argues that one of the key functions of race in United States history has been its role in the legal assignment of property. She notes that we can see this readily in the dispossession of Native Americans from their traditional lands because they did not have the same exclusive understanding of property that the White invaders did (1721, 1724). From the beginning of North American colonial history, Harris argues, whiteness has been defined by the right to own and to exclude others from owning property. Whites cannot themselves be owned;[14] so they cannot be made into slaves as Blacks were in slavery-era America. Thus whiteness not only becomes associated with *owning* property, but it also becomes itself what she calls 'status property.' Status property, in Harris's formulation, constitutes the legal protection of the rights and privileges associated with whiteness (1729). She refers to several historical court cases to illustrate how whiteness operates in the United States as a status property. Among them appears the 1891 case in which a White-looking man named Mr Plessy was barred from a White railway carriage because he was found to have a Black ancestor. Plessy's legal counsel asserted his right to sue, because being called a Black man constituted damage to his reputation and denied him the privileges he could expect from having been known as a White man all his life. He had the right to sue because he had been denied the legally sanctioned expectations accorded to whiteness, and 'property' in legal terms designates not just objects over which exclusive rights can be asserted but also anything to which a person can attach a value or have a right, even if that right is identified by custom. So, for example, an employee can sue an employer for not recognizing the property of a university degree in his or her pay scale. The status property of whiteness guarantees its wages, Harris argues, and these wages amount to the legal protection of class privilege and the right to expect upward social mobility (1759).[15]

Bogle Corbet's desire to establish a reliable link between character and social status not only demonstrates how emigration of the lower gentry is often prompted by the concern to regain status lost in the homeland through the acquisition and improvement of physical property in the colony; it also shows how British character is central to the establishment of status property in British North America. Bogle's orphanhood, and that of the Scottish protagonists of all five novels I examine in this chapter, functions as an allegory for the displacement of the emigrant from the homeland and the justice of his or her pursuit of status property in the colony. More specifically, it emphasizes the removal of Scotland as a viable parent. Whether through the clearances of the Highlands or the industrial and commercial upheavals in the Lowlands in the late eighteenth and early nineteenth centuries, these emigrants have been cast off from the impecunious parent land. The figure of the orphan readily links as well to the Scottish Enlightenment's ideology of self-improvement by means of dispersal into the wider world of the British Empire. Because of the collapse of the Scottish aristocracy and an independent Scottish economy after the Treaty of Union, Scotland no longer represents a place where patrilineal succession can be assumed as the mode of passage for wealth and social standing between the generations. The sons of the English gentry may expect to inherit an estate or at least a living from their fathers, but the Scots are on their own. As Thomas McCulloch's young protagonist, the apprentice Mephibosheth Stepsure, is constantly reminded by Mistress Worthy, 'I was a poor orphan, without parents to take care of me; and, therefore, I must learn to take care of myself' (88).

The figure of the orphan has a further function that is central to the success of these novels' narratives: it solicits empathy from the reader so that the protagonist's ambition to climb the social ladder does not invite the censure of vaulting avarice or doomed Promethean ambition. Orphanhood levers the protagonist momentarily free of the conventions that would normally determine his or her social standing and enables a narrative of unapologetic self-aggrandizement, while at the same time retaining the reader's sympathy for the character's right to secure a higher position on the social scale. The Scottish orphan, then, can freely pursue ever-higher social rank and not be seen to threaten the structure of the social hierarchy itself. Key to the orphan's retention of sympathy, as Bogle shows us, is the belief that the social hierarchy established in the New World will be based upon proven character or merit and not upon inherited or rumoured reputation. The orphan may reinvent him or herself, but because this reinvention is accomplished against terrific odds, it proves the orphan's solidity of character and his or her act of self-invention avoids the charge of artifice or falsely acquired reputation.

It is important to read this allegory of the orphan's self-reinvention against the long history of Scottish self-invention and its function in crafting the Scots' route into their major partnership in the British Empire. Daniel Munro, the deceased father of Frederick Niven's orphan protagonist in *The Flying Years* (1935), used to call Scotland a 'kingdom of the mind' (19, 226), by which phrase he tried to arm himself against his own and his Canadian pioneer family's nostalgia for a place from which they had been treacherously driven by their own clan chieftains. Munro's kingdom of the mind nicely identifies the phenomenon of the Highland myth and its emergence at the same time as an actual independent way of life in the Highlands was in rapid decline. Largely popularized by Lowlanders such as Walter Scott in his historical romances, Robert Burns in his Gaelicized ballads (written in English, however), and James Macpherson in his fake 'translation' of an ancient epic by Ossian, the supposed Homer of a sophisticated Gaelic culture that resisted the Romans, the Highland myth, as represented in the lingering icons of what Ian McKay has called 'tartanism' – bagpipes, kilts, tartans, and so on – is largely bogus. As Hugh Trevor-Roper has shown, the Scots are mostly descended from Irish emigrants; so the truly original musical instrument of the Highlands would be the Irish harp, not the bagpipes. Furthermore, the pleated kilt is a recent creation. It goes back not to time immemorial but to the 1720s (i.e., after union with England in 1707), when it was invented by an English Quaker named Thomas Rawlinson, owner of an iron foundry near Inverness, whose Scottish employees wore the traditional philibeg, which consisted of a plaid belted and thrown over one shoulder. This garment proved awkward and dangerous around the smelters; so Rawlinson had a tailor design the short kilt with its sewn-in pleats, and the practicality of the design caught on and spread through the general populace (20–2). It was not until the Disarming Act, introduced a year after the defeat at Culloden in 1746, that the kilt became associated with Highland identity when it was outlawed, along with 'plaid, philibeg, trews, shoulder-belts, tartans, or parti-coloured plaid,' by a newly victorious but still nervous English government (24).

Trevor-Roper catches James Macpherson – he of Ossian fame – at the game of tartanization quite literally when the latter served as a founding member of the Highland Society of London, which in 1778 busily set about the business of assigning tartans to the various Highland clans. In a campaign to get the Disarming Act repealed, Macpherson and his Highland Society compeers made strong representations about the 'ancient' tradition of tartan kilts and their centrality to Scottish clan identity. Trevor-Roper exposes the hoax by following the career of a specific fabric made by William Wilson and Son of Bannockburn. Their no. 155 fabric pattern became known as 'Kidd' plaid when Mr Kidd purchased it in bulk to clothe his West Indian slaves. Under the historical alchemy of the Highland Society, this plaid later became known as the ancient 'Macpherson' tartan (30). This newly assigned family tradition would have had one of its early official airings when it was worn by the Macpherson chieftains, in the company of the other Highland chieftains who had been invited by the Celtic Society of Edinburgh (established in 1820 under its first president, Walter Scott), to dress according to the new tradition for their attendance upon the state visit of George IV in 1822 (29–30).[16] Although Trevor-Roper takes clear delight in exposing the chicanery involved in the elaboration of these elements of the Highland myth, he notes that this invented tradition remains a lasting triumph in that it elevated Scottish culture from the Celtic periphery to a world-renowned cultural myth celebrated in story, song, and popular history (18). Indeed, an equally valid reading of the power of tartanism would attend to the desperation of people who had suffered genocide, treachery, and displacement to construct for themselves the signs of a coherent, continuous identity that would be transportable and adaptable to the farthest reaches of empire.

The efficiency of such a construction has been recently examined by Ian McKay in 'Tartanism Triumphant: The Construction of Scottishness in Nova Scotia, 1933–1954.'[17] McKay shows how the popular notion of Nova Scotia as North America's 'New Scotland' is largely the product of a very successful tourism campaign orchestrated by Premier Angus L. Macdonald in the 1930s and 1940s (see illus. 8). He points out that, contrary to popular opinion, Scots did not predominate in Nova Scotia's early population, nor were they the original European settler-invaders of the region, not even in that most Scottish of Canadian regions, Cape Breton. Indeed, a coherent claim for Nova Scotia's Scottishness was never voiced until Macdonald began to address the province's economic difficulties in the 1930s with his campaign to attract tourist Scotophiles. The practice of piping visitors across the provincial border, the establishment of Highlands National Park in Cape Breton and the paving of the Cabot Trail, the formation of Gaelic College in St Ann's, and the

8 Tartanization in Nova Scotia: the opening parade at the Canso Causeway between Cape Breton and the mainland, 13 August 1955.

building of the Lone Shieling monument at Pleasant Bay, Inverness, were all part of Macdonald's tartanization of Nova Scotia. McKay's point, however, is not merely to expose the artificiality of the province's quickly invented tradition but also to reflect upon its powerful continuing effects. The image of Nova Scotia as a place where tourists can 'See Scotland without Crossing the Atlantic,' as one promotional article put it (McKay 31), generated a large and enduring tourism industry. Furthermore, McKay notes that the nostalgia and anti-modernism fostered by the 'return' to Scottish traditions allowed Macdonald to keep socialist and Keynesian opposition at bay in the volatile politics of the 1930s and 1940s (40–2). Finally, McKay claims, the 'tartanism [Macdonald] espoused and articulated rooted itself so firmly partly because it gave Nova Scotians of Scottish descent, many of them decidedly marginal in provincial society, a sense of validation. Such people were ambiguously positioned in Nova Scotia and Canada. Many defined themselves as "British" and hence as a "founding people" with special rights and, notoriously, a disproportionate amount of economic and political power' (19). Here we see how the slippage within the category of Britishness allows Scottish-descended Canadians to have it both ways: when the status of being members of one of the founding nations is called for, they are 'British,' and when Scottishness opens the door to opportunity, they become Highlanders. McKay's reference to Nova Scotian Scots' claims to founding-nation status returns us to the other Scottish-invented myth that paralleled the Highland-tartan myth, and that is the myth of Britishness.

If eighteenth-century Lowlanders were centrally involved in the invention of the Highland myth of courageous but ultimately doomed independence, they were also centrally involved in the invention of the pan-ethnic myth of British inclusiveness and thereby of Scottish adaptation to the English state. The sharp contrast between these two myths does not make them as incompatible as might at first appear. The ideology of what Alistair MacLeod calls 'Highland Darwinism' ('Writings' 75) starts with the image of the Highlanders as members of a noble but hopelessly belated culture, but it then calls for their improvement, for all of their culture's hoary grandeur, because they must be brought into step with modern times, usually through Lowland education, anglicization, and Presbyterianization. In fact, despite the venerable aura of the Highland myth, this Lowland myth of progress and its Darwinist assumptions can be discerned earlier than the Highland one elaborated by the likes of Scott and Macpherson. George, Earl of Cromartie, for example, wrote in a 1706 letter to John, Earl of Mar, in Edinburgh: 'May wee be Brittains, and down goe the old ignominious names of Scotland, of England. Scot or Scotland are words not known in our native language; England is a dishonourable name, imposed on Brittains by Jutland pirates and mercenaries to Brittains, usurping on their Lords. Brittains is our true, our honourable denomination' (qtd. in Richards 67). Cromartie echoes the sentiments expressed 150 years earlier by James Harrison in *An Exhortation to the Scottes to Conforme Themselfes to the ... Union betweene ... Englande and Scotland* (1547), in which he longed for the day when 'these hateful terms of Scottes and Englishemen, shalbe abolished, and blotted oute for euer, and we shal al agre in the onely title and name of Britons' (*Oxford English Dictionary*, 1933 ed., 1: 1114). These statements reflect the fact that, regardless of the myth of a proud and independent Highlands, members of the Scottish oligarchy around Edinburgh believed the economic advantages of the union outweighed the virtues of sovereignty and, despite riots in the streets, pushed for union (Richards 73). They had good reasons to do so. Under Cromwell, Lowlanders had fared fairly well, but when Parliament rejected the Calvinistic Westminster Confession of Faith, they felt betrayed. Their fortunes fared even worse with the restoration of Charles II, when the English merchant lobby managed to get Scots excluded as 'foreigners' from the colonial trade (Reid 7). Union meant renewed access to this colonial trade (8) and thus the motive, as Stanford Reid puts it, for a transfer of Scottish nationalism to a new heath (13). The Act of Union, according to Daniel Defoe, opened the 'door to Scots in our American colonies,' and by 1821 Walter Scott described India as 'the cornchest of Scotland where we poor gentry must send our youngest sons' (qtd. in Richards 68 and 90 respectively).

The Lowland ideology of improvement, individual effort, and universal education meant that Lowlanders developed a reputation for practical, economically efficient business practices and well-trained, mobile personnel, all of which stood them in good stead in colonial trade. They developed inventive ways of stretching credit which caused them to attract investors, and they came to dominate West Indies commerce through the first half of the eighteenth century (Richards 78–9). After the Revolutionary War diverted American trade away from the loyal northern colonies, Greenock-based merchant ship companies controlled commerce with Nova Scotia to such an extent that historian David Macmillan claims that between 1775 and 1825 British North America became a sort of 'Scottish commercial preserve' for trade and emigration (26). Because young Englishmen could get posts more easily in England itself and were not as willing to take the risks or move the distances required in colonial posts, young Scotsmen were free to consider the empire 'a profession in itself, an opportunity for power, responsibilities, and excitement on a scale they could never have enjoyed back home' (Colley 133). Thus Scotsmen came to dominate many of the major commercial ventures of the British Empire: the East India Company, the Hudson's Bay Company, the North West Company, and, later on, the Canadian Pacific Railway all had Scotsmen in major positions of power. Linda Colley calculates the benefits to Scotland's joining the union in stark economic terms: between 1750 and 1800, she reports that Scotland's overseas commerce grew by 300 per cent while England's grew by 200 per cent (128). Indeed, she reads this great commercial success as a major reason, along with Protestant solidarity, for the failure of the Jacobite uprisings (80–5): there were simply too many benefits for Scots – many Lowland, but some Highland as well – in solidarity with Great Britain. Like the inventor James Watt, writes Colley, Scots 'do not

seem to have regarded themselves as stooges of English cultural hegemony. Far from succumbing helplessly to an alien identity imposed by
others, in moving south they helped construct what being British was all
about' (131).

Thus, while the Scots enjoyed great latitude in the colonial trade, they
also made significant inroads in England itself. Samuel Johnson's quip
about the Anglo-Scottish relationship being one of exploitation – of
England by the Scots – betrays an anxiety felt by many Englishmen (qtd.
in Bailyn and Morgan 17). This anxiety was vociferously expressed by the
mercurial John Wilkes in his anti-Scottish campaign of the 1760s, in
which the future lord mayor of London protested against the popularity
of the term 'Great Britain' because, he claimed, fundamental liberties
such as those outlined in the Bill of Rights were specifically English and
not 'British' achievements; thus all lovers of true freedom should prefer
'England' to 'Britain' (Colley 114–22). Wilkes's cult-of-England campaign rose out of his and other Londoners' resentment of the power of
the Scotsman John Stuart, 3rd Earl of Bute, who was prime minister at
the time and who was viciously rumoured to be having an affair with
George III's mother, the Princess Dowager (Colley 127). If his salacious
fantasies were far-fetched, Wilkes's political anxieties were well founded.
Scots were indeed inserting themselves into the very highest echelons of
English political and economic power, and they continued to do so over
the following century and a half. Royce MacGillivray points out that of
the ten British prime ministers between 1864 and 1908, five were of Scots
descent and another three were born in Scotland (45). The Lowland
ideology of progress through self-improvement and self-reinvention enabled these practically oriented Scots to acquire some of the highest
status property available in Britain and to become major contenders with
the English for power and influence throughout the empire.

If Galt's Bogle Corbet is a scarecrow (which is what 'bogle' means in
western Scots) that warns of what can happen when a weak character
develops a false reputation in the overheated world of colonial trade,
then Thomas McCulloch's *Mephibosheth Stepsure Letters* shows what rewards await a strong and proven character. Published serially in the
Acadian Recorder between 1821 and 1823, in the decade after the Napoleonic Wars, the letters pillory a society that has gotten used to the wartime
inflation of fat government contracts for Canadian timber and is now
unwilling to rely on its own resources. Mephibosheth's letters constitute
a tirade against the kind of weak character that got Bogle Corbet and his
ineffectual partner, Mr Possy, into such trouble. True character, accord-

9   Highland settlers arriving at Pictou, Nova Scotia, from the *Hector*, 1773. Reproduced in John Murray Gibbon's *Scots in Canada*, 17.

ing to the *Letters*, involves improvement of oneself and one's property in the interests of a domestic economy independent of patronage or artificial support.

It is important to recall that McCulloch's writing emerged out of a running battle he waged against the dominance of the English in Nova Scotia. A graduate of the University of Glasgow who had trained for the ministry in the Secession Church, which had separated from the Church of Scotland in 1733, McCulloch arrived in Nova Scotia in 1803 on his way to the parish to which he had been assigned on Prince Edward Island. But his plans changed when he accepted an invitation to stay and preach in the local Presbyterian church in the Scottish settlement at Pictou and to establish a school for the kirk members' children there (see illus. 9). The opening of Pictou Academy launched McCulloch into a long conflict with the Tory-Anglican elite, who reserved entry into the University of King's College in Windsor, the colony's only institution of higher learning, to those who would sign the Thirty-Nine Articles of Anglican doctrine (Hubert 29; Gwendolyn Davies, 'Editing' 92–3). As four out of five Nova Scotians were non-Anglican, the fight to establish the ecumenical Pictou Academy became a battle against the exclusivity of the English ruling class. McCulloch did eventually gain the promise of a yearly grant for his academy, but every year the House of Assembly would approve this grant and every year the twelve-member Legislative Council would veto it (Whitelaw 139; McMullin 70). The council's power to veto the decisions of the elected assembly drew McCulloch into the political forum when he became a regular writer of editorials, under the pen name of 'Investigator,' who called for a council that answered to the people. Indeed, Joseph Howe later claimed that he learned the principles of responsible government from McCulloch (Irving 156; McMullin 74–5). McCulloch's efforts to establish a non-denominational, multiethnic educational system illustrate how the Scottish construction and elaboration of the elastic category of Britishness challenged the power of the English.[18]

Thomas McCulloch's challenge to the exclusive privilege of the English in Nova Scotian pedagogical politics had its roots in the Scottish Enlightenment and its ideology of improvement. Significantly, this pedagogical ideology involved the Scottish invention of 'English' as a university subject. In their separate studies, Robert Crawford, Henry Hubert, and Franklin Court have shown how English literary studies as a university discipline arose out of the pragmatism that determined the curriculum in the Scottish universities of the mid-eighteenth century. Hubert notes that whereas Oxford and Cambridge trained the sons of English gentry, who were guaranteed positions either in the clergy or the civil service, the Scottish universities tended to train the sons of the middle class, who had no such guarantees (9–12). Presbyterianism's insistence on literate parishioners who could read the Bible for themselves and therefore participate in the election of their kirk elders meant that Scottish education was aimed at the general populace and was not the exclusive property of the upper class (Hubert 11; Bumsted 5). English higher education served the aristocracy by investing its sons with the patina of classical languages, the knowledge of which served as one of the signs of refinement that distinguished them from the vernacular-speaking lower orders – this especially after the restoration of the monarchy in 1660, when vernacular language retained its association with Puritan republicanism (Hubert 18). The English universities therefore

concentrated on impractical classical studies, while the Scottish universities, by contrast, emphasized subjects such as science, agriculture, math-
ematics, and especially moral philosophy, a discipline intended to
inculcate moral purpose as a central value for daily business and ethics
(Bumsted 12; Court 1–3).

The study of English literature as a university subject emerged from
moral philosophy. Moral philosophy involved the education of refined
sensibilities since, as the Scotsman Francis Hutcheson had argued in *An
Inquiry into the Origin of Our Ideas of Beauty and Virtue; in Two Treatises*
(1725), a refined aesthetic sensibility contributed to a refined moral
sensibility. In an effort to improve his students' moral and aesthetic
sensibilities, Hutcheson therefore asked his students to write abstracts of
passages from the *Spectator* and the *Guardian* (Court 9). The study of
belles-lettres in English vernacular fitted moral philosophy's objectives
perfectly, for it linked together aesthetic refinement with practical function. Adam Smith expanded upon Hutcheson's method by providing his
law and theology students with examples of English belles-lettres and
then by introducing a series of lectures on rhetoric and belles-lettres at
the University of Edinburgh in 1750. 'Our words must not only be
English and agreeable to the custom of the country but likewise to
the custom of some particular part of that nation,' he wrote. 'As those of
the higher rank generally frequent the court, the standard of our language is therefore chiefly to be met with there' (qtd. in Crawford 29). So
the study of English letters killed two birds with one stone: it trained
the aesthetic-moral sensibility at the same time as it provided entry into
the English-dominated worlds of law, politics, and commerce. This espousal of English in the Scottish universities may appear one more
instance of the assimilation of Scottishness to English/Britishness, but in
fact the assimilation often worked in the opposite direction. For, as
Franklin Court observes, 'Proficiency in English was essential to the
education of Scottish lawyers defending, particularly, Scottish interests
in the English metropolitan arena' (10). This emphasis on a practical,
vernacular education, oriented towards the aspirations of the rising
middle classes, explains why Scottish higher education provided not only
the model but also the professors for the dissenting universities in Great
Britain and for institutions of higher education throughout the empire
(Crawford 42; Hubert 19; Bumsted 5).[19]

McCulloch, educated in Glasgow during the Scottish Enlightenment,
was one of those who brought this commitment to a local, practical
education to Nova Scotia. And *The Mephibosheth Stepsure Letters* accord-

ingly inculcates the Scottish university values of reading in carefully crafted English, the moral philosophy of self-improvement, and a practical, scientific approach to agriculture. Although a rivalry between Scottish and English values never receives explicit mention in the letters, Mephibosheth's constant references to the superiority of 'homespun' to 'genteel' values conveys the anti-aristocratic, anti-elitist message which exactly parallels McCulloch's battle with King's College and the Halifax Tory elite. The caricatured villagers – the Mr Goslings, Jack Scorems, Mr Gypsums, Boniface Soakems, and Mrs Grumbles – all suffer from the 'fyke' or restlessness excoriated by Bogle Corbet. Their love of 'bravery' and the 'superfine' – what twenty-first-century readers would call conspicuous consumption – causes them to live beyond their means, and they fall further and further into debt to Mr Ledger at the general store. Sooner or later their debts make them turn to drink, which only increases their penury, and they end up enjoying the hospitality of Sheriffs Holdfast and Catchem at the debtors' prison. In virtuous contrast to these gadabouts and spendthrifts stand the very Scottish, very Presbyterian, very Lowland Mephibosheth Stepsure (who writes most of the letters), his adviser, Pastor Drone, and his friend and fellow farmer, Alexander Scantocreesh. These sturdy characters constitute the satiric norm (Sharman 619) against which the frivolous Mr Trots and Mrs Whinges are measured and found wanting.

McCulloch's Stepsure letters appeared two years after John Young had published the 'Agricola' letters in the *Acadian Recorder* in an effort to support Lord Dalhousie's establishment of a provincial agricultural society, whose objective was to turn the Nova Scotian economy from resource exploitation for foreign markets to locally based agriculture. Thus Young's letters called for a reassessment of the social status of the Nova Scotian farmer: 'He was of the lowest caste in society, and gave place here to others who, according to the European standard of rank and consequence, are confessedly his inferiors. This sense of degradation was perceptible among husbandmen themselves. Such of them as were under the necessity of working, set about it with great reluctance and always under a mortifying sensation of shame. They would blush to be caught at the plough by their genteeler acquaintance' (qtd. in Matthews, *'Stepsure'* 131). Like Young and Galt's Bogle Corbet, McCulloch's Stepsure distrusts the false reputations upon which mercantile and urban status are based and advocates a return to the land and to rural values, where merit can be demonstrated and true character assessed. In this sense, these novels are simultaneously conservative and anti–status quo. The pastoral myth of a return to a simpler, rural-based value system is deeply conservative,[20] and yet because this return constitutes a protest against the inefficiency and corruption of the existing state of things, it is 'progressive.'

Mephibosheth's letters trace his success as a farmer to the character he has developed by overcoming adversity in life. Like his namesake in the Old Testament, Mephibosheth is an orphan who was born lame. In accordance with a remarkable eighteenth-century Nova Scotian poor law, he was 'sold' upon the town's charity when his parents died soon after their arrival in the village. According to this arrangement, townships without poorhouses would pay householders to feed and lodge an orphan, who would then earn his or her keep by serving in their homes (McCulloch 297, editor's note). Mephibosheth is taken in by Squire Worthy, to whom he becomes a farmer's apprentice. In this position, the lame lad must be inventive about fencing in cattle and remembering where he laid down his tools. 'Nature had not qualified me for running races,' he explains. 'There is, however, scarcely any disadvantage in life, which may not be turned to some good account ... To me, to whom even a moderate pace was always a painful exertion, it soon became a subject of study, when walking was necessary, how many steps might be saved ... this calculating disposition arose out of hard necessity' (88). Mephibosheth's misshapen feet mean that he must plan his every action carefully because it is simply too hard for him to go back and do it again.[21] His condition also means that he cannot gad about town much or go drinking or dancing. When he comes to the end of his apprenticeship with Squire Worthy and his guardian offers him the choice of a financial payout or a piece of woodland, Mephibosheth wisely chooses the piece of property, which he soon turns into a thriving farm. Because he has no pretensions to gentility, he has no qualms about doing menial tasks such as manuring his fields himself, with the result that he reaps larger crops than his neighbours Mosey Slack and Mr Pumpkin, who plough more land than he does but cannot be bothered with such repugnant jobs (165). He marries Dorothy, daughter of the Widow Scant, not because she is good-looking but because she shares his background of poverty and knows how to make much with very little. He and Dorothy and her mother therefore stay close to their new home, working, reading, and improving themselves and their property in a quiet, orderly life that soon turns them, despite Mephibosheth's twisted feet and their unpromising starts in life, into leading villagers with the surest financial and moral foundation.

The parallel McCulloch draws between Mephibosheth's triumph over adversity and the solution to Nova Scotia's economic decline becomes clear. Parson Drone avers that 'the distresses of the province originate in the idleness, extravagance, and ill applied labour of the community' (74), and he goes on, in his sermon on 'Economy' to affirm the virtues of the Protestant work ethic:

> Many ... view labour, only as the wages of sin; and without quarrelling with the sin, they avoid the labour. But to man in his present state, industrious exertion is one of heaven's best gifts. It is the wise arrangement of merciful providence, to curb his vices and protect him from misery. It is the means to collect around him an abundance of individual and social enjoyments. But those who escape from the activity of an industrious life, do not escape to a life of happiness: they become the debased and profligate; and at last, the wretched dregs of a miserable world .... [U]pon the earth transgression has entailed a curse, which man must remove by an industrious life. This and this only, will gladden the wilderness and solitary place, will make the desert rejoice and blossom as the rose. (139)

Parson Drone's sermon connects the improvement of one's character to the improvement of one's property as a mutual relationship: the improvement of land trains one in the qualities of perseverance, discipline, orderliness, consistency, and thrift that constitute character, and character, in turn, guarantees the success of one's economic endeavours. Like Bogle Corbet's comment about the Welland Canal atoning for the displacement of Aboriginals, Parson Drone's sermon suggests that the improvement of property constitutes a redemption of character which justifies the enterprise of British colonial settlement.

As several scholars have observed, this emphasis on economy as aimed primarily, not at the making of profits, but at the more idealistic values of establishing a comfortable home and a good character distinguishes McCulloch's version of the Protestant work ethic from Benjamin Franklin's more explicitly capitalist program of self-improvement.[22] I raise this comparison because it highlights a key point about the Britishness of Mephibosheth's values, especially in the way they distinguish character from vulgar ambition by showing how true character keeps a clear sight on the ultimate goals of one's enterprises. As the caricatures of the treasure-seekers who seek fruitlessly after buried gold or the Mr Gypsums who chase after the quick turnovers of cross-border smuggling of gypsum or plaster emphasize (McCulloch 64 and 32 respectively), money-making in itself must never dislodge moral and domestic improvement as one's ultimate priority. The letters outline a very clear order for true improvement; in the words of Parson Drone, 'activity expended on industrious pursuits, acquires property; and property enables [one] to enjoy the comforts of life' (153). Comfort remains the true goal, and property functions merely as a means to that end, not the end in itself. Furthermore, comfort is the end result, not the starting point, of the prudent life. Character is demonstrated by keeping this order straight. Indeed, Mephibosheth's ability to keep the sequence and therefore to triumph over adversity demonstrates that character *is* economy; that is to say, the *Letters* argue that character overcomes the conditions of production as the ultimate determinant of economy. The traits of this character – efficiency, thrift, cleanliness and orderliness, and the ability to exert oneself and persevere, in addition to a general optimistic outlook that believes in the ideology of improvement and progress – produce Mephibosheth's financial stability and establish his status property as an exemplary, solvent settler in British North America.

McCulloch makes sure that Mephibosheth's satiric norm occupies a middle position between the crass materialism which British North Americans associated with American-style resource exploitation and the kind of rarefied elitism they associated with (English) aristocratic classicism.[23] After the first seventeen Stepsure letters had run in the *Acadian Recorder* in 1821, an anonymous critic under the pseudonym of Censor wrote to the *Recorder* attacking the letters for their vulgarity and infelicitous prose. Stepsure rebuts his critic in the second series of letters, published in 1823. In Letter Twenty-Three he narrates a dream in which he and the villagers take Censor's advice to drink from the Castalian fountain, pluck the flowers of Parnassus, and beseech Apollo, god of poesy, for more sophisticated tongues. Predictably, Apollo ridicules Censor's classicist pretensions, and Pegassus kicks him off the mountain and into the great pile of manure that Mephibosheth's friend Scantocreesh has been eyeing for the improvement of his garden (252–60). Mephibosheth's ridicule of Censor's classicist affectations is built by contrast with his own persona of ham-fisted yeomanry: 'it is out of the question for the like of me to think of going to Parnassus. The Muses, I know, have not a good word to say of me; for I never sell my potatoes for flowers ... It is my misfortune to be a plain man: and my mistake, to have told a plain story to plain people in plain terms' (247–8). Here we have the Scottish professor of Pictou Academy pillorying the effete ostentation of the classicist King's College Anglican elite. True character is preached to Nova Scotians by a plain man speaking in plain English terms, and plain English is the property of a practical Scottish education.

The Stepsure Letters allows us to observe how very specifically Scottish values become generalized in colonial society as the universal values of the model British colonist. They demonstrate how, in the Scottish-derived ideology of practical education and self-improvement, class ascendancy becomes linked with moral development and how both are demonstrated by labour invested in private property. The famous doctor, poet, and editor of McGill's *University Magazine,* Andrew Macphail, identifies the basic logic of this ideology over a hundred years later in *The Master's Wife* (1939), the posthumously published remembrance of his childhood in the Scottish village of Orwell, Prince Edward Island. 'A man who lives on his own land and owes no man anything,' writes Macphail, 'develops all the dignity inherent in his nature' (18). As proof of the way in which good character results from owning private property, Macphail points to the Jacobite uprisings and the fact that the Highlanders had Prince Charlie lodging among them for nine months during the 1745–6 rebellion with nobody betraying his whereabouts, whereas in the 1715 revolt the Lowlanders, who did not own their lands and therefore had their loyalties divided between national allegiance and fealty to landlords, had betrayed his father, James. Macphail draws the parallel to his islanders: 'these people at Orwell lived upon their own land in their own houses, and correct behaviour is inseparable from that high estate' (88).

This linking of reliable character to private property adds a further layer of complexity to Charyl Harris's concept of status property, because it shows how the colonial dream of independence manifests itself in the desire for *private* property, which of course is based upon the concept of exclusiveness – the right to exclude other potential owners. Scottish Canadians such as McCulloch and Macphail were writing for readers who were very conscious of the traumatic removals of Scots from their lands in the old country, and for such readers, the ownership and improvement of land in the colony was the primary objective and cardinal virtue of the settler generation. The cultivation of wilderness into private lands, in this system of values, becomes the training ground as well as the proof of virtuous character. Without this superior character, the acquisition of property is merely vulgar materialism and no sign of respectable social status. Stepsure's good character, proven through his having overcome the adversities of orphanhood and disability, places him in a higher caste than his crassly materialistic neighbours, even if they own more land than he does. *The Mephibosheth Stepsure Letters* demonstrates that good (Scottish) character makes the difference between admirable and reprehensible status property in colonial British North America.

Mephibosheth Stepsure and Bogle Corbet would applaud the improvement of character that the protagonists undergo in Margaret Murray Robertson's *Shenac's Work at Home* (1866), Ralph Connor's *The Man from Glengarry* (1901), and Hugh MacLennan's *Barometer Rising* (1941). Each of these novels opens with an orphan protagonist who must battle adversity and emerge from under the shadow of an unsteady reputation. Each traces the establishment of a solid character through Highland Darwinism, the process by which Scottish characters 'become "more English" by going into and mastering the English world' (MacLeod, 'Writings' 74). This kind of movement from a parochial Highland Canadian place of origin (Glengarry and Cape Breton) to a wider, cosmopolitan arena functions centrally not only in MacLennan's but also in Robertson's and Connor's novels to enact a maturation process that widens these novels' purviews from local-colour narrative to larger social or national vision. In Robertson's novel, this wider vision involves the expansion of Shenac MacIvor's concept of feminine work from the domestic sphere of her own family to the wider world beyond Glengarry, while in Connor's and MacLennan's male-oriented novels, Ranald Macdonald and Neil Macrae emerge from rural, family embroilments in Glengarry and Cape Breton respectively into urban spheres of operation that have national consequences. In Connor's and MacLennan's national allegories, the Scottish character negotiates with and eventually overcomes a corrupt English hierarchy in the process of emerging as the allegorical figure for the nascent Canadian nation. In all three cases, the substance of the protagonist's good character derives from the kind of Scottish values advocated by Mephibosheth Stepsure and learned in the parochial Scottish home.

Although Robertson published sixteen novels to international acclaim between the 1860s and the 1890s, she is now much less widely known than either her nephew Ralph Connor or Hugh MacLennan. She was part of a prominent Scottish Presbyterian family. Her maternal uncle was Andrew Murray, the eminent religious thinker and writer, and her father was a minister in the Congregational Church, an evangelical movement that had withdrawn from the Church of Scotland in the late eighteenth century over the official church's resistance to progressive social initiatives such as the establishment of Sabbath schools and libraries for the children of the poorer classes. After her mother died when Margaret was nine, the family emigrated from Stewartfield, Scotland, first to Vermont and then to Sherbrooke, Quebec. Her brother Joseph went on to become mayor of Sherbooke, a position he held for close to twenty years, before he was elected member of the provincial parliament and went to Quebec City. Three other brothers became prominent lawyers in Montreal (McMullen 82–4). She and her sister Mary benefited from the Scottish value placed on education when both were sent to Mount Holyoke Female Seminary in Massachusetts, where Emily Dickinson was among Margaret's classmates in 1847. Both sisters were brilliant scholars – so much so that Mary was invited to become principal of Mount Holyoke, a position she relinquished in order to marry Daniel Gordon, a Presbyterian minister, with whom she went to live in Glengarry. There she gave birth to Charles William Gordon, later known by the pseudonym Ralph Connor. Margaret, on the other hand, did not marry, but taught for many years at Sherbrooke Ladies' Academy before turning in 1865 to full-time writing. She published her first two novels, *Christie Redfern's Troubles* and *Shenac's Work at Home*, the following year.

Shenac was possibly the most popular of Robertson's novels: it was originally published by the American Sunday-School Union Press of Philadelphia in 1866, reprinted by the Religious Tract Society of London in 1868, 1883, and 1884, and then reissued in both Britain and the United States by Thomas Nelson of London, Edinburgh, and New York in 1889, 1892, 1901, and 1904 (Guth, 'Introduction' xxxv, n2). The novel is typical of Robertson's fictional didacticism, which employs the form of sentimental romance to convey quiet sermons on self-improvement, domestic efficiency, and the principles of Christian forgiveness and love. Orphanhood features regularly in Robertson's books as a situation in which social conventions, particularly those related to girls' and women's involvement in making a living, must be momentarily lifted. By being called upon in adverse circumstances to provide for siblings or a disabled parent, her young female orphans develop a self-reliance and comfort in leadership that counterbalances the tradition of women's sacrificial labour on behalf of others. '[N]o one could have been long in the house without seeing,' Robertson's narrator asserts, 'that Shenac was the ruling spirit there. It was right it should be so. It could not have been otherwise; for her mother was broken in health and spirits, and Allister was away. Hamish was not able to take the lead in the labour, because of his lameness and his feeble health … As for Dan, his will was strong enough to command an army … but he was two years younger than his sister, quite too young and inexperienced, even if he had been steady and industriously disposed, to take the lead. So of course the leadership fell upon Shenac' (131). Importantly, the young orphan girl rules the house and makes money, and though she usually spends it on behalf of her dependants, it remains significant that she becomes the family's primary decision-maker and economic agent.

As I mentioned earlier, orphanhood elicits readers' sympathy in such a way that they are invited to judge these characters' entry into unconventional roles not as rebelliousness but as admirable responses to difficult and unchosen circumstances. *Shenac's Work at Home* is set in Glengarry between the families of two cousins, both named Angus MacIvor; one is light-haired and therefore known as Angus Bawn (meaning fair), and the other is dark-haired and known as Angus Dhu (meaning black or dark). Angus Bawn, despite his sunny disposition, never does well on his farm and eventually falls into debt to his 'closer,' more abstemious cousin, Angus Dhu. The oldest sons of both families head off to the California gold rush to try to bolster the families' fortunes, but soon after, Angus Bawn dies of heart attack during a tragic journey to collect the body of his second son, who has drowned in a river accident. Tragedy strikes yet again before the bodies are even in the ground, for Bawn's house burns to the ground. Angus Dhu decides that it would be best for his cousin's family if he not only claimed the half of the land owed him but also bought out the rest of their farm. The family would then be dispersed – the one able-bodied boy, Dan, to work with him, and the others to various positions throughout the Glengarry community. But the two oldest remaining Bawn MacIvors, the sixteen-year-old twins Shenac and Hamish, decide they will not let the farm go nor let their family be separated, which means they must run the farm, at least until the return of Allister, their brother in California, who has no mailing address and no idea about the tragedies plaguing his family at home. Shenac is a plucky, determined worker, and Robertson is at pains to point out that her work involves both the physical labour of farming and the spiritual or emotional work of lifting her feeble mother's and frightened siblings' spirits. Hamish struggles with depression from his being lame and prone to rheumatism, but Shenac reminds him that his wise counsel and his care for the details around the garden and home are his 'higher' work. And under Shenac's leadership, the children do it; they successfully plant and harvest their crops and, by so doing, keep themselves not only in body and soul but together and on their own property for two years before Allister returns with money gained in the gold mines. With this windfall, he cancels their debt to Angus Dhu and restores the family to their own property.

Shenac demonstrates, perhaps even more clearly than *Bogle Corbet* and *Mephibosheth Stepsure,* that preoccupation with property is more than a matter of individual self-aggrandizement or class ascendancy. For the Bawn MacIvors, retaining their property means defending the family's integrity and thus their collective independence. They may work them-selves to exhaustion on their own farm, but this independence is infi-nitely superior to going into servitude to Angus Dhu and others in the neighbourhood. Indeed, the distinguishing mark of character is this self-sacrificing commitment to the family's collective independence. Their family 'must cling together and do the best they [can] until Allister come home,' Shenac tells her despairing mother. '[T]hink of Allister coming and finding no home! ... [T]he land would be gone, and it would be no home long to Allister or any of us without the land' (51). In order to retain the land, Shenac must live by Stepsure's formula for reliable character: while her little brothers rest after meals, she makes sure the house is not in 'disorder' before going back to work in the fields (65–6); she gets up before dawn to milk the cows and churn the butter long before the others have their breakfasts; she is too busy to go visiting neighbours' farms (78); and she echoes Mephibosheth's calculating disposition when she purchases a new spinning wheel and her mind gets 'busy calculating how many days' work there might be in the wool, and how long it would take her to finish it' (121).

Shenac's 'work at home' therefore involves more than merely manag-ing a domestic economy. It means developing the kind of character around which a family unit can cohere. In this regard, the narrative presents her as a character who needs to mature. Early in the novel she resents her Uncle Angus Dhu's intention to purchase the farm and break up the family, and she sharply accuses him of avarice. She speaks caustically to her fourteen-year-old brother, Dan, whose energy she desperately needs if they are going to plant and harvest their crop. Indeed, her very success as farm manager makes her 'less lovable as the years went on' (132–3), and the narrator admits that Shenac sometimes leans to 'triumphant self-congratulation' (125). Shenac herself tells Hamish that she fears what her many responsibilities are doing to her: 'I am getting as hard as a stone, and as cross as two sticks' (214). Most significantly, her total commitment to making the farm pay exhausts all her energies, so that she fails to set aside time for the 'higher duties' of prayer, for moments when she and Hamish can discuss books together, and, most troublingly, for attendance at worship. When she does go to church, she is so tired that she often falls asleep (137). This higher work of inner self-reform becomes the key realm for the next stage of labour, which takes up the second half of the novel now that she and the other children have saved their farm.

Indeed, having worked so hard to avoid surrendering the farm, Shenac faces her most difficult task when she must surrender everything for which she has worked. When her brother Allister finally comes home from California, not only must she give up her 'rulership' of the family farm to his superior management – the narrative assumes his superiority because he is older, he has experienced the wider world, and he is male – but she must also give up the management of his domestic arrangements when he marries her cousin Shenac Dhu. As if this were not trying enough, she must then surrender her twin and confidante, Hamish, into God's hands when the illness that has plagued him since infancy finally takes his life. The narrative suggests that this series of renunciations constitutes a process of softening that loosens the callousness Shenac had developed through her fierce self-discipline. Twenty-first-century readers might be tempted to interpret the process of surrender she undergoes as the recuperation of the independent woman back into the traditional female roles of self-sacrifice and abnegation, but Robertson works against such a ready subsumption of her feisty protagonist to patriarchal convention. Close to the end of the novel, Mr Stuart, Hamish's good friend, who had recently been assigned as minister to a distant Presbyterian parish, offers her an escape from her diminished position as spinster sister in Allister's household by asking her to marry him. But despite her attraction to him, Shenac resolutely refuses his proposal because she wants to get an education first. She does not deny his contention that her many adversities and sufferings on behalf of others have educated her beyond what any school could do, but she nonetheless insists that she will attend two years of school in Montreal before she will marry him. She does not wish to appear a backcountry girl to his parishioners, and so she insists, over his objections, that she will delay the wedding until she has gained some higher education (397–407). Like all the younger people of Glengarry, who have learned English so that they can read the papers and explain what is happening in the wider world to their Gaelic-speaking parents (9, 79), Shenac recognizes that the sequestered life among the Glengarry Highlanders is coming to an end, and she must prepare herself for entry into a wider, public world.

Shenac's higher work of inward transformation occurs through a process of religious conversion that reflects a significant shift underway in Scottish Presbyterianism in the late nineteenth century. The novel is deliberately set during the famous Glengarry revival which followed upon the building of the Gordon Free Church in 1864,[24] and Shenac's softening is meant to reflect and affirm the general loosening of Calvinist rigidity in the decreased emphasis on law and judgment and increased emphasis on love and forgiveness that were central to the revival and to the separation of the Free churches from the Church of Scotland. When Shenac attends her first revival service at the new church, however, she is struck by how nothing about the service seems out of the ordinary. The same psalms are sung, the same scriptures read, and for the most part the same people are in attendance as at the old church. Rather, she thinks that there is a new life hidden in the old content and form (244–5). The narrator explains that the transformation taking place in the community is not dramatic or sensational in any way. Indeed, 'God does not always choose the wisest and greatest, even among his own people, to do his noblest work,' and Shenac's inner 'turn' takes place under the preaching of a humble neighbour and not a great orator (260). In this very low-key description of conversion, we might rightly hear the echo of Stepsure's plain man speaking in plain language to plain people and its reiteration of the Scottish common sense philosophy of quiet, steady improvement.

And as Lorraine McMullen observes, we might also note that the novel's careful detailing of Shenac's conversion functions as a fictionalized sermon which calls its readers to a similar surrender to the gospel. In this way, novels such as Robertson's evince a new position possible for women in Scottish Presbyterianism and in evangelical Protestantism more generally; and this is the role of the woman writer whose domestic fiction enables her to proclaim the virtues of private life and the domestic values of forgiveness, cooperation, self-sacrifice, and self-improvement as instances in microcosm of the values necessary to wider social organization (McMullen 106). The emergence of the Sunday-School Union Press and the Religious Tract Society made it possible for Robertson to launch a career as a writer of such sermons, and her subsequent reprintings with secular commercial presses such as Thomas Nelson in New York and Hodder and Stoughton in London show that the audience for such materials was much wider than the small Highland outpost of colonial Glengarry would suggest. This audience read in English; so Shenac's Scottish virtues, specifically forged in the environment of Scottish Presbyterianism and its evolution from old to new church, were disseminated to a general English reading public.

Charles William Gordon was six years old when his aunt published *Shenac's Work at Home*, with its evocation of the community and values in which he was raised in Glengarry. So although he claimed, after his success as Ralph Connor had been well established, that he never intended to become a writer with serious artistic pretensions (*Postscript* 150–1), his aunt had modelled for him how a combination of local colour, sentimental romance, and religious didacticism could find an international market. Gordon made a phenomenal success of this formula, first raising funds for the Presbyterian Church's Canadian missions by writing descriptions of his adventures in the Northwest for the Presbyterian *Westminster Magazine* and then going on to sell millions of copies of his novels through his friend and Canadian-cum-American publisher, George H. Doran (Lennox 104). *The Man from Glengarry*, Connor's third novel, sold 98,000 copies in its first edition, and its sequel *Glengarry School Days* sold over five million copies (Waterston 186). Gordon's experiences as a missionary in the Northwest when Canada was expanding into the prairies, in addition to his involvements in nationwide ventures such as the formation of the United Church of Canada out of the Presbyterian, Congregational, and Methodist churches, made it natural that he should think in terms that stretched across the emerging nation. He therefore precedes Hugh MacLennan as a significant formulator of Canadian national allegory, not just in *The Man from Glengarry*, which follows the emergence of a young orphan from Glengarry onto the national stage, but also in his stories of the taming of the West, such as *Corporal Cameron of the North West Mounted Police* (1912) and *The Foreigner: A Tale of Saskatchewan* (1909).

In many ways, *The Man from Glengarry* follows the theme and moral intent of *Shenac's Work at Home*. Ranald Macdonald is an orphan from a Glengarry Highland family (Connor inverts Robertson's family arrangements because this time the protagonist's father is the dark one, Macdonald Dhu, and his uncle is the fair-haired one, Macdonald Bhain) who is forced into early maturity by the decline and death of his father and by having to take on heavy physical labour to maintain his father's and now his property. As in *Shenac*, the process of maturation not only involves the ethic of hard work and responsibility but also means the kind of inner spiritual transformation that allows Ranald to forgive the French Canadian logger whose unfair attack on his father inflicted the wounds that eventually took Macdonald Dhu's life. Significantly, this spiritual transformation involves mental improvement in the form of Bible study and theological discussion with Mrs Murray, the Presbyterian minister's wife, whose warm and practical concern for Glengarrians' welfare makes her the spiritual heart of the community. Mrs Murray could easily have been a heroine in one of Margaret Murray Robertson's novels; in fact, she is quite clearly modelled on Margaret's sister and Charles Gordon's mother, Mary. Like Mary, Mrs Murray has attended college and therefore has all the benefits of an advanced education. She is an English-speaking Lowlander, and yet because of her concern for her husband's parishioners, she has taught herself Gaelic since giving up the sophisticated urban life of her college years and moving to Glengarry (57, 218). Whereas her husband urges a strict application of scriptural law in his curt dismissal of Ranald as a hoodlum from a bad family who will only bring trouble upon himself and his community, Mrs Murray advocates the new emphasis on the softer values of grace and forgiveness that I traced earlier in *Shenac's Work at Home* (see also Wood 135). Through her instruction and because of her belief in him, Ranald comes to give up his murderous vendetta against his father's killer. Like Shenac, he learns the paradox that real strength of character is demonstrated by the willingness to surrender. Moreover, Mrs Murray teaches him that a good character always finds its reward. Indeed, the novel makes Ranald's good character pay off – literally, not just figuratively – and it emphasizes his good character by contrast with corrupt Englishness.

After his father's death, Ranald accompanies the Glengarrians' log boom downriver to the sale yards in Quebec City. There his dexterity of mind and limb gets him a position in the firm of the Montreal-based Englishman Mr St. Claire. Ranald is hired to survey some of St. Claire's outlying lumber tracts, and he soon faces a difficult test of character when St. Claire asks him to lie about the value of a certain tract so it will bring a high price. St. Claire hints at promotions and even marriage to his daughter if Ranald will comply. After consulting with Mrs Murray, however, Ranald rejects this Englishman's temptation, even though it may cost him his job. This is where the New World environment of the colonies displaces the absolute domination of the English; for there are other commercial players in the picture, and Ranald's honesty impresses Colonel Thorpe, the American buyer whom St. Claire would have swindled. So Thorpe offers the young Scot a position in the significantly named British-American Coal and Lumber Company as manager of its British Columbian operations. Character, then, clearly emerges as a status property when Ranald quickly rises to influence, not only establishing reading rooms for his BC lumber workers' improvement but also being elected to represent British Columbia in the province's negotiations with Sir John A. Macdonald over the rail link and the Terms of Union. One can almost hear Mephibosheth Stepsure, Bogle Corbet, and Shenac MacIvor applauding as the novel's curtain descends.

Ranald's ascending status contrasts clearly with that of other characters. At the most basic level, his whiteness and his Presbyterian Britishness enable him to emerge as a national figure in a way that is simply not available in Connor's imagination to any of the French or Irish Catholic loggers with whom the Glengarry Scots compete for Ottawa Valley timber. Nor does it seem possible for Connor to imagine such a leading role for any of the St Regis Mohawks, who never appear in the novel but whose lease of land to the Highlanders haunts the narrative through the repeated reference to this part of Glengarry as the 'Indian Lands' (36; McMullen 89). So Ranald's redefinition of the loose category of Britishness away from the kind of Englishness represented by St. Claire constitutes the Scottish Canadian's entering qualification for national allegory. But as he ascends onto the national stage, he departs from his primary identification with Glengarry. At the conclusion of the Highlanders' timber sales in Quebec, they prepare to return to Glengarry. Uncle Macdonald Bhain turns to Ranald, who will be staying in the city to take up his new job with St. Claire, and says, 'Ye are taking the way that will be leading you from us all, and I will not be keeping you back …You will be a true man, and you will keep the fear of God before your eyes, and you will remember that a Macdonald never fails the man that trusts him' (259). Although Macdonald Bhain's words clearly recognize the Highland Darwinism at work here, they also emphasize the Scottish character – 'a Macdonald never fails …' – upon which Ranald's allegorical figuration as national representative is based.

This point is key, for it identifies the process by which Scottish virtues are transformed into Canadian ones, even as the distinctly Scottish communities out of which they emerge gradually erode into the amorphous terrain of Britishness. As Terrence Craig puts it, Connor 'looked into the Canadian future and saw a romanticized Scottish past' ('Religious' 107). This erosion does not mean that the Scottish element disappears in the English Canadian story, for Connor retains within his allegory the familiar contest between Scottish practicality and effete English patronage. Not only does Ranald stand in sharp contrast to St. Claire of the shady business ethics, but he is also clearly separated from the affectations of his romantic rival, Lieutenant De Lacey: 'the lieutenant, handsome, tall, well made, with a high-bred if somewhat dissipated face, [had] an air of *blasé* indifference a little overdone, and an accent which he had brought back with him from Oxford, and which he was anxious not to lose. Indeed, the bare thought of the possibility of his dropping into the flat, semi-nasal of his native land filled the lieutenant with unspeakable horror' (228). De Lacey's aristocratic pretensions, his being a graduate of the impractical English university system, and his snobbish attitude towards local Canadian English make him a sad contrast to Ranald's down-home values, his work ethic, optimism, and sincerity. De Lacey is well matched with Maimie St. Claire, whose values are as misguided and character as unstable as her father's and whom Ranald ultimately rejects as a suitable fiancée.

De Lacey represents a version of the English 'remittance man,' a stock figure of scorn that had spread from the specifically Scottish competition with Englishness that I have been tracing in this chapter throughout Canadian fiction more generally during the late nineteenth and early twentieth centuries. Again and again, the English remittance man is represented as a city-bred greenhorn, dependent upon the remittances he receives from his family back home and therefore unprepared for the rigours of rural pioneer life. His untested book knowledge makes him regularly misjudge situations and people and leaves him the laughing stock of anyone with a little common sense. The pioneer ethos was so well prepared for this object of ridicule, therefore, that one can easily lose track of the specifically Scottish element which pits an orphan such as Ranald who must make do for himself against the Englishman who has an inheritance and has never been forced by adversity to develop character as a result.

Connor's elevation of simple rural over complex urban values has caused some commentators to suggest that his novels hearken nostalgically to a world that was 'already passing as he wrote about it' (Watt 10) and that they are therefore 'signposts of a Canada that no longer exists' (Lennox 149). But this reading too readily separates the rural and the urban parts of the novel from one another. Connor's novels do indeed espouse the pastoral myth, with its assumption that it is 'easy to be good here' in the country (*Man* 196), but this goodness or virtue is not allowed to remain a perpetual property of the backwoods. What qualifies Ranald to represent the bold new Canada in which Jack's as good's (or even better than) his English master is that the character forged in the Presbyterian smithy of Glengarry proves itself as readily in the commercial centre of urban Quebec as in the resource frontier of British Columbia. As Susan Wood suggests, Ranald's maturation demonstrates that 'Connor offers, instead of the static opposition of pure country and wicked city, a dynamic view of society's moral evolution' (138). The old Scottish values are the source of the model citizen's virtues, but to become a leader of the Canadian nation, Ranald must leave the woods, contend with the corrupt English oligarchy of the city, and adapt his rural traditions to the contemporary problems of growing, urbanized commercialism. Thus his efforts to reform labour relations in the company he manages are practical applications of the Scottish Presbyterian values of self-improvement to the new circumstances of the expanding nation in British Columbia. The character qualities and ideology of his Scottish parochial background are removed from their original context and become generalized onto English Canada as a whole.

Hugh MacLennan's *Barometer Rising* takes the Highland Darwinism of this model of national allegory into the next generation, for while Connor concentrates on the protagonist's departure from his rural community, MacLennan picks up the story long after the young man's family has left the rural Highland district. As with Ranald's Glengarry, Neil Macrae's Cape Breton represents a touchstone for enduring values – this time of loyalty, nobility, and craftsmanship – but it is too narrow a venue for the national drama MacLennan intends to stage in the novel. So Neil derives his genius for ship design from his father's training as a shipbuilder in Cape Breton, but he must adapt these skills to the modern circumstances of a Canada that is playing a new role on the international stage of the Great War in Europe.

As in *Bogle Corbet, The Mephibosheth Stepsure Letters, Shenac's Work at Home,* and *The Man from Glengarry,* redemption of character lies at the heart of *Barometer Rising.* Indeed, the barometer in MacLennan's novel of the Halifax explosion of 1917 traces the emergence of Neil's character from under a dark cloud and into brighter prospects after a terrible trial by fire. Neil has been accused by his English commanding officer, Colonel Wain, of cowardice in battle that cost the lives of many of his fellow soldiers. Despite his being Neil's uncle and despite his daughter Penny's love for Neil, Geoffrey Wain would have eagerly court-martialled Neil had the latter not apparently been killed in a bomb attack in Flanders. But we soon learn that, in fact, the colonel has blamed Neil for disobeying orders so confused that disaster would have been total had not Neil abrogated his directives. The plot tension rises from Neil's urgent need to contact the only man who knows how confusing those orders were, Big Alec MacKenzie, before Colonel Wain learns Neil is alive and has a chance to silence his old army mate. Neil and another Cape Bretoner, Dr Angus Murray, eventually get a sworn affidavit from MacKenzie that proves Neil's innocence, despite the fact that it may cost MacKenzie his job as dock foreman in Colonel Wain's shipyard. They succeed partly because they are all three from Cape Breton and MacKenzie places clan loyalty above the English colonel's pay-off in the form of his job at the shipyard and partly because the big man's homespun values insist that honesty always finds its reward. The national allegory that is played out here receives overt comment from the novel's philosopher-doctor, Angus Murray. Geoffrey Wain, he thinks, represents the corrupt and waning English colonial patriarchy that has exploited the colony but never contributed to its independent improvement. The Gaelic-speaking MacKenzie represents the primitive Highland pioneer whose noble values save Neil's reputation. MacKenzie is also representative in that he has realized the inevitable and brought his family to the city so that his son can get an English-language education that will serve as his ticket to the future.[25] Neil and Penny represent the new, urbane cosmopolitans with whose technical expertise the Canadian nation will go forward, while Dr Murray represents himself as the Canadian caught between England and America, between the old and the new (208).

Much of the existing criticism of *Barometer Rising* is divided between critics' taste or distaste for MacLennan's allegorical mode. Those who approve insist that his work brilliantly produces for the first time a strongly realized fictional representation of Canadian national identity, and those who disapprove complain that he sacrifices his characters to the nationalistic theme.[26] For the most part, the critical discussion of the allegory itself follows Angus Murray's schema, whereby Neil represents the orphaned young Canada, which has been incompetently directed by its outmoded English colonial commander and which is now maturing through adversity into an independent, self-directed nation. Few scholars, however, observe the ethnic dimension of MacLennan's allegorical scheme.[27] But all the elements we have observed in relation to the Scots-English conflict in previous novels are here: five generations of the Wain family have lived since 1812 in their prominent Halifax home (19), long enough for Geoffrey Wain's ancestors to have sat on the Tory-Anglican council that denied Pictou Academy's yearly grant. Wain himself is portrayed as a man who 'had been born at the top of things with no wider horizon to aim for' (66). Nothing he owns is the product of his own efforts. He has inherited a library of books that he has never read (189). Only the war, with its inflated economy, has given him a chance to better his prospects, and he would gladly sell his Canadian properties to better his international prospects. Like Lieutenant De Lacey, he has no real respect for his local birthplace; 'he merely felt it was a little less inferior than the rest of North America' (70). Yet despite his own complete lack of character, he disparages Neil, and in specifically Scottish terms. According to Wain, 'Like a lot of the Highland Scotch [Neil] was shiftless unless he had everything his own way' (96).

Neil, by contrast, inherits nothing but his father's knowledge of boat-building. Like Bogle Corbet and Ranald Macdonald, he is plagued by a bad reputation and must clear his name through the demonstration of his own integrity and the exercise of his own abilities. This he does under great duress after the explosion and during the subsequent blizzard, when his capacity for decisive action and effective leadership leaps to the fore as he organizes rescue teams and a temporary hospital in the Wains' old home. Whereas Wain disparaged his inherited colonial home, Neil and Angus Murray transform it into a place of healing. Whereas Wain thought his birthplace second-rate, Neil feels his own future is tied up with Canada's: 'The life he had led in Europe and England these past two years had been worse than an emptiness. It was as though he had been able to feel the old continent tearing out its own entrails ... There was no help there. For almost the first time in his life, he fully realized what being a Canadian meant. It was a heritage he had no intention of losing' (79). The young man born in the Highland community of Cape Breton links himself wholeheartedly with the emerging nation, whose entire geography he envisions bound together by the railway line 'with one end in the darkness of Nova Scotia and the other in the flush of a British Columbia noon' (79).

We can be fairly confident that the Scottish-English tensions that animate this national allegory were clearly linked in MacLennan's view to Canadian-colonial tensions, for his own recollection of the first time he realized what it meant to be Canadian, like Neil's, highlights rivalry with an Englishman. In the essay 'On Discovering Who We Are' (1949), MacLennan describes the time he returned to Halifax after his years as a Rhodes scholar at Oxford and applied for a position at Dalhousie University. The department head told him he had lost the competition to another applicant because, 'After all, you're a Canadian and he's an Englishman. It makes all the difference' – this, despite the fact that the English candidate had graduated from MacLennan's own class at Oxford with exactly the same credentials (40). He had the experience repeated when he applied for a university job in western Canada and was once again bypassed for an Englishman (41).[28] This preference and his resentment of it, MacLennan recalls, made him aware of himself as a Nova Scotian and a Canadian for the first time. To return to the opening paragraphs of this chapter, we might say that whereas Sandor Hunyadi asserts an identity between Canadianness and Englishness, MacLennan describes the emergence of Canadianness out of conflict and disaffection with Englishness. And underneath that Canadian disaffection lies a significant element of Scottishness.

Two days before the terrible explosion in Halifax in 1917, Angus Murray, the philosophically minded doctor of *Barometer Rising,* stands near the harbour watching a troop ship embark for the European war. A pipe band in the dock shed is playing 'Lochaber No More,' and the sound makes every nerve in Murray's body quiver. 'This was the lament the village pipers had played a hundred years ago when the clansmen who were the ancestors of half the people in Nova Scotia had left Scotland,' Murray thinks. 'Now Nova Scotian pipers were playing their men back to the Old World again. Was this another of England's baits, or did the pipers really feel their music?' (53). Sandor Hunyadi, too, hears the bagpipes playing, but whereas we might dismiss his calling them 'English' as the error of an outsider untuned to the differences between Scottishness, Britishness, and Englishness, Murray's Highland Cape Breton ancestry makes it clear that he is sensitive to the tensions within and between these categories. He ruminates as he watches the men march onto the deck of the troopship: 'Perhaps some scientist of the future ... would be able to analyze the nature of the chain which bound Canada to England ... Hardly anyone in Canada really understood the legal obligations of his own country to England. Hardly anyone cared. Yet the chain was stronger than the skeptics guessed' (53).

It takes no scientist of the future to take the hint from those bagpipes and to show how the chain binding Canada to 'England' was made of Britishness and that its links were forged largely by Scots in their own interests as well as those of the Celtic populations of Britain's peripheries. This chain was made precisely to tie the colonies together into a larger empire that exceeded the exclusive grip of the English. The flexible category of Britishness served the Scots and other White, non-English colonists as a status property that facilitated their upward social mobility and allowed them to capitalize on the opportunities of empire to the extent that they became senior administrators of what has become known as English Canada. The elasticity of Britishness enabled Celts such as the Scots to claim British status when it suited them without relinquishing their Scottish identity. As Simon Gikandi has noted, 'the invention of British identity did not obliterate older loyalties (those of Scottish Presbyterianism, for example) but proffered a conduit through which such loyalties could be synthesized and, indeed, legitimated' (33). Thus, as we have seen, Mephibosheth Stepsure, Ranald Macdonald, and Neil Macrae enter wholeheartedly into the national project of establishing English Canada, and they feel no need to repudiate their Scottishness in the process. In this way, the properties of Scotch permeated the basic character that came to define the anglophone Canadian nation.

4 The Muscular Christian in Fictions of the Canadian West

Ever since T.C. Sanders coined the term 'muscular Christianity' in Britain in 1857, it has functioned as an expression of dismissal. Writing in the *Saturday Review* about Charles Kingsley's recently published *Two Years Ago*, Sanders quips that the book presents Kingsley's 'love of a muscular Christianity' personified by a 'man who fears God and can walk a thousand miles in a thousand hours, who … breathes God's free air on God's rich earth, and at the same time can hit a woodcock, doctor a horse, and twist a[n iron] poker around his fingers' (qtd. in Donald Hall 7). The hyperbolic masculinity of such manly characters has made them ready targets for this kind of dismissive satire over the past one hundred and fifty years. Seventy years later, for example, a nationalized version of the muscular Christian had crossed the Atlantic, only to be dismissed again in A.J.M. Smith's 'Wanted – Canadian Criticism' (1928). In this manifesto for Canadian modernism, Smith rejects the 'inspiration stuff and He-man Canadiana' that has dominated Canadian literary tastes up to the late 1920s and calls, by contrast, for a more intellectual, 'realistic' sensibility (221). Forty-five years later again, Susan Wood Glicksohn picks out the same figure for dismissal in her 1973 portrait of the turn-of-the-century Canadian readership that Smith decried: 'A lingeringly Victorian, prudish society, it demanded pure romance mixed with uplifting morality, an emphasis on the ideals of progress and Christian manliness; and it regarded with horror European and American experiments with "realism"' (xi). In a 1997 article on the figure of the Mountie in twentieth-century fiction and film, Michael Dawson, though he does not use the term 'muscular Christian,' points out that the Mountie, a paragon of high-minded and manly values, was fundamentally an expression of 'Canadian antimodernism' (129). Linked as it has been with the general optimism of the mid-Victorian glory days of empire, the figure of the muscular Christian appears in twentieth-century scholarly commentary as an oft-repeated representative of that embarrassing period of bumptious naiveté in Canadian literary culture before the disillusionments of the First War and the Great Depression. In Canadian literary criticism, in particular, this figure has often been used to characterize what was wrong with the first two decades of this century, when Canadian fiction floundered hopelessly in pie-in-the-sky romance before it was rescued by the tough-minded existentialism of the prairie realists in the mid–1920s.[1]

These ready dismissals overlook the way in which a serious study of the figure of the muscular Christian can enable us to trace the interweaving of nationalist ideas about ethnicity, gender, religion, class, and race in early twentieth-century Canadian fictional and social texts. Such dismissive views obscure the fact that muscular Christianity was a site where significant social ideologies were negotiated and contested, and by doing so, they deprive us of a very useful way to locate and trace the historical renewal of White, British, male norms in Canadian public life. They participate in a presentist myth of literary progress which envisions the history of Canadian literature as a development from juvenile romance to intellectually rigorous realism (in criticism between the 1930s and the 1970s) and from realism to the sophisticated multi-perspectival forms of postmodernism, multiculturalism, or postcoloniality (in criticism of the 1980s and 1990s). In so doing, these scholarly dismissals fail to consider the significance of the powerful movement of social progressivism in class, gender, and ethnic politics of which muscular Christianity, like its counterpart, maternal feminism, was a key element. By disregarding the social context that made these idealized gender images popular, dismissive criticism produces the naive romanticism it vilifies and thus displaces onto another era its own social amnesia.

I do not propose this chapter's reappraisal of the popular, allegorical figure of the muscular Christian in order to defend the values it represents. Rather, I intend to demonstrate how this figure functioned powerfully to popularize and inculcate normative ideals of British civility during the era of national consolidation after Canada expanded into the prairie west subsequent to its purchase of Rupert's Land from the Hudson's Bay Company in 1870. The figure of the muscular Christian, with his untiring and virile physical body balanced by his spiritually sensitive heart, made a perfect representation of the ideal Canadian who could carry out the hard physical work of territorial expansion, as well as the equally important social work of building a new civil society. I follow Donald Hall in preferring the term 'muscular Christianity' to its common nineteenth-century parallel term 'Christian manliness' because the former empha-sizes the male body and its representation of a specific set of social values. 'Throughout works written by the muscular Christians,' says Hall, 'the male body appears as a metaphor for social, national, and religious bodies, while at the same time it attempts to enforce a particular con-struction of those bodies' (8). National allegory functions by means of this common trope; as the 1921 poster from the Canadian National Exhibition reproduced in illustration 10 demonstrates, the body of the nation is often figured by means of the body of an idealized individual, and in such personifying tropes, the heterogeneity of the nation is gathered into the homogenizing image of the single anthropomorphic image. The figure of the muscular Christian served as a central represen-tation of the civil ideals of practical social improvement that English Canadian culture derived from the Scottish emphases on practical edu-cation, independent initiative, and self-discipline which I described in the previous chapter. Indeed, the dynamism and energy of the muscular Christian were often linked by means of British versions of the northern myth to the hardy qualities of north Britons and especially Presbyterian Scots. The muscularity of this figure prepared him to wage battle in the causes of justice, and his Christian piety ensured that he resisted the temptations of both American-style capitalism and English over-sophisti-cation. Together, his physical strength and moral conviction distin-guished Canadian civility from both American competitors and British antecedents. As such, this figure was fundamental to the establishment of the British Protestant ethnic norm in Canada, and any comprehensive understanding of how the mainstream was formed in anglophone Canada must include a consideration of the figure of the muscular Christian.

The muscular Christian, even more, perhaps, than the figures of the Loyalist brother and the Scottish orphan, manifests the contradictory structure of civility outlined in my introductory chapter. That is, in providing a coherent image of a Canadian ideal that contributed effec-tively to progressive national movements, muscular Christianity identi-fied the racial, religious, ethnic, and sexual characteristics to be excluded from that coherent ideal. In 'The Politics of Recognition,' the philoso-pher Charles Taylor describes the conflict between the 'politics of uni-versality,' which bases civil society on equal treatment of all, and the 'politics of difference,' which tries to address social inequities by giving special recognition to marginalized groups. Muscular Christianity is riven by this conflict. On the one hand, it is motivated by powerfully demo-cratic values which assume that any person (usually but not necessarily a

10   This poster, created by Francis Robert Halliday, emphasizes the allegorical link between the strong national body and the strong masculine body.

man), regardless of race, class, or creed, can learn and practise the virtues of manly Christianity. But on the other hand, its commitment to social service and moral uplift requires the constant rediscovery of outsiders and of those who are seen as morally weak and who therefore need the muscular Christian's help. It designates and reinscribes the other's difference, even as it recognizes the muscular Christian's responsibility to build an equal relationship with that other. In this sense, the Canadian figure of the muscular Christian operated in an allegorical discourse that was paradoxically progressive and conservative, radical and reactionary, and as such, it reminds us how social discourse is not dogma but the site of lively cultural and ideological contestation.

I begin with a scene taken from *The Foreigner,* a best-seller by Ralph Connor published in 1909 and made into a movie in 1922 with the rather frightening title *God's Crucible.*[2] It is 1884, and two stock characters of turn-of-the-century Canadian fiction are riding in a buckboard out to a ranch in Canada's newly annexed Northwest. The first is Kalman Kalmar, a Ukrainian teenager recently rescued by Presbyterian mission workers from a life of squalor in Winnipeg's immigrant ghetto. The second is Jack French, an English remittance man, who has reluctantly taken on the responsibility of giving Kalman useful employment and a healthy place to live on his ranch on the South Saskatchewan River. Jack rounds a corner too quickly in the buckboard and accidentally runs an ox cart from the nearby Ukrainian colony off the narrow road. When he and Kalman go back to help the farmer reload the tipped cart, the furious colonist attacks Jack with a club. Jack responds by first disarming the fellow, then cheerfully setting the cart to rights (the word 'cheerful' appears six times in the short scene), and finally, at the request of the now-mollified and repentant Ukrainian farmer, giving him a bare-knuckled lesson in what Connor calls 'the manly art' (216). When Kalman translates the farmer's apology for the attack, French replies,

'Tell him ... only a fool loses his temper, and only a cad uses a club or a knife when he fights.'

'A cat?' Kalman asks, puzzled.

'No, a cad. Don't you know what a cad is? Well, a cad is – hanged if I know how to put it – you know what a gentleman is? ... Well, the other thing is a cad' (216).

Connor's narrator makes sure that Jack's lesson sinks in deeply when he tells us, 'To Kalman the day brought a new image of manhood ...

[T]his man of rugged strength and forceful courage [possessed] a subtle something that marks the finer temper and nobler spirit, the temper and the spirit of the gentleman. Not that Kalman could name this thing, but to his sensitive soul it was this in the man that made appeal and that called forth his loyal homage' (219). The 'subtle something' Kalman cannot name is the British-derived gentlemanly code of muscular Christianity. But the lesson is not lost on the Englishman who teaches it. When Jack sees the admiration in Kalman's eyes, he realizes that his new responsibility for the boy's upbringing requires a general clean-up in his own dissipated life, and that he would be a cad himself if he shirked his job as role model to the young foreigner of the novel's title (220).

This scene sketches in simple strokes the significance of muscular Christianity to the discourses of westward expansionism that animated turn-of-the-century visions of the emerging sea-to-sea dominion. Jack French's lesson in the manly art expresses British anxiety about maintaining cultural dominance in the face of increasing numbers of non-British immigrants, and it placates that anxiety by staging a contest between manly Christian (read 'White, Anglo-Celtic Protestant') civility and unmanly foreign (read 'Catholic, non-Anglo-Celtic') backwardness. This contest dramatizes the belief that the new Canadian dominion, the colony best situated to realize the original ideals of the British Empire, is engaged in the production of an orderly, civil society that will be a model to the world. One reason why Canadian society can claim exemplary progressive status, during and after Clifford Sifton's aggressive campaign to recruit eastern European farmers for the newly annexed prairies, is because of British Canadians' capacity to accommodate and civilize what they considered to be foreigners. Jack's pedagogy assumes that foreigners such as Kalman and his countryman are not essentially different from Jack himself despite their different ethnic, linguistic, and religious backgrounds. Anyone of whatever race or ethnicity who can admire the 'subtle something' of gentlemanly conduct, learn to discipline his violent passions, and convert his own behaviour to the muscular Christian's double code of justice and forgiveness can become a welcome member of the new society.

It is significant that Jack's lesson takes place in the region that will soon become Saskatchewan because the Canadian expansionists figured the Northwest simultaneously as the future breadbasket of the empire (Owram 112–13; Murphy, *Janey* 9, 146) and as the crucible in which the character of the new nation would be refined (Watt 14; Thompson and Thompson 166; Berger, 'True'). The adversities of prairie homesteading would burn away the excesses of dissipated English remittance men and release a pure vigour not merely of body but, more importantly, of spirit. The physical sturdiness and discipline required on the homestead were believed to contribute to a moral rectitude and orderliness that would produce citizens of the highest character. And these citizens, in turn, would produce the bread that would guarantee the economic future of the empire. Thus the muscular Christian provided Canadian imperialists with a representative figure that linked westward expansion to the refining of the nation's moral character, and in turn, that refinement could contribute to the moral, political, and economic renovation of the British Empire. As even this short discussion demonstrates, then, an examination of the muscular Christian can bring to light important formations in popular images of Canada that can easily elude analysis. It gives us one way to study the transparent assumptions that have established and continue to maintain the figure of the White, British male as a national norm.

The muscular Christianity popularized in Victorian England by such novels as Charles Kingsley's *Westward Ho!* (1855) and Thomas Hughes's *Tom Brown's School Days* (1857) valued manliness as a primary agent of Christian social activism. By linking physical sturdiness and vigour with moral discipline and spiritual vitality, these authors attempted in their novels, sermons, and journalism to chart a path for practical, socially engaged Protestant Christians between two other-worldly pietisms: that of evangelicals, on the one hand, and that of Anglo-Catholic Tractarians, on the other (Vance 29–41). In such publications as Hughes's *The Manliness of Christ*, they rejected the image of a meek-and-mild Jesus and argued instead that God had given men strong bodies to labour and fight for justice and social improvement. As Norman Vance explains, theirs was a democratization of the aristocratic codes of chivalry for the middle classes, making heroism possible for the emerging figure of the bourgeois gentleman (21). A man need not be a member of the landed gentry to be responsible for the administration of justice and charity among the wider populace. According to Kingsley and Hughes, all men of conviction should roll up their sleeves and get to work on behalf of the poor, the labouring classes, and the disenfranchised. Thus these two authors purveyed a widening of the ideals of noblesse oblige that had previously been limited to the aristocratic code. Their middle-class gentleman, like his chivalric predecessor, must demonstrate his virtue both in the public affairs of state and within the privacy of his own character.[3] For the muscular Christian, the personal was political, to borrow a phrase from 1970s feminism. Indeed, the man's personal body was political, for from its outset, the discourse of muscular Christianity linked the physical ideal of a vigorous male body with the spiritual ideal of a passionate but disciplined morality. This composite ideal was, in turn, linked to the patriotic ideal of a heroic citizenry dedicated to the protection of the weak and the punishment of those who took unfair advantage. The muscular Christian's well-defined biceps must be as ready to lift a weaker brother as to knock down an oppressor.

The class-reorganizing project of muscular Christian discourse can be readily traced in the deliberate attempts that Christian activists made to introduce the sporting and military drill ethos of the Rugby School of *Tom Brown's School Days* to lower-class boys through such institutions as William Alexander Smith's Boys' Brigade, Baden-Powell's Boy Scouts (which was a later, secular version of Smith's Brigade), and the Religious Tract Society, which published the immensely popular *Boy's Own Paper* and many of R.M. Ballantyne's and G.A. Henty's adventure novels for boys, as well as Margaret Murray Robertson's domestic romances of orphans who make good by dint of hard work and by learning the important balance of Christian compassion. Each of these institutions glorified the combination of vigorous, forceful masculinity with disciplined self-restraint that was central to the code of the muscular Christian gentleman; this would have been why, for example, the Boy Scouts of Winnipeg invited a writer of vigorous, manly novels about self-discipline such as Ralph Connor to inspect their activities, as illustration 11 shows. They idealized this combination with the purpose, as Smith put it in the 1883 passage that still serves as the mission statement of the Boys' Brigade, of 'the advancement of Christ's Kingdom among Boys and the promotion of habits of Obedience, Reverence, Discipline, Self-Respect *and all that tends towards a true Christian manliness*' (qtd. in Springhall 53, original emphasis). Historians have debated the effectiveness of this middle-class campaign to socialize lower-class boys into manly Christian values (see Springhall; Mangan and Walvin; MacKenzie 183–5), but my point at present is to observe the aim to restructure class hierarchies that was central to the ideals of muscular Christianity.

Fundamental to the renovation of British manhood was Kingsley's theory of *thumos*, a kind of rage or primitive vigour that could reanimate the man enervated by the decadence of modern Victorian society (Rosen 30; Wee 68). Kingsley likened this primal energy to a volcano's lava bubbling within men; it was a product of biological maleness and an active agent of virtue. Rosen observes, '"Animal passion,"' in Kingsley's

11   The Reverend Charles William Gordon inspecting a Boy Scout group, most likely on the occasion of the visit of Lord Baden-Powell, 1910.

term, 'a hot rage, becomes the primal stuff of virtue that stamps male nature and seeks expression through sex, fighting, and morality. Manliness can only be achieved by allowing this primal source to flow' (30). The problem, according to Kingsley, was that the over-refinements of civilized British society so strongly suppressed this natural energy that it only rarely surfaced. He theorized two ways that one could tap into primitive vigour and turn it to healthy effects. First, one could recapture primal British vigour through historical-imaginative activity: one could turn one's atavistic energy into healthy patriotism through a renewed appreciation of Britain's pre-modern Teutonic ancestry. In a series of lectures on the Roman and the Teuton, Kingsley used a British version of the northern myth to contrast manly and disciplined northern Teutons against effeminate and luxuriant southern Romans in an effort to inspire his British audience to reassert their Germanic vigour (Vance 86). His juxtaposition served two functions at once: he was able to enlist a mythos of Anglo-Saxon aggressiveness in the service of patriotism, and he was also able to vilify the Catholic Normanism that threatened his vision of a Protestant nation and empire (Wee 68, 85). Thus Kingsley's muscular Christian ideology proposed virile Protestant Britishness as central to, and effete non-Anglo Catholicism as antithetical to, its code of patriotism.[4]

Whereas the first way of regaining primitive vigour was historical-imaginative, Kingsley's second method was contemporary and imperialist. A young British man could reacquaint himself with his own raw vitality in the testing grounds of the colonies, where competition with Indigenous people whose energies were not yet constrained by modern civilization called upon new levels of energy and discipline (Wee 68; Rosen 30). This imperialist theme operated not only as the base plot of the adventure stories of Ballantyne and Henty and the *Boy's Own Paper* but also as the subtext of the woodscraft and outdoor adventurism of the Boys' Brigade and the Boy Scouts (see Springhall; MacKenzie). Through the chivalric struggle to bring British enlightened principles to the darkened, backward world, the muscular Christian firmed up his own character and found a productive outlet for his volcanic energy.

These imperialist elements of muscular Christian discourse gave it ready application in Canada, especially for the Canadian imperialists, who used it to support their campaign for a sea-to-sea dominion. Canadian imperialists, as Carl Berger explains in *The Sense of Power*, represent a peculiar progeny of British imperialism in that they advocated loyalty to Britain at the same time as they believed Canada's newly acquired wealth of resources (once it had annexed the Northwest) would cause the young, giant nation to supplant Britain as the centre of the British Empire. Canadian imperialists advocated the maintenance of British institutions of governance at the same time as they believed Britain's economic and political decline was imminent as a result of the degeneration of the original ideals of the British Empire (Berger, *Sense* 5, 152, 219). Canada offered a hinterland where primal British manhood could be regained. Its rugged northern climate and untapped natural resources posed a challenge that would thicken the blood and callus the hands of any delicate British young man (Hulan 18–19). Canada presented the ideal place for Britons to refurbish their lost Teutonic vigour in a bracing new atmosphere. As Canada First group member Robert Grant Haliburton, in *The Men of the North and Their Place in History* (1869), and McGill professor of medicine William Hales Hingston, in *The Climate of Canada and Its Relation to Life and Health* (1884), argued, the cold climate of the North constituted a eugenic, social Darwinist advantage for the new dominion. Its northern location would appeal more to Nordic peoples than to southern peoples and thus would weed out citizens too weak physically or morally to endure its stern conditions.

In this way, nature reinforced the borders of Canadian civility, and Canadians were doing non-northerners a favour by keeping them out of a region that would only bring them grief. At the same time, the demands of this northern life would refine the characters of those who did call it home, requiring of them a strenuous work ethic, a cooperative spirit, and resilient courage (Berger, 'True' 5–11). The physical tendency among Canadians, Dr Hingston testified, 'is unmistakably in favour of increased muscular development,' such that 'the future occupants of the soil will be taller, straighter, leaner people – hair darker and drier and coarser; muscles more tendinous and prominent and less cushioned' (qtd. in Berger, 'True' 11). Thus the Canadian version of the discourse of muscular Christianity enabled the Canadian imperialists to weave together the primal vigour and Christian activism of British manliness with a nationalist vision of Canada as the loyal son who would reinvigorate the aging empire by producing a strengthened and improved character in the hinterland. Muscular Christianity gave the Canadian imperialists a way to argue for Canada's separation from its colonial motherland at the same time as they could emphasize the contribution the country could make to a reformation of a British character that had been in decline (see Berger, *Sense*, 49, 259; Coleman, 'Immigration'; Cannadine).

Thus, when Jack French gives Kalman Kalmar and his fellow Ukrainian a lesson in the art of fisticuffs, that single lesson plunges teacher and students into a far-reaching curriculum on the values of vigorous Protestant activism, British supremacy, the chivalric code of the middle-class gentleman's social responsibility, and Canadian nationalist imperialism. And the rest of the novel shows that they learn their lessons well: Kalman leads a revolt against the avaricious Polish Catholic priest, renounces his vendetta to kill his mother's murderer, learns the work ethic that makes a success of the prairie ranch, and eventually marries the Scottish-born daughter of a CPR shareholder. This 'Canadian foreigner' (384) almost literally marries into Sir John A. Macdonald's National Policy. The Englishman, Jack, meanwhile, renounces his alcoholism, shoulders his responsibilities to the foreign boy in his care, and thereby rediscovers a manly dignity that is worthy not merely of his British lineage but even more of the new nation that has given him this opportunity for a second start.[5]

Such Canadian testings and reformations of masculine mettle appear again and again throughout Connor's immensely popular novels. While *The Foreigner* usefully delineates his idea of what constitutes Canadianness through the assimilation of an eastern European outsider to the ideal of muscular Christianity, his best-known novel, *The Man from Glengarry*, shows in even more detail than in the case of Jack French the process by which ostensible insiders must be converted to this ideal. The novel opens in Connor/Gordon's own boyhood environs of the Glengarry lumber shanties and among the Scottish Highlanders who work in them. But the narrative shows that even these Presbyterians of Gordon's own ethnic group need to be converted, that they need to undergo Alistair Macleod's Highland Darwinism and evolve to a new cultural identity, in order for them to emerge from their narrow religiosity and eye-for-an-eye legalism into the full light of Canadian progress. In charting this evolution, Connor was following the liberal theology of the Scottish theologian-scientist Henry Drummond, whose *Natural Law in the Spiritual World* (1882) and *The Ascent of Man* (1894) had a great impact on the optimistic thinking of many Canadian progressives. Connor had encountered Drummond's Darwinian-influenced Christian progressivism during his studies at New College, Edinburgh, but Drummond went on to have great influence in Canada, moving in 1894 to the position of principal of McGill and becoming well-known by such Canadian luminaries as Salem Bland, Mackenzie King, and Lord and Lady Aberdeen (Mack 144–5). Drummond harmonized Christian theology with Darwinist theory by suggesting that the universe evolves spiritually as well as physically, that the current evolutionary phase of the late nineteenth century was progressing beyond the simple, patriarchal 'Struggle for Life' to the 'Struggle for the Life of Others,' and that this phase was most fully nurtured by the figure of the self-sacrificing mother. Thus the contemporary phase of evolutionary development meant a shift from a rigid patriarchal struggle for survival to the female-nurtured struggle for the lives of others. The sign of true social and spiritual evolution, then, meant an increased feminization of culture (see Mack 143–6), but not one that entirely abandoned the energy and aggression associated with the masculine struggle for life. Rather, true spiritual evolution tempered that male primal energy with the gentle and caregiving elements of the maternal struggle for the lives of others. This is precisely the evolution that Connor outlines as the ideal in the Glengarry community and especially in the growing-up story of Ranald Macdonald, the novel's protagonist.

Connor's attitude towards the strict Calvinism of the Glengarry Presbyterians is affectionately ironic. He writes in his preface to the novel,
'Their religion may have been narrow, but ... [i]t was the biggest thing
in them. It may have taken a somber hue from their gloomy forests, but
by reason of a sweet, gracious presence dwelling among them it grew in
grace and sweetness day by day' (9). This sweet and gracious presence is
that of the minister's wife, Mrs Murray, whose advocacy of a softer
version of Christian doctrine, with an emphasis on mercy, forgiveness,
and self-sacrifice, makes an important counterbalance to the vigorous
elements in muscular Christianity. Whereas her minister husband and
the other Glengarry Calvinists manifest plenty of Charles Kingsley's
thumos, the novel shows how they develop true strength of character
when they balance righteous energy with the maternal capacity to forgive others' faults and to control their fighting instincts. The figure of
the muscular Christian, as outlined among Connor's Glengarrians, combines the ideals of manly vitality with spiritual sensitivity and emotional
self-control.

A key moment in the evolution of the Glengarry community occurs
when they hold a series of communion services to dedicate the new
church building. The narrator observes that hard-line church members
such as Peter McRae were disappointed with the visiting preacher's
message about God's love, since they believed sermons of hellfire and
damnation were more effective in restoring the ardour of the faithful
(203–4). Ironically, this supposedly weak and disappointing message,
combined with Mrs Murray's advocacy of forgiveness and her practical
kindness, changes the whole course of the Glengarrians' future. For she
visits the sickbed of Macdonald Dubh, one of the leaders of the Glengarry
shantymen, and by her influence convinces him to renounce his vow to
avenge himself against the French logger who inflicted his fatal injuries.
This conversion powerfully galvanizes the community and initiates eighteen months of daily revival meetings, as community members open
themselves to a new understanding of the message of love and forgiveness. (These meetings are based on the historical revival services that I
mentioned in my discussion of *Shenac's Work at Home* in the previous
chapter.) As Macdonald Dubh is the protagonist Ranald Macdonald's
father, the narrative poses this incident as a critical moment in Ranald's
maturation into a manly Christian leader of the expanding Canadian
nation.

Since Ranald's bildungsroman serves as the novel's allegory of the
maturation of Canada into an independent nation, it is crucial to note
that his emerging identity is defined by the ideals of muscular Christian-

ity. Ranald starts his story in the brawling ethos of the historical Shiners' Wars between 1837 and 1845, which resulted from territorial disputes between French and Irish lumbermen along the Ottawa Valley.[6] The novel traces his rejection of the code of violence that characterized these disputes, his training at the hands of Mrs Murray in Christian belief and ethics, and his eventual success as a manager of the British-American Coal and Lumber Company in British Columbia. The novel ends after Ranald, elected by British Columbians to represent their concerns in Ottawa, encourages John A. Macdonald to offer the Terms of Union that bring the western colony into the new dominion. We are to understand that Ranald's emergence from the petty squalor of the Shiners' Wars in Glengarry to the prestigious status of political representative of the future-oriented West was made possible through two things: his physical development, through hard work, into a man with a vital, well-trained body and his spiritual development through his indoctrination in the tenets of muscular Christianity by Mrs and Reverend Murray.[7]

The allegorical relation between a healthy, well-disciplined body and a healthy, well-disciplined spirit is fundamental to Ranald's figuration as an ideal muscular Christian. At the point of the novel when he is about to move from being a rural Glengarry lumberjack into his new position as cosmopolitan, nationwide company manager, we are given this description of his physical and spiritual readiness for his new role:

> Four years of hard work and clean living had done for him everything that it lies in years to do. They had made of the lank, raw, shanty lad a man, and such a man as a sculptor would have loved to behold. Straight as a column he stood two inches over six feet, but of such proportions that seeing him alone, one would never have guessed his height. His head and neck rose above his square shoulders with perfect symmetry and poise. His dark face, tanned now to a bronze, with features clear-cut and strong, was lit by a pair of dark brown eyes, honest, fearless, and glowing with a slumbering fire that men would hesitate to stir to flame. The lines of his mouth told of self-control, and the cut of his chin proclaimed a will of iron, and altogether, he bore himself with an air of such quiet strength and cool self-confidence that men never feared to follow where he led. Yet there was a reserve about him that set him a little apart from men, a kind of shyness that saved him from any suspicion of self-assertion. (288–9)

The eroticism of the first half of this description presents the ideal male body as the product of hard work in the outdoors and of self-discipline. Ranald's training in the Canadian backwoods has turned him into the prototype of Dr Hingston's future Canadian with 'muscles more tendinous and prominent and less cushioned.' And the second half of the description shows how his physical attributes link seamlessly with his ideal character: there is fire in his eyes, but his mouth indicates self-control. His strength is quiet and indicates a self-confidence that need not assert itself. Here is the ideal body of Canadian civility, for it exudes imperial confidence and enterprise, without needing to make ostentatious displays of (Yankee) wealth or of effete (English) sophistication. Furthermore, Ranald's body is ideal because it manifests the good health of his spirit; it is as though his body is the physical expression of that spirit, a spirit whose values are shaped between the two poles of Christian doctrine represented by Mrs and Reverend Murray.

While Reverend Murray plays a less-obvious role in Ranald's maturation than does Mrs Murray, nonetheless he does perform a significant function. In him, as with Reverend Brown in *The Foreigner* and all of Connor's many ministers from *The Sky Pilot* onwards, we encounter an overt linkage of the muscular and the Christian. Early in the novel we read that the young men of the Glengarry church,

> filled the back seats under the gallery. And a hardy lot they were, as brown and brawny as their fathers, but tingling with life to their finger-tips, ready for anything, and impossible of control except by one whom they feared as well as reverenced. And such a man was Alexander Murray, for they knew well that, lithe and brawny as they were, there was not a man of them but he could fling out the door and over the fence if he so wished; and they knew, too, that he would be prompt to do it if the occasion arose. Hence they waited for the word of God with all due reverence and fear. (100)

Here we encounter the fundamental tension between the primal vigour of masculinity and its need for disciplinary restraint. The young men, including Ranald, already have their muscles; what they need now is the kind of discipline that deploys these muscles in constructive, rather than destructive, ways. The muscular Christian minister must be prepared to use violence if necessary to compel the young men to self-disciplined, rather than chaotic, vitality.

But the narrative suggests that Reverend Murray, like his backwoods congregation, tends to err on the side of severity. When he dismisses Ranald, who gets in a fight with another young man at church, as a young 'savage,' readers are made to realize that Mrs Murray's administration of 'grace' is the necessary complement of her husband's strict

application of the 'law' (116–20).[8] Ranald's development into a muscular Christian surpasses Reverend Murray's example in that Ranald comes
to incorporate as much of Mrs Murray's gracious charity as he does of
the minister's forceful discipline. And this balance (or tension) is demonstrated when Ranald, later in the novel, not only inspires fear in the
brawling lumberjacks in British Columbia with the skill of his fists (335)
but also supplies them with libraries, reading rooms, fair prices at the
camp stores, and the best wages going (331, 340). The muscular Christian's
raw material consists of *thumos*, which is expressed in physical vitality. But
this physical energy and passion for justice must be disciplined or tempered through the experience of 'gethsemane' ('Not my will, but Thine'
[33–4]) which in turn produces the kind of compassion for the weakness
and suffering of others that results in social concern and activism. Aware
of having received grace during his own gethsemane, the ideal muscular
Christian remains as ready to dispense grace and compassion as he is to
enforce justice.

E. Anthony Rotundo's survey of American middle-class masculine
ideals during the nineteenth century provides a useful comparative
framework for identifying the function of muscular Christianity in turn-
of-the-century Canada. Rotundo takes three gender ideals earlier speci-
fied by Charles Rosenberg and examines their appearance in over one
hundred middle-class men's letters and diaries of the period. He finds
that the Masculine Achiever, characterized by 'accomplishment, autonomy and aggression' and oriented to competition in the market
place (37), the Christian Gentleman, characterized by compassionate
and ethical idealism (38–9), and the Masculine Primitive, characterized
by forceful action and personality (40–2), consistently reappear as masculine ideals in these men's papers. Rotundo theorizes that the first two
ideals operate in a dialectical fashion whereby the Christian Gentleman's
concern for moral order and communal cooperation restrains the
Achiever's tendency to bare-knuckle capitalist competition (38). He
suggests, along lines that echo the gender division between the influences of Reverend and Mrs Murray on Ranald's education, that fathers
tend to emphasize hard-edged Achiever values, whereas mothers tend to
focus on temperate Christian Gentlemanly values in their letters to their
sons. He also observes that Primitive values are assimilable to Achiever
values, but that they are not intentionally taught by parents (43–5).

I would argue that a similar dialectic between Achiever/Primitive and
Christian Gentlemanly values animates the Canadian ideal of the muscular Christian, but that since the concept of achievement is usually de-

fined in spiritual, rather than material, terms, the preference in turn-of-the-century Canada goes to the Christian Gentleman over the Achiever. Indeed, this Canadian emphasis of spiritual values over material ones is one of the main ways in which Canadian nationalists attempted to clarify the difference between Canada and the United States. The Canadian muscular Christian's business and individual interests must take second place to his ethical and communal ideals.[9] If Ranald's first gethsemane occurs when he must forgive his father's enemy, his second one occurs in the scene I discussed briefly in chapter 3, when he must decide to give a truthful report about the less-than-ideal commercial value of the timber tract his employer wishes to sell to the American representative of the British-American Coal and Lumber Company. His truthful report means that he must be prepared to lose his job and the good graces of his English employer. The belief that virtue will ultimately receive its compensation clearly guides the plot here, however, for Ranald's honesty is rewarded by a better job with the American buyer.

Lee and John Thompson provide a useful summary of how Connor took what he considered the best of British and American ideas and rejected their less-appealing aspects to construct his set of Canadian ideals. From Britain, Connor valued the sense of 'fair play' and its attendant high valuation of law and order, while from the United States, he valued classless egalitarianism, enterprise and initiative, and openness to immigrants. He criticized Britain for its class stratification and its over-cultured ineffectuality, while he criticized American lawlessness (as demonstrated in the 'Wild' West) and its crass materialism. Ranald's commitment to the values of compassion and community, then, makes him bring about labour reform in his new job, when his institution of reading rooms and fair company store prices causes his employers to readjust their myopic focus on the profit margin. These values of cooperation, ethical integrity, a fierce commitment to just dealings, and compassion for the less-advantaged make the figure of the muscular Christian a powerful representation of progressivism in the domains of class, religion, ethnicity, and gender that animated social activists such as the Reverend Charles Gordon and the readers of his Connor books.

Since the idealized figure of the muscular Christian I have traced from Britain with Kingsley and Hughes to Canada with Ralph Connor was so clearly meant to appeal to males, it would be easy to assume that it was part of an essentially patriarchal discourse committed to the establishment and maintenance of exclusive male privilege. And to some extent, this assumption is valid. As the historians Nancy Christie and Michael Gauvreau explain in *A Full-Orbed Christianity*,

> The theme of muscular Christianity which so pervaded Gordon's religious fiction was a deliberate strategy to attract the increasingly large number of men who, in the estimation of many clergymen, had spurned the conventional worship of the orthodox Protestant churches. More particularly, novels such as *The Prospector*, *Corporal Cameron*, and *The Sky Pilot*, set against the backdrop of the resource frontiers of Canada in the Prairie West and British Columbia, aimed at introducing Christian values to single, male workers who lived beyond the well-established moral and social norms of Ontario and the Maritimes. (37)

But it is important to note here that maternal feminists such as Emily Murphy and Nellie McClung did not perceive the masculine ethos of muscular Christianity as hostile to their interests. For these women writers, who opposed the masculine hegemony assumed in Connor's Canada, the muscular Christian was, nonetheless, a potential ally.

Murphy published *Janey Canuck in the West*, the second book in her popular Janey Canuck series, in 1910, one year after Connor's *The Foreigner*. Janey Canuck was her female parallel to the popular nationalist cartoon figure Johnny Canuck, which had first appeared as a parallel to Uncle Sam and John Bull in the 1870s and later became the name of a newspaper between 1911 and 1918.[10] Janey exhibits all of Johnny's confidence and energy. Indeed, her representation as counterpart to the male figure illustrates the way in which feminists of the turn of the century theorized gender in essentialist terms, arguing that women's natural maternal instincts for nurturing and compassion made them a necessary counterbalance in the political arena to male instincts for aggressive competition (Strong-Boag, 'Ever' 311–12). Such essentialist understandings of gender enabled early Canadian feminists to argue for the unique contribution that women could make to social and political life and, at the same time, to reassure the male hierarchy of the day that their ostensibly God-given male traits were not being dismissed out of hand. The spunky feminist nationalism of Janey complements the muscular nationalism of Johnny. This said, the counterpart model used by Murphy does mock masculine complacency through its parodic doubling. As a parodic literary figure, Janey Canuck both assumes and casts doubt upon the normative masculinity symbolized by Johnny.[11] Indeed, Murphy's representation of herself in the voice of a national superheroine layers the book's parodic effects, for not only does she mock the gender divide that assumes superheroism to be the province of men, but she also mocks her own grandiosity in casting herself in such a role.

Janey Canuck in the West is composed of a series of transparently autobiographical sketches based on Murphy's move to Manitoba and then to Alberta with her convalescent husband, the Anglican minister Arthur Murphy. A doctor in Ontario had prescribed the clean air and vigorous outdoor life of the Northwest as a remedy for Arthur's long struggle with typhoid (Bassett, 'Introduction' xi–xiii). So their journey is a literal application of what we might call Dr Hingston's 'regimen of the north.' Janey's commentary on the journey is a compendium of popular ideas about the West, laced with gentle feminist irony. She repeats the expansionist view that the prairie landscape is an empty waste anxious to be put to agricultural use (58–9), she parrots the optimism that portrayed the West as the wheat-financed centre of the future empire (9, 146), and she repeats the racist ideology that imagined Native peoples as a waning race (77). And throughout the book, she repeatedly refers to the nationalist figure of muscular Christianity. 'The life [in the Northwest] is calculated to produce hardy, self-reliant, self-poised men,' she asserts, as she rides west with her convalescing husband. 'It is a bad day for a race, too, when it becomes over-civilized. Brutality is a sign of strength and health ... The nations cast in the manly mould, are not those who have been polished till all the fibre is rubbed away' (90).

Taken at face value, Janey's affirmation of the necessity of brutality to the health of a nation would confirm the paradox of civility I have been tracing throughout this book; that is, that the civil circle must be defended, even savagely, against external threats. It is impossible, however, to tell how far Murphy's tongue is in her cheek. She and her weakened husband move to the prairies in obedience to the discourse of the manly-making Northwest, yet her regular subversions of her husband's authority destabilize the easy linkage of manly vigour, religion, and nationalism. After a disagreement with Reverend Murphy, whom she archly calls 'the Padre,' Janey Canuck observes: 'Now I make it a daily – indeed, an hourly – habit to treat the Padre as if he were in the right ... I score heavily every time by giving him either his due or a compliment. A man likes to be head and shoulders in advance of his wife. He likes to wonder at his amazing cleverness, and to brighten his spare hours with a little comfortable adulation' (61–2). And so she undermines the paternal assumption, even as she reinforces the imperialist agenda, of the Canadian version of muscular Christianity. In light of such statements, her deployment of muscular Christian discourse might seem dismissive, but as we shall see more clearly in the writing of Nellie McClung, Murphy's attitude indicates that first-wave Canadian feminists distinguished between progressive and non-progressive masculinities – or, at least, progressive and non-progressive masculine behaviours. And it is clear that they viewed muscular Christians as partners in the campaign for social reform, which included social welfare for the labouring poor, activism on behalf of non-charter-group immigrants, and the feminist platforms of temperance, homesteading legislation, and suffrage. For Murphy and her women colleagues, a new social polity, energized by its expansion into the Northwest and enlightened by the active participation of women, would function as a beacon of progress for the rest of the civilized world.[12]

Fifteen years after the publication of *Janey Canuck in the West* and after a roller-coaster ride that first thrilled feminists with the success of the long campaign for enfranchisement and the election of women to provincial legislatures and then disillusioned them with the failure of prohibition and the tokenism that characterized the roles assigned to female members of the legislature, Murphy's good friend Nellie McClung published her last and angriest novel (Warne 59–60). *Painted Fires* departs from McClung's popular Pearlie Watson stories about the maturation of a young Irish girl from the context of her rural Manitoba farm family to being a politicized Canadian feminist and describes instead the many adversities encountered by Helmi Milander, a young woman who migrates from Finland to the Canadian West. Helmi's good humour and hard work are thwarted again and again by the Anglocentric, patriarchal domination of everything from jobs to housing to law courts. This White, British patriarchy devalues her labour, counts her non-English ethnicity as evidence of criminal behaviour, and poisons those who would be her friends with suspicion of her integrity and virtue. Nonetheless, McClung's novel, like Connor's *The Foreigner*, shows how the non-English immigrant can, by dint of hard work and conversion to Protestant values, overcome this adversity to become the ideal empire-making, future-oriented, western Canadian. McClung is concerned to show how such a narrative necessitates a reform in Canadian dealings not just with non-charter-group immigrants but also with women.

Moreover, McClung parallels Connor by having her female protagonist deal with her adversaries by means of the 'manly art.' Throughout the book, Helmi bloodies the noses and blackens the eyes of a range of men who represent the various faces of a corrupt patriarchy. The muscular Christian context of her *thumos* is made explicit, for example, when she throws Mr Wymuth, the Brocklehurst-like disciplinarian of the women's reformatory in which she is unjustly incarcerated, into a glass china cabinet. Her righteous satisfaction breaks forth in a biblical Psalm: 'Now is my head lifted up above mine enemies ... [T]hey are as chaff that the wind driveth away' (101). Helmi's muscular righteousness is regularly rationalized in ethnic terms. Characters repeatedly comment, 'Ain't that just like a Finn ... clean and neat, but high tempered?' (25). McClung's rationalization of Helmi's *thumos* as inherent in her Finnish blood parallels Kingsley's attempt to locate the rage for justice in Teutonic ancestry. Such theories of the racial or ethnic heredity for personality traits and social values fuelled eugenicist discussions of the formation of the Canadian national character. Robert Grant Haliburton, for example, was not alone in tracing a common ancestry for English and French Canadians to their Norse antecedents. He theorized that the impulses to liberty and justice were essentially Nordic passions and therefore inherent in Canadians' common ancient bloodlines (8–10). While McClung glories in Helmi's primal (ethnic) vigour, she does, however, feel the need to Christianize and moderate Helmi's Old Testament passion for justice. Later in the novel, at the moment Helmi is poised to pull the trigger on the drunken Magistrate Blackwood, whose character blackmail has driven her husband away, *Deus* appears out of the *machina* and saves her from committing murder by striking the man dead with a lightning bolt. On the surface of it, McClung's heroine learns to trust in God's justice so that she need not take the law into her own hands.

But McClung's lightning bolt also conveys her anger over the delays to national reform in no uncertain terms (Warne 60), for the destruction of Magistrate Blackwood constitutes her dire solution to the conflict between the forces of good and evil, an opposition she sketches between outmoded, xenophobic patriarchalism and progressivist Christian activism. Helmi's wrongful detention in the Girls' Friendly Home for suspected drug smuggling outlines McClung's clear distinction between the old-boy, liquor-funded politics represented in the courtroom scene by Magistrate Windsor (and later in the novel by Magistrate Blackwood) and the Christian social activism represented by Miss Rogers and the young Reverend Edward Terry. Helmi falls afoul of the law when she picks up a package from a Chinese restaurant for her English tutor, the wealthy Eva St. John, and is discovered by the police to be carrying heroin.[13] Helmi's refusal to disclose Eva's name gets her charged with

12   A meeting of members of the Canadian Girls in Training organization, possibly in Toronto, c. 1919. CGIT groups usually met in churches; some continue to meet to this day.

drug trafficking. The only two people to speak on Helmi's behalf in court are Miss Rogers, leader of the Canadian Girls in Training group that Helmi had been attending, and the Reverend Terry, minister of the Young Methodist church where the CGIT group meets (see illus. 12). Magistrate Windsor, 'late of Stockton-on-Tees' (67), has prejudged the 'naturally red' Finn (69) guilty, and he resents the intrusions of Rogers and Terry. He discredits Rogers's character reference by dismissing women's groups in general: '"She belongs to a girls' club, does she?" the magistrate seemed to bite the words off. "Well, … I don't believe in girls' clubs or women's clubs either. Women and girls have too much liberty these days, and that's why they are going to the devil … The old-fashioned girl stayed at home and worked with her mother. But now the mothers are out reforming the world, and the girls are on the street or in their clubs. I blame the club women of this city for the devilment that goes on among the young people"' (75–6). McClung carefully aligns the English magistrate's regressive comments with class privilege when the narrator follows this speech with the observation 'The cliff dwellers [of the wealthy district of the town] were enjoying it. They did not belong to the women's organizations, so he didn't mean them' (76).

Magistrate Windsor continues to stand in for old-boy, upper-class complacency when we read of his annoyance at Reverend Terry's initiative to ensure a fair trial. 'What right had a parson,' grumbles the judge, 'who should be meek and appealing and apologetic, to look like this young chap, who had the physique of a light-weight boxing champion?' (67). McClung's narrator goes on to gloss the magistrate's complaint thus:

> There was ... the sudden antagonism of the administrator of the law, who resents civilian interference, particularly from the person he called 'Parson.' Let the church mind its own business.
>   Mr. Terry, reared in the new school of thought, would have stoutly insisted that he was minding his business as a minister when looking after the straying members of his flock. (67–8)

For McClung, the law has become corrupt through its ties to upper-class, English privilege. Later we are told that the well-off spectators at the trial share Windsor's view. According to them, 'The modern preacher who comes boldly into public life without apology is a jarring note in the complacent philosophy of their class ... Preachers should be simpering, tea-drinking, bazaar-opening curates, pallid and dandruffy, with decayed teeth' (76–7).

McClung's association of the law with the corrupt Christianity of upper-class self-protection and of grace with social progressivism is emphasized in the shift in management at the euphemistically named Girls' Friendly Home from the progressive administration of the young matron to the unctuous sadism of the Wymuths. The board, dominated by businessmen, disapproves of the matron's attempt to make the girls' stay at the reformatory truly educational by means of outings to cinemas, lectures, and concerts. When its members remonstrate with her for treating these fallen girls so kindly, she objects to the double standard that finds the girls 'fallen' and does nothing about the men, 'fathers of families some of them, and regarded as respectable men in society' (81), who caused these girls' fall in the first place. At this, the board dismisses the matron and replaces her with the Wymuths, who 'believed in hell and spoke of the "world" in a tone which implied both horror and contempt. They knew that Christ was coming soon to take His own out of the world, leaving the other odd millions to their well-merited punishment' (82). McClung clearly posits the muscular Christian as an ally in the matron's struggle against such regressive views. In fact, she employs the figure of the muscular Christian to place the cause of chivalry and justice on the side of the young immigrant woman, who does eventually triumph over her naysayers and establish a flourishing home in Canada's Northwest. Thus for progressives such as Emily Murphy and Nellie McClung, the muscular Christian represented by new activist clergymen of the likes of Edward Terry constituted an ally in the coalition for national reform in gender, ethnic, and class relations.

The assessment of the effects of Canadian Protestant progressivism, however, is a matter of vigorous and continuing debate among historians. On the one hand, historians such as Mariana Valverde observe that, while Christian feminists achieved enfranchisement and some concessions on liquor laws, they did so only by reinforcing the values of the White, British, Protestant, middle-class, and male elite, whose dominance went largely unchallenged (Valverde 33, 60–1).[14] Valverde writes, for example, of the Woman's Christian Temperance Union that 'racism was integral to their view of feminism, of woman's mission as 'mother of the race' ... [S]ince women's nurturing role was the keystone of their feminism, and this nurturing was perceived as involving the reproduction not of human beings in general but of their race in particular, racism and feminism were integral parts of a single whole' (60–1). On the other hand, historians such as Randi Warne and Nancy Christie and Michael Gauvreau argue that the feminists and their Protestant progressivist allies were not the racists Valverde claims (Warne 72–5; Christie and Gauvreau 188–90), and that to suggest so undervalues not only their success in producing compassionate and inclusive social welfare policies in Canada but also their radical ideas about racial fusion as Canada's future ideal (Christie and Gauvreau xiv, 190). The debate points up my interest in the figure of the muscular Christian as a significant element in the building of Canadian ideas of civility, for it highlights the contradictory impulses within progressivist notions of civility. Rather than representing a single-voiced political coalition, muscular Christianity, maternal feminism, and the progressivism of which they were parts encompassed a set of social ideals whose interpretation and application involved intense debate and conflict. Through this tracing of muscular Christianity's Canadian genealogy, we can see how normative figurations convey authoritative ideology at the same time as they attempt to manage the tensions between contestatory possibilities within that ideology.

My claim so far has been that the figure of the muscular Christian was central to the portrayal of British, Protestant, masculinist, and middle-class values as constituting the ideal values of the citizen in expansion-era Canada. But I have also tried to show that, alongside its privileging of this homogeneous national standard, muscular Christianity pressed for progressive liberalization of the narrow ideologies of ethnicity, religion, gender, and class of the day. A.W. Beall, the popular WCTU-sponsored author of *The Living Temple: A Manual on Eugenics for Parents and Teachers* (1933), had his listeners repeat the slogan 'JESUS CHRIST AND CANADA EXPECT ME TO BE AN A.1 BOY' at the lectures on social purity he delivered throughout the first three decades of the twentieth century. This 'A-oneness,' formulated in terms of muscular Christianity's composite ideal of self-discipline, moral virtue, bodily purity, and physical vitality, was making, according to Beall, 'CANADA'S MOST VALUABLE PRODUCTS. / EVERY BOY AND GIRL HERE TODAY / IS WORTH TO CANADA AT LEAST / $50,000' (qtd. in Valverde 27 and 71, capitals in original). Muscular Christianity, as characterized in the works of Connor, Murphy, and McClung, was, along with other discourses of social progressivism such as maternal feminism, social purity, and Protestant activism, crucial in the making of this product of English Canadian nationalist-imperialist optimism. Insofar as the product could be made from boys and girls of any class, ethnicity, or race, it was, for its time, a remarkably inclusive civil ideal; but insofar as that product required assimilation or conversion to White, British norms, it was also homogenizing. The theoretical possibility of egalitarian inclusion means that early twentieth-century Canadian progressivism did not hold a biologically based, racist view that outsiders were automatically disqualified from becoming A.1 Canadians on the basis of hereditary bloodlines. But the demand of assimilation shows that it was unquestioningly ethnocentric and therefore culturally racist.

What happened, then, to the optimistic prognosis of Canada's emergence as a producer of A.1 citizens for the world stage? To trace the figure of the muscular Christian beyond its emergence in Canadian imperialism, we must take into account the profound changes in Canadian self-images that occurred in response to the First World War, the economic boom in prairie agriculture in the 1920s, and the subsequent Depression. For this segment of our exploration, I will turn our attention to the prairie realist writers who rose to prominence after the mid–1920s and who succeeded Connor, Murphy, and McClung. In examining the three writers most often associated with the emergence of prairie realism – Frederick Philip Grove, Martha Ostenso, and Robert Stead – I am struck by how much the residual values of muscular Christianity pervade their novels. In all three writers, the division of male muscularity from Christian or more generalized spiritual values contributes substantially to the themes of suffering and oppression that characterize their realism. To return to Rotundo's terms, the removal of the tempering ideals of the Christian Gentleman from the aggressive and primitive instincts of the Masculine Achiever plays a significant part in producing the oppressive domestic relations we find in *Settlers of the Marsh, Fruits of the Earth, Wild Geese, The Homesteaders,* and *Grain.* Indeed, I would claim that it is the loss of the compassionate or sensitive value of grace associated with the muscular Christian ideal of masculinity that is repeatedly mourned in the tyranny of the ubiquitous prairie patriarch of post–1920s western Canadian fiction.[15]

While Grove has been widely recognized for his concern, expressed in essays and in fiction, that Canada might be tempted to follow the American error of allowing material values to overwhelm spiritual ones in determining the nation's character,[16] this concern pre-dated Grove's emergence as a Canadian novelist. As I mentioned in chapters 1 and 2, the advocacy of spiritual over material values was fundamental to the Loyalist story of Canada's rejection of American-style capitalism. This theme also had an earlier voice among prairie writers, particularly Robert Stead. Stead is a key figure for tracing muscular Christianity's passage from expansion-era to post-war Canada not only because he himself negotiated this critical juncture of Canadian history but also because he has often been featured by Canadian critics as a writer in whose works the transition from sentimental romance to modernist realism takes place.[17] In Stead we can observe how the muscular Christian values of physical energy, moral rectitude, social responsibility, and spiritual sensitivity retain their status as social ideals, even as the nationalist optimism of which they were integral parts begins to lose its confidence.

Of Stead's eleven published books of poetry and fiction, I will examine *The Homesteaders* (1916) and *Grain* (1926), the first because in it the tensions between romance and realism are played out in identifiably muscular Christian terms, and the second because it has been widely heralded by critics as one of the triad of books that mark the advent of prairie realism in 1925 and 1926 – *Grain, Settlers of the Marsh,* and *Wild Geese.* At first, one might think *The Homesteaders* could have been written by Connor or McClung, because it narrates the pioneer romance of an Ontario couple's migration to a homestead in Manitoba, where their back-breaking toil is eventually rewarded by a successful farm. But Stead departs from his predecessors' model after chapter 5, when he leaps ahead twenty-five years in John and Mary Harris's lives and describes what happens after the initial stages of pioneer romance. John Harris, who had been a schoolteacher in Ontario, full of high ideals, male gallantry, and youthful energy, has now become the slave of his own success. His obsession with financial accumulation causes him to marshal all of his family's and his own energies to a never-ending cycle of work.[18] He retains the muscular ideals of thrift, hard work, and strict discipline, but he has abandoned the Christian or spiritual ones. He quits going to church (132, 304), represses his emotions (141), abandons responsibility for the spiritual and emotional well-being of his family, particularly his daughter and wife (152–3), and foregoes several possible gethsemane moments when Connor's muscular Christian hero would have admitted his own mistakes and been called upon to forgive others' errors in kind (216). Having started out as an educated young man of high ideals who throws in his lot with the expansionist narrative of empire-building in the Canadian Northwest, Harris achieves a commercial success that ironically causes him to lose sight of the original ideal.

Stead makes sure we do not miss the social critique contained in Harris's story when his narrator explains that 'the old sense of oneness, the old community interest which had held the little band of pioneers together amid their privations and their poverty, began to weaken and dissolve, and in its place came an individualism and a materialism that measured progress only in dollars and cents. Harris did not know that his gods had fallen, that his ideals had been swept away' (96). The contrast between the old community values and new materialistic ones is clearly sketched between the men Harris entrusts himself to before and the ones he engages after the novel's twenty-five-year hiatus. When he and Mary first arrive in Manitoba, they fall under the benevolent care of the Scottish guide and land agent Aleck McCrae, who makes sure they file on good farmland within range of helpful neighbours. In the second part of the book, Harris's greed causes him to sell the Manitoba farm and speculate on the land boom in Alberta. There he falls into the hands of two confidence men from Stead's earlier novel *The Bail Jumper* (1914). This is the kind of unsavoury company you fall in with, the narrative suggests, when money becomes your god. And Harris's misplaced faith almost costs him his family. First, his independent-minded daughter, Beulah, leaves in search of a less-stifling Life (with a capital 'L') away from the endless grind of work on the farm. Then his wife, Mary, departs when she learns that the farm they worked so hard to establish is nothing

more than real estate to her husband and that he has made arrangements to sell it without consulting her. And finally, he nearly loses his
own and his son's lives in a shoot-out with the confidence men, who steal
the money he took out of the farm sale. It takes the loss of everything he
has – family, farm, and finances – to bring Harris to his senses. But
Stead's overarching commitment to the ideals of Canadian expansioinist
optimism and the romance of prairie progress ensures that Harris does
come to his senses by the end of the book. He realizes the error of his
ways, encounters his own gethsemane when he confesses his wrongs to
Mary and Beulah, and is rewarded with the unexpected restoration of
the quarter of land on which the Manitoba homestead stands.

The method by which the homestead is restored has significant gender implications. In the final pages of the novel, a delayed letter from
Harris's lawyer explains that when he had gone about finding a buyer for
Harris's farm, he discovered that, to afford an earlier transaction, Harris
had transferred the home quarter into Mary's name. The transfer made
it impossible for the lawyer to include the homestead in the sale without
Mary's signature, and this unlooked for circumstance ends up saving the
family home. In short, Harris's salvation, and the material 'reward' for
his return to Christian Gentlemanly ideals, comes about through women's
ownership of property. Stead's mode of salvation is significant in a novel
published in 1916, the year women gained the franchise in Manitoba
and significant steps were taken towards other objectives of the feminist
platform, such as temperance and reform of the male-privileging clauses
of the Homesteaders Act, which allowed men to sell homestead lands
without consulting their wives.[19] Once again, we see that muscular Christian values are presented as fully compatible with feminist ones – when
women own land, men's own higher interests are kept in reliable hands.
Indeed, a renewed appreciation of conventionally female values (Beulah's
desire for aesthetically pleasing surroundings and intellectual stimula-
tion; Mary's loyalty to the homestead, which is more than real estate to
her because it represents the years of effort they have put into making a
home) is central to the rescue of the deluded Masculine Achiever and
his return to the ideals of the Christian Gentleman.

So Harris's forgotten muscular Christian values return as the ideal in
Stead's *The Homesteaders*, but the protagonist's commitment to those
values is shaky, and significantly, that commitment is shaken by the
success of the expansionist dream. Whereas in Connor and McClung the
secure establishment of the pioneers and the material success of their
homesteading constituted the reward for their moral and ethical ideal-

ism, in Stead that very establishment and success challenge the original ideal. This is not to say that Stead rejected the expansionist agenda of Canadian imperialism, but that, compared to Connor, he had a greater distrust of the effects of capitalism on emerging prairie civilization and on the motives of its individual members. 'Let there be no misunderstanding,' Stead wrote on 11 October 1906 in the *Southern Manitoba Review,* of which he was editor. 'Capital itself is not a menace; it is only where the control of capital, which should be vested in the public generally, passes into the hands of a few that danger exists ... Every blow at wealth monopoly should be aimed, not at wealth itself, but at the unequal division of wealth' (1; qtd. in Mundwiler 187–8). Thus Stead reinforces the muscular Christian valuation of spiritual-ethical responsibilities over material profits, but he does so in a society where the temptations of capital are more readily available to the prairie residents than they were in the sodbusting generation.[20]

In comparison with *The Homesteaders,* we might say of Stead's most critically celebrated work, *Grain,* that the social ethos of the prairies in this 1926 novel is so thoroughly secularized that the figure of the muscular Christian is conspicuous by its absence. In part, this apparent absence is a product of Stead's attempt in this novel to redefine the meaning of heroism. 'Perhaps the term hero, with its suggestions of high enterprise, sits inappropriately upon the chief character of a somewhat commonplace tale,' says his narrator in the novel's opening paragraph. '[T]here was in Gander Stake little of that quality which is associated with the clash of righteous steel or the impact of noble purposes. Yet that he was without heroic fibre I will not admit' (7). Although Gander does indeed lack the 'high enterprise' and the 'righteous steel' and 'noble purposes' we might associate with muscular Christianity, Stead's story about how Gander's maturation comes through a gradual emergence of a quieter, less-dramatic, and less-public heroism does retain significant elements of muscular Christianity.

Like John Harris, Gander goes through a conversion at the end of the novel, and also like Harris before that conversion, he evinces many muscular but few Christian or spiritual values. He shares with Harris the capacity for vigorous outdoor work (61–2), manual dexterity, and an interest in the new technologies of farm machinery (55). But while Christianity forms the 'background' of the Stake family's values, it is not a vital factor in their everyday lives (66). Gander shows an aversion to education and books (52, 81, 179), and this aversion is part of his general lack of interest in spiritual or emotional refinement (112), which, in turn, makes him inarticulate about his feelings (107, 177). At different points in the novel, two young women, Jo Burge and Jerry Chansley, both find his narrow perspective and experience too stultifying to consider him as a possible romantic partner (121, 194). When Gander finally comes around to his gethsemane at the end of the novel, the narrative leads us to believe that his neglect of the life of the mind and of the heart up to this point has been his greatest impediment.

But in the meantime, Stead uses Gander's stolid character to pose a post-war critique of the myth of heroic high enterprise and noble purposes that fed the armed forces with ready recruits during the Great War. Gander's myopic focus on his own farm and its immediate vicinity makes him impervious to the ideology of war heroism which had been readily grafted onto the discourse of muscular Christianity during the early phases of the war (see Karr, 'Robert' 39). His cynical response to full-grown men being trained in parade-ground marching drills and 'form-fours' (145) questions the heroism of men who have been trained not to think for themselves, and his view that grain production is as important to the war effort as manning the front lines in Europe refuses a rigidly monadic image of patriotism (121, 147). Gander's resistance of considerable pressure from the enlistment of other boys in the community, from the patriotism which insists that each family must make its sacrifice for the war effort, and above all, from his sister Minnie's and his sweetheart Jo's desire for him to perform the romantic role of male hero indicates a kind of inarticulate strength of character that will not allow him to sign up for a cause in which he has no faith. For this refusal, he loses Jo to a returning veteran, and he suffers the disapproval of members of his own family as well as of the neighbourhood.

This kind of publicly misunderstood self-reliance is a common feature of muscular Christian virtue, which holds that true courage requires that one be prepared to suffer public censure if necessary to maintain personal integrity. (Compare, for example, Ranald's telling the truth about the timber tract, even though it costs him his job, or Helmi's protecting the identity of Eva St. John, even though it lands her in a penitentiary.) Indeed, Gander's final spiritual triumph, his self-sacrificing decision at the end of the novel to leave the community to which he has been so consistently committed because his and Jo's continuing love will threaten her marriage, constitutes just such a manly commitment to integrity which can never be explained to the community at large. Significantly, what brings Gander to this moment of profound self-assessment and unheralded heroism is a series of plot developments that replace the oft-

cited realism of the novel with the conventions of romance. These
developments include the introduction of a subplot from Stead's earlier
novel *The Smoking Flax* (1924) and its story of the domestic heroism of
Cal Beach in raising his illegitimate nephew, Reed, as his own son; the
villainy of Gander's older brother, who is Reed's irresponsible biological
father; and the eventual marriage of Gander's sister Minnie to Cal.
Gander's conversion to a more sensitive, socially responsible masculinity
involves his reluctant admission that the city-educated, ethically high-
minded, and child-raising Cal can also work hard enough on the farm to
qualify as a 'he-man' (185). Under Cal's influence, Gander takes on
responsibility for Jo's ailing husband by building him a cottage in which
to convalesce by the lake. When this beautiful retreat begins to restore
the veteran's health, Gander realizes that his rather too-obvious love for
the married Jo can only cause trouble. This realization makes him
confide his emotions for the first time to another person when he bursts
into tears in his sister's arms (240), hears the wisdom in her redefinition
of heroism when she tells him, 'Sometimes it is the brave man who runs
away' (243), and ultimately looks himself in the face 'for the first time in
his life' (245), before driving off in his car to explore the possibility of a
mechanic's job with Jerry Chansley's brother in the city.

As Frank Davey observes, this resolution to the narrative shows that,
rather than representing the triumph of modernist realism over outmoded romance, *Grain* actually moves from realism back to romance.[21]
In Davey's view, *Grain* is 'the story of a novelist who began to care for his
main character ... losing his initial amused detachment from him, losing
his will to see him as a mere pawn of deterministic forces. The story of a
novelist who cares so deeply for his main character that he breaks with
credibility to introduce in the concluding chapters new characters and a
pastoral, anti-realistic, subplot, to give his character some faint hope in
the novel's last pages' ('Rereading' 133). Davey suggests that this anti-
realistic turn at the end of the novel in fact makes 'the overall movement
of the novel ... a persuasive one' (134), since it allows Stead to express
his fondness for his character, enables the character to grow in a lifelike
way, and satisfies readers' desires for this potential. Davey's reading of
Grain's movement from realism back to romance helpfully questions the
myth of progress common in 1960s and 1970s criticism of prairie fiction,
according to which realism, like a superior species, gradually evolves
from romance, which is becoming extinct. One of the silent corollaries
of this literary Darwinist myth has been the belief that muscular Christian ideals – A.J.M. Smith's 'he-man Canadiana' – became as extinct as

outmoded romance. But it seems to me that the return of romance in *Grain* (and similar arguments could be made for the romance endings of the other two exemplars of prairie realism, *Wild Geese* and *Settlers of the Marsh*) shows how the optimistic discourses of Canadian western imperialism and their valuation of spiritual, if not overtly Christian, manliness remain very close to the surface of these post–First World War novels.

How then does one determine the stages by which a rhetorical figure loses its social authority? The post-mortem on major values that I have been linking in this chapter to the figure of the muscular Christian, such as western expansionism, nationalist-imperialist optimism, and Protestant progressivism, is still, in each case, a matter of vigorous debate among Canadian historians. Doug Owram argues that expansionism had played itself out even before the era represented by Connor and McClung. He suggests that expansionist optimism in Ontario fell into decline in the 1880s as a result of the economic depression during and after 1883, the Riel Rebellion in 1885, and growing western resentment of the eastern monopoly in the CPR (184–9, 220). He does suggest that expansionist optimism reappeared in the West, but that it was suspicious of the profit motives of Ontario. This remaining western version of expansionist-imperialist optimism runs as a powerful current through the fictional texts from the first two decades of the twentieth century that I examine in this chapter, and it remains a powerfully residual influence in texts that date well into the mid-twentieth century. Alternatively, the First World War has often been cited as a key episode in the decline of Canadian imperialist optimism because the war exposed the vacuity of so many of its tenets. The eugenic theories that had linked Canadian imperialists' myth of the North with Teutonic ancestry lost their appeal once Germany became the enemy (Berger, 'True' 22), the myth of manly self-sacrifice that was central to muscular Christian dogma grew absurd in the new kind of warfare that included disease-filled trenches and gas attacks (Karr, 'Robert' 39), and the unparalleled slaughter of Christian nations by other Christian nations in supposedly civilized Europe made blind faith in the natural evolution of civility untenable. Thus some scholars have identified the post-war period of the 1920s as one of disillusionment and of corresponding secularization in Canada, when the Protestant churches and their progressivist program for the nation lost their leading influence on Canadian society (see Marshall; Cook; Lennox 146). Yet others have argued that Protestant progressivism flourished between the wars and that, far from receding in social influence, it reached its 'apogee of cultural authority' in Canada precisely in the 1920s. These scholars suggest that, by fusing the notion of individual Christian conversion with the collective pursuit of social science research and the campaign for social welfare, Christian activists maintained a broad influence well into the 1940s (Christie and Gauvreau xi). As for the imperialism of Canadian nationalists, it has been suggested that with the settlement of the Northwest by the 1920s, the urgency of rivalry with the United States waned and, along with it, the need for British-inflected imperialist rhetoric (Berger, 'True' 22). However, others insist Canadian imperialism remained dominant in popular images of Canadian national identity until well after the Second World War, and it was not until the parcelling out of the empire in and after the 1950s that it went into decline (Cannadine 13; Francis 53, 84–5).

Contrary to what we might at first expect, Sinclair Ross's strong critique of Christian hypocrisy in *As for Me and My House* (1941) demonstrates how socially influential the ideals of muscular Christianity remained even after the Depression and during the Second World War. Unlike in *Grain*, there is no return of romance at the end of *As for Me and My House* that brings a belated salvation to the novel's leading characters.[22] Nonetheless, its delineation of the desiccated lives of a Protestant minister and his nameless wife relies for its pessimistic theme on a critical engagement with ongoing, or at least residual, progressivism in prairie society and its muscular Christian ideals in particular. By this I mean that the falseness of the Bentleys' many 'false-fronts' signifies most powerfully by contrast with the still-popular myth of integrity associated with the muscular Christian virtues expected of the prairie minister. If Ross's readers did not expect ministers to uphold the true-sterling image of the Protestant clergyman we have identified in Connor and McClung, the scandal of Reverend Bentley's hypocrisy would have little salience.

The Reverend Philip Bentley fails in every way to live up to the set of muscular Christian ideals we have traced from Kingsley and Connor to Murphy, McClung, and Stead. He lacks, or at least suppresses, *thumos*, or the primal passion that motivates Kingsley's champion of justice. This absence of emotional dynamism manifests itself in his bottled-up physicality. We are told he is a big man, yet he never acts forcefully in the cause of justice, never initiates uninhibited and joyful sexual relations with his wife. He lacks the physical vitality of the muscular Christian. In addition, he avoids what Connor would call gethsemane moments when he could experience his own need of forgiveness and thus be able to forgive the faults of others. Because he avoids these moments of vulnerability and self-surrender, he has no experience of grace, which would enable him to offer compassion to others. In short, he completely lacks muscular Christianity's double code of law, the passion for justice, and grace, the ability to offer others compassion and forgiveness.

Significantly, Mrs Bentley's narration of hers and Philip's false-fronted lives opens with a meditation on his feeble muscularity. 'It's been a hard day on him,' she reports on the first page. Philip has been putting up stovepipes and nailing down old linoleum as the couple move into the latest of a series of prairie-town parsonages. Mrs Bentley explains, 'He hasn't the hands for it' and she could do a better job with nail and hammer herself, but for the conventional parish opinion which insists that these are the tasks of men, and so 'today I let him be the man about the house' (5). This scene launches a series of references to Philip's large but useless hands, ineffectual at any manual enterprise but painting and drawing (10, 31, 35, 59). The only time in the novel Philip does prove himself capable in a physical undertaking occurs when the townsmen fight the fire at Dawson's store, and even then Mrs Bentley ascribes this moment of vital activity to their neighbour *Paul's* hands and Philip's *head* in organizing the firefighters (170, my emphasis). Such scenes show how Mrs Bentley constructs Philip's muscular ineffectuality by negative contrast with the assumption of masculine manual dexterity and physical vitality I traced earlier in the characterization of Reverend Murray and Reverend Terry.[23]

Indeed, Philip's entire relation to Christianity is shown to be illegitimate. Himself the bastard son of a minister, he demonstrates his own cynical relation to the church by using it to get a college education and to gain an income, even though he has little faith in the existence of God. Furthermore, if Mrs Bentley's suspicions are correct, his fathering of Judith West's baby figures Philip's reproduction of illegitimacy in others. His attempt to adopt the Catholic, eastern European boy Steve Kulanich may appear to redeem this illegitimacy and to fulfill the muscular Christian ideal of compassion for those marginalized by class, religion, or ethnicity, but Mrs Bentley makes sure that we see through Philip's ruse of altruism. 'It's plain enough,' she writes. '[A]s he thrusts out his chin to meet the town it's his own fight still. As he starts in to dream and plan for the boy it's his own life over again. Steve is to carry on where he left off. Steve is to do the things he tried to do and failed' (70). After she and Philip have gone around the church community suggesting the altruistic version of the adoption story, she makes sure we as readers understand that the adoption has more to do with a desperate attempt to compensate for Philip's bitterness about his own childhood and the hollowness of their marriage than with social justice. '[N]one of them knows,' she writes of the parishioners. 'They can only read our shingle, all its letters freshened up this afternoon: *As For Me and My House – The House of Bentley – We Will Serve the Lord*' (81, emphasis in original).

Indeed, the entire fiasco of Steve's adoption highlights Philip's lack of *thumos*. When the boy gets in a fight with one of the Finley twins during his first visit to Sunday school, Mrs Finley gives him a sharp slap across the face. Philip's ineffectual defence of Steve is telling: 'He worked his lips helplessly a minute, then said thick and hard, "If ever you dare do it again ..."' Whereupon Mrs Finley slaps the boy again right in front of Philip and freezes his threat by fainting immediately (87–8). The next time Steve gets in a fight with the Finley twins, Mrs Finley slaps Philip himself with her purse. His 'might have been a face drawn in chalk,' Mrs Bentley reports, 'pressed so close and still against the woodshed wall ... When I looked again his head was down, and he had a hand across his eyes. There was a small trickle of blood from his mouth, but it may have been from biting his lip to keep himself controlled' (151). In both cases, Philip's large hands and body remain passive. Whatever rage he may feel remains unexpressed. Predictably, on the next page we read that 'someone' has informed a Catholic official about Steve, and priests from an orphanage have come to reclaim the boy. 'Philip didn't argue or protest,' reports Mrs Bentley. He stands helplessly by when they take Steve away (152–4). He has no righteous indignation that can burst forth in a verbal or physical effort to keep Steve from going. His physical impotence and emotional inhibition, according to Mrs Bentley, stems from his spiritual illegitimacy: 'The constant sense of deceit and hypocrisy has been a virus, destroying his will and sapping his energy. Lack of self-respect has meant lack of initiative to try something else [other than the church] – it's been a vicious circle' (88; see also 112). This self-inhibiting cycle undermines Philip's ability to rise up in defence even of Steve, a relationship about which he appears to care passionately. And so he remains unable to 'take hold and do things like other men' (175).

Philip's lack of *thumos*, as traced above, results largely from his constant self-containment. Over and over again throughout the novel, he and Mrs Bentley forego gethsemane moments when they could be honest with one another, when they could admit inadequacy or the need for reconciliation. After Steve's removal, for example, Philip delivers one of his longest speeches in the novel. 'Steve's been good for me,' he tells Mrs Bentley. 'The last few days I've been really down to earth, looking myself over.' Yet, instead of expressing his disappointment over the boy's loss, he covers over any signs of vulnerability: 'The way he dropped out on me – the unimportance of it to everyone else – it made me realize you're a fool not to be just as casual with life as life is with you. Take things as they come – get what you can out of them. Don't want or care too much about anything' (156–7). Mrs Bentley characteristically tries to take responsibility for Philip's disillusionment by saying that she's sorry she has been a hindrance to him. Rather than using her comment to engage in an honest conversation about their marriage, however, he recontains the moment with an aphorism: 'If a man's a victim of circumstances he deserves to be' (157). And so the novel goes, with moments of potential vulnerability between the two regularly bypassed. Having closed himself off from the possibility of grace, Philip cannot offer it to others. He is unable to offer comfort to parishioners suffering economic tragedy on their drought-stricken farms and mourning the loss of undernourished, sickly children (143). His inability to speak honestly about his lack of faith produces his inability or unwillingness to express any true emotions at all, with the result that the closed door of his study remains his most eloquent mode of communication with Mrs Bentley.

Philip's most important departure from muscular Christian ideals, however, occurs in his elevation of the immaterial over the material. 'Religion and art,' he explains, 'are almost the same thing anyway. Just different ways of taking a man out of himself ... They're both a rejection of the material, common-sense world for one that's illusory, yet somehow more important' (148). This statement is heresy to the doctrine of practical Christianity that we have traced from Kingsley to the Canadian social progressives. It was precisely against this preference for the other-worldly over the worldly that Kingsley directed his criticism of Tractarianism in England. And it was against a similar preference for the theoretical over the practical among the nineteenth-century theological colleges in Canada that Protestant reformers such as Connor and McClung called for an activist Christianity (Christie and Gauvreau xii–xiii, 6–7). According to muscular Christian values, Philip makes the opposite error to that made by John Harris and Gander Stake. Whereas their devotion to the material world left them ineffectual in the immaterial realms of emotional and spiritual life, his embroilment in the immaterial worlds of artistic endeavour and spiritual agnosticism leaves him ineffectual in the realm of material reality. Indeed, one can read Ross's novel as a protest against the prevalence of material, common sense values in prairie society that leave little room for artists such as Philip. 'It's been one of

Philip's hard days,' Mrs Bentley reports, 'when the artist in him gets the upper hand. Reality as the rest of us know it disappears from him. It isn't that he sits daydreaming or lost in the clouds – at such times there's actually a vitality about him that you're relieved to get away from – but rather as if he pierces this workaday reality of ours, half scales it off, sees hidden behind it another. More important, more significant than ours, but that he understands it only vaguely. He tries to solve it, give it expression, and doesn't quite succeed' (133).

This is a characteristic statement from Mrs Bentley because it contains an assertion within an equivocation. On the one hand, she asserts that Philip does have moments of vitality, when 'the artist in him' penetrates beyond a mundane and stifling world. But on the other hand, she immediately undermines this vitality by insisting that he fails to give his perspicuity adequate expression. Even in moments when the novel poses a possible criticism of the kind of pragmatism that runs through muscular Christian and progressivist discourse, this criticism is recuperated by the reasserted code of manly vitality that was also central to that discourse. In both instances, prairie society's assumed muscular Christian values remain the standards against which Philip Bentley is measured. His distance from the manly ideal of the progressive Protestant minister, therefore, measures the distance of Ross's critical departure from the romance of Canadian prairie optimism. This criticism becomes salient by contrast with the widely assumed norms of muscular Christianity that Ross's readers would have expected of his Protestant minister.

The attempt to explain the vacuity in the Bentleys' house and the unreliability of Mrs Bentley's narration has so fascinated critics that this novel is one of the most written-about works of fiction in Canadian literature – this despite the fact that the novel, like other founding works of prairie realism, was not a popular success on its first printing. Whereas one can, with a fair amount of confidence, read the novels of Connor, McClung, and the early Stead (including *The Homesteaders*) as representative of popular opinion because of their enormous sales in Canada, Stead's *Grain*, Grove's *Settlers of the Marsh,* and Ross's *As for Me and My House* were not popular successes. *Grain* and *As for Me* received favourable reviews from literary scholars, while *Settlers* launched a teapot tempest over its blunt discussion of sexual matters, but *As for Me* sold only a few hundred copies (Stouck, 'Reception' 6; Harrison 154), *Settlers* went largely unnoticed (Harrison 154), and *Grain* represented a dramatic fall-off in Stead's sales (Varma 144; Glicksohn xiii). All three of these books came belatedly to national prominence as a result of their being reissued in the canon-making New Canadian Library series in the 1950s and 1960s. The contrast between the lack of popular interest in and scholarly acclaim for these 'classics' of realism led Dick Harrison to observe in 1977 that the 'ascendancy of the tragic view of prairie life outlined by Grove and Ross has been largely the work of critics and the academic community over the last twenty years' (154). I would suggest that, in large part, *As for Me* has generated the remarkable critical industry, in the first instance, because of its complex narrative form, and in the second, more recent instance, because of its queer subtext. But the suggestive opacity of Mrs Bentley's narration means that this large body of criticism reveals more about the perspectives of critics than it discloses incontrovertible facts about the plot or characters themselves. For example, assessments of Mrs Bentley range from 'pure gold and wholly credible' (Daniells, 'Introduction' 37) to 'perverse Pygmalion turning her spouse into a statue' (Cude 94), while assessments of the novel's theme range from salvific narrative that replaces perverted religious convention with repentance and rebirth (Djwa 54–5, 57) to feminist subversion of the patriarchal order represented by the Christian church (Buss 196). My own tracing of the echoes of muscular Christianity in the novel is no exception to the rule: it reveals more about my own critical preoccupations than about the plot or characters themselves. But it also presents some significant perspectives on the way that assumptions of muscular Christian ideology subtend a good deal of the critical reception of *As for Me and My House* even up to the present day.

T.J. Matheson, for example, asserts that the extended debate about the novel's ambivalent narration can be resolved when we realize that the novel presents a tension between self-reliance and conformity. Matheson proposes manly nonconformity as the thematic hub of Ross's narrative. He suggests that the novel's evasive narration parallels the many compromises and failures of integrity that constitute its subject matter. He says of Philip that 'he is still a withdrawn, passive man, rarely capable of initiating action. Furthermore, it is obvious that he is stagnating, and in this respect is [a] conformist whose force has been so scattered there is no energy left whereby he could impel himself into a more dynamic relationship with the world' (165). To impose my own terms on Matheson's argument, the Bentleys' hypocrisy (he suggests that Mrs Bentley is as much a conformist as Philip), and thus the opacity of Mrs Bentley's narration, can be traced to the lack of forthright muscular Christian *thumos*.

This reading of the lack of manly righteousness and concomitant spineless conformity in the novel takes an ironic turn when we consider it in the light of more recent bio-critical discussions of Ross's homosexuality and its function as a possible subtext of this novel. For the whole meaning of 'integrity' and 'conformity' take on remarkable complexity if we consider that Philip's false-front may be the closet of his homosexuality and that his adoption of Steve may be motivated by homoerotic desire.[24] On the one hand, Philip's hypothetical gayness might explain why he cannot enact the transparent integrity of the muscular Christian minister, while, on the other, it might explain why he remains in the white-collar profession of the church, one of the few places in a Depression-era prairie town where a man of unrugged sensibilities could make a living. In addition, the implication of paedophilia, if Philip's fascination with Steve is in fact sexual interest in a minor, would go a long way to explaining why any impulse to transparent self-revelation might be plagued not just by anticipated social censure but by internalized self-censure (Fraser 82). Whether or not a reading of the novel's homoerotic subtext would supply 'the' missing clue to understanding the multiple levels of dissimulation in the novel's narration (i.e., Mrs Bentley's narration cannot make clear what she herself may not know or may unconsciously disavow, which is Philip's perhaps unacknowledged sexual orientation), it nevertheless clarifies by contrast how strong the discourse of muscular Christianity, with its valuation of integrity, self-sacrifice, vital assertion, and religious conviction, remains not just in the generic Depression-era prairie town represented by Ross's Horizon but also in recent critics' assessments of his novel. Philip's opacity, and the concerted efforts of critics to pierce through to clarity, registers how powerful the residual codes of forthright Christian manliness remain.

Tracing the allegorical figure of the muscular Christian in western Canadian fiction of the first half of the twentieth century allows us to sift through a complex set of widely held Canadian national ideals. Because it was ideologically useful to the projects of the expansion-hungry Canadian imperialists and of the later generation of Canadian Protestant activists and feminist reformers, muscular Christianity developed a multivalence that has given it remarkable longevity in Canadian national discourse. From the romances of Connor and McClung to the romantic realism of Stead and even the critical realism of Ross, the muscular Christian combination of righteous *thumos* and responsible self-discipline, of individual integrity and social cooperation, and of rigid law and flexible grace remains a constant ideal for the Canadian national character. Indeed, the ongoing critical debates about Ross's novel show that muscular Christian values remain residual in Canadian social commentary to this day.

Muscular Christianity's multivalency makes it a site where we can trace the tensions of White civility's competing and contradictory values. On the one hand, its valorization of masculine aggression and even violence made it a purveyor of specifically male domination, while, on the other hand, its social activism was appropriated by reformers such as first-wave Canadian feminists as a model for and ally in the campaign for progressive gender reform. Or, in the realms of class and ethnic politics, we can observe its ethnocentric assumption of White, British, Protestant, and middle-class values in its promotion of the Christian gentleman's responsibility for apparently helpless others who have been marginalized from privilege on the basis of class or ethnicity. Yet we must also note that this commitment to social responsibility rejected racist essentialism and the assumption of immutable class boundaries, and promoted instead – within the framework of British Canadian normativity – the inclusion of non-charter-group immigrants and members of the lower classes in the Canadian polity. Indeed, muscular Christianity contributed significantly to the movements of Canadian progressivism and their campaign for social policies that improved the material conditions of women, ethnic-minority settlers, and the labouring poor in Canada. In this sense, it undergirded its characteristic narrative of romance with a kind of practical realism that used fiction to motivate its readers to social and political activism. Romance, interestingly, was the seduction by which it sought to convert its readers to the realism of social engagement. As a rhetorical figure in which Canadian ideals were both contested and consolidated, then, muscular Christianity's virtue was also its vice. It purveyed an ideal of social responsibility and so required the distinction between agents and recipients of that responsibility. Even as it promoted a society of justice and equality, it assumed that access to these benefits would be accorded to those Canadians who could most readily assimilate themselves to the normative values of White, British, Protestant, middle-class, heterosexual masculinity. Muscular Christianity was indeed, as Connor put it in *The Foreigner*, a 'subtle something,' and its subtlety has often been misrepresented by the broad caricatures that have been used to dismiss it. But a serious study of this enormously influential ideal image shows that it consisted of a remarkable tenacity and adaptability which enabled it to navigate the romances of imperialism and expansionism in Canada as well as the realisms of two world wars and the Great Depression.

5 The Maturing Colonial Son: Manning the Borders of White Civility

In the opening lines of *Strangers within Our Gates; or Coming Canadians* (1909), J.S. Woodsworth wrote:

> Within the past decade Canada has risen from the status of a colony to that of a nation. A national consciousness has developed – that is, a nation has been born. A few years ago Canadian-born children described themselves as English, Irish; Scotch or French, according as their parents or ancestors had come from England, Ireland, Scotland or France. To-day our children boast themselves Canadians, and the latest arrivals from Austria or Russia help to swell the chorus, 'The Maple Leaf Forever.' There has not been sufficient time to develop a fixed Canadian type, but there is a certain indefinite *something* that at once unites us and distinguishes us from all the world besides. Our hearts all thrill in response to the magical phrase – 'This Canada of Ours!' We are Canadians. As yet we have not entered fully into our national privileges and responsibilities, but great national problems are already forcing themselves upon our attention. In grappling with and solving these we shall attain our national manhood. (16)

As I mentioned in my discussion of Woodsworth in my opening chapter, his book identifies immigration as Canada's number one problem and calls upon Canadians to legitimize their newly minted national status by addressing the problem directly. His allegorical logic is as simple and homely as a preacher's parable: Canada is entering a critical point in its maturation, for it has outgrown its colonial dependency upon its elderly British parent and must now prove its independent manhood by bravely facing its responsibilities. And the primary proof of Canada's maturity, that 'certain indefinite *something* that at once unites us' (Ralph Connor's 'subtle something' echoes loudly here) will be manifested in the nation's civility – that is, in the courtesy and fair-mindedness with which it deals with incoming immigrants.

Woodsworth's allegory bears the markings of a grandly masterminded national experiment in eugenics, the new 'science' that was enthusiastically taken up by social progressives in his time.[1] But the anxiety in his tone reflects the precipitousness with which Canadians felt they had been plunged into this experiment. For the new dominion needed urgently to populate the Northwest if it was not only to pay for the transcontinental railway, not merely to check the encroachments of American interests in the region but also – and most importantly – to turn the prairies into the breadbasket that Canada would need if it were to realize its youthful hope of succeeding England as the reinvigorated centre of an ageing empire (see illus. 13). Accordingly, Prime Minister Laurier's energetic minister of the interior, Clifford Sifton, had embarked upon a scheme of aggressive immigrant recruitment that bypassed the usual British immigrants and called instead, in the words of one of his officials, for 'men of good muscle who are willing to hustle' (qtd. in D.J. Hall 71). More often than not, these hustling, muscled 'men in sheepskin coats' (Sifton's much-quoted phrase) were farmers from Poland, Austria-Hungary, and Ukraine to whom the agricultural conditions of the prairies were more familiar than the veneer of British civilization that was being quickly glued over the social landscapes of the Métis and Cree at Red River, Frog Lake, and Batoche. Put baldly, English-speaking Canada's rapid expansion into what was then called the Northwest introduced a sobering challenge to British dominance in the immigrant farm labourers imported to realize its dream of succeeding Britain as the centre of a renewed empire (see Harney 56, 63–4).

The allegory of manly maturation, such as that deployed in Woodsworth's and many other popular Canadian social and literary texts, functions to shore up British normativity by producing and reinforcing the image of White civility, a civility demonstrated by muscular Christian, gentlemanly, fair treatment of 'strangers.' In Woodsworth's case, the beneficiaries of this mature civility are immigrants, whereas in other versions of the allegory the beneficiaries are figured as Natives or French Canadians.[2] To build upon the division I sketched at the end of the previous chapter between the agents and the recipients of muscular Christian social activism, the allegory of manly maturation establishes the moral high ground of White civility on a productive contradiction: Canada's 'maturity' depends upon extending civil treatment to others,

Foreigners build our railways
1 A construction gang – foreigners do most of the rough work
2 Foreign workmen unloading the first car of steel on the Grand Trunk Pacific

13 Woodsworth called attention to the contribution that 'foreigners' were making to the development of western Canada in photographs such as these. Reproduced in *Strangers within Our Gates*, 111.

but in the very process it constantly repositions these others 'at the gates' in its need to reiterate its maturity. For maturity, like the attainment of Woodsworth's full manhood, is always a constantly deferred ideal, and this teleological structure makes it productive insofar as maturity, like manhood, is never fully possessed but must always be performed and performed again.[3] For this reason, the allegory of manly maturation recurs throughout English Canadian nationalist rhetoric as it anxiously reiterates scenes of the civil incorporation of non-British people into the body of the nation, even as it detains these people at the nation's margins. Focused on demonstrating the maturity of Canada, this process of reiteration and deferral reproduces the predominance of White, British Canadians by inexplicitly stated contrast with the French, Natives, and immigrants, who are always beneficiaries of and never agents in the nation's civil order.[4] Several widely popular literary and social texts by Ralph Connor, John Murray Gibbon, Philippe-Joseph Aubert de Gaspé, Gilbert Parker, and Frederick Niven show how the national allegory of maturation repeatedly mans the national borders by deploying and redeploying the stranger at the gates, and that it does so not to produce understanding or acceptance of the stranger but to convey evidence of White, British, masculine civility.

The allegory of the young colonial Canada growing to maturity and separating from its British parent is ubiquitous in early Canadian public discourse – and, I would argue, remains common in residual form to this day. Robert Brown and Ramsay Cook note in *Canada, 1896–1921: A Nation Transformed* that the 'process of growing up' was a common analogy used by Canadians during the years of optimism and expansion under the Laurier and Borden governments, and Daniel Francis writes in *National Dreams: Myth, Memory, and Canadian History* that in the first half of the twentieth century, 'the maturation of a child to responsible adulthood' was an image fundamental to Canada's master narrative of the gradual evolution of Canadian society from colonial dependency to equal partnership with Great Britain in the empire (54). With Confederation and the expansion of the dominion into the Northwest, Canadian boosterism imagined Canada as the emerging youth that would eventually shoulder its parent aside. As Stephen Leacock put it, 'The old man's got old and he don't know it ... [C]an't kick him off the place, but I reckon that the next time we come together to talk things over, the boys have got to step right in and manage the farm' (qtd. in Berger, *Sense* 261). Independence from the British parent was matched in Canadian maturation rhetoric with moral superiority to the American sibling, and this moral superiority was demonstrated by civil treatment of francophones, immigrants, and Natives. Thus the allegory of maturation depended heavily on the idea of character-building, which, as Valverde explains, was 'the individual equivalent of nation-building ... It involved learning to lead a morally and physically pure life, not only for the sake of individual health and salvation but for the sake of the nation' (27).

That the process of national character-building is commonly (though not exclusively) figured in masculine terms is no accident, for the gendered ideology which assumed that males were naturally fitted for roles in public life and that females were suited to the domestic sphere meant that for the nation to progress, it needed to develop what the popular sex educator A.W. Beall called 'A.1' boys (Valverde 27). Women could contribute to this process of maturation by raising the boys in their families to become men of good character. As Anne McClintock argues, 'Despite many nationalists' ideological investment in the idea of popular *unity*, nations have historically amounted to the sanctioned institutionalization of *gender difference*' (353, emphasis in original). She identifies 'domestic genealogies' such as the 'family trope,' with their hierarchical ordering of fatherly headship in the family and of men's public over women's domestic spheres, as oft-repeated national narratives that convey the naturalness of gendered national hierarchies (357). The allegory of national maturation therefore articulates the hierarchies of race and gender in such a way that categories of privilege such as whiteness, Britishness, heterosexuality, and masculinity are naturalized as leading the vanguard of modernity, and people are placed at higher or lower stages of civil advancement on the basis of how many of these categories they can claim. Moreover, the cross-articulation of these hierarchies establishes rankings not just *between* categories such as feminine and masculine but also *within* them, so that masculinity, for example, becomes internally differentiated when it is articulated with categories of race, class, or ethnicity.

The Australian sociologist Robert Connell departs from the monadic conception of masculine privilege represented by a homogeneous patriarchy and instead schematizes a hierarchy of masculinities from *hegemonic masculinity*, which is fully able to legitimize and benefit from patriarchal power, to *marginalized* and *complicitous masculinities*, which because of poverty, ethnicity, race, sexual orientation, or physical ability, do not have full access to what Connell calls 'patriarchal dividends,' and finally to *subordinated masculinities*, which are excluded from legitimation by social taboo, such as miscegenation or homophobia (77–80). My point here in regard to the allegory of maturation is not to insist that Canada has always been figured in masculine terms (as a boy growing up), for there are many instances of its maturation figured as a female narrative (the most popular instance would be the Miss Canada cartoon figure that was ubiquitous in late nineteenth- and early twentieth-century newspapers). Rather, my point is to observe that the ideologies of gender, which assumed the public domain to be the realm of men, were merged with those of race and ethnicity, in particular, to naturalize White, male, British normativity in Canada. And the elaboration of this hierarchy involved the ordering of diversity.

If the ambivalent position of settler-invader status between European civility and Indigenous authenticity increased the pressure on Canada's narrative of White civility, so too did its undeniable history of internal difference. Whereas European or American nationalisms might have succeeded in producing fairly coherent narratives of homogeneous development and civility (although no such narratives can be absolutely coherent), the hard-to-avoid, very public facts of Native and French prior inhabitation in what became Canada meant that the allegory of the young nation's maturation must figure its civility precisely in terms of its accommodation of diversity. Eva Mackey argues that, for this reason, the history of Canadian nationalist rhetoric poses a challenge to theories of nationalism which argue that the modern nation obliterates internal differences in the effort to produce a homogeneous culture. She surveys Canadian nationalist narratives from early Canadian imperialism to contemporary multicultural policy to demonstrate that, instead of suppressing its 'others,' Canadian public discourse consistently *féatures* images of Natives, francophones, and immigrants in the effort to produce what she calls its myth of 'tolerance' (5–12; 83).

In the preface to Connor's novel *The Foreigner*, published the same year as Woodsworth's *Strangers within Our Gates,* we find an almost exact repetition of Woodsworth's allegory of the maturing colonial son:

> In Western Canada there is to be seen to-day that most fascinating of all human phenomena, the making of a nation. Out of breeds diverse in traditions, in ideals, in speech, and in manner of life, Saxon and Slav, Teuton, Celt and Gaul, one people is being made. The blood strains of great races will mingle in the blood of a race greater than the greatest of them all.
>
> It would be our wisdom to grip these peoples to us with living hooks of justice and charity till all lines of national cleavage disappear, and in the Entity of our Canadian national life, and in the Unity of world-wide Empire, we fuse into a people whose strength will endure the slow shock of time for the honour of our name, for the good of mankind; and for the glory of Almighty God. (n.p.)

The story of the fusion of a heterogeneous population into one people in this novel takes the form of a bildungsroman about the process by which a Ukrainian youth matures into a Canadian man. The novel charts Kalman's escape from poverty and squalor in Winnipeg's North End immigrant ghetto and eventual achievement of respectability in specifically British Canadian terms. Kalman rejects the values of his Old World father, leaves his family, abandons their language and culture, and conforms instead to British – specifically, Scottish Presbyterian – manners and customs. But *two* maturing immigrants – and this is what makes the novel especially revealing for my study of the allegory of maturation – are made into true Canadian men in Connor's novel. The first is Kalman, the obvious foreigner of the title, but the second is Jack French, less obviously a foreigner because he is an immigrant from England.

Let me first deal with Kalman, whose story runs like this: he passes his early life under a slumlord's thumb in an overcrowded boarding house in Winnipeg's immigrant ghetto. Eventually, a Presbyterian missionary named Margaret French delivers him from the ghetto's disease, violence, alcoholism, and Old World political sectarianism, which constantly threaten him, his sister, and his stepmother. Margaret sends him to the care of her brother-in-law, Jack French, who owns a ranch on the South Saskatchewan River. There Kalman is converted by the clean air and vigorous outdoor life – along with some mentoring from Jack and the Presbyterian missionary, Reverend Brown – from the intemperance of what Connor calls his 'Slavic blood' to the disciplined and responsible maturity of Canadian Presbyterianism. And Connor follows up Kalman's conversion with the appropriate rewards: the ownership of a wealth-producing coal mine and marriage to the daughter of an Edinburgh CPR shareholder. 'How wonderful the power of this country of yours to transform men!' exclaims Kalman's Scottish wife-to-be, in explicit affirmation of the masculine paradigm operating in this narrative of maturation. 'It is a wonderful country, Canada' (378).

The contrast between Kalman's two mentors is important to understanding how the allegory of maturation operates as more than a simple assimilation story about the way a foreign boy can grow up into a Canadian man. For while Reverend Brown, a Presbyterian missionary, represents the admirable muscular Christian social activist I examined in the previous chapter, Jack French reminds the reader of the figure of the English remittance man. Until Kalman is sent to live with him by his sister-in-law, Jack has been a casual, rather than an earnest, rancher, having given more of his time and attention to broncos, buckboards, and whisky than to caring for his homestead, potatoes, or cattle. Jack is a far cry from Thomas McCulloch's thrifty, hard-working Mephibosheth Stepsure. His lack of attention to the improvement of his homestead constitutes much more than an agricultural or economic failure. It is also a moral and a national one, since the economy of settlement depends on cooperation among all the settlers in a region to develop their own properties and thereby to generate the productivity that necessitates local roads, canals, and other infrastructures. The shorthand for Jack's neglect is that he lacks the kind of character modelled by Stepsure. The context of immigrant assimilation makes his lack of character even more of a moral and national failure because the whole civilizing mission of the British Empire assumes that not just Natives but also 'backward' eastern Europeans will be improved when they internalize the superior scientific and social practices of British civility. Jack's lack of commitment to his own improvement – let alone that of the neighbouring Ukrainian colony – makes him, in Connor's world, a man sorely in need of conversion.

Jack therefore represents British Canadians who have not yet awakened to their responsibilities to build up Canada's White civility. These responsibilities are made very clear when he and Kalman are out riding across the prairies in search of a lost horse, and they encounter a newcomer to the region named Mr Brown. Brown explains that he is a Presbyterian missionary who has come to the South Saskatchewan out of concern for the Ukrainians who have recently established a colony in the region. '[M]y main line is the kiddies,' he says. 'I can teach them English, and then I am going to doctor them, and, if they'll let me, teach them some of the elements of domestic science; in short, do anything to make them good Christians and good Canadians, which is the same thing' (253). Jack responds with the kind of individualism and disinterest that Connor condemns among people of privilege who refuse to recognize their responsibilities to the larger community. 'Don't be an ass and throw yourself away,' he advises Brown, apparently not thinking of Kalman listening silently to the two men beside the fire. 'Give it up ... I know [the Ukrainians]. You can't undo in your lifetime the results of three centuries. It's a hopeless business. I tried myself to give them some pointers when they came in first, and worried a good deal about it. I got myself disliked for my pains and suffered considerable annoyance. Now I leave them beautifully alone' (253–4). But Brown insists that he's got to do it, 'Partially for my health, and partially for the good of the country.

These people here exist as an undigested foreign mass. They must be digested and absorbed into the body politic. They must be taught our ways of thinking and living, or it will be a mighty bad thing for us in Canada' (255). Jack then changes tack. Instead of arguing that the immigrants cannot be changed, he contends that they might change too radically. He warns, 'You go in and give them some of our Canadian ideas of living and all that, and before you know they are striking for higher wages and giving no end of trouble ... if you educate these fellows, you hear me, they'll run your country ... and you wouldn't like that much' (256). Brown takes up Jack's point and uses it to press his progressive, interventionist argument: 'they'll run your country anyhow you put it, school or no school, and, therefore, you had better fit them for the job. You have got to make them Canadian.' And he names the two institutions that will accomplish this Canadianization: the church and the school (256).

The debate between Jack and Reverend Brown echoes exactly the widespread debates over immigration policy that ran throughout the opening two decades of the twentieth century. Andrew Macphail, author of *The Master's Wife*, for example, wrote in a 1920 article entitled 'The Immigrant': 'Immigration is war, – war by the new comers upon those already in possession ... There are breeds of men as there are strains of animals and classes of plants ... When all immigrants are equal before the law, and have the same power over government through the instrument of the vote; when mental attainments and physical courage count for naught, the lower breeds will prevail' (136–7; qtd. in Craig, *Racial* 6). In comparison to those who, like Macphail, argued that because of their inherent inferiority, eastern and southern European immigrants should be excluded from citizenship, Connor and Woodsworth were progressive liberals who believed that a policy of exclusion would constitute putting one's head in the sand. For them, Canadian expansion necessitated settlers who could successfully farm the prairies, and this meant eastern Europeans.

So, given that these immigrants were necessary to Canada, the challenge became one of civilizing and assimilating them. Woodsworth and Connor were progressives insofar as they rejected the essentialist theory that the hierarchy of races outlined, for example, by Macphail was immutable and insisted instead that people considered backward could be improved, given proper education and enabling social conditions. But this progressivism did not question the assumption that Britishness represented the pinnacle of social evolution. 'Our democratic institutions are the outcome of centuries of conflict,' wrote Woodsworth. And this long history of evolution meant that 'we have been fitted for self-government' (240). By contrast, '[p]eoples emerging from serfdom, accustomed to despotism, untrained in the principles of representative government, without patriotism – such peoples are utterly unfit to be trusted with the ballot' (239). Woodsworth went on to argue that immigrants' eligibility to vote ought to be delayed until they had been sufficiently Canadianized, for, he explained, they were often manipulated by political parties' unscrupulous agents, who would enter immigrant communities with casks of free whisky on election days and proceed to buy votes. As J.W. Sparling put it in the introduction to Woodsworth's book, 'Either we must educate and elevate the incoming multitudes or they will drag us and our children down to a lower level. We must see to it that the civilization and ideals of Southeastern Europe are not transplanted to and perpetuated on our virgin soil' (8).[5] The assimilation of immigrants to British Canadian norms, therefore, becomes crucial to protecting the civility – represented as feminized and vulnerable 'virgin soil' – of the Canadian political and social system.

The only mature or progressive response to the fact of immigration for early twentieth-century liberals such as Woodsworth and Connor, therefore, is to elevate non-anglophones to British standards, as Reverend Brown does in Connor's novel. With the help of Kalman, he converts the members of the Ukrainian colony from subsistence-level peasants who are subservient to an avaricious Polish priest into wage-earning workers at Kalman's coal mine who are educated in Brown's school, liberated from Old World priestcraft by an honest French Canadian priest, and taught rudimentary health and hygiene by Kalman's anglicized sister, who works in Brown's clinic. Connor is careful to point out that this general narrative of elevation reminds degenerate Englishmen such as Jack French that their responsibility to contribute to the improvement of these so-called foreigners is not just a matter of practical help but also of moral or spiritual education. At one point, Jack asks Reverend Brown if they can divide up the responsibility for Kalman's education: 'I will undertake to look after the boy's physical and – well – secular interests, ... while you take charge of his moral training' (280). But Brown will have none of it, for he insists that improvement is taught by the example of one's character: 'For good or evil, you have that boy's life in your hands. Did you ever notice how he rides, – his style, I mean? It is yours. How he walks? Like you ... He models himself after you ... And it is your fate to make him after your own type ... You may refuse this responsibility, you may be too weak, too wilful, too selfish to set upon your own wicked indulgence of a foolish appetite [for alcohol], but the responsibility is there, and no living man or woman can take it from you' (281–2). Seen in this light, immigration represents a civilizing mission for Canadians, not just in the challenge to civilize the strangers at the nation's gates but also to recall those whose British ancestry gives them ready access to power and privilege in Canada to commit themselves to self-development and the improvement of their own characters as essential to the process of maintaining the nation's standard of civility and inculcating it in the nation's newcomers.

But while Kalman and Jack French are readily assimilated to Canadianness in Connor's novel, there remain characters in the novel who never qualify as candidates for Canadianization, and it is important to attend to these exclusions, for they define the borders of Connor's vision of civility. The first is Kalman's Cossack father, Michael Kalmar, whose whole life has been dedicated to a secret brotherhood of zealots opposed to the tyranny of the czar. As a 'nihilist' (126) who is fanatically committed to a violent vendetta against an equally violent system, Michael Kalmar represents a paternity that must be broken if the Canadian immigrant is to become capable of participating in a civil democracy. Kalman must renounce the oath of retribution that has been the driving force of his father's life if he is to become Brown's Christian and Canadian – which, as we recall, is the same thing. Michael Kalmar marks one of the borders of Connor's liberal inclusiveness: Ukrainian children should be welcomed and educated into Canadian civility; they should even be encouraged to emphasize the positive (hard-working, thrifty) virtues of their cultural inheritance; but they must renounce the specific traumas of their cultural history and the (unenlightened, usually passionate) attachments resulting from these. But if Michael Kalmar remains inassimilable to Canadian civility, so too is his nemesis, Rosenblatt, who is identified as a 'Bukowinian' in the novel (45) but whose name and role as the slumlord exploiter of his fellow immigrants figures him as the stereotype of the avaricious Jew.[6] Connor reproduces in Rosenblatt this stereotype to remind his readers that Canadian civility separates itself from money-driven societies by its commitment to non-material spiritual and moral values. In confirmation of those higher values, the vengeful Michael Kalmar and the greedy Rosenblatt are both killed in a hail of bullets and dynamite at the end of the novel.

Another figure that cannot be assimilated to the progressive British ideal is Malcolm Mackenzie, the Scottish-Cree man who works as a hired hand on Jack French's ranch and whose 'savage blood' overwhelms his civil blood whenever he indulges in some of Jack's whisky. One day, out of concern for Jack's and Mackenzie's regular binges, Kalman steals Mackenzie's last bottle of whisky while Jack lies comatose in the ranch house. Mackenzie's 'smiling face became transformed with fury,' we read; 'his black eyes gleamed with the cunning malignity of the savage, he shed his soft Scotch voice with his genial manner, the very movements of his body became those of his Cree progenitors' (233). He gets a gun and tries to shoot Kalman until Jack intervenes (234). This is pretty much the extent of Mackenzie's contribution to the novel. He does not participate in finding or establishing Kalman's mine or in helping Brown Christianize and Canadianize the Ukrainians of the district. Mackenzie fades from the author's notice, having been dismissed by the social evolutionary myth that requires primitive Indigenous people to become a vanishing race. When the laying of railway tracks reaches the region of the South Saskatchewan, the narrator describes what it means to all three men on the ranch: 'That surveyor's flag was the signal that waved out the old order and waved in the new... Mackenzie and his world must now disappear in the wake of the red man and the buffalo before the railroad and the settler' (286). Indeed, since the extension of the railroad had allowed General Middleton to get his troops into Saskatchewan in record time to defeat Louis Riel and Gabriel Dumont at Batoche, its appearance in the region did indeed mark the defeat of Métis and mixed-race people's hopes for cultural and political agency in the region.

By contrast with Mackenzie, however, we are told that to 'Jack French the invasion brought mingled feelings. He hated to surrender the untrammelled, unconventional mode of life, for which twenty years ago he had left an ancient and, as it seemed to his adventurous spirit, a worn-out civilization, but he was quick to recognize, and in his heart was glad to welcome, a change that would mean new life and assured prosperity to Kalman, whom he had come to love as a son' (286). Whereas the approach of technology and a permanent link to the markets of central Canada, and through them to the world, means the erasure of Mackenzie, to Jack it means the necessary conversion from indolent immaturity to responsibility. It means that he must shift from understanding himself as an adventurer who escaped the confines of England to understanding himself as a citizen who must take on the commitments of Canada. Finally, we are told that to 'Kalman that surveyor's flag meant the opening up of a new world, a new life, rich in promise and of adventure and achievement ... "We will have no trouble selling our potatoes and our oats now," said the boy' (286–7). Whereas the advent of modern commerce means opportunity for Kalman and transformation for Jack French, it means extinction for Mackenzie.

The exclusion of the Cossack zealot, the Jewish slumlord, and the 'half-breed' at the borders of Connor's progressive, civil society emphasizes how assimilability becomes the flexible, ostensibly civil apparatus by which inclusion in the nation can be shifted conveniently between *moral* criteria (e.g., vengeance, avarice, alcoholism) and *racial* ones (being Cossack, Jewish, or mixed-race). If a foreigner shows, like Kalman, a malleability to the codes of White civility, race is dismissed in favour of individual moral character, and he or she can be welcomed into the national community. But if that foreigner is less malleable to these codes, then the slippage between moral character and race enables the exclusion of that person on the basis of morality as determined by race – one's moral character is represented as inherited from one's cultural history (e.g., nihilism is the product of the long history of czarist tyranny, alcoholism of savage blood, etc.). This slippage, therefore, allows a civil exclusion; that is, the Canadian nation is seen not to reject specific individuals or to reject specific races *as races*; rather, it is seen to disallow generalized groups of people whose social backgrounds ill suit them for assimilation to the norms of White, British values.[7]

The movement between moral character and race that operates in Connor's text to separate the included from the excluded also functions centrally to rationalize the hierarchy of desirable-to-undesirable races in *Strangers within Our Gates*. But as Woodsworth's text shows, it could also be used to criticize the races at the top of that hierarchy. It gave Frederick Philip Grove, for example, a way to insert an anti-English and pro-European element in the vision of Canada he promoted in the nation-building speeches he delivered during his cross-country tour of the Canadian Clubs in 1927–8. In speeches entitled 'Canadians Old and New,' 'Assimilation,' and 'Nationhood' (the first two were published in *Maclean's*), Grove entered the debates about immigration popularized by writers such as Woodsworth and Connor and carried out in the English Canadian press throughout the 1920s. Having already published four books about life in North America, Grove had by this time established a reputation as a sophisticated man of letters, and he deliberately used his continental learning to play upon the feelings of colonial provincialism felt by the English Canadians who attended his lectures (Craig, *Racial* 57; Padolsky; Hjartarson). Addressing 'Mr Canadian' in

'Canadians Old and New,' for example, Grove observed wryly: 'First of all, you call [the European immigrant] a "foreigner" – a title of honour, indeed, since it implies that likely he has seen more of the world than you have seen – unless you have traveled. But it is well-known that this title, within the British Isles, has from time immemorial had a sinister sound. A strange thing to say, seeing that the population of Great Britain is itself a mixed population, compounded of many different racial strains' (170). Not only does Grove undermine the myth of British purity here, but he also reminds his listeners that Britishers are just as foreign to Canada as central Europeans, and they are often less willing to adapt to Canadian ways, whereas '[s]o-called "foreigners" rarely make themselves obnoxious in that way' (170).

As in all interventions in a previously existing discourse, Grove's use of the allegory of manly maturation repeats some of its common elements and rejects others. His argument, for instance, that European immigration is advantageous to Canada's maturation because continental Europeans bring with them the well-aged spiritual values that a youthful, unformed Canada needs in order to ward off the crass influences of American-style materialism ('Nationhood' 146; 'Canadians' 171–3) repeats the familiar anti-American, anti-materialistic values that recur in Canadian national maturation discourse, but his emphasis on European civility by contrast with British civility contests that discourse's assumption of British Canadian dominance. Nonetheless, his description of the rich character Europeans bring with them remains decidedly masculine: 'The peasantry of Europe has always fed the cities not only with bread and wine,' Grove states, 'but with new blood and new manhood.' And he goes on to question by contrast the new nation's manliness: 'is Canada reproducing that manhood which did the pioneering work of a hundred years ago? Is it not a fact that the Canadian-born in Western Canada today, in the country and in the small towns, are becoming soft, mentally and physically … ?' ('Assimilation' 180).

Grove's reorientation of the way that national maturation premises itself on the courteous assimilation of immigrants is most clearly evident in the echo from Connor and Woodsworth that can be heard in what he calls 'Canada's mission in geo-politics.' In this reorientation of the concept of the nation's civilizing mission, Grove claims that Canada could prove itself superior even to Europe through its accommodation of a multi-ethnic populace. 'Canada is the meeting-place of many races,' he says. 'Only through such a meeting place where Slav rubs elbows with Anglo-Saxon, Teuton with Frenchman – and where they can learn, not only to respect each other's gifts, but also to recognize that they have more that unites than separates them – only through such a meeting-place of all its children can Europe be redeemed. The children must reconcile the parents' ('Assimilation' 187). Grove has a different model of assimilation in mind from that promoted by Woodsworth and Connor insofar as Grove envisions assimilation as a two-way exchange: Canadian-born people must adjust to and accept immigrants' values and contributions, just as immigrants must do for Canadians' ways ('Assimilation' 183–5; 'Canadians' 171–4; 'Nationhood' 149). Grove's term for this form of proto-multiculturalism is 'federation,' or the 'peaceful definition of the races against each other' ('Assimilation' 183). And he illustrates this process by reference to the British Empire: 'in order to make peaceful definition [between races] possible on the large scale, we must first of all learn one important lesson: namely, that no racial strain is intrinsically superior to any other. To learn that lesson would be easy for us who are members of a great empire in which only eleven per cent of the total population is British. Some bond must hold that empire together. What is it? What should it be if not mutual toleration' ('Assimilation' 183).

Thus Grove turns Britishness against itself, boiling down the success of the British Empire, not to the superiority of ethno-national Britishness nor to homogeneity of race or culture, but to tolerance, the British gentlemanly code of 'fair play' ('Assimilation' 187) between people of diverse backgrounds.[8] But, as with Connor and Woodsworth, this multi-ethnic or multi-racial liberalism retains a colour border, for Grove's entire argument is framed by the assumption that Canadian maturity and spiritual progress was premised upon the nation's willingness to welcome and find homes for immigrants from 'all white nations' ('Canadians' 169). The Black Oklahoma farmers in Alberta, the sizeable population of Métis around his home in Manitoba, the owners of the Chinese restaurants and laundries in small towns across the prairies – these were not candidates for Grove's process of federation.

John Murray Gibbon's Governor General's Award–winning book, *The Canadian Mosaic: The Making of a Northern Nation* (1938), follows Grove, and even more clearly Woodsworth, in producing another fascinating proto-multicultural vision that allows an intriguing extension of my study of the construction of Canadian civility. Gibbon was a respected British journalist who had been appointed by the CPR in 1907 to the position of supervisor of European propaganda, in which capacity he visited Russia, Austria, Hungary, and Scandinavia for the purposes of promoting immigration to Canada.[9] In 1913 he moved as the CPR's head of publicity to

Montreal, where he became active in the movement to gain copyright protection for writers in the country and in 1921 took up the founding presidency of the Canadian Authors Association. Gibbon is significant to the history of Canada's representations of its multi-ethnic population not just because he popularized the image of the 'mosaic,' which went on to become the central symbol of multiculturalism, but also because he pioneered the establishment of ethnic heritage festivals across the country as a way to celebrate the nation's diverse population.[10] It is a telling fact that these festivals were tied, from the very beginning, into the commercial-national enterprise of the CPR. Between 1927 and 1930 Gibbon organized fourteen festivals of folk arts and music that served as promotional events for the railway-owned hotels. These included festivals of French Canadian culture at the Château Frontenac in Quebec, a series of European ethnic festivals in Winnipeg, Regina, Edmonton, and Calgary (featuring Polish, Ukrainian, Hungarian, and Scandinavian performers), the annual Banff festivals called 'Indian Days' and the 'Highland Gathering and Scottish Music Festival,' and British-oriented festivals in major cities, such as the Sea Music Festival held in Vancouver. Influenced by a national-romantic approach to folklore studies, Gibbon believed that folk music expressed the popular spirit of a group's particular consciousness and therefore that the collection and study of folk music and arts could offer insights into the distinctive aspects of various national groups' cultures. By extension, then, he hypothesized that awareness of one another's folk traditions could bring Canadians of different cultures together into mutual understanding (McNaughton 68–9). That this noble mission could readily serve the economic advantage of the CPR demonstrates how progressive nationalists could blithely blend the nation's economic and cultural development. With the commercial depression of the 1930s, however, the crowds became too small for the railway to continue to sponsor Gibbon's festivals; so, with the help of his many informant contributors, he translated the folk and ethnic music he had gathered into English, produced recordings of these translations, and presented them to the public through a CBC radio series entitled 'Canadian Mosaic.'

Out of the research he had done for the radio show, Gibbon developed his book's central idea of presenting a history of the various 'racial types' – given visual concreteness by a series of half-tone reproductions such as those in illustrations 14 and 15 – that make up Canada's 'mosaic.' He prefaced the book with his own version of the allegory of maturation, according to which Canada was too young to have established its own

14   The 'French-Canadian Type,' from Gibbon's *Canadian Mosaic* (1938).

15   The 'Polish-Canadian Type,' from Gibbon's *Canadian Mosaic* (1938).

racial type yet. This fact made it important to understand the back-grounds of the various groups in Canada, so that as the country grew up, Canadians could try to give positive shape to its melange of peoples:

> The Canadian race of the future is being superimposed on the original native Indian races and is being made up of over thirty European racial groups, each of which has its own history, customs and traditions. Some politicians want to see these merged as quickly as possible into one standard type, just as our neighbours in the United States are hurrying to make every citizen a 100 per cent. American. Others believe in trying to preserve for the future Canadian race the most worthwhile qualities and traditions that each racial group has brought with it. (vii)

Gibbon is consciously writing not only against the American 'melting pot' model, which reduces all cultural distinctions into one national form, but also against the model of racial purification that is on the rise in Nazi Germany in 1938 (2). In contrast, he portrays Canadian civility by means of the mosaic and its trope for the worth of each separate, distinct cultural fragment that collectively constitutes the nation, but through-out the book he also freely uses the concepts of assimilation and absorp-tion, which would seem to contradict this image of valued diversity. Like Woodsworth's series of chapters, Gibbon's list proceeds down the hierar-chy of racial-national origins from France and Britain at the top to northwestern Europe in the middle and finally to eastern Europe and Jews at the bottom; unlike Woodsworth, however, Gibbon excludes Blacks, Chinese, and other Asians completely (he discusses Europeans of many 'races' who worked on the CPR but omits any mention of Chinese, see 44).[11] Having opened with the observation that an emerging Cana-dian type is being formed from the superimposition of European races upon 'the original native Indian races,' the book abandons any further mention of Aboriginal people, except that an elderly Stoney chief at the Indian Days festival in Banff reminds Gibbon of Crô-Magnard (*sic*), the Stone Age man modelled by the sculptor J.H. McGregor on the basis of contemporary archaeological scholarship (1). As with Connor, Woods-worth, and Grove, Canada's inclusive civility, imaged here as a multi-coloured mosaic, actually insists that all of its tiles will be various shades of white.

And assimilation to British norms returns as the shifting criteria for inclusion. At times, Gibbon seems to echo Grove's idea of two-way assimilation, but then at others he seems to fully endorse a one-way adaptation. For example, at one point he quotes A.J. Hunter, superintendent of the Mission Hospital at Teulon, Manitoba, saying that the 'word "assimilate" has a terrible significance to the Ukrainian patriot. He understands that the lion assimilates the lamb when he eats him, and is resolved that his people shall not be assimilated in that way' (291), and Gibbon also quotes with approval Lord Tweedsmuir's speech to the Ukrainian Canadians at one of his festivals to the effect that the new Canadian nation depends on strong races who retain their cultural traditions (as Tweedsmuir's own Scottish people have done): 'You will all be better Canadians for being also good Ukrainians' (307).[12] But Gibbon quotes with equal approval from *The Education of the New Canadian* by J.T.M Anderson, former premier of Saskatchewan: 'No better material can be found among our newcomers from which to mould a strong type of Canadian citizen than is found among these Ruthenians. The parents, it may be said, almost unanimously desire their children to learn the language of this country' (301). Moreover, he cites the second-generation Ukrainian Myron Masnik, twenty-five-year-old leader of the Institute Prosvita Choir in Winnipeg, as saying, 'If we could ask for anything at all, it would be just to fit in' (304).

The apparent contradiction between the 'mosaic' ideology of the importance of protecting and maintaining cultural difference and these latter citations of the immigrant's desire to assimilate should remind us of the way in which the slipperiness between moral character and race functions to define a civility that can retain its image of courtesy at the same time as it excludes those who will not or cannot accommodate themselves to the codes of White civility. The instances Gibbon provides, for example, imply their negative interpretations: a young Ruthenian who refuses to learn English or a Ukrainian choir leader who does not want to fit in can fairly be rejected from full citizenship on the basis of their having chosen themselves not to agree to the terms of modernization and progress. Such people would be choosing to retain outmoded Old World allegiances over adaptation and education. In this way, Gibbon's image of the mosaic presents the trope of cultural difference as a value but retains the value system of White civility as the 'cement' in which the various tiles of the mosaic are embedded. As Gibbon writes in the conclusion to his volume, 'Whether Time, the artist, will ever design and create a masterpiece out of the Canadian scene remains for a mythical judge in some remote future to decide. All we can do today is to collect and separate and perhaps ourselves fabricate the tesserae or little slaps of colour required for what that artist seems to have in mind as a mosaic ... One contribution we can deliberately make is to discover, analyze and perfect the cements which may best hold the coloured slabs in position' (413). And he concludes, 'The finest and strongest cement for the Canadian Mosaic is the training provided in Canadian schools. This catches the children of the newcomers when their minds readily accept the life and thought of the country which their parents have chosen for their home' (425). In the end, then, the tiles of Gibbon's Canadian mosaic may represent a range of cultural differences, but they all come from Europe and they are all embedded in white cement.

Gibbon's and Woodsworth's books both identify the welcome of White, European immigrants, prioritized by their perceived assimilability, a criterion that shuttles conveniently between moral character and race, as the demonstrated proof of Canadian maturity. They both, along with Connor and Grove, assume a White border for the civil hierarchy that characterizes the Canadian nation. One major and striking difference between their books, however, is the status they assign to French-speaking people. Because Woodsworth's book aims at an investigation of immigration and outlines its hierarchy of Canadian peoples under that rubric, francophones get literally one page of comment in the book, and this page is restricted solely to French and Belgian immigrants, who, we are told, are readily absorbed by francophone Canada. The assumption seems to be that, because British Canadians have taken on the administration of westward occupation and settlement, they must carry on with the task of assimilating the majority of the new immigrants. The French Canadians of such settlements as St Boniface, Manitoba, St Albert, Alberta, and Gravelburg, Saskatchewan, must look after the few French immigrants brave enough to pioneer in the predominantly anglophone West, just as Ukrainian or Mennonite settlers must look after later Ukrainian and Mennonite arrivals. For Woodsworth, this seems to be the end of the problem and therefore the end of the story, but because Gibbon uses the concept of the mosaic to organize his book, he is not limited to first-generation immigrants and must narrate a history of the French in Canada, just as he does for the English, Scottish, Finnish, and all the other ethnic groups. This difference between the two books is significant in that it offers an early example of how the concept of mosaic (as with multiculturalism later on) absorbs French Canada into its common list of Canada's ethnic and racial groups.

Gibbon's chapter on the French is very much oriented towards a demonstration of English Canadian civility by means of a historical narrative of generous treatment of French difference under British rule.

He argues, for example, that British Canadians should not be blamed for the expulsion of the Acadians because that vicious measure was carried out by New Englanders: the order was given by William Shirley, governor of Massachusetts, and the deportation was carried out by Lieutenant-Colonel John Winslow, who used transports from Boston (32). This deflection of blame to New England suggests that, already in the 1750s, the separate paths of American aggression and Canadian civility were discernible, even though all the North American colonies were still administered by a common British colonial system of governance. Gibbon goes on to elaborate on British Canadian magnanimity towards the conquered people of New France when he quotes General Amherst's instructions to British soldiers to treat the French populace humanely during the conquest of Quebec (33) and Bishop Briand's famous *mandemant*, issued at Quebec on 22 May 1778, which urged French Canadians to show their gratitude for being able to keep their language and religion by siding with the British against the American revolutionaries (35).

Gibbon's representation of the conquest of New France by the British as a blessing in disguise is a staple of English Canadian representations of the history of English-French relations in Canada. Daniel Francis traces it to the wide influence of Francis Parkman's series of historical volumes *France and England in America*, published between 1865 and 1892 (94). This reading of British liberality towards French Canadians has remained popular, despite many dissenting voices that go back to the period when Parkman's histories first popularized it. Henri Bourassa, for example, argued in 'The French-Canadian in the British Empire' (1902) that French Canadians need not feel beholden to British civility for the protection of church and cultural privileges under British rule (58), because the protection of these rights was self-serving in that it enabled the British government to keep French Canadians from being tempted to join the American rebels in 1776 and in 1812 (62–3). Nonetheless, the notion of disinterested British civility towards the French continues to recur in representations of Canadian political history. For example, the *Report of the Special Joint Committee on a Renewed Canada* (1992) refers to the Quebec Act of 1774 and to the Royal Proclamation of 1763, which granted certain land rights to Native people in the West, as 'cornerstones of early Canadian life' that set the tone for the Canadian civility which has expressed itself in the commitment to social programs and the tolerance of diversity that have characterized Canada ever since (qtd. in Mackey 24).

This theme of British rule as a blessing in disguise is a repeated feature of popular novels about the Conquest such as Philippe-Joseph Aubert de Gaspé's much-translated *Les Anciens Canadiens* (1863), William Kirby's *The Golden Dog* (1877), and Gilbert Parker's *The Seats of the Mighty* (1896). Indeed, the narrative of the Conquest made ready material for popular, national romance not only because of the high drama of the famed Battle of the Plains of Abraham in 1759 and the French assault on Quebec in 1760, but also because it could so readily be used to demonstrate how the maturation story of Canada depended on the civility represented by British law and order in relation to French Canadians. Born in Quebec City in 1786, de Gaspé was perfectly situated to write his novel about the British conquest of New France. He was descended from an aristocratic Quebec family with a seigneury at Saint-Jean-Port-Joli, and he studied law under Jonathan Sewell, the chief justice of Lower Canada. The earliest of the three Conquest novels I have mentioned, de Gaspé's was immensely and immediately popular not only among French Canadians because the septuagenarian author could recall a rich archive of family stories to convey a detailed account of life in New France under the seigneurial system, but also among English-speaking Canadians because it allegorized a reconciliation between French and British brothers in the relationship between the novel's two representatives of the younger generation: Jules d'Haberville and Archibald Cameron of Lochiell.[13] The maturation of these two schoolmates into officers on opposite sides of the battle for New France and eventually back into reconciled brotherhood represents the process, for de Gaspé, by which former antagonists can be reunified as a family.

There are two main points that I want to emphasize about this process of forgiveness and unification. It is important to recognize, first, that the civil relations necessary for reconciliation are managed through the 'Auld Alliance' between French and Scottish Catholics, rather than directly with what the novel calls the 'English,' and second, that this alliance is realized in the colonies and therefore marks out a set of civil relations which are distinct from Old World relations. This move deploys the figure of the Scot as a way to emphasize the point that British civility as developed in the colonies is distinguishable from Englishness. Archie Cameron's father was among the Highlanders killed at Culloden, and his mother was a French Catholic. This heritage explains why his Jesuit uncle in France removed the orphan from Scotland and found a place for him in a colonial Catholic college in Quebec, where he met Jules and, through him, the d'Haberville household, who become his surrogate family. Archie's complex Scottish history allows de Gaspé to recognize and applaud a form of British civility without appearing to capitulate completely to English rule.[14] It enables him to show that Lieutenant Archibald Cameron would never have burned down the houses of his childhood friends and neighbours in New France had his hand not been forced to these inhuman acts by his English superior officer, Major Montgomery. Indeed, de Gaspé has Archie warn the French inhabitants of the homes all along the proposed route of attack so that they can save as much as possible before his troops arrive with the firebrands (153). By portraying the Scots as fellow sufferers under the domination of the English – at one point the character Dumais explains to an Abenaki named Big-Otter that 'the Scotsmen are the redskins of the English' (165)[15] – and by using the Scottish Archie to represent the Britishers who stay on after the Conquest to settle in Canada, de Gaspé makes it possible for the devastated d'Habervilles to retain a semblance of dignity when they are reconciled with this representative of the new British regime.

Indeed, de Gaspé's text reveals a great deal of anxiety to defend the dignity of the defeated people of New France. Rather than simply narrating the now-mythical Battle of the Plains of Abraham in which both Montcalm and Wolfe were killed, as many of the English-language versions of the national story have done, de Gaspé spends considerable time describing the assault of 1760 in which the outnumbered French retook the city, only to have an 'indifferent Louis XV' cede it back to the English three years later (180). Thus, 'like the wicked step-mother in the fable, the motherland had abandoned her Canadian children' (150). The French Canadians have nothing to be embarrassed about in de Gaspé's version of these events, for they more than proved their courage and loyalty in defending New France, and they have since proven their valour in fighting under England's flag in the American war – all the while maintaining 'their national heritage for more than a century' (152). Thus, de Gaspé concludes, 'I, for one, am far from thinking that all is lost. On the contrary, we may have benefited from the cession of Canada, for the [anti-religious, anti-aristocratic French] Revolution of '93 with all its horrors barely touched this fortunate colony, then under the protection of the British flag' (151). So, even if the romance between Blanche d'Haberville and Archie Cameron is never consummated, nonetheless Archie is welcomed back into the bosom of the d'Haberville family, and Jules marries an Englishwoman (247), having taken the oath of allegiance to the British crown with his father's blessing (213). De

Gaspé's text, then, combines a number of the discourses of national formation that I have traced throughout this book: it uses the Loyalist allegory of fraternity to portray the maturation story of two Canadian brothers, makes one of them French and the other not English but Scottish, and shows how they go through trials by fire that distance them from their European ancestral lands and how, by this process, they acquire the status property and maturity of character that qualify them to become the founders of a new civil order in the nation that is emerging from its colonial dependency.

Rather than organizing his novel around the allegory of a maturing fraternity as de Gaspé does, Gilbert Parker uses a romantic triangle to allegorize French, British, and French Canadian relations in *The Seats of the Mighty: Being the Memoirs of Captain Robert Moray, Sometime an Officer in the Virginia Regiment and Afterwards of Amherst's Regiment* (1896). The twenty-three volumes of Ontario-born Sir Gilbert Parker's mostly romantic and adventure fiction set in the Canadian Northwest, picturesque rural Quebec, and heroic New France were written during his rise from an ordained deacon in the Anglican church in Ontario to a popular journalist in Australia and the South Pacific and eventually to a knighthood (1902), baronetcy (1915), and membership in the Privy Council (1916) in London. Parker's novels were popular worldwide, including Canada, where his books appeared eight times among the top ten bestsellers between 1899 and 1918 (Vipond's 1979 appendix), and none was more popular than *The Seats of the Mighty*, which, like de Gaspé's novel of the Conquest, relies on the Auld Alliance between Scots and French to explain why French Canadians would choose British civility over French corruption. In Parker's text, this choice is figured in the preference of Alixe Duvarney, the young French Canadian heroine, for the plain and high-minded virtues of British sincerity, represented by the Scottish Robert Moray, over the mercurial and spectacular charms of Parisian sophistication, represented by the cynical Tinoir Doltaire. (Parker explains that for this character he simply replaced the initial letter in Voltaire's name [ix].) Parker's novel occupies the same gothic terrain William Kirby's *The Golden Dog* does, not just in its setting during the corrupt end times of Intendant François Bigot's 'La Friponne' in Quebec but also in the whole apparatus of dungeons, hermetical convents, secret passages in palaces, alcoves in cathedrals, and madwomen who speak garbled prophecies.[16] The story takes place during the late 1750s leading up to the Battle of the Plains of Abraham in 1759, and it details the corruption that made the British victory at Quebec a relief to the honest habitants.

Before the narrative present of the novel, Robert Moray's adoptive parent, Sir John Godric, had served Bonnie Prince Charlie in the '45 and retired to France after the defeat at Culloden. When Godric died, he passed on lands in Virginia and a packet of letters to Robert. These letters were written by a Parisian noblewoman to Prince Charlie and they compromise her. Doltaire, the bastard son of the king and a peasant woman, is in league with La Pompadour ('La Grande Marquise'), who wishes to oust this unnamed noblewoman as a rival influence with Louis XV. Operating on behalf of La Grande Marquise, Doltaire demanded the letters from Robert when the latter was captured by the French in a battle in Ohio, and when Robert refused to give them up, Doltaire spirited him away to Quebec. At first, Robert lived under house arrest at the home of Seigneur Duvarney, where he and Alixe fell in love, but at the beginning of the novel, he is taken away to the dungeons at the Citadel, where he will await trial as a spy. Most of the novel consists of Robert's adversities in prison, where Doltaire continually tries to wear down his high-minded refusal to give over the letters. One of Doltaire's tactics is to pay court to Alixe, whose interest in Robert he surmises. She soon realizes that she must feign disinterest in Robert and pretend to just enough interest in Doltaire's suit to be able to bring about better conditions for Robert in prison. She does this brilliantly, but as her intrigue gets more risqué, she grows concerned about the corruption of her own integrity as she plays Doltaire at his own deceptive game. She enjoys the power of influencing important matters of state through wielding her sexual and intellectual attractions, but she prefers the image of herself as a pure, innocent woman. Nonetheless, she manages to negotiate this difficult position and successfully resists Doltaire's very powerful arguments to abandon the marriage she and Robert had sealed while the latter was prison. Robert finally escapes and manages to sail down the St Lawrence in time to join General Wolfe's and Admiral Saunder's assault on Quebec. In fact, it is Robert who shows Wolfe the all-important route up the cliffs to the Plains of Abraham that gives Wolfe the victory. After years of imprisonment and many desperate scenes in prison, in drawing-room intrigue, in riotous debauchery at Bigot's infamous palace, and in pitched battle, Robert and Alixe are finally peacefully reunited, and the British flag flies high over Quebec.

That the love triangle represents an allegory of French-British rivalry over New France is made explicit several times in the novel. In his introduction to the 1913 Imperial Edition of the novel, Parker declared that the novel 'has crystallized some elements in the life of the continent of America, the history of France and England, and of the British

Empire' (ix), and at a point late in the novel, Robert reflects that now that Alixe's marriage to him is publicly known among the populace of Quebec and she is being made an object of hatred, even being pressured by the Catholic bishop to annul the marriage, their union has become 'a national matter – of race and religion' (316). Alixe's attractions to Doltaire's dashing intrigue and to Robert's plain-style sincerity (not to mention her own erotic enjoyment of power) give the allegorical narrative its plot tension. Will Quebec prefer corrupt, urbane French rule or honest, single-minded British power? Again, as with de Gaspé, the Auld Alliance between Scots and French Canadians allows a dignified union between representatives of the British and the French that bypasses the hegemony of Englishness and also distinguishes New World civility based on plain-speaking honesty from Old World artifice and dissimulation. Alixe's final choice of Robert over Doltaire signals that French Canada may be temporarily enticed by the urban sophistication of the corrupt Parisian, but in the end her fundamental honesty and practicality cause her to prefer the Scot.

The masculine rivalry between Doltaire and Moray is expressed not only through their competition for Alixe's affections but also through their homosocially charged, running debate over the nature of civility. Indeed, this ongoing debate is a major part of Doltaire's cat-and-mouse game with Robert; as Alixe once puts it, 'Monsieur Doltaire and Captain Moray ... either hate each other lovingly, or love hatefully, I know not which, they are so biting, yet so friendly to each other's cleverness' (90). In this loving, hateful debate, Robert insists that the essential sign of a great man is 'Mercy' (195) – and the novel is at pains to show that he proves his greatness several times by acts of mercy to his French enemies – while Doltaire sneers at this sentimental view and argues that the strongest survive and some deaths must be allowed on the road to great deeds (196). Whereas Robert heroically refuses the offer of freedom in exchange for the incriminating letters in his possession on the grounds that such an act would constitute a betrayal not only of his own integrity but also of British political relations with France, Doltaire has no loyalty to such lofty ideals and insists instead, 'Expediency, monsieur, expediency is the real wisdom, the true master of the world' (142). The cynical pragmatist goes on to declare his own philosophy: 'Be heartless, be perfect with heavenly artifice ... and you may rule at Versailles or Quebec' (151). Doltaire may be handsome in a darkly Byronic fashion, but there is no real competition here. Alixe is shown by Parker to make the only realistic choice possible when she chooses to marry the civil, high-minded Scot.

In figuring the national allegory in *The Seats of the Mighty* as a woman's process of maturation when she is forced to choose between the societies represented by these two contrasting men, Parker may be seen to have reversed the gender order that usually places men at the centre of the process of maturation and allows women only supporting or peripheral roles.[17] I do not wish to deny the much larger role Alixe plays in this novel as compared with the females in any of the other novels I discuss in this chapter, but I would argue that this variation of the maturation narrative still figures the realm of choices in decidedly masculine terms. The entire plot derives from international conflict played out on the basis of women's sexuality and its uses: Robert's possession of the noblewoman's letters to Prince Charlie and Doltaire's campaign to purloin them (76–7). Alixe must decide between the homosocial rivals: expediency-only Doltaire and merciful Moray. She calls herself 'one weak girl ... matched against powerful and evil men' (119), and though she confesses that she enjoyed the game of dissimulation by which she outwitted Doltaire and that she loves power (163), like the heroine of most gothic sensation novels, this moment of female excess and agency is contained by the ideology of romance. She confesses to Robert that God has protected her from being seduced by her own enjoyment of power and intrigue by putting 'something here – she placed her hand upon her heart – "that saves me"' (163). For, when it comes down to her French Canadian heart, like Robert, she too is a decent, conservative, loyal person whose love for her Scottish suitor overwhelms the blandishments of cynical intrigue. John Murray Gibbon could have been describing Alixe's final decision when he wrote in *The Canadian Mosaic*: 'If there is one characteristic of the [French Canadian], it is the respect for tradition ... The Church has encouraged him to be a believer in authority, and his instinct is to be conservative and thrifty' (22, 24). The future of the nation lies with such practical and salt-of-the-earth goodness. The habitants, by contrast with the intrigue-ridden upper class, are represented as simple, honest folk. Says Doltaire in one of his few sincere moments: 'These are they ... who will save the earth one day, for they are like it, kin to it' (49). Alixe aligns herself with these humble virtues and by so doing, demonstrates the kind of measured, sober maturity that makes her an appropriate partner for the plain-speaking Robert Moray. The novel leaves us with the idea that their union will guarantee the restoration of a civil society from an abused and dissolute one.

Neither Parker's nor de Gaspé's novel about the Conquest gives any significant role to Indigenous people, and those who do appear in these texts function largely as foils to set off the characteristics of White characters and practices.[18] As in Gibbon and Woodsworth, these novels assume that the 'Canadian race of the future is being superimposed on the original native Indian races' (Gibbon vii), who represent civilization's 'prehistory,' as in Gibbon's Cro-Magnon man. The makers of the allegory of manly maturation, like Connor in regard to Mackenzie in *The Foreigner,* assume that Natives will simply disappear with the advent of modernity. Even Charles Mair, praised by Pauline Johnson for his 'Indian-loving pen' (3), expressed this view in 'An Appreciation,' printed in Johnson's *The Moccasin Maker* (1913): 'In our history the Indians hold an honoured place ... They had to yield but before quitting the stage, they left behind them an abiding memory and undying tradition' (qtd. in Monkman 98). Mair's elegiac mode here is typical and revealing of the stratagem of White civility, which ennobles and mollifies a history of brutality and bad faith by representing the Natives' yielding of the national stage as a grand series of *tableaux vivants* in which earlier players are replaced in succeeding scenes by later ones. As we saw in the remarkable story of the Aitkow valley stone, the process of memorializing the vanishing race – Mair's 'abiding memory and undying tradition' – places Native people firmly in the past so that the posthumous process of ennobling can be carried out by sympathetic Whites on their behalf.[19] In his outline of the economy of Indigenous representations that recur in White texts in Australia, Canada, and New Zealand, Terry Goldie observes that Aboriginal figures are often associated with 'orality' and thus with the 'pre-history' that must give way before White writing (151). This positioning of the Native in prehistory accomplishes two objectives at once: it frees White writers to take up the role of memorialization (and thus to indigenize themselves by means of the imaginative intimacy with Native ways that memorialization is presumed to authenticate), and it also disqualifies living Aboriginal people from being authentically Native. As Goldie points out, the contemporary Indigenous person can never match up to the idealized image of the prehistoric Native and so is presented through such ubiquitous stereotypes as drunkenness or prostitution, which chart how far he or she has degenerated from the noble original (168). Dramatically descended from the impossible nobility of a figure such as Mair's Tecumseh, the contemporary Native person is degraded into a 'social problem' (155). What may appear as sympathy for Indigenous people, therefore, often represents what Margery Fee has called a 'literary land claim' (17–18) insofar as the apparently civil act of memorialization premises itself upon a claim of intimacy with Natives who are figured as approaching the verge of extinction, leaving their memorializers to inherit their words and land.

But Natives did not disappear. Despite devastating pandemics caused by European diseases for which their bodies had not developed immunities and despite being made invisible to the majority of the White population and to some extent to themselves by the reserve and residential school systems, First Nations people in Canada survived. And their survival, their undeniable contemporaneous existence, continues to haunt the disavowing narratives of the White civil nation. It is revealing to trace, therefore, how popular novels of the early twentieth century dealt with their continued presence, for after the near-universal assumption of Native disappearance that we have witnessed in late nineteenth- and early twentieth-century texts by Connor, de Gaspé, and Parker, what Deputy Minister of Indian Affairs Duncan Campbell Scott called the 'Indian problem' seems to re-emerge in the 1920s and 1930s with the increased uncertainty that the First World War and the Great Depression introduced to the national dogma of civilization's progress.

Published fifteen years after Frederick Niven had emigrated from Scotland to live near Nelson, British Columbia, and based on several journalistic trips the adventure-fiction writer had made to the Canadian West before emigrating, *The Flying Years* (1935) was the first of three novels by Niven that span the years of western Canadian settlement (the other two in the trilogy were *Mine Inheritance*, 1940, and *The Transplanted*, 1944). This diffuse novel provides a kind of historical panorama of the prairie region's development between 1850 and 1920, from the end of the fur-trade system to the restriction of Plains First Nations to reserves, and from the early settlement of refugees from the Highland clearances among the Red River Métis to the emergence of Calgary as a centre of industrial and commercial power. The narrative follows the life of Angus Munro, who emigrates at the start of the novel from Loch Brennan after the clearances and who passes through a series of representative careers: he starts off as a young apprentice to a Hudson's Bay Company riverboat builder and later travels to Scotland in search of investors for Canadian coal mines and transportation companies; next he returns to the Jasper area as a fur trader, before taking up a position as transportation company manager in Calgary; he finishes his working life as an Indian agent on a Cree reserve in central Alberta. Over all these years, Angus's life is juxtaposed with that of his fellow Scottish immigrant, Sam Lovat Douglas. Whereas Angus feels great ambivalence over the changes caused by the development of the West, Sam is its uninhibited and tireless promoter. Sam, who moves from transport company founder to owner of coal mines and insurance companies to eventually become Sir Sam, jokingly suggests that what keeps Angus from leaping up the ladder of success is his 'Indian kink.' Sam means this phrase to refer to Angus's constant sympathy for Native peoples and the way the development of the prairies has sidelined if not harmed them (e.g., Niven includes a scene in which Angus witnesses the decimation of a Cree village by smallpox), but Sam does not realize that he has put his finger on Angus's secret pathology, a pathology that the allegorical structure of the novel figures as generally representative in this story of the prairies' social, political, and economic maturation.

Early on in his life in Canada and unknown to Sam, Angus had married a bilingual Cree woman named Minota in Rocky Mountain House.[20] They had maintained a fairly open relationship in which she was free to accompany her people when they went on hunting trips and he was free to return to Scotland with Sam to promote investments in Canadian industry. But Angus's stay in Scotland had extended to four years, during which time he received news that Minota had died of measles. Many years after his return to the Canadian west, Angus drives a wagon of supplies for Sam from Calgary to the meeting place where Captain Macleod of the NWMP has gathered the chiefs of the Blackfeet, Stoneys, Bloods, Sarcees, and Crees for the signing of Treaty 7. Here Angus meets a young Cree named All Alone who is wearing the collet ring he gave Minota before leaving for Scotland all those years ago. Because Angus knows Cree, he learns from the boy's adoptive father that All Alone is likely his son – a surprise, since he had not known Minota was pregnant when they parted. Angus says nothing to the young man about his paternity, and the years pass. Angus marries Fiona Fraser and takes a job as Indian agent at the High Butte reserve. It turns out that this is where his son, All Alone, lives, though Angus never tells anyone, not even Fiona, about his past marriage to Minota or about his son. All Alone has a drinking problem and almost loses his wife over it, but Angus's gentle guidance as Indian agent plays a major role in reforming his unacknowledged son. Meanwhile, Angus and Fiona have a boy of their own, Daniel, who grows up to be a doctor and is eventually killed in military service in the First World War. By the time Angus retires from the agency, the Crees all love him, and he has seen All Alone's children – his own unacknowledged grandchildren – grow up to be 'promising' people: Louise trains as a nurse, and Angus (named after the White 'father' who has been such an excellent Indian agent for the reserve but who is still not known to be his grandfather) is a pilot who is going to McGill to become a doctor. So Angus Munro approaches the end of his life regretting the loss of the old free-range days of the West, fond of his memories of Minota, glad for his cheerful Scottish-descended wife, Fiona, who predeceases him, and proud of his good work as Indian agent and as secret grandfather of successfully assimilated Crees.

Niven's story of Angus Munro and the maturation of western Canada is intimately tied up, however, with the secret of what Sam called his Indian kink. Although Minota does represent the sexual temptation that Goldie says is ubiquitous to White representations of Indigenous figures, particularly women, her early death ensures that she does not become the stereotype that Goldie calls the 'squaw,' whose sexual temptations represent negative indigenization and the destructive takeover of the White soul; instead, she becomes what he calls a sacrificial 'maiden,' a memorial to missed opportunity, to Angus's failure to embrace the 'optimism that the land holds, the potential of a positive indigenization' (72). Whatever missed opportunity Angus's intimacy with Minota may have produced in the abstract, in the literal world of sexual reproduction it produces disavowed mixed-race children, and so it is significant that, true to the overall structure of disavowal in the book, the Northwest Uprising and Riel's hanging are passed over in this historical novel in just one sentence (197). For, despite Niven's boldly taking up the central pathology of the settler-invader nation when he addresses the displacement and disavowal of Indigenous peoples at the beginning of the prairies' narrative of development, his novel is motored by a problem that is never addressed directly. The Crees survive and must be attended to, but Angus Munro is never brought to any proactive measure: he never tells All Alone that he is his son, and he never tells his mixed-race grandchildren about his relationship to them. He thinks 'if only' he had not left Minota in the first place (143), and he remains sceptical of the modernization being hurried onto the prairies by his friend Sam Douglas, but he denies his children's and grandchildren's membership in a publicly recognized family. In the end, then, although Niven's text addresses the contemporaneous existence of Natives in Canada, it offers no real development of the problem: Angus's Indian secret becomes a matter of his own nostalgia and resigns Natives once again to prehistory. So contemporary Aboriginals such as All Alone struggle with alcoholism or become postcard Indians, or else, like his grandchildren Louise and Angus, they assimilate themselves as best they can to whiteness.

Surprisingly perhaps, Ralph Connor – whose *Corporal Cameron* (1912) and *The Patrol of the Sundance Trail* (1914), along with *The Foreigner*, present virulently racist depictions of Native savagery and the necessary doom of Indigenous ways of life – also wrote a novel that attempted to address head-on the issues left secret in Niven's book.[21] In *The Gaspards of Pine Croft* (1923), Connor addresses the fact of mixed-racedness directly, but what is revealing about this address is that it remains directed to White, middle-class readers to reinvigorate their commitment to the demonstration of White British civility, and it does not address the Métis (or 'half-breeds,' as the children of Scottish-Native parents were called) as an existing, let alone potential, society.[22] Like most of Connor's novels, this book, which ranked fifth on the Canadian best-seller list in 1925 (Vipond, 1986, 102), is a romantic bildungsroman that clearly allegorizes the maturation story of the ideal Canadian citizen in the figure of the male protagonist of the book, Paul Gaspard. His father, Hugh Gaspard, of mixed Scottish and French ancestry, leaves his Glasgow home and settles on Pine Croft ranch in the Windermere Valley between Golden and Crow's Nest Pass in British Columbia. He has a saintly, anemic Scottish wife named Marion (whose earlier loss of a baby seems to have stolen her will to live) and a lively boy named Paul, who shares his father's artistic energy and intuitions. But Hugh is not a man of strong character: despite his artistic talents, he never finishes his paintings, nor does he complete his brilliant off-the-cuff piano compositions. Connor ascribes this lack of discipline to his mixed ancestry: 'From both strains he drew his fiery, passionate, imaginative temperament, his incapacity, too, for the hard grind in life' (8).

This inherited lack of self-discipline develops more damning ramifications when he has a child by a Chipewyan woman named Onawata while he is away on a hunting expedition in the Athabasca country. When Onawata comes to Pine Croft to seek out her baby's father, Marion learns of the child and dies of the shock. Right from the start, then, *The Gaspards of Pine Croft*, as Terrence Craig points out, 'is a novel about miscegenation, and not just about the Métis in the West but about the whole concept of mixed races in the world' ('Religious' 104). He goes on to add that 'Gordon's attitude to [mixed-race people] is best described as a distortion of polygenic theory, a distortion made much of by white-supremacist propagandists of the times, who insisted that, when two so-called races are mixed, the product is innately inferior to both originals, physically, intellectually, and sometimes even morally' ('Religious' 105).[23] In a move that should be by now familiar to critics of racist rhetoric, Connor generalizes this distorted polygenic doctrine in such a way that it is not represented as the belief of White supremacists alone. He has the Chipewyans show themselves to be just as horrified by the mixing of races as are Whites. We are told that Onawata's father, Chief Wah-na-ta-hi-ta, 'Proud of his race and rank, ... had kept his tribe aloof from the life and manners of the white man. He had seen the degradation of other tribes through contact with white civilization and, following the tradition of his ancestors, he had built up in his people a fear of the white man's power and a contempt for his vices ... He permitted no mingling of blood strains in his tribe, no half-breed could find a home in his wigwams' (50–1). So miscegenation is presented as a universal taboo and not specifically a defensive code employed by British Whites. Nonetheless, Connor reveals a certain lack of conviction in the theory of polygenic degeneration when he applies it unevenly between humans and animals. At one point, we read that Hugh Gaspard has been developing a superior strain of horses by breeding Indian ponies with Arabian sires and that Paul's much-admired pinto, Joseph, represents the success of this experiment (74).

I draw attention to this detail because it demonstrates the consistent belief in this novel and in popular Canadian discourse of the period, regardless of inconsistent applications of the theory of polygenic degeneration, that progress and development were understood to involve the careful management of the borders of sexuality and species or race and that the wise and charitable management of this charged border constituted a mature civility. Connor's didactic point in the novel is to censure representatives of the local elite such as Mrs Augusta Pelham for allowing a combination of racism and sexual prudery to overwhelm the charity and kindness that should mark truly Christian responses to Hugh and his mixed-race family. Despite this creditable pedagogy, however, the novel censures bigotry without questioning either the taboo of miscegenation that subtends bigotry, or the doctrine of Natives as a waning race that lies at its root. According to the logic of early twentieth-century eugenics, miscegenation was taboo because it prolonged a problem that otherwise would take care of itself; that is to say, if Natives were a waning race, then sexual reproduction with Natives prolonged the pain of their extinction by mixing the blood strains of the ascendant races with that of waning ones. This condensation of sexuality, race, and nationalism, as Valverde explains, gave impetus to the eugenics-informed social purity movement that had such widespread influence in the nationalist rhetoric of social reformers in the opening decades of the twentieth century. For first-wave feminists, temperance activists, and political progressives alike, 'Reproduction and nurturing constituted the link between women and the race; since women's nurturing ... was perceived as involving the reproduction not of human beings in general but of their race in particular' (60–1). Kalman, in *The Foreigner,* can marry the daughter of a Scottish railway baron because the marriage is understood to reproduce White British Canadians, but Hugh's interracial marriage with Onawata will not produce White British Canadians.

The colour line drawn in terms of miscegenation and sexuality replicates exactly the line drawn by Woodsworth and Gibbon in terms of assimilability and culture. 'Some peoples may not intermarry,' Woodsworth writes. 'The Mongolians, the Hindus, and the negroes will probably remain largely distinct ... But in time most of these peoples will intermarry – Slavs and Celts, Latins and Germans, Hungarian and Semitic peoples, in varying combinations and proportions' (181). He does not explain why the latter may and the former may not intermarry; likely, the obvious but unspoken colour line was self-explanatory. In the case of Indigenous people such as Onawata, Connor's novel suggests that their inevitable demise is only prolonged and complicated by intermarriage. Halfway into the novel, Hugh is killed during a struggle when the novel's villain, Sleeman, attempts to sexually assault Onawata. Subsequent to her White husband's death, we are told, 'It seemed as if her loneliness and grief were driving her away from the newer environment of the White man's civilisation and back to the ancient racial and primeval precincts of her own people' (161). The implication is that the a priori doom that hangs over the Indigenous person means that intermarriage does not invigorate the primeval race through its contact with the advanced, but that the downward pull of the declining race is irresistible. In a telling, literal application of degeneration theory, Tannawita, the second child of Hugh and Onawata, is born blind. The novel suggests that noble Chipewyans like Wah-na-ta-hi-ta and his daughter would gradually die off as their wilderness home gives way to modernization. The production of mixed-race children imports, as it were, the waning genes into the upcoming generation, leaving that generation to deal with the burden of the weak and dependent half-race that was heedlessly produced by White irresponsibility, a point that is underscored by the narrator's repeated reminder that the problem of what to do with the mixed-race children was Hugh's problem before it was Onawata's (31, 37).

The allegorical structure of this bildungsroman, then, goes on to show how the re-establishment of mature civility (recall the constant need to repeat the performance of maturity) falls upon the shoulders of the next generation. After the death of his mother, Marion, and the ashamed flight of his father, Hugh, into the wilderness with his Chipewyan family, the boy Paul Gaspard is raised in the English home of Colonel and Mrs Pelham. In contrast to his father's dissolute behaviour, Paul maintains the strict self-discipline he learned from his mother. He never skips his piano practices or catechism lessons, even when other children tempt him to go out and play. When his father returns after three years of vagabondage, the young boy learns of his father's adultery and witnesses the self-indulgent life that Hugh takes up at the Pine Croft ranch. (We are to understand that Hugh's inability to forgive himself for his treachery to his Scottish wife has made him cynical about being able to live a moral life, of course leaving him with no resources with which to resist the temptations of alcohol, gambling, and lassitude.) Being the responsible, other-oriented person that he is, Paul decides he must leave the Pelhams and go back to Pine Croft to try to influence his father for the better. For Mrs Pelham and others in the valley, this is a scandalous decision, because the pure Paul will be associated not only with his father's dissipated ways but also with his mixed-race half-siblings, and, in her words, they will 'drag him down.' Some months after Hugh's death in the struggle with Sleeman, Sleeman tries to assault Onawata again, and she stabs him and burns down his house. Despite Colonel Pelham's warning that he need not mix himself up with this affair, Paul joins Onawata and her two children in the resulting six-year flight from the police.

The book then skips the intervening years, during which Paul lives in the bush with her and her Chipewyan relatives. The plot picks up again when Paul, an exhausted and dying Onawata, and the children are caught in a blizzard on a dogsled trip toward Fort Reliance, far up on the Yukon River. She is suffering from an undisclosed ailment – overexertion? starvation? sorrow? dying-race theory? It is impossible to tell, and the six-year gap conveniently sidesteps the necessity of explanation. Eventually the beleaguered family makes it to the fort, where they encounter a NWMP officer who explains that Sleeman survived; so there is no murder charge waiting for Onawata. She dies soon after, having received Paul's promise that he will look after his half-siblings, Peter and Tannawita.

It is important to note that, despite the six years among the Chipewyans, Onawata does not want Paul to become Indigenous. When she is on her death bed, she tells him that Peter and Tanna can go back to her tribe and he should go back to his people: 'I bring the son of my man back to his people,' she tells Paul and the listening policeman. 'He is not Indian, and he must not join himself to my people. I have kept him clean. He will be great among his own people' (203). Paul, however, as representative of the new generation of mature and progressive White men, rejects this rigid separation of the races. He insists that Peter and Tanna are his father's children, despite her saying, 'You do not know what you say. They are of my blood. They will be a burden on you. They will spoil your life. Your father, Paul, did not wish that, I know ... They will drag you down as I dragged your father down' (206). But he replies, 'They are my father's children. They are my brother and sister,' and he alludes to Tanna's blindness and the possibility of getting treatment for her in the White world (206). Onawata is clearly pleased with this response – indeed, the reader is meant to see that she had not dared to hope for this possibility (207). Paul's willingness to commit himself to looking after his half-brother and half-sister does not deny Onawata's warning that they will drag him down; in fact, the measure of his heroism, the sign of his extraordinary civility – especially if we compare it to Angus Munro's suppression of the secret of his relationship to All Alone – is that Paul is willing to take on such an obviously onerous duty.

This story of how the younger generation Canadian must redeem the faults of the older generation in relation to First Nations people occupies only the first two-thirds of the novel. If the novel were to conclude here, we would have the theme of White civility demonstrated by its representatives' willingness to own up to the sins of the earlier generation (i.e., irresponsibility as ultimately signalled by miscegenation) and to commit themselves to manfully taking on the liabilities created by that generation. The paradigm in which the demonstration of civility took place would be strictly racialized in the sense that responsibility and maturity would be figured by a return to proper management of the (sexual) borders of race. But as in *The Foreigner*, where Connor insists that not only Ukrainian immigrants but also dissipated Englishmen must mature into progressive, Christian Canadians, here too he does not allow the theme of maturation and responsibility to remain solely a question of the pathological relationship to Indigenous people. For in the last third of the novel, Paul sets about the redemption of two degenerated White, English Canadians. After leaving Peter and Tanna in the care of good missionary teachers at Fort Reliance (twenty-first-century readers must suppress what they know about the abuses common in residential schools if they are to go along with the plot's assumptions here), Paul reluctantly leaves his ranching, mountain life and goes to Vancouver, where he hopes to make enough money to pay off his father's gambling debts to Sleeman and to train as an engineer.

Very quickly, his rock-solid integrity and muscular Christianity get him a partnership in Tussock, Gaspard and Dalton because he rescues Tussock and Dalton from their alcoholism and degeneracy. Tussock is a gifted construction boss who repeatedly gambles away his fortunes, and Dalton is a drunken, unemployed lawyer. They both need a friend and a 'keeper' – someone who can guard them from their vices. Paul has no problem distracting them from bars and gambling joints by busying them in the establishment of their construction business and in volunteer work at the local downtown mission.

This section of the book widens the central theme of the novel: the White Canadian man of the future is indeed his brother's keeper, whether Métis, Native, or degenerate White. Marvelling at how his life had turned around under Paul's management, Tussock declares that Paul is 'a man, straight grained and white to the core' (266). As Craig explains, 'The word "white" had a meaning in the novels of Gordon, Gibbon, and Stead beyond colour. To call a man "white" was to praise him as a fair and honest man of integrity. Their use of the word implied that Britons had a monopoly on such virtues and that such behaviour could hardly be expected of non-whites' (*Racial* 47). Roy Daniells further specifies the barely masked ethnocentrism of this concept of 'white' when he writes that Connor's narrow Scottish Calvinist concept of excellence means that others (Irish, Americans, English, Methodists, Baptists, and Roman Catholics) are not denigrated in his novels; they just fail to measure up to Presbyterian Calvinist standards ('Glengarry' 21). Paul's manliness and his whiteness, therefore, are proven by his muscular Christian capacity to lift up others to this high moral (and ethnic) ground. Tussock and Dalton agree that all their previous friends have 'helped them down' rather than up. What they need instead is 'something to work at, something worth working for, and, yes, more than anything else, a friend to climb up with. We both want a keeper' (271). It is symbolically significant that the company of Tussock, Gaspard and Dalton is a *construction* company, for the maturity of Paul's White manliness ties into one dense ideological bundle the values of self-discipline, improved character, meaningful enterprise, and responsibility for others that together ensure the build-up of Connor's ideal community. The allegory of the maturing colonial son, as in *The Foreigner, Strangers within Our Gates,* and *The Canadian Mosaic,* conveys the virtues of White civility, not just by showing how its representatives bravely take on the responsibilities of offering a helping hand to those lower down on the scale of civilizations but also by policing and shoring up its own flagging and

wayward members – by providing them with a 'keeper.' The company of
Tussock, Gaspard and Dalton quickly makes plenty of money; so Paul
can go back to Pine Croft with Dalton as legal adviser to pay out
Sleeman. When he gets there, he meets his childhood girlfriend, Peg
Pelham, and their old mutual attraction rekindles instantly, despite her
family's arrangement to have her engaged to Guy Laughton, the son of
one of the colonel's old, English soldier friends.

The concluding scene of the novel returns to a final demonstration of
Paul's mature civility, for in the dinner at the Pelhams' house he proudly
proclaims his connection to his Chipewyan stepmother, much to the
shock of Laughton and the embarrassment of the Pelhams. The dinner
conversation turns to Paul's years among the Chipewyans, and the dinner guests are troubled by his defence of the dignity of their culture and
religion. 'It is not our religion,' he says, 'but I would say [it is] a real
religion, with very noble elements in it. They believe in and worship a
supreme spirit whose favour they seek and whom they strive to obey ...
Yes, we call them pagan, but I often wondered what God would call some
of them. For some of them, those who really practise their religion, are
good men' (306). In this conversation, the upper-class and generally
disdainful-of-colonials Guy Laughton makes the classic move that liberals often make when they wish to discredit another race or culture: he
says he has heard that Natives treat their women badly, as beasts of
burden. This pseudo-feminist assertion really functions as a form of
White racial bonding whereby Whites can reaffirm the superiority
of their civilization. But Paul will have none of it, and he insists: 'They
treat their women pretty much as my ancestors and yours treated their
women a few generations ago' (307). So Aboriginals may be delayed, but
they are not inherently inferior or hopelessly pagan. The progressive
Reverend Fraser then enters the fray by describing the treatment of
women – 'painted women, poor unhappy creatures that they are!' – that
he witnessed in pagan London and grieves these signs of degeneration at
the heart of empire (307–8). Ironically, the conversation is set up as a
rivalry between men over a woman – between Paul and Laughton over
Peg – and Paul proves his moral superiority to the English gentleman by
refusing to denigrate First Nations people as savages and by instead
identifying boldly and publicly with his Chipewyan stepmother (309).
Mrs Augusta Pelham still thinks Paul's family members are 'horrid connections,' but Peg, representative of the new generation of Canadians
who are unfettered by these old class-based racial biases, gladly and
proudly associates herself with him and them, and rejects Laughton as a

suitor (313). The novel therefore presents a younger generation who face squarely the racialized problems created by the older colonial generation, and through defending the nobility of the assumedly waning race of Natives and through identifying with and attempting to assimilate the mixed-race children who survive, they demonstrate that they and their civil order are 'straight-grained and white to the core.'

Following Anne McClintock's reminder that 'nations are not phantasmagoria of the mind but are historical practices through which social difference is both invented and performed' (353), my argument in this chapter has been that the Canadian story of the maturing colonial son is a social practice which produces demonstrations of White civility by means of elaborate engagements with racial, ethnic, and cultural difference. This nation-making allegory repeatedly represents ethnic-minority immigrants, French Canadians, and Indigenous people, not as beings for themselves or in order to inform readers about the circumstances of their lives, but as demonstrations of White British civility. The performative element of the injunction to repeatedly recite these instances of White civility makes the allegory of maturation an endlessly deferred narrative, for the need to produce strangers at the borders of White civility means that the demonstrations of civility – the welcoming of these strangers into full belonging, the process of lifting up weaker or backward people, the bestowing of benefits upon the needy – must be constantly re-enacted, and thus no sooner is one stranger incorporated than another one must be invented. Far from undermining the power of this allegory, this structural contradiction makes it endlessly productive and creative, for it constantly reinvents others whose neediness will draw forth the civility of the nation that is the evidence of its ongoing maturation.

I have examined the development of the allegory of manly maturation during the period of Canadian expansion into the prairies because it came to such prominence in public discourse at that time, and I have traced it in the works of popular writers such as Woodsworth, Gibbon, Niven, de Gaspé, Parker, and Connor in order to show how wide its appeal was. But the problem with examining the allegory in these popular (rather than high-culture) writers is that it can allow later critics to dismiss the continued power of these ideas after these authors fall out of the public limelight. Take the example of Ralph Connor, the most widely read of all early twentieth-century Canadian writers, whom critics have overwhelmingly consigned to the dustbin of the past. Roy Daniells, for instance, restricts his relevance to the 'four or five decades following Confederation' ('Glengarry' 24), while the Thompsons say that, because immigrants and French Canadians retained their cultures and demonstrated the unworkable nature of the monoculturalism that Connor's works envisioned, his popularity faded early on (169). Frank Watt insists that his version of the Canadian West 'was already passing as he wrote about it' (10), while John Lennox flatly asserts that Connor's books are 'signposts of a Canada that no longer exists' (149).[24] In more general terms, historians, too, have suggested a variety of dates for the death of the British connection and the idea of Canada as inheriting the mantle of British imperial civility. Berger says that the First World War and French Canadian resentment over conscription wrote the epitaph for the predominance of Britishness represented by Canadian imperialism (*Sense* 264), and Owram concludes that British Ontarian optimism over expansion into the West, and the associated idea of Canada as stepping in to take over the reins of the British Empire, faded after the economic depression between 1883 and 1890 disappointed central Canadian investors' hopes (220).

But other critics suggest later dates for the devolution of Anglophilia and the predominance of the imperial connection in Canada. Francis, for example, sees Canadian worship of the imperial connection enjoying cult status in school textbooks and curricula into the 1950s (53), and he stresses that this cult promoted the idea of Canada's role in the larger empire as being a leader in 'spreading justice, freedom, and prosperity around the world' (63). Isabelle Bassett argues against the prematurity of Berger's death certificate for Canadian imperialism by referring to the residual forms of imperialism that she traces in the post-1918 writings of Connor and even of Hugh MacLennan in *Barometer Rising* (1941). She points out that Neil McRae's identification in MacLennan's novel of Canada's new civilizing mission as mediator of conflicts between Europe and America translates the allegory of maturation from the paradigm of empire into that of post-war international politics, but that its function remains the same: to demonstrate the maturity of Canadian civilization ('Transformation' 59, 62).

And indeed, there are many other examples of the persistence of the allegory of maturation throughout Canadian nationalist discourse. In a 1988 article, Lorraine Weir examines the way in which a gentlemanly discourse of civility has so overdetermined literary histories of Canada written by a wide range of Canadian critics from Lorne Pierce, J.D. Logan, and Donald French to Desmond Pacey, Carl Klinck, and W.J. Keith, whose values of moderation, unselfconsciousness, and judiciousness meant that experimental, radical, and female writers went without

much notice in their narratives of the development of Canadian literature. (Her focus in the article is not on the linkages of the discourse of
civility to whiteness or issues of race.) She observes that this discourse of
literary civility tends to use a 'lexicon of maturation' which imagines a
single narrative of growth or development for Canadian literature, and
she warns scholars about the dangers of falling into the evolutionary
narrative and its illusions of movement and progress even in their
critiques of it (24–5). Her warning is well taken, for a major sign of the
residual power of the trope of maturation can be seen in the resurgence
of the allegory even in the writings of those who strongly oppose its
linkages with the demonstration of White, British, masculine civility. I
have already traced its usage in Grove's 1920s speeches to the Canadian
Clubs, which contested British claims to superiority, but it recurs also in
the early Ukrainian Canadian writer Vera Lysenko's rebuttal of dismissive attitudes towards 'non-Anglo-Saxons' in her 1947 book *Men in Sheepskin Coats*: 'Canadian culture as such will not come of age until it
embraces in its entirety the manifold life of all the national groups which
constitute its entity' (qtd. in Craig, *Racial* 76). The allegory even appears
in the anti-racist writing of Terrence Craig, upon which I have relied
heavily throughout this chapter, when he suggests that 'with the acceptance of refugee contingents such as the Ugandan Asians and Vietnamese boat people [in the mid-1970s], Canadians achieved a new level of
international maturity' (*Racial* 18).

The discourse of Canada's maturity continues to this day to be premised upon the extension of civil treatment to non-White strangers. And
the comparison to inferior American practices remains ubiquitous in
these representations of Canadian civility. Eva Mackey refers to *Land,
Spirit, Power: First Nations at the National Gallery of Canada*, an exhibition of
Indigenous art organized by Indigenous curators, and to the response to
the exhibition by James Luna, a US Native artist, to the effect that 'in
comparison to Canadian Natives who are very visible,' US Natives are still
at the bottom of the political and social heap. 'Certainly ... there hasn't
been anything like this show – anything of this scope – in the US, so it
helps confirm the view that your Natives are much further ahead' (qtd.
in Mackey 87). Mackey's gloss on this statement reveals how the allegory
of maturation invades even the most progressive forms of anti-racist
criticism: 'Canadian nationalism can appropriate Aboriginal people's
hybridity and self-representation into its own redemption of its sins; in
this redemption, crimes against Native people become conveniently
located in the *past* ... This celebration of Canadian tolerance, and how

far *Canada has come* by celebrating how far the nation has *let "them" come*, erases the difficult questions of how far the nation still needs to go in order to have genuine justice and equality for Aboriginal people' (87, emphasis in original). The teleology of the nation in the phrase 'how far the nation still needs to go' echoes the allegory of maturation and its injunction to the repeated, and therefore endlessly deferred, performance of its civility as demonstrated by reference to its non-White, non-British others. Donna Palmateer Pennee observes that Canada's image of itself as a colony that has developed into a postcolonial nation depends on demonstrating its progressive relation to the chronology of modernity, and that it does so by linking its cultural expressions to the concepts of development, independence, and mature relations with other nation states (87). She illustrates the way in which this campaign for Canadian legitimacy desires an external stamp of approval by citing the 1995 statement of the federal government entitled *Canada in the World*, which claims that 'one of the clearest international expressions of *Canadian values and culture* [is] Canadians' desire to help the less fortunate' (qtd. in Pennee 89; emphasis in original). Pennee comments that this 'rhetoric of maturity' allows Canada to self-identify between centre and periphery (i.e., privileged and underprivileged countries) in external affairs and to minimize modernity's inequities within the domestic (i.e., national) sphere (91).

These examples, then, show that the allegory of maturation cannot be relegated to a long-eclipsed and embarrassing past and that it remains a staple of English Canadian discourse. Although the contexts of its expression may have changed dramatically over the years of the twentieth century, and although the overtly racist elements of its early usage may have been modified, nonetheless the concept of national maturation is repeatedly demonstrated by the civility of its largely British and male elite towards others, who usually are figured as either ethnic- or racial-minority immigrants, French Canadians, or First Nations people.

6 Wry Civility

My argument throughout this book has been that English Canadian whiteness has been modelled upon a specific form of British civility, a form of Britishness that is a uniquely settler-colonial project, and that this British-inflected White civility was formulated and popularized by means of (at least) four ubiquitous allegorical figures in late-nineteenth- and early-twentieth-century Canadian writing: the Loyalist brother, the Scottish orphan, the muscular Christian, and the maturing colonial son. There is a danger in this kind of genealogical argument that my efforts to demonstrate the predominance of these norms and assumptions can make them appear to be universal, as if all Canadians equally and unequivocally ascribed to the values represented by White British civility. A brief examination of several Canadian literary texts that criticized or rejected the claims of White British civility, however, can serve to remind us of the contestatory and uneven, rather than single-voiced, nature of public discourse. In these texts' critical engagement with White civility, we can discern the lineaments of what I call wry civility.

Carl Berger has already done this kind of counter-discursive work when he lists Goldwin Smith's *In the Court of History: An Apology for Canadians Who Were Opposed to the South African War* (1902), John S. Ewart's *The Kingdom of Canada* (1908) and *The Kingdom Papers* (1912), Henri Bourassa's *Great Britain and Canada* (1902), and O.D. Skelton's *Life and Letters of Sir Wilfrid Laurier* (1921) as examples of statements by influential Canadians who opposed the kind of pro-British thinking which fuelled the Canadian imperial federation movement. Literary texts, however, tend not to present these kinds of counter-arguments in the oppositional terms used in the non-fictional texts Berger cites. Instead, they often launch their criticism from within the discourses themselves. For example, ironical texts such as John Marlyn's *Under the Ribs of Death* (1957), Sara Jeannette Duncan's *The Imperialist* (1904), and James De Mille's *Strange Manuscript Found in a Copper Cylinder* (1888) present ironic engagements with the kinds of dominant ideals I have been tracing throughout this book and therefore remind us that some Canadians at least, across the whole period of this study, questioned these ideals. Furthermore, the referential nature of these ironical texts, which must identify a widely recognizable target for their mockery if readers are to comprehend their critical intent, affirm my argument that these values and ideals were indeed predominant in Canadian public awareness. If they had not been perceived by the authors to have considerable social power, they would not have been worthy of satire or critique. In this sense, then, irony, which is a form of double speech, allows us to make both of these opposite-facing observations at once.

I should add, too, that I will discuss these texts in reverse order to their publication dates in order to resist the assumptions of post-Enlightenment modernity that envision civility as progress from ancient primitivism to sophistication and civilization. This evolutionary assumption persists in English Canadian literary criticism, which tends to construct a maturation narrative for the nation's literature that imagines crude and parochial romance giving way to modern and realist complexity and eventually to the multi-perspectival sophistication of the 'posts': postmodernism, poststructuralism, and postcolonialism.[1] By arguing for an increasing sophistication and perspicacity in these three ironical texts as we proceed *backwards in time*, I mean to resist the presentist hubris which assumes a narrative of progress that would place ourselves at the pinnacle of critical insight and sophistication.[2] My strategy to close with irony has another rationale, too. Throughout this book I have examined the pedagogical function of allegorical figures to naturalize abstract concepts of the nation by linking them to familiar, domestic life. I have tried to show that this is the political project of national allegory: to conflate the heterogeneity of the nation's diversity into homogeneous, readily comprehensible figures. But, as Paul de Man and Ross Chambers have observed, irony, while closely related to allegory's method of double-speaking, denaturalizes the tropic structure by emphasizing the artificiality and inadequacy of the comparison in the first place.[3] In this sense, irony is the deconstructive shadow that haunts allegory; it is the ever-present noise of disarticulation in the project of national articulation.

I referred briefly in chapter 3 to John Marlyn's *Under the Ribs of Death* and to the protagonist Sandor Hunyadi's conflation of the Scottish pipers with the 'English,' whose privileged status makes the twelve-year-old boy insist that 'the only people who count are the English. Their fathers got all the best jobs. They're the only ones nobody ever calls foreigners. Nobody ever makes fun of their names or calls them "bologny-eaters" [*sic*], or laughs at the way they dress or talk ... 'cause when you're English it's the same as bein' Canadian' (17–18). Sandor's repeated and discouraging repulsions from the ethnocentric fortress of middle-class British Canadian privilege make Marlyn's novel a counter-discursive answer to Ralph Connor's *The Foreigner* in the way it so clearly echoes but also twists the maturation story of the immigrant boy in Winnipeg who rises in social status as he gradually assimilates to (British) Canadian ways. In fact, Marlyn, who grew up the child of Hungarian immigrants in Winnipeg's North End, seems to have a writer such as Connor in mind when he breaks the novel's plot into two halves at the protagonist's encounter with a novel of sentimental morality and ready redemption reminiscent of Connor. From earliest youth, Marlyn's Sandor Hunyadi, the counterpart here to Connor's Kalman Kalmar, has determined to distance himself from his poor Hungarian family on Henry Avenue and carve out for himself a place among the genteel homes and sumptuous offices of Winnipeg's business class. Throughout the book, Sandor maintains a running disagreement with his father over what constitutes a successful life. His father is an idealist who loves the social philosophies of the great European humanists, whereas Sandor is a materialist who directs every creative thought toward the accumulation of wealth and status.

The novel opens in 1913 and places Sandor's adolescence in the years leading into the First World War, when the rise in Canadian nativist discrimination against those whose ethnic backgrounds associated them with the Austro-Hungarian Empire branded them as enemy aliens and as many as 8,579 males were eventually interned (Brown and Cook 376n50). In Sandor's experience, this prejudice is embodied in a gang of English boys who give him regular beatings after school. The second part of the novel skips to 1924, when Sandor has anglicized his name to Alex Hunter and achieved modest success as a slumlord over his childhood neighbours on Henry Avenue. This part leads up to the stock market crash of 1929 – the great ironic leveller that undermines the entire illusion of the maturation narrative of the nation's collective progress – when Alex's fortunes are completely crushed, along with those of his British Canadian business associates. He is then forced to return to Winnipeg's North End and a recognition of his need for and dependence upon the Hungarian family he rejected.

These two parts of the novel are marked off from each other by young Sandor's reading of a book that could as easily have been written by Connor as by Horatio Alger.[4] The book contains the moral melodrama of a poor young orphan (it does not say whether or not he is Scottish) in desperate need of work who restores the lost wallet of a rich business-man. His honesty pays off, and he is given a place in the rich man's firm. Through hard work and night-school classes in self-improvement, the young entrepreneur turns this opportunity into a business partnership and marriage to his boss's niece. When Sandor finishes reading the novel, we are told, 'He stood there filled with wonder that there should be such a book, giving him back his own dream, his own secret longings that had stirred within him so long.' He reflects, 'The great ones in this book were the doers, the men of wealth and power, the men who counted, whose words people listened to. And one had only to work hard and devote oneself whole-heartedly to the things they believed in, to become one of them' (126). And so, as Julie Beddoes observes, Sandor becomes a subject-in-process, 'reading the various texts that are at the same time writing him as subject' (9). In portraying his protago-nist as the dupe of melodramatic texts of assimilation, and then in showing how the whole fantasy of commercially secured status is under-mined by the Great Depression, Marlyn pokes a pin in the sentimental dream of immigrant assimilation, unhindered class mobility, and the allegory of maturation.

He shows how Sandor cannot live out the beautiful vision a writer such as Connor popularized throughout Canada. Whereas Connor's immi-grant hero, Kalman, is rescued by the missionary lady from having to negotiate his manhood in the fierce underworld dominated by the landlord, Sandor's own efforts to move from marginalized to empow-ered masculinity are rebuffed at every turn. Finally, he decides that the only way to achieve his ambitions is to apprentice himself to Nagy, the parallel character to Connor's Rosenblatt and the slumlord of *Under the Ribs of Death*. Marlyn is careful to point out how Sandor is sidelined into this complicitous form of masculinity by the ethnocentric protectionism of Winnipeg's British upper class. As an aspiring young entrepreneur, Sandor, now Alex Hunter, has an interview with Mr Atkinson, manager of the significantly named Imperial Crown Investments company, situ-ated in the city's business centre at the intersection of Portage Avenue and Main Street. Alex's confidence in his application, however, is crushed when he realizes that Atkinson has no interest at all in his business skills. Instead, the man's questions are aimed entirely at finding out who Alex's people are so that he can ascertain his placement in Winnipeg's vertical mosaic. When Alex reluctantly confesses that his parents are Hungarians from the North End, the door to employment at the British-owned company abruptly closes.[5] Instead of meeting with the benevolence of Jack French, Reverend Brown, and Margaret French as Kalman does, Alex encounters only courteous rejection from the likes of Atkinson.

Marlyn therefore exposes the naïveté of Connor's romance of assimilation not only by showing how British Canadians do not behave like mature, muscular Christians – they do not take on the responsibility of welcoming the strangers within their gates – but also by setting the novel between two historical events, the First World War and the Great Depression, which Berger says finally shattered the imperialist optimism that subtended the national maturity allegory. John Roberts points out that Marlyn uses the stock market crash to implode the myth of Canada as a place of limitless economic opportunities and to expose the ruthless essence of its capitalist culture (41), while Latham Hunter argues that Sandor consistently has his hopes of inclusion betrayed in a series of potential but failed 'brotherhoods': the Henry Avenue immigrant boys' gang, the English gang at school, the humanist 'brotherhood of man' that his father believes in, and the brotherhood of British Canadian businessmen who keep him always on their margins (106). Through these historical and social betrayals, Marlyn's novel shows how 'real' civil relations defied the allegory of maturation, with its peculiar Canadian mix of high-mindedness and ambition, hospitality and ethnocentrism, diversity and masculinist monologism. More specifically, Marlyn's novel shows how Britishness itself is the flaw in Canadian civility; rather than functioning as the pan-ethnic sign of the civil as English-speaking Canadians liked to assume, Britishness operates in this novel as a fortress, an impervious social echelon that keeps people considered enemy aliens, such as Sandor, in their inferior positions in the vertical mosaic. Ironically, however – and this is why I have emphasized the necessity of a wry approach to the genealogy of civility – in the very exercise of Marlyn's exposure of the illusions in the Connor-style romance of immigrant assimilation, the two books share a very similar ethical purpose, albeit from opposite ends: both novels argue for the desirability of a civil reception of immigrants, Connor by means of idealistic romance and Marlyn by ironic exposure of the failure of that romance. They generally agree on this central principle of reception and accommodation as constitutive of civility, but their different historical and cultural positions, the Scottish Presbyterian Connor writing early in the history of prairie immigration and settlement and the second-generation Hungarian Marlyn writing after the main period of settlement, cause them to evaluate the realization of that civility very differently. Marlyn departs from Connor in refusing Britishness as the sign of the civility they both value.

In a sense, *Under the Ribs of Death* deploys what we might call a simple irony, for it is a situational irony that reveals by one-to-one contrast that an ideal has not been realized in the real world. The target of the irony is readily identifiable – Sandor's naive belief in the social mobility that is possible within British Canadian civility – and therefore the moral of the story, the irony's pedagogical intent, is also fairly clear: Canadians should live up to the kind of civility on which they pride themselves by hospitably welcoming the strangers at the nation's gates. In this sense, the novel fulfills the modernist mandate of its time: its ironic recognition of the discontinuities of the world come together in a coherent aesthetic-ethical resolution.[6] The next two texts that I will discuss, however, involve much more complicated kinds of irony, ones that identify an array of targets for their irony and entail such complex narrative positions that critics have made veritable industries out of trying to determine their intent.

Of the three novels that I discuss in this closing chapter, Sara Jeannette Duncan's *The Imperialist* engages most completely and directly with all of the main elements of British Canadian White civility that I have traced throughout this book. It takes up the question of imperial federation as it is championed by a young, enterprising, optimistic, Scottish Canadian (though not an orphan this time), whose role in the text is explicitly marked as representing the young and vigorous ambitions of the Canadian nation, conscious of its youth (and belatedness) on the international stage and desirous of coming into its maturity by means of a reinvented but loyal relationship with its English colonial parent (despite his Scottish ancestry, Lorne Murchison consistently uses 'England' to refer to Canada's Old World heritage). As compared with the fairly straightforward intentions of Marlyn's irony, Duncan's are something of a puzzle.[7] On the one hand, she indulges an affection for her hero, who, as far as we can tell from Duncan's own statements of support for the imperial federation movement, seems to carry forward the author's views on the desirability of forging a new and dynamic empire between Britain and its former colonies. On the other hand, her representation of her hero's political and romantic naïveté and the failure of his campaign, 'broken,' as she herself predicted while she was still writing the novel, 'on the wheel of economic fact,' mocks the impracticality of his ideals.[8] Like Marlyn's irony, Duncan's records the obstruction of idealism by reality, but whereas Marlyn's irony marks a distance between the author's and the (pathetic) hero's views, Duncan's affection for her idealistic hero (and his even more idealistic sister in the novel's subplot) troubles readers' certitude about the author's critical intentions.

Lorne Murchison, the imperialist of the title, grows up in a well-established, middle-class family in Elgin, Ontario, a small manufacturing town based on Brantford, Ontario, where Duncan was born. The story opens around 1880 and concludes in 1903, during the middle of the debate around imperial federation, which Thomas Tausky says was the leading political topic of the Edwardian era, both in Britain and in Canada ('Writing' 334). Although the Imperial Federation League had been formed in London in 1884, the issue came to a crisis at the beginning of the twentieth century when American financier J. Pierpont Morgan purchased so many shipping companies that he controlled almost all transatlantic shipping other than the English Cunard line and the Canadian Allan line. This prospect raised British and Canadian fears to the extent that in June 1902 the British government gave a subsidy of £150,000 to the Cunard line (Tausky, 'Writing' 333). On 15 May 1903 Joseph Chamberlain (fictionalized as 'Wallingham' in the novel) made a dramatic speech calling for preferential trade between Britain and its former colonies despite the fact that this position was not the official policy of the Cabinet, in which he was a member. By September both Chamberlain and his opponents had resigned from Cabinet, and eventually the Conservative government of which he had been a part lost the next election by a wide margin; 'but for months Chamberlain's vision of a united Empire looked like a potential reality rather than a mirage' (Tausky, 'Writing' 334). On the Canadian side, the Laurier government, which had initially pushed for imperial unity, remained passive, insisting this was a matter England had to resolve internally, a position that Tausky says would have frustrated Duncan to no end, since affirmation from Canada might have helped Chamberlain tremendously. This bold espousal of the imperial idea is the stance she therefore has Lorne Murchison make, to his own detriment, towards the end of the novel. Tausky notes that when *The Imperialist* began its serialization on 3 October 1903, the imperial question was still in the balance ('Writing' 335). Misao Dean adds that ever since the American Revolutionary War, the value of the empire had been questioned in Britain and that the debate often divided between economic and moral reasons (i.e., empire as a civilizing mission) for maintaining it. The imperial federationists argued both rationalizations, but tended to downplay the economic ones and to emphasize the moral ones. Duncan, as a federationist, has her hero locate 'the ideals of Empire in the "human product" of British culture, the heroic individual who is able to see beyond self-interest and the narrow application of formulas towards the final end of mutual help and trust among peoples' (Dean, *Different* 109). As Lorne himself puts it, 'They didn't grow so fast in England, to begin with, and now they're rich with character and strong with conduct and hoary with ideals ... They've developed the finest human product there is, the cleanest, the most disinterested, and we want to keep up the relationship' (110). As a true federationist, Lorne leads a campaign that uses the movement for an economic union to promote what he considers to be a superior civil arrangement.

Although this background helps us to see how the novel was a serious engagement with lively politics of the day, the story itself reads like a comedy of manners whose narrator takes an arch but indulgent tone towards the provincialism of the town's characters. These include the Presbyterian Scots family of the Murchisons, their tenacious minister, Dr Drummond, his junior, Mr Finlay, who pursues a spiritualized love relationship with Advena Murchison, and the Milburn family, who stubbornly protect their business interests and their Tory-Anglican upperclass status. Much of the novel's main plot has to do with the debate over imperial federation and the idealism that runs through Canadian political history over ties with the 'British motherland,' especially the higher function of these ties to form a moral bulwark against American-style free-market commerce, which, ironically, is what runs the political machine in Elgin, despite the high-flown rhetoric. 'It is a fact, or perhaps a parable,' quips the ironic narrator, 'that should be interesting to political economists, the adaptability of Canadian feet to American shoes' (144). The sanitized myth of loyalty subtends the imperial idea in the sense that the Scottish Canadian hero is presented as more loyal to the fundamental values of a British constitutional monarchy that oversees a society protected to some degree from the ravages of unimpeded capitalism than are many English colonials, who readily sell out this morally integrous tradition for immediate economic opportunities. Octavius Milburn, the 'father of the Elgin boiler,' for example, represents the manufacturing interests in Canada, whose concern to keep out the tariff-free British products proposed by the imperial federationists makes them blind to Lorne's vision of the long-term benefits of loyalty – the possibility of an imperial economic alternative to American dominance that Lorne envisions.[9] As Clara Thomas has noted, 'There is nothing subtle about the racial aspect of Duncan's social mythology. In Canada she shows the Scotch and their offspring to be builders, men to usher in the future; the English are reactionary, cautious, conservative and ridiculously class-ridden in a society which sees itself as classless. In effect, Duncan polarizes the two racial strains to the point of substituting her own elite establishment, Scotch and Presbyterian, for the old colonial elitism of British and Anglican' (360).[10] Duncan's novel works very much in the tradition of the enterprising Scot, whose admirable character causes him to rise in social status and whose espousal of Britishness signals a progressive Canadian nationalism that rejects Old World sectionalism as well as New World (read American) commercialism. Because the novel is focused on this figure and its negotiation with political power, it neglects entirely, as Clara Thomas and Teresa Hubel have observed, any direct engagement with the working classes. Typical of the kind of Scottish humour that we can trace back to Thomas McCulloch and John Galt, the narrative sets up its hero as a kind of satirical norm by turning him into a target of affectionate mockery when his human failings and naïveté make him the dupe of much more scathingly satirized characters.

Lorne gets his early break in public life when a senior lawyer in his firm passes on a widely publicized case involving the son of the Indian agent on the nearby Moneida Reserve and Lorne successfully defends the young man. The prosecuting lawyer from Toronto, Henry Cruikshank, is impressed by Lorne's intelligence and oratorical skill and realizes he would be useful in the deputation of Canadian Chambers of Commerce he is taking to London to campaign for the 'Imperial Idea.' Lorne performs so well on the deputation that he gains his second lucky break, a nomination for the Liberal candidacy back home in Fox County. However, his youth (he is only twenty-eight) causes him to make the mistake of associating himself too fervently with the imperial idea, and so, despite their admiration for his high ideals, the county constituents' fear of the bottom line leaves them ambivalent, and he barely wins the seat in a traditionally Liberal riding. In a plot development that mirrors an actual election scandal in Brantford and about which I will have more to say presently, the election is contested by the Conservatives over alleged vote-rigging carried out on the Moneida Reserve, and Lorne is asked by the Liberal party organizers to step down, which he does. On the very same day, Richard Hesketh, the self-absorbed English friend

Lorne had invited back to Canada after the deputation to England, announces that he has become engaged to Dora Milburn, whom Lorne has been courting. The political and romantic plots are explicitly linked, not only in the narrator's observation that two illusions were crushed upon the same day (300) but also by means of the subplot of the novel, which traces the idealized relationship of Hugh Finlay, Presbyterian junior minister, and Lorne's intelligent and bookish sister Advena. After forming a fast (and unacknowledged romantic) friendship with Advena, Finlay announces that his aunt has arranged an engagement for him with a woman in Scotland. The two lovers bravely give each other up. Seeing that these two idealists are about to destroy their own happiness, Dr Drummond saves the day by stepping in and marrying the Scots fiancée after she arrives in Elgin, thus freeing the lovers to marry. In both the major plot and the subplot, the context of idealism and practicality is resolved in favour of practicality. We may admire the sincerity, good intentions, and high ideals of the imperialists and the romantic lovers, but when these ideals need to be acted upon in the real world, practical, material concerns rule the day.

Curiously, the novel's subsumption of imperial ideals to material practicalities ran contrary to Duncan's own instincts as she described them in a letter of 22 October 1902 to R.W. Gilder: 'Is it any wonder my sentiments are Imperial, with a husband in India, and a family in Canada and everybody else in England!' (309).[11] Duncan's clear affection for Lorne and Advena and her personal advocacy for imperial federation beg the question 'Why, then, should Duncan write a novel which, as most critics would have it, ran counter to the feelings which she so vehemently expressed in her non-fictional writing?' (Heble 405). First, I would argue that she was too good a writer to allow her personal views to determine the course of the novel; her accurate perception of the political conservatism of her Brantford childhood home made her aware of the passive strength that would resist the risky vision represented by imperial federation. Second, I agree with Janice Fiamengo, who reads the novel as an elegy, written under the cover of self-protective irony, for the higher ideals of the British connection, which Duncan realized were already being undermined by the economic pressures that would eventually destroy the imperial campaign ('"Susceptible"' 132). Read this way, *The Imperialist* constitutes an act of wry civility, one that anticipates George Grant's *Lament for a Nation,* Dennis Lee's *Civil Elegies,* and George Elliott Clarke's 'What Was Canada?' in its regret for the missed potential of Canada to take the best of what it had inherited from Britain – a Red

Tory suspicion of laissez-faire approaches to industrialization, free trade, and what George Grant later called technocracy – and to create in North America an alternative, more civil modernity than that which was emerging in the United States. Like Grant's, Lee's, and Clarke's texts, Duncan's mourns the failure of a distinctly Canadian form of civility, but in comparison to theirs, hers is presented, as Fiamengo suggests, by means of a self-protective, less-vulnerable authorial stance, since her irony allows her to expose the illusions of her characters and thereby to project an image of the author as too clever for such illusions, even though they were ones she cherished.

But the reach of irony in *The Imperialist* has not been as easily contained within the purview of the novel itself, or even within the possible range of Duncan's intentions, as this reading would suggest. For there has emerged of late among critics of the novel an awareness of a kind of 'post-textual' irony that I was originally tempted to call 'extra-textual' but for the fact that its referents were very deliberately included in the novel by Duncan. I refer to what she called, in a letter to her Canadian editor, her 'Indian anachronism.' In this letter to John Willison of 24 February 1904, after the novel had run in serial form in England and the United States and when she was anticipating that the bound version would appear in bookstalls within a few days, Duncan writes: 'The Indian anachronism I considered upon, but it is only a matter of a few years, and I was in the difficulty of either having to sacrifice the whole Imperial situation – as it is now – or my "Indian interest" neither of which I could make up my mind to do. So I left it' (Tauksy, ed. 309). Duncan's anachronism refers to her decision to extend Prime Minister John A. Macdonald's 1885 inclusion of Natives in the federal franchise into the 1903 imperial debates, even though the vote had been taken away from Natives by Prime Minister Wilfrid Laurier's Liberal government in 1898. It is important to observe that while many commentators on the novel explain the failure of Lorne's campaign for the Liberal seat in Fox County as resulting from his intemperate advocacy of the imperialist cause in his final opera-house speech, surprisingly few have noted that he actually *wins* the election. Admittedly, his ill-judged speech is blamed by the narrator and by the party organizers for reducing the margin by which Lorne should have won, but it is actually election fraud carried out by his own party supporters on the Moneida Reserve that loses him his seat when the Conservatives threaten an inquiry and Lorne's advisers counsel him to step down rather than risk a full-blown court case. To adapt Advena Murchison's dismissive phrasing, 'Indian evidence' (282), more than misguided fervency, is what finally blocks the rise of Duncan's beloved imperialist.

Malcolm Montgomery's article 'The Six Nations and the Macdonald Franchise' and Thomas Tausky's 'The Writing of *The Imperialist*' together show that the 'Indian anachronism' which Duncan alludes to in her letter to Willison refers to events that occurred on the Six Nations Reserve in the 1896 election but which she has transposed to the novel's present. In the spring of that year, the Conservatives were defeated for the first time in twenty years by Wilfrid Laurier's Liberals. In the riding of South Brant, however, William Paterson, a politician Duncan's Liberal family supported, who had held the seat for the Liberals since 1872, was defeated by 86 votes.[12] Because of the narrow margin, Conservative Robert Henry's victory was contested by the Liberals. 'In both cases [in 1896 and in the novel], Indian votes, allegedly gained through irregularities, were said to be responsible for the victories' (Tausky, 'Writing' 327). Henry had won at the two largely Native polling stations of Onondaga and Tuscarora on the Six Nations Reserve by 71 and 66 votes respectively (Montgomery 23; Tauksy, 'Writing' 327). The Liberals quickly mounted a protest that the Conservatives had bought votes on the reserve. The Liberal Brantford *Expositor* of 4 December 1896 reported that a backroom deal had been agreed upon between the two political parties so that charges would be dropped if Henry agreed to vacate the seat, while the Conservative Brantford *Courier* reported on the event under the headline 'Mr. Henry Unseated / On the Testimony of a Pagan Indian / Who Would Not Take the Oath, but Affirmed that he was Paid Money' (Tauksy, 'Writing' 329). Tausky says Duncan's representation of the situation has great accuracy, but 'her "Indian interest," as she chose to call it, may be regarded, not only as regrettably racist from a present-day perspective, but also as selective in its attempt to depict the realities of Indian voting patterns' ('Writing' 327).

Montgomery's research on changes in voting status for Natives in the late nineteenth century reveals that Natives had been given the federal vote in Sir John A. Macdonald's Electoral Franchise Act (1885), and that this move was opposed vociferously by the Liberals. He links the Liberals' racial panic to the fact that the act was first proposed four days before the beginning of the second Northwest Rebellion (Montgomery 15), but also observes that they were concerned that, since Indian agents were government appointees and Native people could therefore be manipulated by these agents' power to withhold treaty benefits or annuities, the granting of the franchise to Natives would simply be a scoop for

Conservative votes. This is the background for Squire Ormiston's all-important change of political parties in Duncan's novel from Conservative (he had been a member of the Family Compact) to Liberal after Lorne's successful defence of his son in court and Ormiston's accompanying promise to make sure the Liberals 'can count on Moneida too' in the upcoming election (195). Once they were in power, Laurier's Liberals moved in 1898 to remove the Native franchise – thus Duncan's need to apologize for her anachronism, since they would no longer have had federal voting rights at the beginning of the twentieth century during the imperial federation debates. Montgomery concludes his article by observing that First Nations people lost the franchise and it was not restored until 1960: 'The Indians had committed the crime of not voting the right way ... The punishment that the Indians received was that of being deprived of the right to vote for sixty-two years' (25). Tauksy, for his part, concludes with the following speculations about Duncan's motives for including the 'Indian anachronism': 'we can see Duncan as a loyal Liberal and friend of Paterson creating a fictional episode which presents Indian corruptibility in the darkest terms while conveniently ignoring the motive the Indian voters might have had for feeling ill-treated by the Liberals, as well as Liberal participation in bribery attempts' ('Writing' 330).

It is impossible from this distance in time to come to any certain understanding about how important it would have been for Duncan to defend Paterson in her work of fiction. Was it important enough to jeopardize the historical accuracy of the novel by inserting the 'Indian anachronism'? Was it important enough to seriously compromise the idealized image of moral probity that she has associated throughout the novel with Lorne and the imperial cause? For, given the long history of conflict between the Six Nations of the Grand River and the town of Brantford and, more generally, between Iroquoian (Haudenausanee) traditions of governance and federal franchise laws, 'Indian evidence' constitutes such a powerful indictment of the imperial paradigm of civility championed in the novel that for twenty-first-century readers it must surely constitute the most powerful and far-reaching irony of Duncan's novel, even if much of this evidence is not overtly presented in the novel itself. Although Jonathan Kertzer is right to suggest that 'the novel wages a campaign of rhetorical exclusion in order to build a nation that is native but not Native' ('Destiny' 21), Duncan's very deliberate decision to *include* the Indian anachronism in the novel, only to ignore its challenge to her overall imperial project, marks a dramatic instance

of the way the contradictory injunction of nationalist discourse to remember to forget its fantasmatic and traumatic history results in
moments when the repressed violence that is fundamental to the establishment of civility returns to disturb the calm waters of its surface.
Furthermore, it shows that disrupted or elided time is a key strategy for
this kind of determined ignorance. Natives are anachronistically and
literally brought forward in time in the novel, only to be shown to be
hopelessly out of time, primitive, and unprepared for full participation
in modern civil practices such as the democratic franchise. In the end,
anyway, their being moved forward and backward will not matter much,
for they will soon have all vanished anyway. As Duncan wrote in her
report on the unveiling of the monument to Joseph Brant, the Mohawk
leader who negotiated the settlement of the Six Nations on the Grand
River, in the *Week* of 21 October 1886, 'the time ... cannot be many
centuries away, when these people [the Six Nations] shall have vanished'
(qtd. in Higginson 170).

Although this reference to vanishing Natives may appear as a cliché of
settler-colonial writing, it is particularly revealing in the present instance.
For Montgomery's conclusion that the Six Nations were punished for
the 1896 election fraud by being deprived of the vote for more than half
a century completely misses the point that, for the Six Nations, uniquely
of all First Nations communities in Canada, enfranchisement represents
their social, spiritual, and political erasure. What Montgomery considers
a universal civil right and privilege – the right to vote in federal elections – was, for the Six Nations, a cultural threat. As leaders from Joseph
Brant in the late eighteenth century to Roberta Jamieson, elected band
council chief of the Six Nations in 2003, have insisted, members of the
Iroquois Confederacy (whose six constituent nations are Mohawk, Cayuga, Oneida, Onondaga, Tuscarora, and Seneca) fought as allies of the
British in the American Revolutionary War, and after the majority of
them were driven from their homelands in what is now upstate New York
by vengeful patriots, they were given lands along the Grand River in
British North America as a new home where they would re-establish
themselves according to their own traditions of governance, traditions
according to which candidates for chief were nominated by matriarchs
and then voted upon by the multinational members of the Confederacy.
For over two hundred years, and in defiance of several instances of
armed intervention from the Canadian government (in 1922, 1924, and
1959; see Dickason 344, Rick Monture 135, and 'Aboriginals' respectively), the Six Nations have insisted upon their status as allies, not

subjects, of the Crown. Indeed, consistent with this historical understanding of their status, many members of the Confederacy travel abroad
using their own passports (Dickason 346). Canadian enfranchisement,
then, constitutes a nefarious form of civilized invasion for members of
the Six Nations because it reduces them to the status of Canadian
subjects.[13] Duncan's novel, set in the years after governments had flip-
flopped over the enfranchisement of Aboriginal people, was an extremely disheartening time in Six Nations politics, as enfranchisement
threatened to extinguish their sovereignty, while exclusion from enfranchisement signalled a return to the general tendency to consider all
Indigenous people incapable of participating in democracy.

The conflict between the Six Nations and the Canadian government,
as I have rendered it here, tends to represent the Six Nations as standing
heroically united against the encroachments of Canadian cultural hubris. But the fact is that external pressures have produced disillusionments and divisions within the Confederacy. Right from the foundational
legislative acts that established the Canadian dominion and its relation
to First Nations, such as the British North America Act of 1867 and the
Indian Act of 1876, it became clear that Canada would depart from the
British policy of regarding the Haudenausanee as allies and consider
them instead as subjects (Rick Monture 121). Despite efforts by Iroquoian
leaders in the late nineteenth century to translate their oral codes of
governance (such as the Great Law of Peace and the Two Row Wam-
pum) into written English so they could be perceived by Europeans as
sophisticated instruments of governance (Rick Monture 133–4), and
despite a Six Nations petition in 1890 that Ottawa recognize their autonomy and exclude them from the Indian Act, their sovereignty was
consistently denied (Dickason 344). In 1895 the federal government
made on-reserve elections, instead of traditional hereditary chieftain-
ships, mandatory for most bands in Ontario, Quebec, and New Brunswick.
By 1899 the elective system was mandatory for all bands in these provinces as well as in Nova Scotia and Prince Edward Island. For some
Native groups whose forms of governance were less formal, this mandate
may have seemed less invasive, but for the Six Nations it constituted a
political takeover (Dickason 301).

So, at the point when Duncan composed her novel, the Six Nations
were simultaneously legally *required* to elect their own local band leaders
by the imposed Canadian system and *disqualified* from voting in federal
elections. The Iroquois entered a twenty-year struggle to maintain their
own Confederacy Council until 1924, when Duncan Campbell Scott,

deputy minister of Indian Affairs, ordered an armed RCMP detachment, commanded by C.E. Morgan, to forcibly remove the hereditary chiefs from the Council House and impose the government-mandated elective system (see Rick Monture for a detailed examination of these events and their consequences). Despite an appeal to the League of Nations by Deskeheh, a hereditary Cayuga chief, and despite the lament in the *Toronto Star Weekly*'s report of the forced closure, which mourned 'the official passing of the oldest continued parliamentary body on the American continent' (Rick Monture 135), the imposed elective system has remained in place ever since. The forced change did not obliterate the traditional leadership system, however; it only pushed the system underground, with the result that to this day some Six Nations people assent to the leadership of the government-approved and duly elected band council, and some remain loyal to the traditionally chosen hereditary chiefs, while others divide their loyalties between the two. Signs of continued resistance can be seen in the fact that the RCMP were sent once again in 1959 to evict traditional chiefs who had again seized control and had declared the reserve separate from Canada ('Aboriginals'), and evidence of the complex positions on the Six Nations can be seen in the fact that in 2003 Roberta Jamieson, elected and not hereditary chief of the Six Nations, attended a hearing of the House of Commons Standing Committee on Aboriginal Affairs on yet another proposed First Nations Governance Act, at which she insisted that Bill C-7 'is an effort to give legislative support to what has long been the Government's policy from the time of John A. Macdonald to today: do away with our governance, do away with our people, do away with our territories and lands. By taking control of our style of government, our selection of leadership, the government will be able to go on to impose its will as it wishes' (Jamieson).

   This brief survey of the struggles over enfranchisement constitutes an 'Indian evidence' that radically recontextualizes the election scandal in *The Imperialist*. Rather than going along with the Murchisons' assumption that the Moneida Reserve fraud consists simply of the manipulation of Indian drunkards, we can understand the Native participation in the 1896 scandal as at the very least the product of radical disillusionment in and even more likely as resistance against the enfranchisement process as a whole. Furthermore, the date I have mentioned above for the most recent removal of the hereditary chiefs from the council, 1959, alludes to another important connection to Duncan's novel, one that relates to the very land upon which the town of Brantford stands and in particular to the Market Square, which the novel portrays as its very centre. To understand this connection we must inquire back to the Halidmand deed of 1784, when the Six Nations were first granted approximately one million acres that spread six miles (for a total of twelve miles) from each of the two sides of the Grand River, from its mouth to its source (Jamieson; see also Dickason 164–5). Within five years, Joseph Brant, acting under the guidance of the Iroquois Confederacy Council (though some have debated with how much approval) and hoping to raise money with which the Six Nations could set about settling upon their new lands, had sold the northern half of the grant to buyers who never fully paid or sometimes acquired their purchases by suspicious means. For example, Rick Monture notes that Brant's signature has been found on purchases that were made up to five years after his death (see also Higginson 180n5).

Thus began a long history of the whittling away of the original reserve lands. The Six Nations lost 369 acres for towpaths, dams, and locks in the 1830s and 1840s when the lieutenant-governor expropriated $160,000 in band funds to purchase stocks in the short-lived Grand River Navigation Company, a river-improvement scheme that failed to compete with railway transportation systems (Dickason 214–15), and, more famously, they lost 807 acres in 1830 when these were purchased by the dominion for the townsite of Brantford. In this arrangement, three blocks of land, Alexandra Park, Victoria Park, and – most important for our purposes – the Market Square, were reserved for public use.[14] Nonetheless, the city council succeeded in 1958, over protests from the Six Nations, in the multi-million-dollar sale of the Market Square for commercial use (Higginson 146). I am not claiming that the sale of these lands was the sole cause for the attempt by the hereditary council to reassert its authority over the Six Nations a year later, but the conflicts with the town over land and the federal government's collusion with the town were certainly among them. Contested land acquisition, purchased by what the Haudenausanee consider an alien government for whom they have consistently refused to vote, constitutes an important part of the history of the Brantford Market Square (see illus. 16).

Given this history, one cannot help but perceive a powerful post-textual irony in Duncan's selection of the Market Square as a symbol of her hero's capacity to perceive the essential core not only of the people of Elgin but also of the British in Canada:

> Elgin market square, indeed, was the biography of Fox County, and, in little, the history of the whole Province. The heart of it was there, the enduring heart of the new country already old in acquiescence. It was the deep root of the race in the land, twisted and unlovely, but holding the promise of all.

16   Brantford Market Square, Market Day, 1899.

Something like that Lorne Murchison felt about it as he stood for a moment in the passage ... and looked across the road ... these were his people, this his lot as well as theirs ... He was as much aware of its potential significance as any one could be, and what leapt in his veins till he could have laughed aloud was the splendid conviction of resource ... A tenderness seized him for the farmers of Fox County, a throb of enthusiasm for the idea they represented ... At that moment his country came subjectively into his posses-sion; great and helpless it came into his inheritance as it comes into the inheritance of every man who can take it, by deed of imagination and energy and love. He held this microcosm of it, as one might say, in his hand and looked at it ardently. (81–2)

Neither Lorne Murchison nor Sara Jeannette Duncan could have known about the future sale of the Market Square in 1958, although controversy over ownership and use of the public lands in Brantford certainly existed during Duncan's youth there. The point of her intra-textual irony is that her hero sees perspicaciously and lovingly into the 'heart' of the country in the Elgin market place, and that it is this very heart – the fundamental commercial priority that no politician can ignore – that undermines his ideal vision for the people of Fox County. The post-textual irony, however, is that when Duncan's narrator identifies Elgin market square as 'the deep root of the race in the land, twisted and unlovely, but holding the promise of all,' she is saying much more than she knows. For the history of the Brantford Market Square is indeed twisted and unlovely, not just because the market represents what Lorne perceives as the struggle of White settlers against early poverty and difficult physical circumstances to produce a commercially viable society, but also because that struggle, bolstered by the 'splendid conviction of resource,' involved a struggle against other Loyalist settlers who had come from across the American border and who, too, were trying to establish a viable way of life along the Grand River in the new country of Canada. And the tragedy is that neither Lorne nor Duncan ever imagine, not for an instant, that these Iroquoian neighbours are allies who have resources of their own with which to contribute to the 'promise of all.' For if Duncan's novel is about the hope for and failure of political confederation, her characters and narrator ignore and denigrate right next door a confederation of Six Nations with a two-hundred-year history of political, economic, and military alliance (Kertzer, 'Destiny' 24), and if the novel's subplot charts the limited options available to Advena, a woman equally gifted as her brother, the novel takes no hints of how to construct a better way from the Haudenausanee system of matriarchally informed governance.

There are further post-textual ironies, too, for if the novel constitutes an elegy for the loss of a British connection for Canadians, and if it, like Marlyn's *Under the Ribs of Death,* uses the celebration of Victoria's birthday to introduce the importance of that British connection, then it is significant to note that members of the Six Nations Reserve continue to celebrate Victoria Day much more enthusiastically than Canada Day, for when they participate in the annual distribution of bread and cheese on Victoria Day as a reminder of the sustaining alliance they had formed with the British, they too participate in an elegiac act, mourning the coming of an allegedly postcolonial Canada, with its insistence on their subjection, and hearkening back to the days of British colonial rule, when they were allies. Ironically, the Iroquois, too, would agree with Duncan that the British connection represented a superior form of civility, but they would disagree with the Canadian view that colonial tilt had produced an improvement on it.

Although James De Mille's *A Strange Manuscript Found in a Copper Cylinder* also questions British civility as a superior social project, in contrast with Marlyn's and Duncan's novels, it does not address this question in a Canadian context, for it is not set in Canada (or even in the world, for that matter); nor does it ever refer directly to Canada. De Mille's novel also departs from *Under the Ribs* and *The Imperialist* in that it does not affirm a satirical norm; which is to say, it does not criticize the failures of society in order to reconfirm a standard set of values. Instead, the novel makes a travesty of the whole discourse of European, and particularly British, civility itself, lifting it quite literally out of the world as we know it and resituating it in a defamiliarizing fantastical realm so that we can actually see its presumptions and not assume them as inevitable.[15] A central focus of this lampoon of European civility falls upon the hubris of European epistemology itself, which presumes the reliability of its own cultural standards for evaluating the cultures it encounters in colonial exploration and travel. Whereas a significant element of Marlyn's and Duncan's irony derives from the narrator's knowing more than the characters do (on Duncan, see Davey, 'Narrative' 427), De Mille allows no such confidence to any character, narrator, or interpreter (there are several of each featured in this novel). In this way, *Strange Manuscript* constitutes a brilliant, chaotic challenge to European assumptions of civility and the narrative of progressive enlightenment upon which they are based.

De Mille's novel opens with a frame story in which four Englishmen, vacationing on Lord Featherstone's yacht, find themselves becalmed in the Mediterranean. While the idle yachtsmen drift aimlessly at sea, they come upon a copper cylinder floating in the water which contains a brief letter and a papyrus manuscript describing the adventures of Adam More, whose name alludes to the first human as well as to Sir Thomas More, author of *Utopia*. The manuscript describes Adam More as an English sailor who had got separated from his ship on the return from Tasmania, where he and the crew had delivered a cargo of convicts. Off the coast of Antarctica, he and a companion, Agnew, are carried by a powerful current under the polar ice into a strange, tropical world at the South Pole. Agnew, the sacrificial lamb, as his name suggests, is murdered and possibly cannibalized by the first inhabitants they meet, but More saves himself by killing a few 'savages' with his gun and leaping into the boat, which carries him further on to the verdant, orderly, well-cultivated world of the pre-industrial Kosekin. These people at the bottom of the world hold values and perceptions that are the exact reverse of European ones: they value darkness, death, adversity, and self-sacrifice above all else. They live in caves during the six months of light to avoid the harsh sunshine and celebrate the return of darkness, when they can resume their active lives outdoors. They eagerly embrace death and poverty and try to divest themselves of power and wealth in order to compete with one another for the exalted state of pauperism in hopes of eventually being granted the highest reward of all: ritual sacrifice and cannibal consumption by their fellows in the ceremonial banquet of the Mista Kosek.

Adam More's name is pronounced 'Atam-or,' which means man of light in Hebrew, by the Kosekin. He is attracted by the Kosekin's civility and kindness and revolted by their barbarous disregard of human life. Among these people, he meets another foreigner, Almah, a woman who is a sacrificial hostage and who values life, light, and wealth as he does. They fall in love, but this development is disastrous because the Kosekin have been waiting for Almah to fall in love with someone who can then be her co-victim in a ritual sacrifice. Despite an attempted escape when More uses the affections of the beautiful Layellah, the rebel daughter of the wealthiest (and therefore most despised) Kosekin, the Kohen Gadol, to literally fly out of the Kosekin's land, he and Almah are brought gently and inexorably to the sacrificial moment when gunfire from More murders the would-be murderers and quick thinking on Almah's part not only saves them from being killed but also establishes a new, self-perpetuating colonial order according to which the Kosekin's desire to dispossess themselves and acquire the gift of death is perfectly met by More and Almah, when they set themselves up as rulers who accept a quarter of everyone's wealth and More takes on the role of the Sar Tabakin, or chief executioner of the Kosekin.

De Mille turns his satirical hand in many directions throughout More's narrative,[16] but repeatedly a central object of mockery is More's assumption that he is the civilized and the Kosekin are the savages, that he is the enlightened and they are the benighted. He is utterly nonplussed, for example, when his kind host, the Kohen, is shocked at More's repugnance for the blessing of death that the Kosekin have prepared for him and Almah. When More begs the Kohen to help them escape this fate, the Kohen replies that 'these feelings which you profess are utterly unnatural. We are so made that we cannot help loving death; it is a sort of instinct ... This is human nature. We cannot help it; and it is this that distinguishes us from the animals' (131). When More protests that it is not human nature to love death and that, in fact, his own society fears death and tries to avoid it at all costs, the Kohen replies: 'Have you not told me incredible things about your people, among which there were a few that seemed natural and intelligible? Among these was your system of honoring above all men those who procure the death of the largest number ... Your most renowned men are those who have sent most to death' (157). After realizing that he and the Kohen can never compre-hend each other, More despairs at ever meeting anyone during his sojourn among the Kosekin whom he can understand; so when he meets the Kohen Gadol, whose cunning and lack of virtue have made him the wealthiest and most despised of all the Kosekin, his heart leaps up: 'I longed to find someone among this singular people who was selfish, who feared death, who loved life, who loved riches, and had something in common with me' (166), he explains. 'If I could only find someone who was a coward and selfish and avaricious ... how much brighter my life would be!' (167).

And so, the further we read into More's narrative, the more we come to realize that the Manichaean allegory of colonial contact, the binary between the civilized European and the savage Aboriginal, is becoming so perforated that it becomes very difficult to tell which side is the civilized and which the barbaric. More is not as diametrically opposed to savagery as he thinks he is: he is much more violent than the Kosekin are; he is cowardly and inconsistent in comparison to them; he operates by subterfuge and stratagem, while they are straightforward and honest; and he indulges a xenophobia and an avarice that expose him as small-minded and self-centred in contrast with their generosity and open-mindedness. Meanwhile, their strange customs constitute an ex-treme literalization of Christian ethics as outlined in Christ's Sermon on the Mount: 'If anyone comes to me and does not hate ... even his own life, he cannot be my disciple' (Luke 14:26); 'Blessed are you poor' (Luke 16:20); 'Love your enemies' (Matt 5:44); 'Greater love than this no one has, that one lay down his life for his friends' (John 15: 13) (cited in La Bossiere 47–8).

De Mille's novel plays a cagey, enticing game with the act of interpre-tation and especially with the assumed norms or standards on which it is based. In fact, this is De Mille's trap – and he makes the game so delightfully compelling that it is almost impossible to resist stepping into it. The plot of More's adventures is regularly interrupted by chapters in which the four yachtsmen of the frame narrative pause in their reading of his story to engage in the game of interpretation. Melick, a 'littérateur' from London, declares the manuscript a fraud, a 'satirical romance,' while Oxenden, a philologist, considers it a narrative of 'plain facts,' and he uses his knowledge of Hebrew and Grimm's Law of linguistic variation to insist that More has discovered one of the Ten Lost Tribes, which disappeared after the dispersion of the Israelites. Dr Congreve, based on his knowledge of palaeontology and geographical exploration, insists that More's narrative is believable because the monsters he mentions correspond to dinosaurs and because various topographical details match those mentioned in the narratives of colonial explorers such as Captain James Cook and Sir James Ross. Featherstone, as his lightweight name suggests, remains more interested in food and wine than in committing himself to one reading or another, but as a good sport, he expresses interest in both Oxenden's and Congreve's credulity in the literal truth of the manuscript, and he enters into banter with Melick's sarcastic view that not only is the manuscript a hoax, but it is poorly written. 'The style is detestable,' Melick complains, 'this writer is tawdry; he has the worst vices of the sensational school – he shows everywhere marks of haste, gross carelessness, and universal feebleness. When he gets hold of a good fancy, he lacks the patience that is necessary in order to work it up in an effective way' (228). In statements such as these, De Mille uses Melick's voice to announce his own satirical mode[17] and thereby anticipate potential critique, even as he focuses attention within the novel upon the process of interpretation itself as a major theme, particularly upon the way in which interpretations are always shaped by the epistemological orientation of the interpreter. For in all levels of the book, whether in the contrast between More's and Agnew's respective pessimistic and optimistic apprehensions about whether they will survive their ordeal or whether the natives are friendly (they are both right and both wrong), whether in the mutual incomprehension of More and the Kohen about what constitutes human nature (they are both right and both wrong), or whether in the conflict between Melick's incredulity and the willingness of Congreve and Oxenden to believe More's tale is literally true (they are all wrong, mostly), we are constantly reminded that the interpreter – whether separated from the text by culture or by time and distance – makes sense of his experiences (the interpreters in the novel are all male) on the basis of incommensurate experience and inadequate knowledge.

It is striking, as Gwendolyn Guth has observed, that for all the yachtsmen's intelligent attempts to authorize a specific understanding of More's story, they are such poor readers ('Reading' 48–9). For in their complete absorption with the question of the literal authenticity of

More's manuscript – whether the papyrus on which it is written is authentic or whether it could have been obtained by a nineteenth-century writer comfortably situated in England who wished to foment a hoax, whether the monsters are this or that dinosaur, and whether the volcanoes correspond to those mentioned in Cook or Ross, and so on – they fail to discuss its meaning. Melick suggests vaguely that it may be a satire of 'things in general,' of 'the restlessness of humanity,' but his suggestion that the narrative 'mocks us by exhibiting a new race of men, animated by passions and impulses which are directly the opposite of ours' misses the way in which the Kosekin are very similar to Europeans. And when he opines that the manuscript 'teaches the great lesson that the happiness of man consists not in external surroundings, but in the internal feelings, and that heaven itself is not a place, but a state' (226–7), he privatizes what is clearly a social critique and then reduces the whole to a cliché from Milton's *Paradise Lost*.

The four yachtsmen seem like allegorical figures in a Foucauldian parable about the way in which discourse makes certain objects of knowledge possible and others impossible for perception. They seem completely oblivious to the satirical inversions of central principles of European civilization and its role in rationalizing colonial expansion. They never comment on the reversal of gender roles that makes Layellah and Almah agents of decisive action, while More, far from a muscular Christian spreading civility among the less fortunate, is repeatedly overwhelmed by his experiences and then overreacts to them either by falling into a faint or by opening fire and killing yet another passel of Kosekin. The yachtsmen never really discuss Kosekin culture in general, and they therefore fail to notice the Kosekin's terrible rituals of sacrifice and cannibalism, as well as the clear parallel to sacrifice and ritual consumption of the body of Christ in Christian ritual. Oxenden does observe that 'the Kosekin may be nearer to the truth than we are' in their recognition of the vanity of mortal life, but he links this kind of wisdom to Hinduism and Buddhism and fails to see any link to Western Christianity (236). None of the four English readers seems to notice how violent More is in comparison to the Kosekin; nor do they see any relationship between their own circumstances, drifting in luxury, drinking excellent wines, and dining upon the creations of Featherstone's French chef, and the supposed wisdom of renunciation as outlined by Oxenden. Indeed, just as the possibility arises that they might turn from their dead-end debate about the manuscript's authenticity to a discussion of its possible relevance to the world in which they live, Featherstone yawns, lays the manuscript aside, and says, 'It's time for supper' (269). And it is at this point that not just More's but De Mille's manuscript abruptly ends.

It is also at this point that the post-textual irony starts, for the critical response to *Strange Manuscript* has continued to focus on the same preoccupations entertained by the yachtsmen. De Mille died suddenly of pneumonia at age forty-six, leaving the novel, in Guth's apt phrasing, 'finished in its incompleteness, ... completely (un)finished' ('Reading' 51), and the ensuing attempts to explicate the novel have been as entirely absorbed with interpreting its authenticity as were the yachtsmen on Featherstone's sailboat. The novel was published by De Mille's widow in 1888, eight years after his death, but without the kind of information that critics need to determine exactly when it was composed (so we can know whether it is a work of original genius or if it is an imitation of Samuel Butler's *Erewhon* [1872] or Rider Haggard's *She* [1887]); what sources De Mille would have had available to gather his information about Antarctica, palaeontology, or zoology; and whether or not the present conclusion was one he was satisfied with (so we can determine if this is a work of art or a fragment that would have been a masterpiece if it had been concluded properly; whether it is a clever idea that was too hastily concluded and therefore an artistic failure; or whether the startling, inconclusive conclusion is such a brilliant way to end a novel about the impossibility of complete exegesis that it constitutes a stroke of genius). Despite repeated claims for the novel's ingeniousness, from R.W. Douglas's assertion in 1922 in the *Canadian Bookman* that *Strange Manuscript* is 'a great book, perhaps the greatest ever produced by a Canadian writer' (qtd. in Parks, 'Editor's' xliv) to Reginald Watters's in 1969 that in 'the whole of Canadian literature, there is nothing comparable to this remarkable novel' (vii), and from Crawford Kilian's claim in 1972 that it is 'the best novel written in nineteenth-century Canada, and one of the best in all of Canadian fiction' (67) to Patricia Monk's in 1990 that it is 'one of the best and more entertaining pieces of social criticism by a Canadian writer of this period' ('James' 94), and finally to David Ketterer's in *Canadian Science Fiction and Fantasy Writers* (1992) that 'there is growing consensus that this provocative philosophical work is not only the best nineteenth-century Canadian novel but one of the best Canadian novels period' (qtd. in Ivision 64), the regular repetition of these claims affirms Carole Gerson's wry observation in 1985 that 'the purpose of nearly all commentary on De Mille has been to call attention to this unduly neglected author' ('Three' 209).

The post-textual ironies of *Strange Manuscript* also include the fact that Malcolm Parks, who observed the welter of ironies and cross-purposes that make solid ground hard to find in the novel ('Strange'), could still not resist supplying thirty-two pages of explanatory notes in his edition of the novel, most of which work to substantiate De Mille's work by supplying the sources for Oxenden's and Congreve's empirical evidence for the authenticity of More's manuscript. The post-textual irony also includes statements such as Gerry Turcotte's assertion, 'One immediately obvious point to make is that the text is resoundingly colonial in its cast' (80), when the critical record indicates that nobody seemed to have noticed this 'obvious point' until postcolonial criticism around the mid-1990s made the colonial context of De Mille's novel into an object of notice, and only then did the welter of postcolonial interpretations begin to appear.[18] Critics continue to debate whether the novel is a utopia (Hughes), dystopia (Watters), 'untopia' (Keefer), or none of the above (Woodcock), and whether it is a Menippean satire or 'anatomy' (Kilian), or a postmodern metafiction (Lamont-Stewart, Wilson) – or both at once (Guth). They debate when De Mille might have written the book, many of the book's early reviewers and many critics before the mid-1980s assuming it was composed late in his life and therefore derivative of Samuel Butler, Jules Verne, or Lord Lytton (Woodcock; Gerson, 'Three') and most, after the publication in the mid-1980s of Parks's careful analysis of letters between De Mille's executors, agreeing that it was likely composed in the mid-1860s and therefore before many of its supposed models.[19] If they agree that the book is satirical, critics debate the targets of the satire: Watters identifies religious cant; Kilian, a general 'philosophical attitude' which is ostensibly religious but practically godless; Woodcock, the 'anti-vitalism' and life-denying puritanism of Victorian society; Hughes, the English aristocracy; and Bush, the gendered order assumed in conventional nineteenth-century romance.

The most recent round of debates have tended to read the novel either as a proto-postmodern parody of the certitudes of interpretation itself (Cavell, Wilson, Guth, Lamont-Stewart) or as a counter-discursive engagement with the discourses that enabled and rationalized colonialism. The latter approach has focused on the novel's deconstruction of the binary between civilization and barbarity (Milnes; Gerson, 'Contrapuntal'), its lampooning of the colonial trope of cannibalism, which functioned paradoxically to divide the civilized from the savage by means of a fantasy of being consumed by the other (Kilgour, Turcotte), or its satire of the assumption of civility upon which the Canadian imperial federation movement was based (Arnold). Predictably, the recent postmodernist and postcolonial readings, based on theoretical formulations that have held most sway in the fields of literary criticism and interpretation during the time of my own writing, seem to me to carry the most weight. But this is precisely the trap De Mille set in the book: readers will interpret what they see, hear, and experience according to the epistemologies that they bring with them to De Mille's text, to More's manuscript, to the land of the Kosekin.

I have saved *Strange Manuscript* for the end of this book because it is a novel that deploys, even as it interrogates, a wry approach to civility. It is a text that reminds us of the contingency of our own understandings, a text that reminds us that civility is a project, a project with a culturally specific genealogy which assumes the knowledge and experience of that specific culture to be universal – until it comes into contact with other cultures, with their epistemologies and experiences. De Mille's book reminds us that very often that encounter, rather than producing self-knowledge or an expanded civil project, turns into exploitation and violence and that, remarkably, even when well-educated, cool-headed, civilized professionals later have the benefit of reconsidering the records of those first encounters, the most glaring challenges to our own assumptions go unnoticed and unexamined. As such, *Strange Manuscript* is a critic's lesson in humility, and it was written, not by a postmodern, postcolonial, post-Holocaust, post-1968 poststructuralist, but by a nineteenth-century, White, British-descended, Canadian professor of rhetoric and history who furiously scribbled boys' adventure stories and satirical sensation novels late into the night. Something, however, about his circumstances – his strict Loyalist ancestry in Nova Scotia, his education in the United States and youthful journey to Europe, his survival of failed business attempts, and his innovation ahead of his times in introducing classes on Canadian and American history into Dalhousie's standard courses on Western civilization – something gave him a wry and acute understanding of the colonial paradoxes of the civility in which he lived.

De Mille's parody of the assumptions of civility that pervade the narrative of colonial contact remains powerfully relevant for recent twenty-first-century narratives of Canadian civility. In *Dark Threats and White Knights,* Sherene Razack, for example, identifies the mythological narrative of the Canadian peacekeeper as a popular image of Canada's role in the new world order in the late twentieth and early twenty-first centuries. As citizens of a middle power, Razack explains, Canadians do not consider themselves aggressors like the Americans and the British, who invaded Iraq in 2003; we prefer to think of ourselves as civil intermediaries, witnesses to the barbarisms of Third World, non-White regions such as Somalia, Rwanda, Afghanistan, or Iraq, but helpless as a smaller power to intervene in arcane ethnic or religious conflicts that are overdetermined by the superpowers' military and economic might. But like De Mille's Adam More, the contemporary Canadian peacekeeper is in fact an ambiguous figure of civility, as readily represented by members of the Canadian Airborne Regiment who tortured and killed sixteen-year-old Shidane Abukar Arone while on a peacekeeping mission in Somalia in 1993 as by General Roméo Dallaire, who has become a pitied national hero for the trauma he suffered after 1994 when his calls for UN military intervention to prevent the Rwandan genocide went unanswered. Razack's point is not to question the severity or genuineness of Dallaire's suffering but to observe that in the popular imagination, the Dallaire figure has sidelined those of the abusive peacekeepers of the Somalia affair – who have largely been represented in the press as a few bad apples – and has been taken up as an icon of Canada's specific form of civility.

The figure of Dallaire is a direct descendent of the figures of White civility I have been tracing in this book. Razack observes that, through documentary films such as *Witness the Evil* (1998), *Unseen Scars* (1998), and *The Last Just Man* (2002), as well as the keen interest in Dallaire's story in the Canadian press – not to mention Dallaire's Governor General's Award–winning memoir and its film version, *Shake Hands with the Devil* (2003 and 2004, respectively), which were released after Razack had submitted her book for publication – the traumatized, noble general has become a Canadian icon of the 'last just man.' The figure of the humane, traumatized general, she writes, 'continues to personify our fragility in encounters with absolute evil, our hesitant but deeply moral stance, and, above all, our non-involvement in the horrors' (25). In this way, she argues, Canadians construct an image of their own superior civility by figuring themselves as what Robertson Davies once called 'the hero's friend' – that is, as the secondary character who is a wise and tempering influence on the American hero's unilateral, aggressive approach to peace-building, and therefore as a more-humane member of the White civilized brotherhood of northern nations who descend when called upon into the heart of darkness in the South to teach, by force if necessary, uncivilized peoples the principles of peace and democracy (36, 23–4). Razack concludes her critique of this figure by asserting that

Canadians should not necessarily stay home and refuse to involve themselves in international peacekeeping efforts; rather, she urges them to resist the narrative erasures that are fundamental to the fantasy of the neutral Canadian peacekeeper who remains outside implication. For this figure operates consistently by reference to a colour line that assumes White civility and non-White, Third World barbarity, and it ignores not only the racism of these assumptions but also the history of Canadians' involvements in the exploitation and violence that have contributed to recent high-profile international conflicts (e.g., Canadian mining companies' illegal operations in eastern Congo near the border of Rwanda, Canadian oil companies' relation to ethnic cleansing in southern Sudan, and Canadian munitions companies' manufacturing ammunition for the forces occupying Iraq).[20]

In this sense, Razack's critique of the Canadian fantasy of the peacekeeper emphasizes in a contemporary context the need for what I have been calling wry civility – a self-aware, self-critical engagement with the project of civility that is cognizant not just of the structural contradictions of civility as a strictly bordered and internally stratified universalism but also of the particular Canadian genealogy of White civility, which has repeatedly figured Canadian values through images such as the loyal brother who continues to negotiate a nervous relationship with the United States, the enterprising Scottish orphan whose prudent, good character produces his economic success, the muscular Christian who meets out justice on behalf of oppressed people, and the maturing colonial son who demonstrates his independence from Britain and America by altruism towards his minority beneficiaries. These figures of Canadian White civility, developed during the nation-building years, have survived numerous challenges to their capacity to present a normative ideal for Canadian citizenship, and they continue to have enormous influence in popular understandings of Canadian identity. The onus falls to cultural critics and scholars, therefore, to dismantle these narratives by means of a critical or wry civility which knows that civility itself has a contaminated, compromised history but which nonetheless affirms that its basic elements as formulated in Canada – peace, order, and good government – are worth having and maintaining. Wry civility remains aware that civil ideals have been partially and unevenly pursued in the past and that we in the present are as likely to be blind to similar exclusions and unevennesses as were past Canadians. Malcolm X famously said that racism is like a Cadillac: there's a new model every year. Wry civility recognizes the improvisational and ongoing nature of Canadians' participation in a flawed process, one that continually encounters new racisms and invents new borders; it is a way to see ourselves as implicated, rather than as uninvolved, observers in a process that remains committed to a continuous dismantling of the borders and hierarchies that are inherent in the ongoing project of civility.

Notes

1. The Literary Project of English Canada

1 For the purposes of consistency, I use the upper case for racializing words that refer to people whether as nouns or adjectives – thus 'Blacks,' 'White settler,' 'Aboriginal knowledge,' and so on – because they parallel the national and ethnic uses of similar terms such as 'Canadian,' 'Chinese,' or 'Mohawk.' I use lower-case when I am referring to the conceptualization of these categories – thus 'whiteness,' 'blackness,' 'indigeneity,' and so on. This distinction is difficult to maintain consistently because the conceptualization cannot be separated from the capacity of these terms to refer to people. I have come to the conclusion that there is no adequate system for referring to these racialized terms and that their typographical awkwardness and inconsistency are signs of their constant capacity for mutation and reinvention.

2 The term 'English Canada' itself demonstrates my larger point, for if 'civility' involves the definition of *civis*, or who will be included among the citizenry, then 'English Canadian' introduces as many exclusions as inclusions. First, one must assume that 'English' refers to language and not to ethnicity, if the term is not to exclude not only Canadians of Scots, Irish, or Welsh backgrounds but also English-speaking Canadians of Ukrainian, Scandinavian, South Asian, or Caribbean descent. So, then, are all Canadians who speak English part of this culture? Clearly, many Canadians who derive significant cultural meaning from their non-linguistic heritage will find this designation inaccurate, if not aggressively engulfing. Nonetheless, the term is commonly used in public discourse to describe the 'rest of Canada' by distinction from 'French Canada.' It is patently an inadequate shorthand, and it is one that demonstrates how the constant discomforts

and renegotiations of civility remain part of everyday discussions of Canadian culture. I am indebted to Benjamin Lefebvre for helpful discussions of the problems involved in such terms as 'English,' 'French,' 'anglophone,' or 'francophone' to describe cultural regions or groups in Canada.

3 I am grateful to Guy Beauregard for drawing my attention to the Diène report.

4 For a minimal list of scholars who have participated in this effort, see Abella and Troper, Kay Anderson, Avery, Backhouse, Dickason, Henry and Tator, and Walker.

5 It seems to me that a capacity to recognize the presence of racism *within* the *real* projects of civility helps to avoid the errors of two polar extremes: one that tends to read the racism of progressives such as first-wave feminists or early reformers and socialists as signs of the hypocrisy of their claims for civility and therefore as reasons to dismiss the impact of the movements of which they were part, and the other extreme, which, out of a desire to defend the accomplishments of these early reformers, ignores or suppresses their racism.

6 Each of these fields of study is too vast for me to discuss properly here. For an overview of masculinity studies, see http://mensbiblio.xyonline.net. Important references in American whiteness studies would extend from W.E.B. Du Bois's *Black Reconstruction in America* (1935) and James Baldwin's 'The Price of the Ticket' (1985) to David Roediger's *The Wages of Whiteness* (1991), Toni Morrison's *Playing in the Dark* (1992), Ruth Frankenberg's *White Woman, Race Matters* (1993), and Theodore Allen's *The Invention of the White Race* (1994). For an overview of Canadian work on race and racism as it relates to literary and cultural studies, see Coleman and Goellnicht's introduction to '*Race.*'

7 Omi and Winant propose the term 'racial project' to suggest both mobility (constant reconstruction and being-madeness) and structural function (that racial projects *form* social relations and realities) (55–6). For a powerfully suggestive use of the concept of social projects in a Canadian context, see Ian McKay's 'The Liberal Order Framework,' in which he suggests that understanding Canada as an ongoing project of liberalism would free historians from thinking of the country in terms of an essence or as empty homogeneous space.

8 I share Balibar's notion of civility as that form of politics that does not suppress all violence but creates a civil space by removing violence to that space's borders ('Three' 29–30), but I do not share his desire to delink 'civility' from 'civilization' and the latter's association with the colonialist-Enlightenment idea of history as progress from barbarism to civilization

(39n6). The continuity between this progressive concept of history and civility is fundamental to my analysis. See also Anindyo Roy for a study of British civility in the context of Indian colonial history.

9 See Foucault's 'Governmentality' essay on the linkage of self-government to state government, and Henderson for the development of this theory in relation to Canadian settler feminism (19ff).

10 R.B. Bennett, then the Conservative MP for Calgary East, gave a speech at an Empire Day banquet sponsored by the Empire Club of Toronto in 1914 that expresses this civilizing mission in its triumphalistic mode: 'We are [in India and Egypt] because under the Providence of God we are a Christian people that have given to the subject races of the world the only kind of decent government they have ever known. (Applause.) We are the only colonizing race that has been able to colonize the great outlying portions of the world and give the people that priceless boon of self-government, and we have educated men year after year until at last those who were once subjects became free, and those who were free became freer, and you and I must carry our portion of that responsibility if we are to be the true Imperialists we should be ... An Imperialist, to me, means a man who accepts gladly and bears proudly the responsibilities of his race and breed. (Applause.)' (qtd. in Berger, *Sense,* 230–1).

11 See Mackey 2–3 and Day 5, 42 for discussion of this process in a Canadian context.

12 See Goldie, ch. 8, on Indigenous people's relegation to 'prehistory.'

13 Lawson indicates that the settler subject who experiences and enacts this inner division is paradigmatically male, because the whole process of land acquisition upon which settler colonies were founded was by and large a masculine enterprise (thus I have used the masculine pronoun throughout my description of the settler colonial complex). See Henderson and Valverde for arguments that figure femininity as central to, rather than peripheral to, this process. Lawson also notes that the settler's complex structure of feeling produces an aggressive impulse to indigenization on the part of the White settler, whereby the Indigenous presence must be displaced and eventually replaced (28). See Goldie (13) and Fee on indigenization as a 'literary land claim' (Fee 17).

14 In 'Wanted – Canadian Criticism,' Smith links this concern overtly to an unwillingness in Canadian literary criticism to attend to temporal matters. In this essay, he asserts that 'Canadian poetry ... is altogether too self-conscious of its environment, of its position in space, and scarcely conscious at all of its position in time' (223). A much more recent assessment of Canada's ongoing concern with belatedness has been made by Donna

Palmateer Pennee, who argues that the pressure towards cosmopolitanism depends on a progressive relation to a chronology of modernity that sutures cultural expression to development, independence, and mature relations to other nation states (87); thus she reads Canada's representation of itself in the 1990s as a champion of constructive multilateralism and as an international mediator as an attempt to compensate for a sense of belatedness by constructing an important cosmopolitan role on the international stage (87–8).

15 In order to emphasize the psychic complexity entailed in the settler-colonial complex, I have been using the singular pronoun. But Jennifer Henderson supplies an excellent example of this anxiety to distinguish the settler colony from later (non-White) colonies at the collective level when she describes the 1907 Colonial Conference in London, at which the prime ministers of the newly independent dominions met. She notes Canadian prime minister Wilfrid Laurier's concern that the term 'dominion' not be too widely applied. For if future conferences were to be attended by 'the Mother Country and His Majesty's Dominions over the seas,' 'Dominions' might 'as well apply to Trinidad or Barbados as to Canada' (qtd. in Henderson 24). The conference participants then decided that the invitation to these conferences should be directed to 'self-governing Colonies,' the implication being that the capacity for self-government was restricted to British Whites, as the British prime minister stated in his opening remarks: 'we found ourselves, Gentlemen ... upon freedom and independence – that is the essence of the British Imperial connection ... Anything which militates against that principle would be wholly contrary to the genius of our race' (24).

16 There were others, however, who distrusted the wholehearted espousal of British values, as, for example, in the anonymous dissenting article 'Imperialism, Nationalism, or a Third Alternative,' signed by 'A Westerner,' which was published in the *University Magazine* in 1910: 'Canada's contribution to history and to civilization is to be that she shall consciously declare her desire to be merely one of a "Union of Nations" who are all prepared to be limited, not merely by the physical power of neighbours, but by a self-imposed legal and contractual bond' (347). This union could only come about by the 'self-repression of the British nationality,' by the development of 'restrained nationalities' in the younger dominions, and by their 'voluntary contractual union on a basis of equality into a new system to be known as "The United Nations"' (355).

17 This constrained emergence theory for Canada's development was not limited to Tories. Various kinds of progressive social movements, including

the social gospel, labour unionism, early feminism, various socialist political parties, and western Canadian reform movements, also operated under the assumption that Canadian society should be a planned society. As recently as 2003, Africadian poet and critic George Elliott Clarke has updated Grant's lament in relation to Canada's increased submission, in the Mulroney-Chrétien era of free trade and NAFTA, to the American empire. Clarke recognizes the Anglocentrism of Grant's Red Toryism but credits it with having a broader public good in mind than the free-enterprise governments of Mulroney and Chrétien (see his 'What Was Canada?').

18 In 'Imperial Federation' (1902), for example, George Parkin observed that the presence of French-speaking prime minister Sir Wilfrid Laurier at the British Jubilee celebrations of 1897 'showed that the free institutions enjoyed under the British flag gave an equal opportunity to men of every race and creed; it proved that the difference fought out in 1759 had been lost sight of in the common citizenship of this great country, and our greater Empire. It proved the assimilating power of a political system which, from the circumstances of our vast national expansion, is compelled to adapt itself to many people and varying conditions' (191).

19 One example occurs in William Kirby's poem 'Pontiac and Bushy Run' (1887) when an Algonquin chief's preamble to his narrative about Pontiac represents Canada as a shining alternative to American greed:

> their treaties – never one
> Was kept by them unbroken: nor will be
> So long as we have lands, or place to dwell,
> Or graves where lie our kindred – which these men
> Covet the more, the more we wish to keep.
> In this Dominion only – God be praised!
> Old English law and justice, and the rights
> Of every man are sacredly maintained
> Here conscience lives, and the bright covenant chains
> Were never broken with the Indian tribes.' (qtd. in Monkman 109)

Statements such as these are common throughout Canadian claims for civility and find their most pithy expression in the title to this article published in the *Young Canadian* (8 April 1891) by H. Coulthard: 'They Shall Covet Their Neighbour's Indians' (reference in Strong-Boag and Gerson 241n32).

20 In his 'Address: Delivered at Niagara, on the 14th of August, 1884,' for example, William Kirby claimed that the first parliament at Fort George (1792), which established the English principles of law, order, and govern-

ment and expressly abolished slavery, made Upper Canada 'the first country in the world which abolished slavery by an Act of the Legislature!' 'These acts,' claimed Kirby, 'prove better than any words the noble and generous character of the men who founded this Province' (173). Of course, Kirby's words should be balanced against the fact that Simcoe's act did not immediately abolish the practice of slavery in Upper Canada. It merely prohibited the purchase or importation of new slaves; existing slaves remained their masters' property. The separate works of Robin Winks (*Blacks*), James W. St. G. Walker, and George Elliott Clarke ('Raising'), which describe the continued practice of slavery in Canada as well as the discrimination that was practised against Black Loyalists, collectively challenge the common belief that Canada was an unqualified refuge for North American Blacks.

21 An example of this 'civil' approach to exclusive immigration policies appeared in the *Nanaimo Daily Free Press* on 9 September 1907, just after the anti-Japanese riots in Vancouver; the writer asserts that 'riots will do no good' and that 'mob action is always to be scorned,' but then goes on to add that now 'that the seriousness of the problem is realized, and all of Canada is alive to the fallacy of taking to herself a race who will ever be alien, our quarrel is no longer with the Orientals, just as long as we can take measures that will lead to prohibiting their entry into Canada' (qtd. in Greer 482).

22 The pamphlet was written by Basil Stewart and published in London. Its full title was 'No English Need Apply, or Canada as a Field for Immigration' (see McCormack 41).

23 See Berger, 'True North'; Hulan 18–19; Grace.

24 Perhaps the most infamous articulation of the myth of the North with Canadian British race-making was made in Canada First member Robert Grant Haliburton's 1869 lecture, published as *The Men of the North and Their Place in History*: 'A glance at the map of this continent, as well as at the history of the past, will satisfy us that the peculiar characteristic of the New Dominion must ever be that it is a Northern country inhabited by the descendants of Northern races. As British colonists we may well be proud of the name of Englishmen; but as the British people are themselves but a fusion of many northern elements which are here again meeting and mingling, and blending together to form a new nationality, we must in our national aspirations take a wider range, and adopt a broader basis which will comprise at once the Celtic, the Teutonic, and the Scandinavian elements, and embrace the Celt, the Norman French, the Saxon and the Swede, all of which are noble sources of national life' (2).

25 Although the Imperial Federation League was formed in London in 1884, its main proponents and ideologues were from the colonies (Berger, *Sense* 3).

Daniel Francis reminds us, for example, that Empire Day was established in 1897 at the instigation of Hamiltonian Clementine Fessenden and picked up by Ontario's minister of education, George Ross (who went on to become Ontario premier). The first celebration of Empire Day was 23 May 1899. Francis notes that it evolved into Victoria Day, a Canadian invention that is not celebrated anywhere else (*National* 64–5). David Cannadine argues that imperialism, not nationalism, has provided the figures and myths which made possible an 'imagined community' of Canadians and that, although Canada has become a state, it has never successfully imagined itself as a nation (4, 7). According to Cannadine, 'the British connection pervaded Canadian life at all levels. In conformity with the British North America Act, most Canadians thought of themselves as Britons, who happened to be living in British North America. There were too many Scots for them to be English: rather, it was a shared sense of Britishness which held them together and linked them to the land of their birth or of their forebears' (9). Cannadine says that the imperial connection was as strong in the 1930s and 1940s as it was at the turn of the century (12); it only declined after the Second World War, but it remains residual in Canadians' use of Britishness to distinguish themselves from the United States (13).

26 In their discussion of imperial federationism, Brown and Cook note that this claim in relation to Britain and the United States is ironic, because the trading 'preference' given to Britain under Laurier's Liberal government only slowed the marked shift from British to American trade. From 1897 to 1912 British imports had shrunk from one-third to one-fifth of Canadian totals; in the same time, American imports had leapt to two-thirds of all imports (30).

27 See Barrie Davies; Berger, *Sense* 3–5; Owram 57, 127.

28 In *The Secular Scripture* (1976), Northrop Frye observes that popular literary forms such as romance are related to class anxieties because they are 'what people read without guidance from their betters' and thus are usually rejected by the critical establishment (23). Generally, according to Frye, romance is populist, anti-hierarchical, and fraternal, although what he calls 'kidnapped romance' can be made to reflect the values of a ruling class (29–30, 56–8).

29 For discussions of popular literature in a Canadian context, see Clarence Karr's *Authors and Audiences* (2000) and Elizabeth Waterston's *Rapt in Plaid* (2001) with their sustained defence of the legitimacy and importance of popular fiction. In their introduction to 'Discourse in Early Canada,' a special issue of *Canadian Literature* (1991), Germaine Warkentin and Heather Murray argue that a proper understanding of early Canadian

culture can only be gained through examination of a much wider range of textual materials than literary scholars since the high modernist and New Criticism movements of the mid-twentieth century have identified as 'literature.' They believe that this wider study of early Canadian "discourse,"' which they define as 'the realm of stories and sense-making, power and persuasion,' 'will best open to study Canadian texts from 'Before 1860" (7) because much pre-1860 writing in Canada was produced when the distinctions between 'science' and 'literature' and 'high and low genres, oral and written, were blurred or not yet hardened.' Indeed, for much of the nineteenth century, the term '"literature" already denoted the "vernacular" in the widest sense – including scientific, practical, and political treatises – and that even where literary study was most aestheticized, its *raison d'être* remained preparation for civil life' (8).

30 Ralph Connor was the pen name of Charles William Gordon (1860–1937), who was born in the Highland community of Glengarry, Canada West, the son of a Presbyterian minister and a well-educated mother. Gordon first came to fame for several sketches he wrote of his early experiences as a Presbyterian missionary in the mining communities around Banff and Canmore in the Rocky Mountains. He sent these sketches to the *Westminster Magazine* in Toronto in an effort to raise awareness and funds for western missions, and they were gathered into his first book, *Black Rock* (1898), which was published under the pseudonym 'Ralph Connor.' Connor's first three novels – *Black Rock: A Tale of the Selkirks, The Sky Pilot: A Tale of the Foothills* (1899), and *The Man from Glengarry: A Tale of the Ottawa* (1901) – became international best-sellers that sold millions of copies in Canada, the United States, Britain, and Australia (Lennox 104). Gordon went on to publish thirty-four books over the next forty years, each of his twenty-three works of fiction selling between 20,000 and 60,000 copies in Canada alone (Karr, *Authors* 53–5).

There are many signs of Ralph Connor's immense popularity: *Black Rock* recorded eleven pirated editions (Watt 11), and *The Sky Pilot* was still selling in the thousands as late as 1927 (Karr, *Authors* 259n4). During Gordon's life, *Glengarry Schooldays* sold over 5 million copies (Waterston, *Rapt* 186), and in 1902 he matched sales with Rudyard Kipling, Hall Caine, and Mari Corelli (Karr, *Authors* 68). Although many critics have represented Connor as a turn-of-the-century flash in the pan, still in the early 1920s, long after the height of his pre-war popularity, the Toronto Public Library could hardly keep its 700 copies of Connor's novels on the shelves (Karr, *Authors* 28). In addition, six of his novels were made into movies in the 1920s (Karr, *Authors* 179–86). Mary Vipond's studies of Canadian best-sellers in the first thirty

years of the twentieth century indicate that Connor was far and away the
most financially successful Canadian writer before the First World War, even
in comparison to Robert Service, L.M. Montgomery, Gilbert Parker, Nellie
McClung, Basil King, and Stephen Leacock. He appeared fifteen times in
the top ten sales in Canada between 1899 and 1918, and he fell behind only
Montgomery in top ten listings between 1919 and 1928 (see Vipond's two
articles). In *The Frontier and Canadian Letters* (1957), a memoir of his growing
up on the prairies, Wilfred Eggleston placed Connor on the same shelf with
Walter Scott and the Bible: 'Most homes had a few books, a Bible, a medical
compendium, *The Sky Pilot* perhaps, a novel by Sir Walter Scott,
a Sunday School prize or two' (qtd. in Eric Thompson 221). Connor was
admired and hosted by Henry Ford (Ferré 60), Teddy Roosevelt, Woodrow
Wilson, Wilfrid Laurier, and Herbert Asquith (Thompson and Thompson
159); on his tours of the United States, when he had been commissioned
by the Borden government to urge the Americans to join the 1914–18 war
effort, police had to control the press of crowds seeking autographs (Ferré
60).

Connor went on to serve as president of the Social Service Council of
Manitoba, president of the Canadian Authors Association, chaplain to the
Highland regiments in the Canadian forces during the First World War,
chairman of the Manitoba Joint Council of Industry after the 1919 strike,
and moderator of the Presbyterian Church in Canada in 1921–2, when he
championed the movement for amalgamation with the Methodist and
Congregationalist churches into the United Church of Canada. He became
a fellow of the Royal Society and was awarded two honorary doctorates, one
by the University of Glasgow and the other by the University of Manitoba
(Lennox 105; Karr, *Authors* 216). I list the wide-ranging accomplishments
and functions of Ralph Connor as indications of the way in which popular
authorship in nineteenth- and early twentieth-century Canada provided a
'public address system' for certain figures not only to generate narratives of
the nation but also to play leading public roles in shaping the institutions of
the state.

31 Recent theoretical discussions about the structure and function of allegory
can help us to examine not only how this condensation is composed but
also the fissures that destabilize its guise of 'naturalness' and that therefore
make it anxiously reproductive. Post-structuralist reassessments of allegory,
taking their cues from Walter Benjamin's 'Allegory and Trauerspiel' (1928)
and Paul de Man's 'The Rhetoric of Temporality' (1969), have focused
mostly on allegory's non-coincidence with itself: as opposed to symbolism's
illusory fusion of signifier and signified, allegory's double discourse – its

reference to an anterior, already familiar, code in the given sign – constantly signals the non-simultaneity of sign and meaning. As de Man put it, 'Whereas the symbol postulates the possibility of an identity or identification, allegory designates primarily a distance in relation to its own origin, and, renouncing the nostalgia and the desire to coincide, it establishes its language in the void of this temporal difference' (210). Seen from this perspective, allegory becomes worthy of great fascination and careful study because it demonstrates the fundamental structural problem of language in general: the sign is arbitrarily linked – by convention, by artifice, by association – with its referent and not by any necessary or essential relation between the two.

32 As a pedagogical instrument, allegory addresses both teachers' and students' anxieties. Deborah Madsen's historical survey of allegory from early Judaism and classicism to post-structuralism portrays it as a literary genre deeply invested in the management of cultural anxiety or instability; its very structure of reading the present literal thing in reference to a pre-existent 'normative' code (146) makes it one of society's 'authoritative responses to the trauma of cultural change' (2; see also 109, 135). Gordon Teskey likewise describes allegory as a contentious rhetorical form. He notes how it operates commonly through the figure of the political body: many individuals are incorporated into a single body and usually silenced by the injunction to speak as one. But this single collective body is a delusion: when the nation risks, for example, it is not the nation that pays but individuals (23, 126, 144–5). Seen from this perspective, the contemporary critical interest in allegory, then, is not the mere assertion of literary scholars who wish to politicize a rhetorical form, which would be the dismissive view of Fredric Jameson's much-criticized claim that all Third World writing is political national allegory (see Jameson; also Ahmad). Rather, allegory is increasingly understood as being fundamental to political thinking, insofar as the very idea of representation, whereby a person or character is abstracted from his or her individual life and made to represent the manners, values, and interests of a constituency or milieu, is precisely the function of anthropomorphic allegory. Allegory is the boiled-down short form, the one-standing-in-for-the-many that enables political representatives to negotiate and politic on their constituencies' behalf. Because of its tropic structure – and this was a good deal of Jameson's point about Third World writing (see 65) – allegory constitutes a public, formulaic form of writing that departs from the psychologized and depoliticized forms that were heralded as 'high art' by Euro-American modernists.

33 Sayre N. Greenfield argues that no allegory remains pure allegory because it

can never confine itself strictly to its vehicle-to-tenor (signifier-to-signified) arrangement. For an allegory to work as a story, it needs to 'fill out' its vehicle. Red Cross Knight, for example, needs villagers to witness his destruction of the Dragon; and Bunyan needs to create riff-raff to make Vanity Fair look like a city market. In both cases, extraneous characters are introduced which are superfluous to the allegory's central conceptual conflict. This enlargement means that the vehicle always brings excess with it. Teskey calls this excess the 'noise' that occurs in the rift between the signifier and the signified in the allegorical sign (23), noise that introduces excessive significations which convey unofficial (not necessarily 'unintended') supplements to the allegory's overt pedagogy.

34 This is a point made in Wander, Martin, and Nakayama 24.

35 I am indebted to David Gray for helping me to understand the political utility of this kind of discursive critical practice.

36 For a Canadian overview of this phenomenon, see Frank Davey's *Post-National Arguments*.

2. The Loyalist Brother

1 I gratefully acknowledge the helpful criticisms I received on earlier versions of this chapter from the two anonymous readers for the *Journal of Canadian Studies* and from my colleague at McMaster University, Grace Kehler.

2 Agnes Maule Machar's *For King and Country* (1874) is the only English Canadian Loyalist novel of the War of 1812 I have encountered to date that does not employ the allegory of fraternity. Rather than setting up the conflict as fratricide between brothers, Machar places it within Ernest's ancestry. His deceased father was a decorated military leader of the American rebels in the Revolutionary War, but since his death, Ernest has been raised in Canada by his Quaker uncle and aunt. He shares their pacifist repugnance for the war, but realizes he will be suspected of disloyalty if he does not enlist in the Canadian militia, and after careful reflection, he does so, believing in the rightness of this defence against American aggression. In his eyes, it is a just cause, if a regrettable one.

3 See Goldwin Smith, Davidson, Berger's *Sense,* Mills, Barkley, Winks's *Blacks,* Walker, Clarke's 'Raising,' Enos Monture, and Potter-Mackinnon for a small selection of the Loyalist debates.

4 Further evidence of the existence of a Loyalist myth as a construct later imposed upon Loyalist experience can be seen in the way that scholars have shown how far removed were the actual demographics of the Loyalist refugees from the elite, anglicized image purveyed in the Loyalist myth.

Dennis Duffy observes that there were more Quakers, Highland Scots, and Brantford Mohawks than there were ethnically English United Empire Loyalists among the refugees who settled in Upper Canada (*Gardens* 20–2); and Norman Knowles observes that of the 7,500 Loyalists who settled in Upper Canada before 1785, 3,500 were British soldiers and their families (i.e., not Loyalists from the rebel states), 2,000 were Native allies (and not British subjects) led by John Deseranto and Joseph Brant. Of the remaining group of refugee UELs, 90 per cent were farmers of modest means (and thus not of the wealthy or professional classes). Over half of those who applied for compensation were 'foreign-born,' and only 8 per cent were English by birth (15–17). Knowles provides the following ethnic breakdown for the 240 UEL claimants of Adolphustown in 1784, the year of the famous arrival at the Bay of Quinte: 37 per cent Dutch, 28 per cent British, 20 per cent French, and 15 per cent German. Against the popular image of the Anglican Loyalist he notes that the overwhelming majority were Methodists (17).

5 My argument takes a cue from Dennis Duffy's 1996 book *A World under Sentence: John Richardson and the Interior,* where he observes that the metaphor of 'filial loyalty,' in which '[f]amily relations model and legitimate political allegiance,' was 'common in the Upper Canada of Richardson's day, and well after,' and he produces a lengthy reading of *The Canadian Brothers* as an allegory that uses fraternity as a trope for the 'foundations of the nation-states of North America' and the 'recognition of common ancestry sundered by history' (115). Duffy here builds on previous scholarship by James Reaney, Jay MacPherson, and Michael Hurley, who have all commented on the 'Cain and Abel' motif in Richardson. But Duffy goes a step beyond these scholars and comes closest to my own concerns when he departs from the tendency in these others to interpret the motif in terms of Jungian psychological archetypes and instead reads it explicitly in terms of a national allegory of Canadian-American conflict.

6 In 'The Reorganization of the British Empire' (1888), one of the many articles and speeches George Parkin wrote in his round-the-world campaign for imperial federation, the Anglo-Saxon race is represented – after a Malthusian manner – as fecund, outgrowing the British Isles, and 'impelled by a spirit of enterprise' to search out larger breathing space in the new continents. 'By inherent inclination,' he asserts, 'the Anglo-Saxon is a trader … It has been found to consist in our history, with all the fighting energy of the Roman and much of the intellectual energy of the Greek. It does not seem incompatible with the moral energy of Christianity, and furnishes the widest opportunity for its exercise' (189).

7 See Cogswell 127 for a different perspective on this matter.

8 This arrangement makes possible what must be one of the most remarkable moments in early Canadian literature. For after dinner, amid the gentlemen's accoutrements of cigars and port, the British Canadians General Brock, Commodore Barclay, and Colonel D'Egville enter into a chapter-long debate with the American Major Montgomerie about the treatment of Indigenous peoples by British and American policies. The British accuse the Americans of a policy of open genocide against Natives in a greedy push for land, while Montgomerie accuses the British of using Aboriginals as paid mercenaries and of establishing the policy of genocide that the United States is simply completing. Richardson allows the British Canadians to claim most of the moral high ground, but not without showing that there is more consistency between the two positions than the British are willing to admit. Of course, when he later republished this work in the United States, he cut this scene, along with most other negative references to American policies. (See Donald Stephens's 'Editor's Introduction' to the 1992 CEECT edition of *The Canadian Brothers* for a discussion of the changes Richardson made in a desperate effort late in life and under duress of poverty to market the novel in the United States under the title *Matilda Montgomerie*.)

9 McIlwraith uses this officer code to show how men on opposite sides of the conflict are like brothers who respect one another's dedication to their opposed causes. After the death of Brock at Queenston Heights, she observes that the Stars and Stripes are flown at half mast over the American Fort Niagara in honour of the great British commander's death (111). Similarly, after the terrible battle between Perry's and Barclay's fleets on Lake Erie, we are told that, while the poor sailors are buried ignobly at sea, the officers of both sides are buried in a joint funeral with 'six coffins, draped alternately with the Stars and Stripes and the Union Jack' and that a chaplain of the Church of England reads the service to the mixed group of officers. Later, Perry cares for the wounded Barclay 'as if he had been his brother,' sending him his own surgeon and making a plea to Congress that the British commodore be released on parole and landed in Canada as soon as he has convalesced (255).

10 Even in texts such as Mair's *Tecumseh*, Cody's *The King's Arrow*, and Raddall's *Yankees* which do not engage their heroes in duels, admirable characters show their nobility by refusing to take advantage of moments when they have clearly reprehensible rivals in their power. In Mair, Tecumseh restrains himself from killing his brother, the Prophet; in Cody, Dane Norwood restrains himself from throttling Seth Lupin; and in Raddall, Davy lets his rival Helyer go free, even though he has him in his rifle sights.

11 The tragic vision of his fiction played out in Richardson's own life. Frustrated on all fronts after his return from England to Canada by his inability to make a living either by patronage or by sales of his books, he eventually moved to the United States, where he republished *The Canadian Brothers* as *Matilda Montgomerie; or, The Prophecy Fulfilled,* having removed from the manuscript all the anti-American references. Ironically, this bowdlerized version of the book went through several reprints after its first appearance in 1851. It became the publishing success that had eluded Richardson, but he did not live to benefit from the income it generated since he died of malnutrition in 1852 in New York City (Stephens lxiii–lxvii).

12 Conspicuously absent in the Loyalist texts I have examined is the French Canadian brother or comrade. Raddall's *His Majesty's Yankees* and Cody's *The King's Arrow,* set in eighteenth-century Nova Scotia, both mention and dismiss the struggle between British and French Acadians as background to their Loyalist narratives (Raddall's *Roger Sudden,* a novel about the siege of Louisbourg, describes this background in detail). McIlwraith has a character report that de Salaberry's French volunteers' battle with the Americans at Châteauguay produced the final victory, but this recognition of French participation in the defence of Canada is kept 'off stage,' in the background of reported events (278). Kirby refers to the parallel rebellion in Lower Canada only to recuperate the event as an affirmation of law and order provided by the British crown. His French are not as driven by ambition for progress as his Englishmen are (II, xv; p. 32), and their relaxed intelligence makes them the easy dupes of demagogues' treacherous tongues; but once 'stern Law' beats loud its 'English drums,' they are saved from the chaos of misinformed revolt (XI, xviii–xxix; p. 163).

13 That Kirby uses Mango more to make an argument for British Canadian virtue and against American hypocrisy than to develop an anti-racist argument is made clear by his repugnance for the miscegenation that produced Mango as half-brother to his master:

> His yellow skin betrayed the mingled vein
> That brands the white man with eternal shame,
> The hideous truth revealing to the sun
> That Africa's revenge at last is won;
> That Europe's blood polluted as the grave,
> Quails 'neath the lash and in the slave;
> By nature's outraged laws condemned to live
> And bear the yoke and chain it wont to give.' (VIII, v; p. 108–9).

14 Machar's *For King and Country* is also structured around the romantic rivalry

of a plain-talking Canadian and an over-polished English officer, but the
novel posits Ernest's integrity in his own character and does not ascribe any
influence to Native people.

15 Many critics have observed Raddall's denigration of Native and Acadian
characters, as well as his monological masculine vision of Nova Scotian
history (see Ferns, Creelman, Beeler, Moody, and Smyth). Most of these
criticisms have focused attention on *Roger Sudden*, but many of Raddall's
assumptions that the White, British, male figure accurately represents the
province's founders are evident in *His Majesty's Yankees* as well.

3. The Enterprising Scottish Orphan

1 See Alfred, Dickason, Lawson, Boire, and Findlay for a small selection of
such critiques.

2 There are, of course, other ethno-national groups such as the Irish whose
contestation of Englishness would make an excellent site for defamiliarizing
the normative status of 'English Canada.' I have chosen to examine Canadian Scots, first, because they infiltrated the category of Britishness much
more readily and at an earlier date than did the Irish and, secondly, as a
result because of this earlier infiltration, they had greater power over a
longer time to influence the formation of English Canada. See Royce
MacGillivray for a comparison of Scottish and Irish access to power in the
empire (36) and David Roediger (*Wages*) and Noel Ignatiev for separate
discussions of how the Irish became 'White' by emigration to North
America.

3 See Li, Kay Anderson, Ward, Cho, and Rick Monture for discussion of these
respective examples of White British racism in Canada.

4 In *Maps of Englishness: Writing Identity in the Culture of Colonialism,* Simon
Gikandi highlights the uneven ways in which the inclusiveness and exclusiveness of Britishness could be applied to various colonial subjects by marking
the different identities available to the nineteenth-century Scottish missionary Arthur Barlow, in contrast to those available to Gikandi's Gikuyu grand-
parents, who learned to read in Barlow's Kenyan school: 'The Scottish
missionary was simultaneously … a citizen of Edinburgh, a Lowlander, a
Scot, and a Briton; but such identities did not necessarily all carry the same
weight. The new Christian "readers" [such as Gikandi's grandparents]
would be simultaneously Gikuyu, Kenyan, and African, but they were also
British subjects, wards of the empire, not its citizens' (36–7). See my summary of Baucom below for a discussion of the distinction between subjects
and citizens in the legislation on Britishness.

5 See Trumpener on empire as reconciliation (254, 270); McMullin on Britishness as brotherhood and ecumenism (70).

6 *Les Anciens Canadiens* is particularly interesting in this regard, because de Gaspé consistently uses 'English' to describe the army in which Archie Cameron serves, even after the English general James Wolfe is replaced by the Scottish general James Murray – Murray is even referred to as the 'English general' (183). But when Murray succeeds to the civil post of governor, he is referred to as the representative of the 'British' government. Apparently, the French resentment expresses itself against the 'English' invaders, whereas the benefits of civil rule (de Gaspé writes that Quebec has more peace and better hopes of prosperity under British rule than under the *ancien regime* [151, 239]) are credited to the 'British.'

7 In her introduction to the 1974 reprint of *The Poetical Works of Alexander McLachlan*, E. Margaret Fulton says that poems such as 'Britannia' and 'The Anglo-Saxon' illustrate McLachlan's regular theme of loyalty (xi) and his view that Scots all over the empire, as McLachlan put it in 'Song' (a poem he wrote for the Scottish Gathering in the Crystal Palace grounds in Toronto on 14 September 1859), 'must ever be faithfu' still to kirk and Queen' (xii). In her entry on McLachlan in the *Dictionary of Canadian Biography*, Mary Jane Edwards likewise notes McLachlan's 'loyalty to queen and country,' as well as his typically Victorian 'faith in the superiority of the Anglo-Saxon.'

8 For summaries of this claim, see Waterston, Reid, Gittings, and Williams.

9 Perhaps the most absurd lengths to which this ambition for Scottish domin- ion can be taken appear in Wilfred Campbell's lavish ethnogenesis *The Scotsman in Canada*, vol. 1 (1911). Early in this pantheon of great Canadian Scots, Campbell traces a racial pedigree for North Britons that reaches back through Aeneas to Adam and therefore to God himself: 'Ap-Aeneas, Ap- Anchises, Ap-Lapsius ... Ap-Noachen, Ap-Lamech, Ap-Methsualem, Ap-Enos, Ap-Seth, Ap-Adda (Adam), AP-Duw (God)' (45).

10 Besides the five novels under consideration here, Scottish orphans in Canadian literature include Archie Cameron of de Gaspé's *Les Anciens Canadiens* (1863), Captain Robert Moray of Gilbert Parker's *Seats of the Mighty* (1896), Allan Cameron of Connor's *Corporal Cameron of the NWMP* (1912), Angus Monroe of Frederick Niven's *The Flying Years* (1935), David Baxter of Niven's *Mine Inheritance* (1940), Alan MacNeil of MacLennan's *Each Man's Son* (1951), Morag Gunn of Margaret Laurence's *The Diviners* (1974), Alexander Macdonald of Alistair MacLeod's *No Great Mischief* (1999), and the protagonists of all of the following novels by Margaret Robertson: *Christie Redfern's Troubles* (1866), *The Bairns* (1870), *The Inglises* (1872), *The*

Perils of Orphanhood (1874), *A Year and a Day* (1874–76?), *The Orphans of Glen Elder* (1879), *The Twa Miss Dawsons* (1880), and *By a Way She Knew Not* (1888).

11 The sexual parallel is apt here, and it is underlined by the Mrs Paddock subplot at the end of the novel, which shows how emigration can result from a woman's sexual 'ruination.'

12 In an essay entitled 'The Free Trade Question,' published the year after *Bogle Corbet*, Galt wrote: 'The variety of endowment which distinguishes individuals is a demonstration by Providence that the establishment of the abstract right of equality is obnoxious to society' (qtd. in Graham 40). See Graham for a discussion of Galt's belief in the unequal distribution of human capacities and the resulting appropriateness of an unequal distribution of private property.

13 See Costain for a comparison and contrast between Bogle's British/Canadian pastoral myth based on the bundle-of-sticks analogy and Lawrie Todd's American myth of individual progress.

14 See my discussion of *Mephibosheth Stepsure* below for a remarkable exception to this rule when, in accordance with Nova Scotian poor laws, the orphan Mephibosheth is sold at public auction. Mephibosheth's sale is something akin to the system of indenture that had displaced many Scots to the West Indies in the seventeenth century (see Macmillan 23), but while indentured workers were often treated as brutally as slaves, the system of indenture, at least in theory if not in practice, assumed that the worker was not a permanent property and that he or she could eventually redeem his or her independence.

15 See Lipsitz for a meticulously researched examination of whiteness as property in the domains of American popular culture and political economy.

16 The tradition of dubious assignments of tartans to various groups continues right up to the present, for example, with the passing of Ontario legislative bill 49, which received royal assent on 23 June 2000, for the adoption of an official tartan for the province of Ontario. Other Canadian provinces with official tartans are Nova Scotia, New Brunswick, Manitoba, Saskatchewan, Alberta, and British Columbia. (See http://192.75.156.68/DBLaws/Statutes/English/00to8_e.htm for the Ontario legislation and http://www.pch.gc.ca/progs/cpsc-ccsp/sc-cs/06_e.cfm for Canadian tartans; sites visited 15 March 2005. I thank Marc Ouellette for alerting me to this information.

17 I am indebted to Grace Pollock for this reference.

18 McCulloch's original proposal for Pictou Academy was for a non-sectarian education, but the members of the Anglican-dominated council amended

the 1816 Act of Incorporation so that it limited teachers and trustees to either the Presbyterian or the established church. By so doing, it deliberately undermined the academy's ecumenical vision as well as its potential to serve as a point for solidarity among an interdenominational and resistant constituency (McMullin 70).

19 In *Masks of Conquest: Literary Study and British Rule in India* (1989), Gauri Viswanathan describes how the belletristic study of English literature that had developed in Scotland and the dissenting universities was formalized into the discipline of English literature by the colonial administration in nineteenth-century India in order to produce Indians of British sensibilities, manners, and tastes.

20 '[W]henever people get to the point of emotional confusion at which the feeling "things are not as good as they ought to be" turns into "things are not as good as they used to be," back comes this fictional image of thrift, hard work, simple living, manly independence, and the like, as the real values of democracy that we have lost and must recapture' (Frye, Introduction, iv).

21 The figure of physical disability is often added to orphanhood in Scottish immigrant fiction to emphasize the theme of character overcoming adversity. Galt's Lawrie Todd is also lame, and Hamish MacIvor, in *Shenac's Work at Home*, suffers from anaemia and rheumatism.

22 Robin Matthews, for example, uses Mephibosheth's choice of land over capital to distinguish Mephibosheth's narrative of self-improvement from Benjamin Franklin's. Whereas Franklin, according to Matthews, aimed at 'turning over' one's money several times so that it multiplied itself, Mephibosheth speaks of 'turning over' his lands, that is, cultivating them, and aims at improving the land itself. Matthews thus claims that the *Letters* lacks the capitalist ethos associated with the Franklin-style Puritan work ethic, and that it instead constitutes a *roman de la terre*, or novel of the land ('*Stepsure*'). See Frye, 'Introduction' iv and vii and Rasporich 97 for similar readings, and Sharman 618–19 for an opposite one.

23 Much existing criticism of *Mephibosheth Stepsure* examines McCulloch's role as a progenitor of Canadian parodic humour (Sharman, Rasporich, Frye, 'Introduction,' Davies, 'Editing'). While it is important to recognize that the satirical form of the letters means that Mephibosheth himself becomes the object of gentle satire (when he begins to take on airs because of the fame his writing is bringing him, so that he begins to sign his letters, 'Mephibosheth Stepsure, Gent.,' in the second series of letters), this criticism is nowhere near as biting as that applied to his feckless neighbours, and so he remains a 'satiric norm' (the term is Vincent Sharman's [619]) against which they are consistently found wanting.

24 *The Man from Glengarry* also highlights this time when a renewal of spiritual commitment throughout the Glengarry community meant that for over a year the Gordon church attracted large congregations to its nightly services.

25 I am influenced here by Alistair MacLeod's reading of the Highland-Gaelic tonalities of the Cape Breton characters. I should add that MacLennan himself remains consistently ambivalent about his Scottish heritage: on the one hand, Cape Breton Highlanders are the source of old-time values, and on the other, they are members of a 'race' cursed by their inheritance of Calvinist guilt, which MacLennan likens to a 'somber beast growling behind a locked door' (Prologue to *Each Man's Son*, x). MacKenzie's following the path of Highland Darwinism reflects MacLennan's suggestion that one of its motivations is the desire to escape this cursed inheritance.

26 For admirers of the allegorical mode, see Arnason, Boechenstein, Hatch, Matthews ('Hugh'), McPherson, and Sutherland; for those who object to the heavy-handedness of the allegory, see Woodcock (*Introducing*), Hoy, Cockburn, and Cameron. Of course, these two categories are too absolute, for many critics object to the sacrifice of characters on aesthetic grounds but see the importance of the allegory on nationalistic grounds. For examples of this position, see Staines, New, Woodcock, and Cameron.

27 MacLeod, himself famously of Cape Breton Highland background, Arnason, and Woodcock are the exceptions.

28 Woodcock says that this experience was central to MacLennan's drive to define a Canadian identity separate from English domination, but he also draws attention to the fact that MacLennan was not an outstanding scholar and may have been passed over for reasons other than purely English preference (*Introducing* 57).

4. The Muscular Christian

1 See Woodcock, 'Introduction' 7; Winks, 'Introduction' vi; Ricou, 'Afterword' 249.

2 *The Foreigner* was second best-seller in Canada in 1909 and tenth in 1910 (Lennox 137). The film adaptation starred up-and-coming Hollywood actors Gaston Glass, Wilton Lackeye, and Bigelow Cooper (Karr, *Authors* 139). Even as late as 1972, long after literary critics had abandoned serious discussion of Connor, J. Lee and John Thompson, among the few critics who did offer a consideration of Connor's oeuvre, called it his 'most important novel' and his 'most exhilarating statement on the development and destiny of the Canadian spirit' (166).

3 Kingsley and Hughes lived out these convictions. Kingsley went door to door

during a cholera epidemic in 1848, dispensing hygiene information and food to suffering families; he was also a founding member of the Christian socialist movement (Vance 80–1); and he worked with women's groups to establish the first women's college, women's learned societies, a woman's trade union, and women's suffrage (Rosen 28). Hughes worked to establish cooperative workshops and was chairman of the first Co-operative Congress in 1869, co-author of *A Manual for Co-operators* (1881), and a Liberal MP from 1865 to 1874 (Vance 138, 134).

4 Kingsley's anti-Catholic views were fuelled by homophobia. Vance reports that although Kingsley never explicitly refers to homosexuality, 'he leaves it open to his reader to suspect that the "maundering, die-away effeminacy" of the "Manichees" [Kingsley's term for Cardinal Newman's Tractarian Catholics] who repress the instinct to marry and be conventionally manly may include this unspoken and unspeakable sin' (112–13).

5 From the date of the novel's publication, commentators of eastern European descent have been offended by Connor's reliance on stereotype and misinformation. In a review of *The Foreigner* published in 1910, W.J. Mihaychuk expresses himself sick at heart at Connor's biased presentation of Slavs and 'Galicians' (487). He expresses dismay at the contrast between the high-flown rhetoric of charity and justice presented in the preface and the degraded representation of Galicians in the sections that describe their squalid living conditions in North End Winnipeg (489). Sixty years later, in *Ukrainian Canadians: A Survey of Their Portrayal in English-Language Works* (1978), Frances Swyripa points out the many incongruities that show how little Connor actually knew about Ukrainian culture: he marries Kalman's father, Michael Kalmar, supposedly a Russian nobleman, to Paulina, a Galician peasant, an impossibility in the old country; then he puts Rosenblatt, a Bukovinian, in cahoots with the Russian secret police; and finally he gives Kalman and Irma Hungarian names that would have been uncommon among Ukrainians and Russians (13–14). Swyripa reports a section from John Murray Gibbon's *Canadian Mosaic* in which Gibbon tells how he encountered opposition when he was organizing the New Canadian Heritage Festival in Winnipeg in 1928 because townsfolk had read Connor's 'somewhat lurid melodrama of the shack-town which had grown up on the skirts of this mushroom city' (Gibbon 276), and Winnipegers felt that such low-living cultures should not be encouraged in Canada. Connor was an old friend of Gibbon's, and so Gibbon invited him to attend a performance of a Polish dance troupe and to meet the dancers. Connor was impressed with the civility of the people he met and confessed to Gibbon, 'I always looked on the Poles as husky, dirty labourers whose chief entertainment was drink,

but these are delightful, cultivated people. I feel that I have done them an injustice in my book. What can I do to make amends?' (Gibbon 277). Because the festival had opened to a poor turnout, Gibbon asked Connor to phone his friends to come to see the rest of the festival. He did, and by the end of the week, there was standing room only (278).

6 For an overview, see 'Shiners' Wars' in *The Canadian Encyclopedia* (1988).

7 The prominent role played by Mrs Murray in guiding Ranald's maturation into the ideal of muscular Christianity is significant in several ways. Certainly, her presence in the novel overshadows that of her husband, so that, in point of fact, she is more active as a minister in Glengarry than he is. But a feminist evaluation of her character would be ambiguous: compared to her husband, she has more perspicacity in her assessment of Ranald's potential, and because of her practical service to the community at large, she is more essential to the Glengarrians' daily lives; but because her virtues are those of self-renunciation and service, she can appear more as a stereotype of female self-denial than as a self-fulfilled woman (see Alison Gordon's afterword to *The Man from Glengarry*). Her appraisal becomes even more complicated when we consider that her self-sacrifice participates in the class restructuring I mentioned earlier in ways that are specific to Canadian concerns over ethnicity and urban/rural values. Mrs Murray, we are told, comes from a well-to-do family in the city, and she has all the advantages of a rich education; one sign of her strength of character is that she has willingly given up these advantages for her ministry in the bush to the Glengarrian Highlanders. She has even taken it upon herself to learn Gaelic in order to speak the language of her parishioners' hearts. Her identification with their ethnicity, her practical work to alleviate their poverty, and her preference for rural rigour to urban luxury distinguishes her from the vapid femininity of Maimie St. Clair, who passes up Mrs Murray's practical Christianity for the hollow values of class status and urbane entertainment.

8 Many critics have noted the tension between violence and forgiveness in Connor's fiction (e.g., Lennox 139, 148; Daniells, 'Glengarry' 22). The tension is fundamental to Connor's narrative technique, for the violent scenes provide the excitement essential to the adventure genre while they also operate as foils for the 'gethsemane' moments when Connor's muscular Christians realize that the way of forgiveness requires more courage than the way of vengeance (*Glengarry* 33–4; *Foreigner* 341–7).

9 In 'Ranger and Mountie: Myths of National Identity in Zane Grey's *The Lone Star Ranger* and Ralph Connor's *Corporal Cameron*,' Ronald Tranquilla examines these two 'Westerns' to compare American and Canadian depictions of the national hero. He finds that, while both protagonists are manly,

self-confident, and strong, the American hero is linked with popular democratic, individualistic, and violent values, whereas the Canadian hero is
associated with oligarchy, community, and the values of self-restraint. Dick
Harrison (159), Pierre Berton (43), and Daniel Francis (34) all point out
that the Mountie's heroism is remarkably 'Canadian' in that, while the
image of his profession is glorified, the man himself remains faceless, the
member of a group rather than an individual.

10 For information on Johnny or Jack Canuck, see www.nlc-bnc.ca/
superheroes/t3-201-e.html and http://www.collectionscanada.ca/2/6/
h6-208-e.html (sites visited 20 May 2005).

11 See Morson 72 and Hutcheon, 'Modern' 91 on how parody operates
through resituating the original utterance in an unfamiliar context or
skewed situation which undermines the original's self-security.

12 Murphy's 1922 book on drugs in Canada, *The Black Candle*, is often cited as
an example of the xenophobic elements of first-wave feminist writing in
Canada (see Anthony and Solomon 3; Valverde 86). It is indisputable that
this book recycles the racist myth of Chinese, African, and southern European men inveigling Canadian women through drug addiction into the
'white slave' trade as prostitutes (17, 233). But to charge Murphy with
xenophobia outright is to overlook her attempt to criticize this widespread
panic over the conjectured trade in White women. 'Much has been said,'
she writes from her years of experience as the first female magistrate in the
British Empire, 'concerning the entrapping of girls by Chinamen in order
to secure their services as peddlers of narcotics ... Personally, we have never
known of such a case ... It is not true ... that a white girl or woman who is
keeping her own preserves is hunted like game ... and trapped by the
Chinaman in order that she may be bent to his criminal purpose' (233).
Of the rumour that the 'yellow peril' plots the demise of the White race by
unmanning the latter through drug addiction, Murphy writes, 'We have no
very great sympathy with the baiting of the yellow races, or with the belief
that these exist only to serve Caucasians, or to be exploited by us' (186).
Because she composed much of the book from newspaper clippings and
from anecdotes from her courtroom, many of her sources employ the
language of racist panic. By quoting them, she unwittingly participates in
their repetition, despite her criticism of this panicked language. Murphy's
assumption of a White readership – she could not have been assuming
Chinese or African readers when she described an African woman as 'as
black as the proverbial ace-of-spades' (67) or a Chinese man 'whose morals
were as oblique as his eyes' (236) – tends to recuperate her critical discourse
into that of the xenophobic panic she wants to critique. Her book provides a

good example of how a liberal attempt to criticize social attitudes overdetermined by racialized panic can trade on the very anxiety it seeks to
repudiate. As with the example of J.S. Woodsworth, discussed in my opening
chapter, *Black Candle* illustrates the contradictions inherent in Canadians'
British-derived code of civility itself, and as such, it allows us to see how
people sincerely committed to building what they understood as a civil
society could have been blind to the incivilities and exclusions that were
essential to the project in which they were engaged. See Kulba for a recent
reassessment of Murphy's legacy.

13 Like Murphy's engagement with anti-Chinese racist discourse in *Black
Candle*, McClung's representations of Chinese people in *Painted Fires* both
repeat and critique bigoted attitudes. A generous reader might claim that
McClung tries to present a rounded image of Chinese restaurant owners by
balancing the villainy of the heroin supplier with the decency of Sam Lee,
who provides Helmi with a job in Edmonton when no one else will (Warne
73). But McClung's clumsy rendition of Sam's broken English readily
reinforces the assumption of Chinese unassimilable foreignness: 'nice liddle
girl carry chop suey – makea nice white apron, liddle cap ...' (249).

14 Veronica Strong-Boag's modification of her views on this issue indicates the
unsettled opinion about maternal feminism's effects, as well as its investment in White, middle-class values. Compare her 'Canadian Feminism in
the 1920s' (1985) with the revised version, "Ever a Crusader" (1991).

15 See Tamara Palmer 57; Harrison 90, 111–13; Karr, 'Robert' 43; and Kroetsch
118 for discussions of the image of the patriarch and of spiritually bankrupt
masculinity in prairie fiction.

16 In 'Nationhood,' the speech he delivered to the Canadian Clubs across the
country in 1928, Grove points to history to warn that 'if a great material
civilization was bestowed upon a people which was spiritually not prepared
for it, it has ever had but one effect, and that a coarsening one which has
necessarily prevented the deeper nature of that people from maturing its
finest blossoms' (139). He therefore urges his listeners: 'if we prize our
spiritual heritage above material things, then, perhaps ... Canada stands a
chance of counting as one of the spiritual units which will go to make up a
greater British Empire' (158). While Grove's emphasis of spiritual values
does parallel the muscular Christian ideals I have been tracing, his use of
the term 'spiritual' has a more secular purview and more closely resembles
Matthew Arnold's aesthetic-humanist notion of the spiritual than a strictly
religious one. Nonetheless, as David Rosen points out, there are many
echoes of muscular Christian values in Arnold's *Culture and Anarchy* (Rosen
40–1), and I would claim the same for Grove's secularized spirituality.

17 See Woodcock, 'Introduction' 17–18; Thompson 221, 223; Ricou, *Vertical* 20; Varma 142.

18 In this regard, Harris anticipates the tyrannical workaholic patriarchs Caleb Gare in Ostenso's *Wild Geese* and Abe Spalding of Grove's *Fruits of the Earth*.

19 The Homesteaders Act allowed only women with dependents to file on land, while men as young as eighteen years old could file. See Susan Jackel's introduction to the reprint edition of the homestead activist Georgina Binnie-Clarke's *Wheat and Woman* (1914), as well as Nellie McClung's fictional discussion in *Purple Springs* (1921) of political activism in regards to homestead and voting legislation in the build-up to Manitoba premier Roblin's political fall in 1915 and the achievement of female suffrage in the province the year after.

20 See Stead's novel *Dennison Grant* (1920) for his fictional outline of an alternative use of capital for public benefit in rural communities. See also Mundwiler and Karr ('Robert') for discussions of Stead's ideas on social and economic reform. On a slightly different note, an indication of his long-standing alignment with Canadian imperialist ideas can be observed in the fact that his *Empire Builders* (1908) was reprinted four times and released again in 1923 with no change to title or theme, despite the selection of some new poems for the 1923 edition (Mundwiler 190).

21 Davey takes his cue in questioning the realism of *Grain* from Mundwiler.

22 I make this claim with the caveat that the opacity of Mrs Bentley's narration renders any certain interpretation of the novel dicey, including mine. See Sandra Djwa for an interpretation that posits a salvific ending for the novel.

23 My comment about Mrs Bentley's construction of Philip's character is meant to call attention to her absolutely central role as narrator of the diary-novel. But I do not mean to participate in the misogynistic interpretations of the novel that treat her as the destroyer of Philip's manhood. See Cude for a particularly hostile reading of Mrs Bentley. Stouck's and Moss's collections of Ross criticism provide useful samplings of differing interpretations of Mrs Bentley's narration.

24 See Keith Fraser for a discussion of the homosexual subtext of Ross's novel. In opposition to Valerie Raoul's and Andrew Lesk's readings of homoeroticism as the obvious theme systematically repressed by critics of Ross's fiction, Fraser presents the homosexual subtext as hidden even from its author. He reflects on his almost thirty-year friendship with Ross to produce the image of a man progressively less timid about his homosexuality but whose characteristic privacy made him simultaneously an artistic master of false-fronts and their victim. Fraser reports that Ross did not think of *As for Me* as a homoerotic book when he was writing it, but that he gradually came to

admit that 'it' was there (42ff). Fraser suggests that Ross's (unconscious?) sympathy for Philip's closeted homosexuality gives the narrative both its compelling power and its tragic flaw, because it blinded him to the narrative violence done to the character of Mrs Bentley, who, Fraser believes, should have left the marriage to fulfill the novel's dramatic demands (53).

5. The Maturing Colonial Son

1 See Angus McLaren's *Our Own Master Race: Eugenics in Canada, 1885–1945* for an excellent survey of the impact of eugenicist theories upon Canadian public thinking – especially among progressive reformers – in the late nineteenth and early twentieth centuries. He observes that eugenics thinking had two high-water marks in Canada: the decade before the First World War and the decade before the Second World War (10).

2 I am thinking here of late nineteenth- and early twentieth-century uses of the allegory. In post-1960s, post-multiculturalism Canadian discourses, the role of beneficiary is often extended to include 'visible minorities' (see Mackey 16, 49; Bannerji, *Dark* 10, 87–124). In each of these discursive periods, we see residual versions of the Loyalist brother's patronizing of African and Native figures that I traced in chapter 2.

3 See David Gilmore's *Manhood in the Making* for an international survey of the way masculinity requires this constant reaffirming performativity in cultures around the world.

4 As Arnold Itwaru puts it, 'in this necessary invention of [the nation's] meaning, the inventor is simultaneously being invented. The stranger categorized in the name and label "immigrant" is already invented as "immigrant," ... a particular *other*, the bearer of a label invented by the "host." This person has become the immigrant – this term of depersonalization which will brand her and him for the rest of their lives in the country of their adoption' (13–14).

5 United Church purity educator and social activist Dr Samuel Dwight Chown wrote in 1910: 'While many of our non-Anglosaxon population are amongst the best of the people from their native lands ... it is lamentable that such large numbers have come to Canada during the last decade bringing a laxity of morals, an ignorance, a superstition and an absence of high ideals of personal character or of national life ... [They] may constitute a danger to themselves and a menace to our national life' (qtd. in Valverde 53).

6 Craig notes that although Rosenblatt is never identified as a Jew, his appearance, behaviour, and name all draw on features of the anti-Semitic stereotype (*Racial* 34).

7 Essentially, the civil mode of exclusion I discuss here is a form of what
Martin Barker, analysing the increased exclusions of British immigration
policy during the Thatcher years, has called 'new racism.' Satzewich summarizes Barker's concept this way: 'the new racism does not make reference to
biological and cultural *inferiority* but rather to inherent cultural, "racial," and
national *difference.* Such differences are defined by new racists as the source
of social antagonisms and are then used as grounds for various kinds of
social exclusions' ('Race' 36).

8 In a recent article that assesses Grove's assimilation to British normativity in
Canada, Paul Hjartarson observes the strong anti-foreign sentiments that
emerged just after Grove arrived in Manitoba in 1912 with the advent of
the Great War and then the Bolshevik Revolution. Canadian xenophobic
responses to these events included the rejection of foreign-language instruction in Manitoba schools (Grove had been principal of a German school)
and the imposition of anti-alien legislation. Hjartarson reads Grove's reluctance to identify his German background, to depict only 'desirable' Scandinavian immigrants in his novels, and his general Anglo-conformity not only
to the problems he had escaped in Europe (a charge of fraud, his abandoned marriage, and his faked suicide) but also to the emergence in
Canada of an anti-foreign 'surveillance state' during the late teens and early
twenties.

9 I am indebted for much of the biographical information about Gibbon to
Janet McNaughton's 'John Murray Gibbon and the Inter-war Folk Festivals'
and to Daniel Francis (81ff.).

10 Gibbon is careful to credit the American writer Victoria Hayward with the
first use of the term 'mosaic' to describe Canada's diverse religious populace
in her *Romantic Canada* (Macmillan, 1922). He then credits Kate A. Foster
of Toronto with the second use in her 150-page survey of 'New Canadians'
called 'Our Canadian Mosaic,' written for the Dominion Council of the
YWCA in 1926 for use by social workers (ix). Ian McKay insists, however, that
Gibbon was central to the popularization of the metaphor: 'Without Gibbon
the now all-pervasive metaphor of Canada as a cultural mosaic might have
died an obscure death as an American writer's conceit. It was Gibbon who
rescued it as the governing metaphor of the new post-colonial liberal
nationalism that gradually overshadowed many Canadians' earlier identification with Britain' (qtd. in Francis 81).

11 The fact that Gibbon was born in Ceylon raises the likelihood that his
exclusion of Asians from the book is more a conscious than an unconscious
decision.

12 In the same speech, Tweedsmuir credits his Ukrainian listeners' ancestors

with defending Christian Europe's White borders: 'for it was your race which for centuries held the south-eastern gate of Europe against the attacks of the East' (Gibbon 307).

13 The first English translation of *Les Anciens Canadiens,* by Georgiana M. Pennée, appeared in 1864, the year after de Gaspé's original publication. A second translation, by Charles G.D. Roberts, was published in 1890. A revised edition of the Pennée translation was issued in 1929, and the Roberts translation has been reprinted many times in the New Canadian Library series. I refer to Jane Brierley's 1996 translation in my discussion of the text.

14 Brierley notes that de Gaspé translated most of Sir Walter Scott's novels into French (10); these would have provided a source for his familiarity with Highland history as well as with the romance genre, which in the nineteenth century was making that history into one of the most widely known myths of a conquered people's dignity.

15 The Indigenous figures in the novel do not enter into its allegorical scheme according to which the brotherhood between Scots and French points the way toward the civil relations that de Gaspé hopes will characterize the emerging Canadian nation. This is to say that there is no indication what form of relations will be established between the reconciled family and the surrounding Indigenous peoples. In addition, it is important to note the fact that Lisette, the d'Habervilles' mulatto slave, is portrayed as preferring to remain in service to the seigneur's household even when she is offered her freedom. Her choice suggests that her servitude will be as welcome and necessary to the new civil order as it was in New France (210–11). I am indebted to Don Moore for alerting me to Lisette's significant marginalization in the novel.

16 See Blair and Stacey for discussions of New France gothic in nineteenth-century Canadian fiction.

17 This feminized form of the national allegory of maturation is not unknown. Georgina Binnie-Clarke's *Wheat and Woman* describes Canada as the 'true daughter of a new day' (312–13), and McClung's *Painted Fires* is an immigrant maturation narrative whose protagonist is a 'foreign' girl who matures into a fully participating Canadian woman. In yet another example, Hugh MacLennan suggests in 'The Canadian Character' (1949) that Canada is not a masculine but a feminine country: 'she' is like a 'good wife' who manages, soothes, and is amused at her American husband's bravado (5–6). Finally, closest in time and setting to Parker's novel, Rosanna Leprohon's *Antoinette de Mirecourt* (1864) presents an allegorical maturation narrative in which the French Canadian female protagonist must choose between a dissipated English officer and a plain-speaking and reliable one.

18 A troop of Native soldiers is mentioned in passing during Parker's description of the Battle of the Plains of Abraham, but besides a dismayingly casual mention of how Robert's party readily kills two Native men during their voyage down the St Lawrence and how the war-loving Clark even takes the scalps, which he says will demand £12 each in New York (286), there is no mention of Indigenous people in the novel. In de Gaspé's novel, Native forces also appear in the battle scenes, and beyond these appearances, Abenaki and Iroquois figures function to contrast with European politics and culture. The reclusive d'Egmont points out the absurdity of debtors' prisons by quoting an Iroquois who asks how a prisoner can pay off his debts if he cannot trap for furs. In neither of these novels do Indigenous people figure at the centre of the national allegory or in its envisioned future.

19 In *Medicine River*, through the words of his character Lionel James, an old Blackfoot storyteller who travels the world relating stories and legends, Thomas King lampoons this tendency to place Natives in the distant past. Lionel notes that his European listeners do not like contemporary stories about First Nations people, and he cannot figure out why they prefer to live in the past like that (175).

20 For historical background on the formation and denial of the interracial marriages that were common in and around Hudson's Bay Company forts, see Venema and also Van Kirk.

21 Barry Mack is right to point out that the price of modernization in the West was the destruction of Native and Métis societies and that Connor's fiction glosses over, rather than addresses, this fact (152–3). *The Gaspards* constitutes a moment in Connor's writing, however, when the gloss wears the thinnest. Terrence Craig notes that the novel was published in the period after the First World War when Connor was less certain of his Anglo-Celtic vision of Canada, and this new uncertainty makes it 'one of the most interesting novels in Canada' ('Religious' 104).

22 The novel never mentions either of the Métis uprisings. While this lack of reference may be explained by the novel's far removal in setting (the Kootenays) and date of publication (1923) from these events in Manitoba and Saskatchewan, the fact that mixed-race people are central to the 'problem' addressed by the novel makes it seem odd that the uprisings would be passed over in silence.

23 A dramatic example of the pathological horror that could be attached to miscegenation as late as 1944 appears in Thomas Raddall's *Roger Sudden*, a historical novel about the French and English contest for sovereignty in eighteenth-century Nova Scotia. At one point, when Roger is a captive of Mi'kmaqs, one of their leading women chooses him for a sexual partner.

Despite his attraction to 'the splendid animal' before him, he thinks: 'To
mate with this wild thing, to produce hybrid things, half beast and half
himself, and to live year in year out among these mockeries, like a man shut
up in a room hung with distorted mirrors … ugh! Darkness! Darkness!'
(166, ellipsis in original). In his subsequent attempt to explain his repugnance at the prospect of having children with her, Roger tells Wapke to look
at the delta where the clear river runs into the sparkling sea: 'Yet where they
mingle … is mud and stink. This is the wisdom of Manitoo who made these
things – and thee and me' (173). If we have been tempted to read a distance
between the novel's overall ideological views and Roger's individual ones on
this matter, Roger later develops this anti-miscegenation taboo into the
novel's concluding explanation for the way the English prevailed over the
French: 'the *coureurs* had mated with savage women and spilled their seed
in the wilderness' (357), while the English 'who were not content to mate
with savages but who took their women with them everywhere, resolved not
merely to penetrate the wilderness but to people it!' (357–8). The power of
Englishness, according to this line of thinking, which forms the centrepiece
of the novel's concluding rationale, rises from its reproduction of a racially
'pure' population untarnished by degrading intimacy with Indigenous
savagery.

24 Clarence Karr rejects this dismissal of Connor and other popular writers
    of the early twentieth century as hopelessly irrelevant to modern Canadian
    concerns. He argues that writers such as Connor, McClung, Montgomery,
    Stead, and Stringer came into their popularity precisely because of modern
    production and distribution technologies (cheap paper; machinery for
    printing, binding, and folding; a national railway for distribution; a better
    mail system, postcard ads, free rural delivery, and mail-order catalogues; and
    movies [27–8, 32]) and because they wrote consciously with the intent to
    intervene in modernization. For Karr, Connor tried, not to evade moder-
    nity, but to retain spiritual and communal values and so to humanize
    modernity (2, 8).

6. Wry Civility

1 See Kertzer, 'Historical'; and Weir.
2 I should also insert a caveat here: I turn to these ironical texts as a critical
   strategy, not because I have any interest in proving or disproving the argument, derived from Linda Hutcheon's *Splitting Images* (1991), that there
   is something inherent in the Canadian situation that leads to ironic expression.

3 See de Man, 218 and Chambers, *Room* 238ff.

4 Itwaru (66) and Beddoes (10) both comment upon the centrality of the Horatio Alger–type book as Marlyn's counter-discursive target, while Thacker (26) reads the novel as targeting Connor's *The Foreigner* and Woodsworth's *Strangers within Our Gates.*

5 Even Lawson, the businessman who denounces Englishmen and Europeans alike who do not count themselves Canadians first (188), and who treats Alex as an equal, is unable to provide him with any practical help or even emotional comfort after the stock market crash destroys their mutual interests (243–4).

6 See Hutcheon's introduction to *Double-Talking* for distinctions between pre-modernist, modernist, and postmodern forms of irony (15–16).

7 Peter Allen writes that the novel's 'narrative voice is the chief puzzle' (370), and Dean reads Duncan's double marginalization as a colonial and as a woman as producing an ambiguous, subversive irony (6–10), while Fiamengo focuses on the question of 'how to read Duncan's irony' ('"Susceptible"' 137) and says that her capacity to stand 'both inside and outside an argument' constitutes one of the chief enjoyments of reading her work ('"Baptized"' 14). Peterman admires Duncan's 'deft balancing of wry sympathy and probing satire' (345), and Thomas refers to her 'double focus-vision' (357).

8 Letter to R.W. Gilder, 22 October 1902, in Tausky, *Imperialist* 307. The Tecumseh Press edition of *The Imperialist,* edited by Thomas Tausky, reprints many of Duncan's letters and the early reviews that appeared after the novel's publication. Subsequent references to letters and reviews all come from Tausky's edition.

9 Milburn is Duncan's scathing portrait of the self-satisfactions of the privileged, conservative English colonial: 'If an important non-entity is an imaginable thing, perhaps it would stand for Mr. Milburn; and he found it a more valuable combination than it may appear, since his importance gave him position and opportunity, and his nonentity saved him from their risks. Certainly he had not imposed his view upon his fellow members [of the Chamber of Commerce] – they would have blown it off like a feather – yet they found themselves very much of his mind' (236).

10 Thomas ties Duncan's admiring representation of the Scottish Canadian to the mythology popularized by Ralph Connor: 'Among our novelists, Duncan and Connor have given us the "classic" statements of the Scotch Hero and Builder mythology …. Connor rewrote the Scotch-Canadian hero in different guises and situations in virtually every one of his thirty-odd novels … There is no other social mythology so pervasive in our literature as that of the Scotch' (367).

11 Tausky reports that when Duncan visited Canada just after the first edition
    of the novel had been published in Toronto, she bravely read a passage
    from Lorne's impassioned advocacy of imperial federation in his disastrous
    opera-house speech at the reception held in her honour by the Canadian
    Society of Authors. In the audience were a collection of professors, govern-
    ment ministers, and literati, including Goldwin Smith, her former employer
    at the *Week,* who was famous for his antagonism for imperial federation
    ('It Is' 470, 482).

12 Montgomery says the margin was 201 votes (23), but Tausky, citing the
    Brantford *Expositor* of 24 June 1896, says the number was 86 ('Writing' 327).

13 That enfranchisement constitutes a form of cultural and even political
    erasure for First Peoples is not just a perception of Native paranoia, for it
    has been an explicit objective in repeated attempts by successive govern-
    ments to enfranchise Indigenous peoples. Here, for example, is Sir John A.
    Macdonald's rationale for the 1885 Electoral Franchise Act: 'the great aim in
    our legislation has been to do away with the tribal system and assimilate the
    Indian people in all respects with the other inhabitants of the Dominion, as
    speedily as they are fit for change' (qtd. in Montgomery 13). And here is
    Duncan Campbell Scott in his introduction to Bill 14 on the compulsory
    enfranchisement of Native peoples in 1920: 'I want to get rid of the Indian
    problem. I do not think as a matter of fact, that this country ought to con-
    tinuously protect a class of people who are able to stand alone. That is my
    whole point. Our objective is to continue until there is not a single Indian in
    Canada that has not been absorbed into the body politic, and there is no
    Indian question, and no Indian Department and that is the whole object of
    this Bill' (qtd. in Rick Monture 133).

14 This arrangement is contested by the town of Brantford (Higginson 146).

15 In this regard, *Strange Manuscript* fits Keith Booker's description of the
    dystopian genre in his introduction to *Dystopian Literature: A Theory and
    Research Guide*: 'I consider the principal literary strategy of dystopian litera-
    ture to be defamiliarization: by focusing their critiques of society on imagina-
    tively distant settings, dystopian fictions provide fresh perspectives on
    problematic social and political practices that might otherwise be taken for
    granted or considered natural or inevitable' (3–4).

16 One vector of the satire compares the unstable civility of the Scots and the
    Irish with that of the Kosekin. At one point, More discovers that the Kosekin
    take an immediate liking for the Celtic music he plays on a fiddle. Noting
    their delight in such tunes as 'Tara,' 'Bonnie Doon,' 'The Land of the Leal,'
    'Auld Lang Syne,' and 'Lochaber,' he makes sense of it thus: 'in their mild
    manners and their outbursts of cruelty they seemed to me to be not unlike

the very race which had created this music, since the Celt is at once gentle and blood-thirsty ... and the eyes that weep over the pathetic strains of "Lochaber" can gaze without a tear upon the death-agonies of a slaughtered friend' (108).

17 Here is De Mille himself describing his own novels in a response to a request for a biographical sketch for the *Literary World* in 1878. After supplying a bibliographical list of his over twenty-five published novels, which of course did not include the posthumously published *Strange Manuscript,* he writes: 'The chief characteristics of the above novels is the union of sensationalism with extravagant humor; the most tragic incidents are brought forward only to be dismissed with playful mockery; the plot is highly elaborated, tragedy & comedy exist side by side, the prevalent atmosphere is one of mock seriousness; and the author while he freely uses the most startling and harrowing details never fails to turn them into ridicule, and thus appears to satirize and burlesque the whole sensational school of fiction' (qtd. in Parks, 'Editor's' xxv).

18 See Gerson, 'Contrapuntal'; Milnes; Kilgour; Turcotte; and Arnold.

19 Kilian speculates, on the basis of drawings that appear in the author's college notebooks from Brown University, that De Mille may have had the novel in mind as early as 1853 (62).

20 See Silbiger, McCullum, and Spanos respectively.

Works Cited

Abella, Irving, and Harold Troper. *None Is Too Many: Canada and the Jews of Europe, 1937–1948*. Toronto: Lester & Orpen Dennys, 1982.

'Aboriginals: Treaties and Relations: 1951–1981 Aboriginal Rights Movement.' http://www.canadiana.org/citm/themes/aboriginals/aboriginals12_e.html. Visited 6 May 2004.

Ahmad, Aijaz. 'Jameson's Rhetoric of Otherness in the "National Allegory."' *The Post-Colonial Reader*. Ed. William Ashcroft, Helen Tiffin, and Gareth Griffiths. New York and London: Routledge, 1995. 77–82.

Akenson, Donald Harman. 'The Historiography of English-Speaking Canada and the Concept of Diaspora: A Sceptical Appreciation.' *The Canadian Historical Review* 76.3 (September 1995): 375–409.

Alfred, Taiaiake. *Peace, Power, Righteousness: An Indigenous Manifesto*. Don Mills, ON: Oxford University Press, 1999.

Allen, Peter. 'Narrative Uncertainty in *The Imperialist*.' In Tausky, ed. 369–88. (Revised from *Studies in Canadian Literature* 9.1 (1984): 41–60.)

Allen, Theodore. *The Invention of the White Race*. 2 vols. London and New York: Verso, 1994.

Anderson, Benedict. *Imagined Communities: Reflections on the Origin and Spread of Nationalism*. Rev. ed. London: Verso, 1991.

Anderson, Kay J. *Vancouver's Chinatown: Racial Discourse in Canada, 1875–1980*. Montreal and Kingston: McGill-Queen's UP, 1991.

Anonymous ['A Westerner']. 'Imperialism, Nationalism, or a Third Alternative.' *University Magazine* 9 (October 1910): 339–58.

Anthony, Brian, and Robert Solomon. 'Introduction.' *The Black Candle*. By Emily Murphy. Toronto: Thomas Allen, 1922; facsimile ed., Toronto: Coles, 1973. 1–3.

Arnason, David. 'Canadian Nationalism in Search of a Form: Hugh MacLennan's *Barometer Rising*.' *Journal of Canadian Fiction* 1.4 (1972): 68–71.

Arnold, Angela. '"To Seize, to Slay, to Conquer": Satirizing the Imperial Mission in James De Mille's *Strange Manuscript Found in a Copper Cylinder.*' *Foundation: The International Review of Science Fiction* 30.81 (Spring 2001): 83–9.

Aubert de Gaspé, Philippe-Joseph. *Canadians of Old: A Romance.* Translation of *Les Anciens Canadiens* by Jane Brierley. Montreal: Véhicule, 1996.

Avery, Donald. *'Dangerous Foreigners': European Immigrant Workers and Labour Radicalism in Canada, 1896–1932.* Toronto: M & S, 1979.

Backhouse, Constance. *Colour-Coded: A Legal History of Racism in Canada, 1900–1950.* Toronto: Osgood Society/U of Toronto P, 1999.

Bailyn, Bernard, and Philip D. Morgan. 'Introduction.' *Strangers within the Realm: Cultural Margins of the First British Empire.* Ed. Bernard Bailyn and Philip D. Morgan. Chapel Hill and London: U of North Carolina P, 1991. 1–31.

Balibar, Étienne. 'The Nation Form: History and Ideology.' 1991. *Race Critical Theories.* Ed. Philomena Essed and David Theo Goldberg. Oxford: Blackwell, 2002. 220–30.

– 'Three Concepts of Politics: Emancipation, Transformation, Civility.' Trans. Chris Turner. *Politics and the Other Scene.* Trans. Christine Jones, James Swenson, and Chris Turner. London and New York: Verso, 2002. 1–39.

Ballstadt, Carl, ed. *The Search for English-Canadian Literature: An Anthology of Critical Articles from the Nineteenth and Early Twentieth Centuries.* Toronto: U of Toronto P, 1975.

– 'Secure in Conscious Worth: Susanna Moodie and the Rebellion of 1837.' *Canadian Poetry* 18 (Spring/Summer 1986): 88–98.

Bannerji, Himani. *The Dark Side of the Nation: Essays on Multiculturalism, Nationalism and Gender.* Toronto: Canadian Scholars' Press, 2000.

– 'The Other Family.' *Other Solitudes: Canadian Multicultural Fictions.* Toronto: Oxford UP, 1990. 141–5.

Barkley, Murray. 'The Loyalist Tradition in New Brunswick: The Growth and Evolution of an Historical Myth, 1825–1914.' *Acadiensis* 4 (Spring 1975): 3–45.

Bassett, Isabel. 'Introduction.' Emily Murphy's *Janey Canuck in the West.* 1910. Toronto: M&S, 1975. ix–xxiii.

– 'The Transformation of Imperialism: Connor to MacLennan.' *Journal of Canadian Fiction* 2.1 (1973): 58–62.

Baucom, Ian. *Out of Place: Englishness, Empire, and the Locations of Identity.* Princeton: Princeton UP, 1999.

Beddoes, Julie. 'Sandor, Alex and the Rest: Multiplication of the Subject in John Marlyn's *Under the Ribs of Death.*' *Open Letter* 6.8 (1987): 5–14.

Beeler, Karin E. 'Divided Loyalties in Eighteenth-Century Nova Scotia/Acadia: Nationalism and Cultural Affiliation in Thomas Raddall's *Roger Sudden* and A.E. Johann's *Ans dunke Ufer.*' *Dalhousie Review* 72.1 (Spring 1992): 66–83.

Benjamin, Walter. 'Allegory and Trauerspiel.' *The Origin of German Tragic Drama.* Trans. John Osborne. London: NLB, 1977. 159–235.

Berger, Carl. *The Sense of Power: Studies in the Ideas of Canadian Imperialism, 1867–1914.* Toronto: U of Toronto P, 1970.

– The True North Strong and Free.' *Nationalism in Canada.* Ed. Peter Russell. Toronto: McGraw-Hill, 1966. 3–26.

Berton, Pierre. *Hollywood's Canada.* Toronto: M&S, 1975.

Bhabha, Homi. 'DissemiNation: Time, Narrative, and the Margins of the Modern Nation.' In Bhabha, ed. 291–322.

– 'Introduction: Narrating the Nation.' In Bhabha, ed. 1–7.

– ed. *Nation and Narration.* London and New York: Routlege, 1990.

– 'Sly Civility.' *The Location of Culture.* New York: Routledge, 1994. 93–101.

Binnie-Clarke, Georgina. *Wheat and Woman.* 1914. Toronto: U of Toronto P, 1979.

Blair, Jennifer. 'The Knowledge of Sex and the Lattice of the Confessional: The Nun's Tales and Early North American Popular Discourse.' In Blair et al., eds. 173–210.

– Daniel Coleman, Kate Higginson, and Lorraine York, eds. *ReCalling Early Canada: Reading the Political in Literary and Cultural Production.* Edmonton: U of Alberta P, 2005.

Boechenstein, Hermann. 'Hugh MacLennan, A Canadian Novelist.' *Hugh MacLennan.* Ed. Paul Goetsch. Critical Views on Canadian Writers series. Toronto: McGraw-Hill Ryerson, 1973. 35–57.

Boire, Gary. 'Canadian (Tw)ink: Surviving the White-Outs.' *ECW* 35 (Winter 1987): 1–16.

Booker, Keith M. 'Introduction: The Turn to Dystopia in Modern Literature.' *Dystopian Literature: A Theory and Research Guide.* Westport, CN: Greenwood P, 1994. 1–9.

Bourassa, Henri. 'The French-Canadian in the British Empire.' *Monthly Review* 24.8 (September 1902): 55–71.

Brierley, Jane. 'Introduction.' *Canadians of Old: A Romance.* By Philippe-Joseph Aubert de Gaspé. Montreal: Véhicule, 1996. 9–16.

Brown, Robert Craig, and Ramsay Cook. *Canada. 1896–1921: A Nation Transformed.* Canadian Century Series. Toronto: M&S, 1974.

Bumsted, J.M. *The Scots in Canada.* Ottawa: Canadian Historical Association, 1982.

Bush, Pippa. 'Romance in Dystopia: A (Re-)Evaluation of James De Mille's *A Strange Manuscript Found in a Copper Cylinder.' British Journal of Canadian Studies* 9.2 (1994): 238–48.

Buss, Helen M. 'Who Are You, Mrs. Bentley? Feminist Re-vision and Sinclair Ross's *As for Me and My House.'* In Stouck, ed. 190–209.

Cameron, Elspeth. 'Will the Real Hugh MacLennan Please Stand Up: A Reassessment.' *Hugh MacLennan.* Ed. Frank M. Tierney. Reappraisals: Canadian Writers Series, vol. 19. Ottawa: U of Ottawa P, 1994. 23–36.

Campbell, Wilfred. *A Beautiful Rebel: A Romance of Upper Canada in Eighteen Hundred and Twelve.* Toronto: Westminster, 1909.

– *The Poetical Works of Wilfred Campbell.* Ed. W.J. Sykes. London and Toronto: Hodder & Stoughton, 1922.

– *The Scotsman in Canada.* Vol. 1. *Eastern Canada, including Nova Scotia, Prince Edward Island, New Brunswick, Quebec and Ontario.* Toronto and London: Musson, 1911.

Cannadine, David. 'Imperial Canada: Old History, New Problems.' In *Imperial Canada, 1867–1917.* Ed. Colin M. Coates. Edinburgh: Centre of Canadian Studies, U of Edinburgh, 1997. 1–19.

Canniff, William. *History of the Settlement of Upper Canada (Ontario), with Special Reference to the Bay of Quinte.* Toronto: Dudley and Burns, 1869.

Carter, Adam. 'Anthropomorphism and Trope in the National Ode.' In Blair et al., eds. 117–44.

Cavell, Richard. 'Bakhtin Reads De Mille: Canadian Literature, Postmodernism, and the Theory of Dialogism.' *Future Indicative: Literary Theory and Canadian Literature.* Ed. John Moss. Ottawa: U of Ottawa P, 1987. 205–10.

Chambers, Ross. *Room for Maneuver: Reading (the) Oppositional (in) Narrative.* Chicago and London: U of Chicago P, 1991.

– 'The Unexamined.' In 'The White Issue.' Special issue, *Minnesota Review* 47 (1996): 141–56.

Chisholme, David. 'Essay on the Advantages That Might be Derived from the Establishment of a Literary Association in Montreal.' In Ballstadt, ed. 5–9.

Cho, Lily. 'Rereading Chinese Head Tax Racism: Redress, Stereotype and Anti-Racist Critical Practice.' In Coleman and Goellnicht, eds. 62–84.

Christie, Nancy, and Michael Gauvreau. *A Full-Orbed Christianity: The Protestant Churches and Social Welfare in Canada, 1900–1940.* Montreal and Kingston: McGill-Queen's UP, 1996.

Clarke, George Elliott. 'Raising Raced and Erased Executions in African-Canadian Literature, or Unearthing Angélique.' In Coleman and Goellnicht, eds. 30–61.

– 'What Was Canada?' *Is Canada Postcolonial? Unsettling Canadian Literature.* Ed. Laura Moss. Waterloo: Wilfrid Laurier UP, 2003. 27–39.

Cockburn, Robert H. *The Novels of Hugh MacLennan.* Montreal: Harvest, 1969.

Cody, Hiram A. *The King's Arrow: A Tale of the United Empire Loyalists.* Toronto: M&S/George Doran Co., 1922.

Cogswell, Fred. 'Charles Mair.' *Canadian Writers and Their Works.* Poetry Series, vol. 1. Ed. Robert Lecker, Jack David, and Ellen Quigley. Toronto: ECW, 1988. 119–55.

Coleman, Daniel. 'Immigration, Nation, and the Canadian Allegory of Manly Maturation.' *ECW* 61 (Spring 1997): 84–103.

– *Masculine Migrations: Reading the Postcolonial Male in 'New Canadian' Narratives.* Toronto: U of Toronto P, 1998.

Coleman, Daniel, and Donald Goellnicht, eds. '"Race" into the Twenty-First Century.' Special issue, *ECW* 75 (2002).

Colley, Linda. *Britons: Forging the Nation, 1707–1837.* London: Vintage, 1992.

Connell, R.W. *Masculinities.* Berkeley and Los Angeles: U of California P, 1995.

Connor, Ralph. *Corporal Cameron of the North West Mounted Police: A Tale of the Macleod Trail.* New York: Grosset and Dunlap, 1912.

– *The Foreigner: A Tale of Saskatchewan.* Toronto: Westminster Co., 1909.

– *The Gaspards of Pine Croft: A Romance of the Windermere.* New York: George H. Doran Co., 1923.

– *The Man from Glengarry.* 1901. New Canadian Library. Toronto: M&S, 1993.

– *Postscript to Adventure: The Autobiography of Ralph Connor.* 1938. Toronto: M&S, 1975.

– *The Runner: A Romance of the Niagaras.* Garden City, NY: Doubleday, Doran, 1929.

Cook, Ramsay. *The Regenerators: Social Criticism in Late Victorian Canada.* Toronto: U of Toronto P, 1985.

Costain, Keith. 'Sticks and the Bundle: *Lawrie Todd* and *Bogle Corbet*: Galt's Portraits of Two Nations.' In 'Scottish Influences in Canadian Literature: A Selection of Papers Delivered at the University of Edinburgh, May 9–12, 1991.' Ed. Michael Williams. Special issue, *British Journal of Canadian Studies* 7.1 (1992). 26–38.

Court, Franklin E. *The Scottish Connection: The Rise of English Literary Study in Early America.* Syracuse: Syracuse UP, 2001.

Craig, Terrence L. *Racial Attitudes in English-Canadian Fiction, 1905–1980.* Waterloo: Wilfrid Laurier UP, 1987.

– 'Religious Images of Non-Whites in English-Canadian Literature: Charles Gordon and Rudy Wiebe.' In King et al., eds. 99–114.

Crawford, Robert. *Devolving English Literature.* Oxford: Clarendon P, 1992.

Creelman, David. 'Conservative Solutions: The Early Historical Fiction of Thomas Raddall.' *Studies in Canadian Literature* 20.1 (1995): 127–49.

Cude, Wilfred. 'Beyond Mrs. Bentley: A Study of *As for Me and My House.*' 1973. In Stouck, ed. 76–95.

Curzon, Sarah. *Laura Secord, the Heroine of 1812: A Drama, and Other Poems.* Toronto: C. Blackett Robinson, 1887.

Daniells, Roy. 'Glengarry Revisited.' *Writers of the Prairies.* Ed. Donald G. Stephens. Vancouver: UBC P, 1973. 17–25.

– 'Introduction' to 1957 New Canadian Library reissue of *As for Me and My House.* In Stouck, ed. 35–40.

Davey, Frank. 'The Narrative Politics of *The Imperialist.*' In Tausky, ed. 422–37.

– *Post-National Arguments: The Politics of the Anglophone-Canadian Novel Since 1967.* Toronto: U of Toronto P, 1993.

– 'Rereading Stead's *Grain.*' *Surviving the Paraphrase.* Winnipeg: Turnstone, 1983. 113–35.

Davidson, John. 'The Loyalist Tradition in Canada.' *Macmillan's Magazine* (Toronto), September 1904, 390–400.

Davies, Barrie. '"We Hold a Vaster Empire than Has Been": Canadian Literature and the Canadian Empire.' *Studies in Canadian Literature* 14.1 (1989): 18–29.

Davies, Gwendolyn. 'Editing the *Mephibosheth Stepsure Letters.*' *Challenges, Projects, Texts – Canadian Editing: Twenty-Fifth Conference on Editorial Problems.* Ed. John Lennox and Janet Patterson. New York: AMS Press, 1993. 89–104.

– 'Editor's Introduction.' *The Mephibosheth Stepsure Letters.* 1821–23 By Thomas McCulloch. CEECT ed. Ottawa: Carleton UP, 1990. xvii–lxxi.

Dawson, Michael. '"That Nice Red Coat Goes to My Head like Champagne": Gender, Antimodernism and the Mountie Image, 1880–1960.' *Journal of Canadian Studies* 32.3 (Fall 1997): 119–39.

Day, Richard J.F. *Multiculturalism and the History of Canadian Diversity.* Toronto: U of Toronto P, 2000.

Daymond, Douglas M., and Leslie G. Monkman, eds. *Towards a Canadian Literature: Essays, Editorials and Manifestos.* 2 vols. Ottawa: Tecumseh P, 1984.

Dean, Misao. *A Different Point of View: Sara Jeannette Duncan.* Montreal and Kingston: McGill-Queen's UP, 1991.

de Man, Paul. 'The Rhetoric of Temporality.' *Critical Theory since 1965.* Ed. Hazard Adams and Leroy Searle. Tallahasee: Florida State UP, 1986. 198–222.

De Mille, James. *A Strange Manuscript Found in a Copper Cylinder.* CEECT ed. Ottawa: Ottawa UP, 1986.

Devereux, Cecily. 'New Woman, New World: Maternal Feminism and the New Imperialism in the White Settler Colonies.' *Women's Studies International Forum* 22.2 (1999): 175–84.

Dewart, Edward Hartley. 'Introductory Essay to *Selections from Canadian Poets.*' 1864. In Daymond and Monkman, eds. 1:50–9.

Dickason, Olive Patricia. *Canada's First Nations: A History of Founding Peoples from Earliest Times.* 3rd ed. Toronto: Oxford UP, 2002.

Diène, Doudou. 'Racism, Racial Discrimination, Xenophobobia and All Forms of Discrimination: Mission to Canada.' United Nations Economic and Social Council, Commission on Human Rights, Sixtieth Session. www.unhchr.ch/

huridocda/huridoca.nsf/Documents?OpenFrameset. Site visited 1 March
2005.

Djwa, Sandra. 'No Other Way: Sinclair Ross's Stories and Novels.' 1971. In
Stouck, ed. 54–65.

Duffy, Dennis. *Gardens, Covenants, Exiles: Loyalism in the Literature of Upper
Canada/ Ontario.* Toronto: U of Toronto P, 1982.

– *A World under Sentence: John Richardson and the Interior.* Toronto: ECW, 1996.

Duncan, Sara Jeannette. *The Imperialist.* 1904. Toronto: New Canadian Library.
Toronto: M & S, 1990.

Duncan Campbell Scott: The Poet and the Indians. Film directed by James
Cullingham. Tamarack Productions/National Film Board of Canada, 1995.

During, Simon. 'Literature – Nationalism's Other? The Case for Revision.' In
Bhabha, ed. 138–53.

Dyer, Richard. *White.* London and New York: Routledge, 1997.

Edgar, Pelham. 'A Fresh View of Canadian Literature.' 1912. In Ballstadt, ed.
110–14.

Edwards, Mary Jane. 'McLachlan, Alexander.' *Dictionary of Canadian Biography.*
www.biographi.ca/EN/ShowBio.asp?BioId+40407. Site visited 31 March 2004.

Fee, Margery. 'Romantic Nationalism and the Image of Native People in Contemporary English-Canadian Literature.' In King et al., eds. 15–33.

Fellows, Jo-Ann. 'The Loyalist Myth in Canada.' Canadian Historical Association, *Historical Papers, 1971.* 94–111.

Ferns, Chris. 'Building a Country; Losing an Empire: The Historical Fiction of
Thomas H. Raddall and J.G. Farrell.' *Time and Place: The Life and Works of
Thomas H. Raddall.* Ed. Alan R. Young. Fredericton: Acadiensis P, 1991. 154–64.

– 'Look Who's Talking: Walter Scott, Thomas Raddall, and the Voices of the
Colonized.' *Ariel* 26.4 (October 1995): 49–67.

Ferré, John P. *A Social Gospel for the Millions: The Religious Bestsellers of Charles
Sheldon, Charles Gordon, and Harold Bell Wright.* Bowling Green, OH: Bowling
Green State U Popular P, 1988.

Fiamengo, Janice. '"Baptized with Tears and Sighs": Sara Jeannette Duncan and
the Rhetoric of Feminism.' In Blair et al., eds. 257–80.

– '"Susceptible to No Common Translation": Language and Idealism in Sara
Jeannette Duncan's *The Imperialist.'* *Canadian Literature* 160 (Spring 1999):
121–40.

Filewod, Alan. 'National Battles: Canadian Monumental Drama and the Investi-
ture of History.' *Modern Drama* 38 (1995): 71–86.

Findlay, Len. 'Always Indigenize! The Radical Humanities in the Postcolonial
Canadian University.' *ARIEL* 31.1–2 (January–April 2000): 307–26.

Foucault, Michel. 'Governmentality.' Trans. from Italian by Rosi Braidotti, rev.
by Colin Gordon. *The Foucault Effect: Studies in Governmentality with Two Lectures*

and an Interview with Michael Foucault. Ed. Graham Burchell, Colin Gordon, and Peter Miller. Chicago: U of Chicago P, 1991. 87–104.

Fowles, John. 'On Being English but Not British.' (1964). *Wormholes: Essays and Occasional Writings.* Ed. Jan Relf. New York: Henry Holt, 1998. 79–88.

Francis, Daniel. *National Dreams: Myth, Memory, and Canadian History.* Vancouver: Arsenal Pulp P, 1997.

Frankenberg, Ruth. *White Women, Race Matters: The Social Construction of Whiteness.* Minneapolis: U Minnesota P, 1993.

Fraser, Keith. *As for Me and My Body: A Memoir of Sinclair Ross.* Toronto: ECW P, 1997.

French, Maida Parlow. *Boughs Bend Over.* Garden City, NY: Doubleday, Doran, 1943.

Frye, Northrop. 'Conclusion to *The Literary History of Canada.*' 1965. *The Bush Garden: Essays on the Canadian Imagination.* Toronto: Anansi, 1971. 213–51.

– Introduction. *The Stepsure Letters.* By Thomas McCulloch. 1821–23. New Canadian Library. Toronto: M&S, 1960. iii–ix.

– *The Secular Scripture: A Study of the Structure of Romance.* Cambridge: Harvard UP, 1976.

Fulton, E. Margaret. 'Introduction.' *The Poetical Works of Alexander McLachlan.* Toronto: U Toronto P, 1974. i–xxiii.

Galt, John. *Bogle Corbet; or, The Emigrants.* 3 vols. London: Henry Colburn and Richard Bentley, 1831.

Gates, Henry Louis, Jr. 'Writing, "Race," and the Difference It Makes.' *The Critical Tradition.* 2nd ed. Ed. David Richter. New York: Bedford, 1998. 1575–88.

Gerson, Carole. 'A Contrapuntal Reading of *A Strange Manuscript Found in a Copper Cylinder.*' In 'Testing the Limits: Postcolonial Theories and Canadian Literatures.' Ed. Diana Brydon. Special issue, *ECW* 56 (Fall 1995): 224–35.

– 'Three Writers of Victorian Canada [Rosanna Leprohon, Agnes Maule Machar, James de Mille].' *Canadian Writers and Their Works.* Fiction Series, vol. 1. Ed. Robert Lecker, Jack David, and Ellen Quigley. Toronto: ECW P, 1983. 195–256.

Gibbon, John Murray. *Canadian Mosaic: The Making of a Northern Nation.* Toronto: M&S, 1938.

– *The Scots in Canada: A History of the Settlement of the Dominion from the Earliest Days to the Present Time.* Toronto: Musson Book Co., 1911.

Gikandi, Simon. *Maps of Englishness: Writing Identity in the Culture of Colonialism.* New York: Columbia UP, 1996.

Gilmore, David. *Manhood in the Making: Cultural Concepts of Masculinity.* New Haven and London: Yale UP, 1990.

Gittings, Chris. 'Canada and Scotland: Conceptualizing "Postcolonial" Spaces.'

In 'Testing the Limits: Postcolonial Theories and Canadian Literature.' Ed. Diana Brydon. Special issue, *ECW* 56 (Fall 1995): 135–61.

Glicksohn, Susan Wood. 'Introduction.' *The Homesteaders*. By Robert Stead. 1916. Toronto: U of Toronto P, 1973. vii–xxvi.

Goldberg, David Theo. *Racist Culture: Philosophy and the Politics of Meaning*. Oxford: Blackwell, 1993.

Goldie, Terry. *Fear and Temptation: The Image of the Indigene in Canadian, Australian, and New Zealand Literatures*. Kingston and Montreal: McGill-Queen's UP, 1989.

Gordon, Alison. 'Afterword.' *The Man from Glengarry: A Tale of the Ottawa*. By Ralph Connor. 1901. Toronto: M&S, 1993. 379–84.

Grace, Sherrill. 'Gendering Northern Narrative.' *Echoing Silence: Essays on Artic Narrative*. Ed. John Moss. Ottawa: U of Ottawa P, 1997. 163–81.

Graham, Robert. 'John Galt's *Bogle Corbet*: A Parable of Progress.' *Scottish Literary Journal* 13.2 (November 1986): 31–47.

Grant, George. *Lament for a Nation: The Defeat of Canadian Nationalism*. 1965. Ottawa: Carlton UP, 1995.

Greenfield, Sayre N. 'The Politics of Allegory and Example.' *Genre* 24.3 (Fall 1991): 233–55.

Greer, Alex. 'Canadian Immigration: An Earlier Perspective.' *Journal of Social, Political, and Economic Studies* 18.4 (Winter 1993): 467–89.

Grove, Frederick Philip. 'Assimilation.' 1927. *A Stranger to My Time: Essays by and about Frederick Philip Grove*. Ed. Paul Hjartarson. Edmonton: NeWest, 1986. 177–87.

– 'Canadians Old and New.' 1927. *A Stranger to My Time: Essays by and About Frederick Philip Grove*. Ed. Paul Hjartarson. Edmonton: NeWest, 1986. 169–76.

– 'Nationhood.' *It Needs to Be Said* ... Toronto: Macmillan, 1929. 135–63.

Guth, Gwendolyn. 'Introduction.' *Shenac's Work at Home*. By Margaret Murray Robertson. 1866. Early Canadian Women Writers Series, gen. ed. Lorraine McMullen. Ottawa: Tecumseh P, 1993. vii–xli.

– 'Reading Frames of Reference: The Satire of Exegesis in James De Mille's "A Strange Manuscript Found in a Copper Cylinder."' In 'De Mille's Utopian Fantasy.' Special issue, *Canadian Literature* 145 (Summer 1995): 39–59.

Haliburton, Robert Grant. *The Men of the North and Their Place in History; A Lecture Delivered before the Montreal Literary Club, March 31st, 1869*. Montreal: John Lovell, 1869.

Hall, D.J. 'Clifford Sifton: Immigration and Settlement Policy, 1896–1905.' *The Settlement of the West*. Ed. Howard Palmer. Calgary: U of Calgary Comprint Publishing Co., 1977. 60–85.

Hall, Donald. 'Introduction: Muscular Christianity: Reading and Writing the

Male Social Body.' *Muscular Christianity: Embodying the Victorian Age*. Ed.
   Donald Hall. Cambridge: Cambridge UP, 1994. 3–13.

Hall, Stuart. *Race the Floating Signifier*. Film directed by Sut Jhally. Media Education Foundation, 1996.

–   'The West and the Rest: Discourse and Power.' *Formations of Modernity*. Ed.
   Stuart Hall and Bram Gieben. Cambridge: Polity P, 1992. 275–331.

Hampl, Patricia. *A Romantic Education*. New York: W.W. Norton, 1981, with a
   new afterword, 1999.

Harney, Robert F. '"So Great a Heritage Is Ours": Immigration and the Survival
   of the Canadian Polity.' In 'In Search of Canada' Special issue, *Daedalus* 117.4
   (Fall 1988): 51–97.

Harris, Charyl I. 'Whiteness as Property.' *Harvard Law Review* 106.8 (June 1993):
   1707–91.

Harrison, Dick. *Unnamed Country: The Struggle for a Canadian Prairie Fiction*.
   Edmonton: U of Alberta P, 1977.

Hatch, Ronald. 'Narrative Development in the Canadian Historical Novel.'
   Canadian Literature 110 (Fall 1986): 79–96.

Heble, Ajay. '"This Little Outpost of Empire": Sara Jeannette Duncan and the
   Decolonization of Canada.' In Tausky, ed. 404–16. (Excerpted from *Journal of
   Commonwealth Literature* 26.1 (1991): 215–28.)

Henderson, Jennifer. *Settler Feminism and Race Making in Canada*. Toronto: U of
   Toronto P, 2003.

Henry, Frances, and Carol Tator. *Discourses of Domination: Racial Bias in the
   Canadian English-Language Press*. Toronto: U of Toronto P, 2002.

Herriot, Trevor. *River in a Dry Land: A Prairie Passage*. Toronto: Stoddart, 2000.

Higginson, Catherine. 'Shelley Niro, Haudenosaunee Nationalism, and the
   Continued Contestation of the Brant Monument.' In 'Cultural Memory and
   Social Identity.' Ed. Roxanne Rimsted. Special issue, *ECW* 80 (Fall 2003):
   141–86.

Hingston, William Hales. *The Climate of Canada and Its Relations to Life and Health*.
   Montreal: Dawson, 1884.

Hjartarson, Paul. '"Out of the Wastage of All Other Nations": "Enemy Aliens"
   and the "Canadianization" of Felix Paul Greve.' *The Politics of Cultural Media-
   tion: Baronness Elsa von Freytag-Loringhoven and Felix Paul Greve*. Ed. Paul
   Hjartarson and Tracy Kulba. Edmonton: U of Alberta P, 2002. 107–29.

Hoy, Helen. 'Hugh MacLennan and His Works.' *Canadian Writers and Their
   Works*. Fiction Series, vol. 5. Ed. Robert Lecker, Jack David, and Ellen Quigley.
   Toronto: ECW, 1990. 149–212.

Hubel, Teresa. 'Excavating the Expendable Working Classes in *The Imperialist*.'
   In Tausky, ed. 437–56.

Hubert, Henry. *Harmonious Perfection: The Development of English Studies in Nine-teenth-Century Anglo-Canadian Colleges.* East Lansing: Michigan State UP, 1994.

Hughes, Kenneth J. 'A Strange Manuscript: Sources, Satire, a Positive Utopia.' *The Canadian Novel: Beginnings.* Vol. 2. Ed. John Moss. Toronto: New Canada Publ, 1980. 111–25.

Hulan, Renée. *Northern Experience and the Myths of Canadian Culture.* Montreal and Kingston: McGill-Queen's UP, 2002.

Hunter, Latham. '*Under the Ribs of Death:* Immigrant Narratives of Masculinity and Nationality.' *Mosaic* 36.2 (June 2003): 93–109.

Hunter, Lynette. *Outsider Notes: Feminist Approaches to Nation State Ideology, Writers/ Reading and Publishing.* Vancouver: Talonbooks, 1996.

Hurley, Michael. *The Borders of Nightmare: The Fiction of John Richardson.* Toronto: U of Toronto P, 1992.

– 'John Richardson's Byronic Hero in the Land of Cain.' *Studies in Canadian Literature* 20.1 (1995): 115–26.

Hutcheon, Linda. 'Introduction.' *Double-Talking: Essays on Verbal and Visual Ironies in Contemporary Canadian Art and Literature.* Toronto: ECW P, 1992. 11–38.

– 'Modern Parody and Bakhtin.' In *Rethinking Bakhtin: Extensions and Challenges.* Eds. Gary Saul Morson and Caryl Emerson. Evanston, IL: Northwestern UP, 1989. 87–103.

– *Splitting Images: Contemporary Canadian Ironies.* Toronto: Oxford UP, 1991.

– and Marion Richmond, eds. *Other Solitudes: Canadian Multicultural Fictions.* Toronto: Oxford UP, 1990.

Ignatiev, Noel. *How the Irish Became White.* New York: Routledge, 1995.

Irving, John A. 'The Achievement of Thomas McCulloch.' *The Stepsure Letters.* By Thomas McCulloch. 1821–23. New Canadian Library. Toronto: M&S, 1960. 150–6.

Itwaru, Arnold Harrichand. *The Invention of Canada: Literary Text and the Immi-grant Imaginary.* Toronto: TSAR, 1990.

Ivison, Douglas. 'James De Mille.' *Canadian Fantasy and Science-Fiction Writers.* Ed. Douglas Ivison. Dictionary of Literary Biography, vol. 251. Detroit: Gale, 2002. 61–5.

Jackel, Susan. 'Introduction.' *Wheat and Woman.* By Georgina Binnie-Clarke. 1914. Toronto: U of Toronto P, 1979. v–xxxvii.

Jameson, Fredric. 'Third-World Literature in the Era of Multinational Capital-ism.' *Social Text* 15 (Fall 1986): 65–98.

Jamieson, Roberta. 'Presentation to the Canadian House of Commons Standing Committee on Aboriginal Affairs, Northern Development & Natural Re-sources.' Hearings on Canada's Bill C-7 First Nations Governance Act.

Toronto, 21 March 2003. www.turtleisland.org/discussion/viewtopic.php?t=
535&view=next. Visited 18 May 2005.

Johnson, E. Pauline. 'A Strong Race Opinion: On the Indian Girl in Modern
Fiction.' Originally published in *Toronto World*, 22 May 1892; available at the
Pauline Johnson Web site at McMaster University. http://www.humanities
.mcmaster.ca/ ~pjohnson/modern.html. Visited 22 February 2000.

Karr, Clarence. *Authors and Audiences: Popular Canadian Fiction in the Early
Twentieth Century.* Montreal and Kingston: McGill-Queen's UP, 2000.

– 'Robert Stead's Search for an Agrarian Ideal.' *Prairie Forum* 14.1 (Spring
1989): 37–57.

Keefer, Janice Kulyk. *Under Eastern Eyes: A Critical Reading of Maritime Fiction.*
Toronto: U of Toronto P, 1987.

Kertzer, Jonathan. 'Destiny into Chance: S.J. Duncan's *The Imperialist* and the
Perils of Nation Building.' *Studies in Canadian Literature* 24.2 (1999): 1–34.

– 'Historical Literary Criticism in English Canada: Within, Beyond, and Back
into the Past.' *100 Years of Critical Solitudes: Canadian and Québécois Criticism
from the 1880s to the 1980s.* Ed. Caroline Bayard. Toronto: ECW Press, 1992.
98–121.

– *Worrying the Nation: Imagining a National Literature in English Canada.* U of
Toronto P, 1998.

Kilgour, Maggie. 'Cannibals and Critics: An Exploration of James De Mille's
Strange Manuscript.' Mosaic 30.1 (March 1997): 19–37.

Kilian, Crawford. 'The Cheerful Inferno of James De Mille.' *Journal of Canadian
Fiction* 1.3 (1972): 61–7.

King, Thomas. *Medicine River.* Toronto: Penguin, 1989.

King, Thomas, Cheryl Calver, and Helen Hoy, eds. *The Native in Literature:
Canadian and Comparative Perspectives.* Toronto: ECW P, 1987.

Kirby, William. 'Address: Delivered at Niagara, on the 14th of August, 1884, at
the Centennial Celebration of the Settlement of Upper Canada by the United
Empire Loyalists in 1784.' *Canadian Idylls.* 2nd ed. Welland, 1894. 163–75.

– *The U.E.: A Tale of Upper Canada.* 1859. Toronto Reprint Library of Canadian
Prose and Poetry. Toronto: U of Toronto P, 1973.

Knowles, Norman. *Inventing the Loyalists: The Ontario Loyalist Tradition and the
Creation of Usable Pasts.* Toronto: U of Toronto P, 1997.

Kroestch, Robert. 'The Fear of Women in Prairie Fiction: An Erotics of Space.'
1979. In Stouck, ed. 111–20.

Kulba, Tracy. 'Citizens, Consumers, Critique-al Subjects: Rethinking the "Statue
Controversy" and Emily Murphy's *The Black Candle.' Tessera* 31 (Winter 2002):
74–89.

La Bossiere, Camille R. 'The Mysterious End of James De Mille's Unfinished
Strange Manuscript.' *ECW* 27 (Winter 1983–84): 41–54.

Lamont-Stewart, Linda. 'Rescued by Postmodernism: The Escalating Value of James De Mille's "A Strange Manuscript Found in a Copper Cylinder."' In 'De Mille's Utopian Fantasy'. Special issue, *Canadian Literature* 145 (Summer 1995): 21–36.

Lawson, Alan. 'Postcolonial Theory and the "Settler" Subject.' In 'Testing the Limits: Postcolonial Theories and Canadian Literatures.' Ed. Diana Brydon. Special issue, *ECW* 56 (Fall 1995): 20–36.

Leacock, Stephen. 'Greater Canada: An Appeal.' *The Social Criticism of Stephen Leacock.* Ed. Alan Bowker. Toronto: U of Toronto P, 1973. 4–11.

Lee, Dennis. 'Cadence, Country, Silence: Writing in Colonial Space.' *Towards a Canadian Literature: Essays, Editorials and Manifestos.* Vol. 2, 1940–1983. Ed. Douglas M. Daymond and Leslie G. Monkman. Ottawa: Tecumseh P, 1985. 497–520.

– *Civil Elegies and Other Poems.* Toronto: Anansi, 1972, 1994.

Lennox, John. 'Charles W. Gordon ["Ralph Connor"] (1860–1937).' *Canadian Writers and Their Works.* Fiction Series, vol. 3. Eds. Robert Lecker, Jack David, and Ellen Quigley. Toronto: ECW, 1988. 103–59.

Leprohon, Rosanna. *Antoinette de Mirecourt: or, Secret Marrying and Secret Sorrowing.* Ed. John C. Stockdale. CEECT ed. Ottawa: Carleton UP, 1995.

Lesk, Andrew. 'Something Queer Going on Here: Desire in the Short Fiction of Sinclair Ross.' *ECW* 61 (Spring 1997): 129–41.

Li, Peter. *Chinese in Canada.* 2nd ed. Oxford: Oxford University Press, 1998.

Lighthall, William Douw. 'From the Introduction to *Songs of the Great Dominion*.' In Daymond and Monkman, eds. 128–33.

Lipstiz, George. *The Possessive Investment in Whiteness: How White People Profit from Identity Politics.* Philadelphia: Temple UP, 1998.

Logan, John E. ('Barry Dane'). 'National Literature.' In Ballstadt, ed. 114–17.

MacGillivray, Royce. 'Celts and Others: Scotland and Ireland.' *The Mind of Ontario.* Belleville, ON: Mika Publishing, 1985. 31–47.

Machar, Agnes Maule. *For King and Country: A Story of 1812.* Toronto: Adam, Stevenson & Co., 1874.

Mack, D. Barry. 'Modernity without Tears: The Mythic World of Ralph Connor.' *The Burning Bush and a Few Acres of Snow: The Presbyterian Contribution to Canadian Life and Culture.* Ed. William Klempa. Ottawa: Carleton UP, 1994. 139–57.

MacKenzie, John M. 'The Imperial Pioneer and Hunter and the British Masculine Stereotype in Late Victorian and Edwardian Times.' In Mangan and Walvin, eds. 176–98.

Mackey, Eva. *The House of Difference: Cultural Politics and National Identity in Canada.* London: Routledge, 1999.

MacLennan, Hugh. *Barometer Rising.* 1941. New Canadian Library. Toronto: M&S, 1989.

– 'The Canadian Character.' *Cross-Country*. Toronto: Collins, 1949. 1–20.

– *Each Man's Son*. Toronto: Macmillan, 1951.

– 'On Discovering Who We Are.' *Cross-Country*. Toronto: Collins, 1949. 35–56.

Macleod, Alistair. 'Afterword.' *Barometer Rising*. By Hugh MacLennan. 1941. New Canadian Library. Toronto: M&S, 1989. 221–35.

– 'The Writings of Hugh MacLennan.' *Brick* 44 (Summer 1992): 72–7.

Macmillan, David S. 'The Neglected Aspect of the Scottish Diaspora, 1650–1850: The Role of the Entrepreneur in Promoting and Effecting Emigration.' *The Diaspora of the British*. Institute of Commonwealth Studies, Collected Seminar Papers no. 31. London: U of London, 1982. 20–43.

Macphail, Sir Andrew. *The Master's Wife*. 1939. Introd. Ian Ross Robertson. Charlottetown: Institute of Island Studies, 1994.

Macpherson, Jay. 'Reading and Convention in Richardson: Some Notes.' *Recovering Canada's First Novelist: Proceedings from the John Richardson Conference*. Ed. Catherine Sheldrick Ross. Erin, ON: Porcupine's Quill, 1984. 63–86.

Madsen, Deborah. *Rereading Allegory: A Narrative Approach to Genre*. New York: St. Martin's, 1994.

Mair, Charles. 'The New Canada.' In Ballstadt, ed. 151–4.

– *Tecumseh: A Drama, and Canadian Poems*. Master-Works of Canadian Authors Series. Ed. John W. Garvin. Toronto: Radisson Society of Canada, 1926.

Mangan, J.A., and James Walvin. 'Introduction.' In Mangan and Walvin, eds. 1–6.

– eds. *Manliness and Morality: Middle-Class Masculinity in Britain and America, 1800–1940*. Manchester UP, 1987.

Marlyn, John. *Under the Ribs of Death*. 1957. New Canadian Library. Toronto: M&S, 1993.

Marshall, David B. *Secularizing the Faith: Canadian Protestant Clergy and the Crisis of Belief, 1850–1940*. Toronto: U of Toronto P, 1992.

Matheson, T.J. '"But Do Your Thing": Conformity, Self-Reliance, and Sinclair Ross's *As for Me and My House*.' 1986. In Stouck, ed. 162–77.

Matthews, Robin. 'Hugh MacLennan: The Nationalist Dilemma in Canada.' *Studies in Canadian Literature* 1 (Winter 1976): 49–63.

– '*The Stepsure Letters:* Puritanism and the Novel of the Land.' *Studies in Canadian Literature* 7.1 (1982): 127–38.

McClintock, Anne. *Imperial Leather: Race, Gender and Sexuality in the Colonial Contest*. London: Routledge, 1995.

McClung, Nellie. *Painted Fires*. Toronto: Thomas Allen, 1925.

– *Purple Springs*. 1921. Toronto: U of Toronto P, 1992.

– *The Stream Runs Fast*. 1945. Toronto: Thomas Allen, 1965.

McCormack, Ross. 'Cloth Caps and Jobs: The Ethnicity of English Immigrants in Canada, 1900–1914.' *Ethnicity, Power and Politics in Canada*. Ed. Jorgen Dahlie and Tissa Fernando. Toronto: Methuen, 1981. 38–55.

McCulloch, Thomas. *The Mephibosheth Stepsure Letters*. 1821–3. Ed. Gwendolyn Davies. CEECT ed. Ottawa: Carleton UP, 1990.

McCullum, Hugh. 'Turn off Sudan's Oil Wells Say Canadian Church Visitors.' *Christianity Today*, 20 April 2001. Available at: http://www.christianitytoday .com/ct/2001/116/55.0.html. Visited 14 April 2005.

McGee, Thomas D'Arcy. 'Protection for Canadian Literature.' In Ballstadt, ed. 21–4.

McGregor, Gaile. *The Wacousta Syndrome: Exploration in the Canadian Landscape*. Toronto: U of Toronto P, 1985.

McIlwraith, Jean Norman. *Kinsmen at War*. Ottawa: Graphic Publishers, 1927.

McKay, Ian. 'The Liberal Order Framework: A Prospectus for a Reconnaissance of Canadian History.' *Canadian Historical Review* 81.4 (December 2000): 617–45.

– 'Tartanism Triumphant: The Construction of Scottishness in Nova Scotia, 1933–1954.' *Acadiensis* 21.2 (Spring 1992): 5–47.

McLachlan, Alexander. *The Poetical Works of Alexander McLachlan*. 1900. Introd. E. Margaret Fulton. Toronto: U of Toronto P, 1974.

McLaren, Angus. *Our Own Master Race: Eugenics in Canada, 1885–1945*. Toronto: M&S, 1990.

McLean, Ken. 'William Kirby.' *Profiles in Canadian Literature*. Vol. 5. Ed. Jeffrey Heath. Toronto and Reading: Dundurn Press, 1986. 33–40.

McMullen, Lorraine. 'Margaret Murray Robertson: Domestic Power.' *Silenced Sextet: Six Nineteenth-Century Canadian Women Novelists*. By Carrie MacMillan, Lorraine McMullen, and Elizabeth Waterston. Montreal and Kingston: McGill-Queen's UP, 1992. 82–106.

McMullin, Stanley E. 'In Search of the Liberal Mind: Thomas McCulloch and the Impulse to Action.' *Journal of Canadian Studies* 23.1 –2 (Spring–Summer 1988): 68–85.

McNaughton, Janet. 'John Murray Gibbon and the Inter-war Folk Festivals.' *Canadian Folklore* 3.1 (1981): 67–73.

McPherson, Hugo. 'The Novels of Hugh MacLennan.' *Hugh MacLennan*. Critical Views on Canadian Writers series. Ed. Paul Goetsch. Toronto: McGraw-Hill Ryerson, 1973. 23–33.

Mignolo, Walter D. 'Globalization, Civilization Processes, and the Relocation of Languages and Cultures.' *The Cultures of Globalization*. Ed. Fredric Jameson and Masao Miyoshi. Durham and London: Duke UP, 1998. 32–53.

Mihaychuk, W.J. Review of Ralph Connor's *The Foreigner*. *Canadian Magazine* 34.5 (March 1910): 487–9.

Mills, David. *The Idea of Loyalty in Upper Canada, 1784–1850.* Kingston and Montreal: McGill-Queen's UP, 1988.

Milnes, Stephen. 'Colonialist Discourse, Lord Featherstone's Yawn and the Significance of the Denouement in "A Strange Manuscript Found in a Copper Cylinder."' In 'De Mille's Utopian Fantasy.' Special issue, *Canadian Literature* 145 (Summer 1995): 86–104.

Mitchell, Tom. '"The Manufacture of Souls of Good Quality": Winnipeg's 1919 National Conference on Canadian Citizenship, English-Canadian Nationalism, and the New Order after the Great War.' *Journal of Canadian Studies* 31.4 (Winter 1996–7): 5–28.

Monk, Patricia. 'James De Mille.' *Canadian Writers before 1890.* Ed. W.H. New. Dictionary of Literary Biography, vol. 99. Detroit: Gale, 1990. 92–4.

Monkman, Leslie. *A Native Literature: Images of the Indian in English-Canadian Literature.* Toronto: U of Toronto P, 1981.

Montgomery, Malcolm. 'The Six Nations Indians and the Macdonald Franchise.' *Ontario History* 57.1 (1965): 13–25.

Monture, Enos T. *The Feathered U.E.L.s: An Account of the Life and Times of Certain Canadian Native People.* Toronto: Division of Communications, United Church of Canada, 1973.

Monture, Rick. '"Beneath the British Flag": Iroquois and Canadian Nationalism in the Work of Pauline Johnson and Duncan Campbell Scott.' In Coleman and Goellnicht, eds. 118–41.

Moodie, Susanna. *Roughing It in the Bush; or, Life in Canada.* 1852. Ed. Elizabeth Thompson. Ottawa: Tecumseh P, 1997.

Moody, Barry. 'The Novelist as Historian: The Nova Scotia Identity in the Novels of Thomas H. Raddall.' *Time and Place: The Life and Works of Thomas H. Raddall.* Ed. Alan R. Young. Fredericton: Acadiensis P, 1991. 140–53.

Morrison, Toni. *Playing in the Dark: Whiteness and the Literary Imagination.* Cambridge: Harvard UP, 1990.

Morson, Gary Saul. 'Parody, History, and Metaparody.' *Rethinking Bakhtin: Extensions and Challenges.* Eds. Gary Saul Morson and Caryl Emerson. Evanston, IL: Northwestern UP, 1989. 63–86.

Moss, John. '*Wacousta* and the Narrative Implications of Trisexuality.' *Wacousta.* By John Richardson. Ed. John Moss. Ottawa: Tecumseh P, 1998. 468–72.

– ed. *From the Heart of the Heartland: The Fiction of Sinclair Ross.* Ottawa: U of Ottawa P, 1992.

Mundwiler, Leslie. 'Robert Stead – Home in the First Place.' *ECW* 11 (Summer 1978): 184–203.

Murphy, Emily. *The Black Candle.* Toronto: Thomas Allen, 1922; facsimile ed., Toronto: Coles, 1973.

– *Janey Canuck in the West.* 1910. Toronto: M&S, 1975.

Nairn, Tom. 'The Three Dreams of Scottish Nationalism.' *New Left Review*. 49 (1968): 3–18.

Nakayama, Thomas K., and Judith N. Martin, eds. *Whiteness: The Communication of Social Identity*. Thousand Oaks, CA: Sage, 1999.

New, W.H. 'The Storm and After: Imagery and Symbolism in Hugh MacLennan's *Barometer Rising.' Critical Views on Canadian Writers* series. Ed. Paul Goetsch. Toronto: McGraw-Hill Ryerson, 1973. 75–87.

Niven, Frederick. *The Flying Years*. London: Collins, 1935.

Noel, S.J.R. *Patrons, Clients, Brokers: Ontario Society and Politics, 1791–1896*. Toronto: U of Toronto P, 1990.

Northey, Margot. 'William Kirby.' *Canadian Writers and Their Works*. Fiction Series, vol. 2. Ed. Robert Lecker, Jack David, and Ellen Quigley. Toronto: ECW, 1989. 79–104.

O'Loane, L. 'Our Chances for a Literature.' 1890. In Ballstadt, ed. 83–5.

Omi, Michael, and Howard Winant. *Racial Formation in the United States: From the 1960s to the 1990s*. 2nd ed. New York: Routledge, 1994.

Owram, Doug. *Promise of Eden: The Canadian Expansionist Movement and the Idea of the West, 1856–1900*. Toronto: U of Toronto P, 1980.

Padolsky, Enoch. 'Grove's "Nationhood" and the European Immigrant.' *Journal of Canadian Studies* 22.1 (1987): 32–50.

Palmer, Howard. 'Strangers and Stereotypes: The Rise of Nativism – 1880–1920.' *The Prairie West: Historical Readings*. Ed. R. Douglas Francis and Howard Palmer. Edmonton: Pica Pica Press, 1985. 309–33.

Palmer, Tamara. 'Ethnic Response to the Canadian Prairies, 1900–1950.' *Prairie Forum* 21.1 (1987): 49–73.

Parker, Gilbert. *The Seats of the Mighty: Being the Memoirs of Captain Robert Moray, Sometime an Officer in the Virginia Regiment and Afterwards of Amherst's Regiment*. 1896. The Works of Gilbert Parker, Imperial Ed., vol. 9. New York: Charles Scribner's Sons, 1913.

Parkin, George R. 'Imperial Federation.' *McGill University Magazine* 1.2 (April 1902): 180–93.

– 'The Reorganization of the British Empire.' *Century Magazine* 37.2 (December 1888): 187–92.

Parks, Malcolm G. 'Editor's Introduction.' *A Strange Manuscript Found in a Copper Cylinder*. By James De Mille. CEECT ed. Ottawa: U Ottawa P, 1986, 1991. xvii–lix.

– 'Strange to Strangers Only.' *Canadian Literature* 70 (Autumn 1976): 61–78.

Pennee, Donna Palmateer. 'Looking Elsewhere for Answers to the Postcolonial Question: From Literary Studies to State Policy in Canada.' *Is Canada Postcolonial?* Ed. Laura Moss. Waterloo: Wilfrid Laurier UP, 2003. 78–94.

Peterman, Michael. 'Humour and Balance in *The Imperialist:* Sara Jeannette

Duncan's "Instinct of Presentation."' In Tausky, ed. 344–55. (Slightly condensed from *Journal of Canadian Studies* 11.2 (1976): 56–64.)

Philip, M. NourbeSe. *Frontiers: Essays and Writings on Racism and Culture.*
Toronto: Mercury P, 1992.

– 'Why Multiculturalism Can't End Racism.' *Frontiers* By M. Nourbe Se Philip.
181–6.

Potter-Mackinnon, Janice. 'Patriarchy and Paternalism: The Case of Eastern
Ontario Loyalist Women.' *Ontario History* 81.1 (March 1989): 3–24.

– *While the Women Only Wept: Loyalist Refugee Women in Eastern Ontario.* Montreal
and Kingston: McGill-Queen's UP, 1993.

Raddall, Thomas H. *His Majesty's Yankees.* 1942. New Canadian Library. Toronto:
M & S, 1977.

– *Roger Sudden: An Historical Novel of Conflict, Adventure, and Passion.* 1944.
Halifax: Nimbus Publishing, 1996.

Rasporich, Beverly. 'The New Eden Dream: The Source of Canadian Humour:
McCulloch, Haliburton, and Leacock.' *Studies in Canadian Literature* 7.2
(1982): 227–40.

Raoul, Valerie. 'Straight or Bent: Textual/Sexual T(ri)angles in *As for Me and
My House.*' *Canadian Literature* 156 (Spring 1998): 13–28.

Razack, Sherene H. *Dark Threats and White Knights: The Somalia Affair, Peacekeeping, and the New Imperialism.* Toronto: U of Toronto P, 2004.

Reaney, James. 'Tale of the Great River: Aubert de Gaspé and John Richardson.'
Transactions of the Royal Society of Canada, ser. 4, vol. 17 (1979): 159–71.

Reid, W. Stanford, 'Introduction.' *The Scottish Tradition in Canada.* Ed. Stanford
Reid. Generations History of Canada's Peoples Series supported by Secretary
of State, Multiculturalism. Toronto: M&S, 1976. ix–xi.

Renan, Ernest. 'What Is a Nation?' Trans. Martin Thom. In Bhabha, ed. 8–22.

Richards, Eric. 'Scotland and the Uses of the Atlantic Empire.' *Strangers within
the Realm: Cultural Margins of the First British Empire.* Ed. Bernard Bailyn and
Philip D. Morgan. Chapel Hill and London: U of North Carolina P, 1991.
67–113.

Richardson, John. *The Canadian Brothers; or, The Prophecy Fulfilled. A Tale of the
Late American War.* 1840. Ed. Donald Stephens. CEECT ed. Ottawa: Carleton
UP, 1992.

Ricou, Laurerce. 'Afterword.' *Grain.* By Robert Stead. 1926. Toronto: M&S,
1993. 247–55.

– *Vertical Man – Horizontal World: Man and Landscape in Canadian Prairie Fiction.*
Vancouver: UBC P, 1973.

Roberts, John. 'Irony in an Immigrant Novel: John Marlyn's *Under the Ribs of
Death.*' *Canadian Ethnic Studies* 14.1 (1982): 41–8.

Robertson, Margaret Murray. *Shenac's Work at Home.* 1866. Early Canadian

Women Writers Series. Gen. ed. Lorraine McMullen. Ottawa: Tecumseh P, 1993.

Roediger, David. 'Introduction: From the Social Construction of Race to the Abolition of Whiteness.' *Critical Race Theory: Essays on the Social Construction and Reproduction of Race.* Ed. Nathaniel E. Gates. New York and London: Garland, 1997. 1–17.

– *The Wages of Whiteness.* London: Verso, 1991.

Rosen, David. 'The Volcano and the Cathedral: Muscular Christianity and the Origins of Primal Manliness.' *Muscular Christianity: Embodying the Victorian Age.* Ed. Donald Hall. Cambridge: Cambridge UP, 1994. 17–44.

Ross, Sinclair. *As for Me and My House.* 1941. Toronto: M&S, 1993.

Rotundo, E. Anthony. 'Learning about Manhood: Gender Ideals and the Middle-Class Family in Nineteenth-Century America.' In Mangan and Walvin, eds. 35–51.

Roy, Anindyo. 'Introduction 'Subject to Civility': The Story of the Indian Baboo.' In 'Civility and the Pleasures of Colonialism.' Ed. Anindyo Roy. Special issue, *Colby Quarterly* 37.2 (June 2001): 113–24.

Satzewich, Vic. 'Introduction.' *Racism and Social Inequality in Canada: Concepts, Controversies and Strategies of Resistance.* Ed. Vic Satzewich. Toronto: Thompson Educational, 1998. 11–24.

– 'Race, Racism and Racialization: Contested Concepts.' *Racism and Social Inequality in Canada: Concepts, Controversies and Strategies of Resistance.* Ed. Vic Satzewich. Toronto: Thompson Educational, 1998. 25–45.

Sedgwick, Eve Kosofsky. *Between Men: English Literature and Male Homosocial Desire.* New York: Columbia UP, 1985.

Sharman, Vincent. 'Thomas McCulloch's Stepsure: The Relentless Presbyterian.' *Dalhousie Review* 52 (1972–3): 618–25.

Shrive, Norman. *The Voice of the Burdash: Charles Mair and the Divided Mind in Canadian Literature.* London, ON: Canadian Poetry P, 1995.

Silbiger, Helen. 'Letter to the Editor.' *Toronto Star,* 23 May 2003, A27.

Smith, A.J.M. 'Nationalism and Canadian Poetry.' *Northern Review* 1.1 (December 1944–January 1945): 33–42.

– 'Wanted – Canadian Criticism.' 1928. In Daymond and Monkman, eds. 1: 221–4.

Smith, Goldwin. 'Loyalty.' *Loyalty, Aristocracy, and Jingoism: Three Lectures Delivered before the Young Men's Liberal Club, Toronto.* 2nd ed. Toronto: Hunter, Rose Co., 1896. 9–34.

Smyth, Donna E. 'Raddall's Desiring Machine: Narrative Strategies in the Historical Fiction.' *Time and Place: The Life and Works of Thomas H. Raddall.* Ed. Alan R. Young. Fredericton: Acadiensis P, 1991. 60–86.

Spanos, Chris. 'Canadian Bullets, Dead Iraqis.' *Znet Blogs*, 8 September 2004. Available at: http://blog.zmag.org/index.php/weblog/entry/canadian_bullets_dead_iraqis/. Viewed 14 April 2005.

Springhall, John. 'Building Character in the British Boy: The Attempt to Extend Christian Manliness to Working-Class Adolescents, 1880–1914.' In Mangan and Walvin, eds. 52–74.

Stacey, Robert David. 'Romance, Pastoral Romance, and the Nation in History: William Kirby's *The Golden Dog* and Philippe-Joseph Aubert de Gaspé's *Les Anciens Canadiens*.' In Blair et al., eds. 91–116.

Staines, David. 'Mapping the Terrain.' *Mosaic* 11 (Spring 1978): 137–51.

Stasiulis, Daiva, and Radha Jhappan. 'The Fractious Politics of a Settler Society: Canada.' In Stasiulis and Yuval-Davis, eds. 95–131.

– Stasiulis, Daiva, and Nira Yuval-Davis. 'Introduction: Beyond Dichotomies – Gender, Race, Ethnicity and Class in Settler Societies.' In Stasiulis and Yuval-Davis, eds. 1–38.

– eds. *Unsettling Settler Societies: Articulations of Gender, Race, Ethnicity and Class*. Sage Series on Race and Ethnic Relations, vol. 11. London: Sage, 1995.

Stead, Robert J.C. *Grain*. 1926. Toronto: M&S, 1993.

– *The Homesteaders*. 1916. Toronto: U of Toronto P, 1973.

Stephens, Donald. 'Editor's Introduction.' *The Canadian Brothers; or, The Prophecy Fulfilled. A Tale of the Late American War*. By John Richardson. 1840. CEECT ed. Ottawa: Carleton UP, 1992. xvii–lxxxii.

Stewart, George, Jr. 'Letters in Canada.' In Ballstadt, ed. 163–8.

Stewart, Ian. 'New Myths for Old: The Loyalists and Maritime Political Culture.' *Journal of Canadian Studies* 25.2 (Summer 1990): 20–43.

Stouck, David. 'The Reception of *As for Me and My House*.' In Stouck, ed. 3–8.

– ed. *Sinclair Ross's* As for Me and My House: *Five Decades of Criticism*. Toronto: U of Toronto P, 1991.

Strong-Boag, Veronica. 'Canadian Feminism in the 1920s: The Case of Nellie McClung.' *The Prairie West: Historical Readings*. Ed. R. Douglas Francis and Howard Palmer. Edmonton: Pica Pica P, 1985. 466–80.

– '"Ever a Crusader": Nellie McClung, First-Wave Feminist.' *Rethinking Canada: The Promise of Women's History*. Ed. Veronica Strong-Boag and Anita Clair Fellman. 2nd ed. Toronto: Copp Clark Pitman, 1991. 308–21.

– and Carole Gerson. *Paddling Her Own Canoe: The Times and Texts of E. Pauline Johnson (Tekahionwake)*. Toronto: U of Toronto P, 2000.

– Sherill Grace, Avigail Eisenberg, and Joan Anderson. *Painting the Maple: Essays on Race, Gender, and the Construction of Canada*. Vancouver: UBC P, 1998.

Sutherland, Ronald. 'The Fourth Separatism.' *Canadian Literature* 45 (Summer 1970): 7–23.

Swyripa, Frances. *Ukrainian Canadians: A Survey of Their Portrayal in English-Language Works*. Edmonton: U of Alberta P, 1978.

Szeman, Imre. 'Belated or Isochronic? Canadian Writing, Time, and Globalization.' In 'Where Is Here Now?' Special millennium issue, *ECW* 71 (Fall 2000): 186–94.

Tait, Michael. 'Playwrights in a Vacuum: English-Canadian Drama in the Nineteenth Century.' *Canadian Literature* 16 (Spring 1963): 5–18.

Tausky, Thomas E. '"It Is the Very Life of Our People": The Audiences of *The Imperialist*.' In Tausky, ed. 466–82.

– 'The Writing of *The Imperialist*.' In Tausky, ed. 324–43.

– ed. *The Imperialist*. By Sarah Jeannette Duncan. Canadian Critical Ed. Ottawa: Tecumseh P, 1996.

Taylor, Charles. 'The Politics of Recognition.' *New Contexts of Canadian Criticism*. Ed. Ajay Heble et al., Peterborough: Broadview, 1997. 98–131.

Teskey, Gordon. *Allegory and Violence*. Ithaca, NY: Cornell UP, 1996.

Thacker, Robert. 'Foreigner: The Immigrant Voice in *The Sacrifice* and *Under the Ribs of Death*.' *Canadian Ethnic Studies* 14.1 (1982): 25–35.

Thomas, Clara. 'Canadian Social Mythologies in *The Imperialist*.' In Tausky, ed. 356–68. (Condensed from *Journal of Canadian Studies* 12.2 (1977): 38–49).

Thompson, Eric. 'Robert Stead and His Works.' *Canadian Writers and Their Works*. Fiction Series, vol. 3. Ed. Robert Lecker, Jack David, and Ellen Quigley. Toronto: ECW, 1988. 213–76.

Thompson, J. Lee, and John H. Thompson. 'Ralph Connor and the Canadian Identity.' *Queen's Quarterly* 79 (1972): 159–70.

Tranquilla, Ronald. 'Ranger and Mountie: Myths of National Identity in Zane Grey's *The Lone Star Ranger* and Ralph Connor's *Corporal Cameron*.' *Journal of Popular Culture* 24.3 (Winter 1990): 69–80.

Trevor-Roper, Hugh. 'The Invention of Tradition: The Highland Tradition of Scotland.' *The Invention of Tradition*. Ed. Eric Hobsbawm and Terence Ranger. Cambridge and London: Cambridge UP, 1983. 15–41.

Trumpener, Katie. *Bardic Nationalism: The Romantic Novel and the British Empire*. Princeton: Princeton UP, 1997.

Turcotte, Gerry. '"Generous, Refined, and Most Self-Denying Fiends": Naming the Abomination in James De Mille's *Strange Manuscript*.' *Seriously Weird: Papers on the Grotesque*. Ed. Alice Mills. New York: Peter Lang, 1999. 77–88.

Valverde, Mariana. *The Age of Light, Soap, and Water: Moral Reform in English Canada, 1885–1925*. Toronto: M&S, 1991.

Van Kirk, Sylvia. *'Many Tender Ties': Women in Fur-Trade Society, 1670–1870*. Winnipeg: Watson and Dwyer, 1980.

Vance, Norman. *Sinews of the Spirit: The Ideal of Christian Manliness in Victorian Literature and Religious Thought*. Cambridge: Cambridge UP, 1985.

Varma, Prem. 'Robert Stead: An Annotated Bibliography.' *ECW* 17 (Spring 1980): 141–204.

Venema, Kathleen. 'Letitia Mactavish Hargrave and Hudson's Bay Company Domestic Politics: Negotiating Kinship in Letters from the Canadian Northwest.' In Blair et al., eds. 145–71.

Verduyn, Christl. 'Reconstructing Canadian Literature: The Role of Race and Gender.' In Strong-Boag et al., eds. 100–12.

Vipond, Mary. 'Best Sellers in English Canada, 1899–1918: An Overview.' *Journal of Canadian Fiction* 24 (1979): 96–119.

– 'Best Sellers in English Canada: 1919–1928.' *Journal of Canadian Fiction* 35–6 (1986): 73–106.

Viswanathan, Gauri. *Masks of Conquest: Literary Study and British Rule in India.* New York: Columbia UP, 1989.

Walker, George W. St. G. *The Black Loyalists: The Search for a Promised Land in Nova Scotia and Sierra Leone, 1783–1870.* New York: Africana Publishing, 1976.

Wander, Philip C., Judith N. Martin, and Thomas K. Nakayama. 'Whiteness and Beyond: Sociohistorical Foundations of Whiteness and Contemporary Challenges.' In Nakayama and Martin, eds. 13–26.

Ward, Peter W. *White Canada Forever: Popular Attitudes and Public Policy towards Orientals in British Columbia.* 3rd ed. Montreal and Kingston: McGill-Queen's UP, 2002.

Warkentin, Germaine, and Heather Murray. 'Introduction: Reading the Discourse of Early Canada.' In 'Discourse in Early Canada.' Special issue, *Canadian Literature* 131 (Winter 1991): 7–13.

Warne, Randi R. *Literature as Pulpit: The Christian Social Activism of Nellie L. McClung.* Waterloo: Canadian Corporation for Studies in Religion/Wilfrid Laurier UP, 1993.

Waterston, Elizabeth. *Rapt in Plaid: Canadian Literature and Scottish Tradition.* Toronto: U of Toronto P, 2001.

Watt, Frank W. 'Western Myth: The World of Ralph Connor.' *Writers of the Prairies.* Ed. Donald G. Stephens. Vancouver: UBC P, 1973. 7–16.

Watters, Reginald E. 'Introduction.' *Strange Manuscript Found in a Copper Cylinder.* By James De Mille. New Canadian Library. Toronto: M&S, 1969. vii–xviii.

Wee, C.J.W.-L. 'Christian Manliness and National Identity: The Problematic Construction of the Racially "Pure" Nation.' *Muscular Christianity: Embodying the Victorian Age.* Ed. Donald Hall. Cambridge: Cambridge UP, 1994. 66–88.

Weir, Lorraine. 'The Discourse of "Civility": Strategies of Containment in Literary Histories of English Canadian Literature.' *Problems of Literary Reception / Problèmes de reception littéraire.* Ed. E.D. Blodgett and A.G. Purdy. Edmonton: Research Institute for Comparative Literature, U of Alberta, 1988. 24–39.

West, Cornell. 'A Genealogy of Modern Racism.' 1982. *Race Critical Theories*. Ed. Philemena Essed and David Theo Goldberg. New York: Oxford UP, 2002. 90–112.

Whitelaw, Marjorie. 'Thomas McCulloch.' *Canadian Literature* 68–9 (Spring–Summer 1976): 138–47.

Williams, Michael, ed. 'Scottish Influences in Canadian Literature: A Selection of Papers Delivered at the University of Edinburgh, May 9–12, 1991.' Special issue, *British Journal of Canadian Studies* 7.1 (1992).

Wilson, Kenneth C. 'The Nutty Professor: or, James De Mille in the Fun House.' *ECW* 48 (Winter 1992–3): 128–49.

Winks, Robin W. *The Blacks in Canada: A History*. 2nd ed. Montreal and Kingston: McGill-Queen's UP, 1997.

– 'Introduction.' *The Sky Pilot: A Tale of the Foothills*. By Ralph Connor. 1899. Lexington: UP of Kentucky, 1970. v–x.

Wood, Susan. 'Glengarry and Péribonka.' *The Land in Canadian Prose, 1840–1950*. Ottawa: Carleton Monographs, 1988. 129–47.

Woodcock, George. 'De Mille and the Utopian Vision.' *The Canadian Novel: Beginnings*. Vol. 2. Ed. John Moss. Toronto: New Canada Publ, 1980. 99–110. (First published in *Journal of Canadian Fiction* 2.3 (1973): 174–9.)

– *Introducing Hugh MacLennan's Barometer Rising*. Toronto: ECW P, 1989.

– 'Introduction.' *Canadian Writers and Their Works*. Fiction Series, vol. 3. Ed. Robert Lecker, Jack David, and Ellen Quigley. Toronto: ECW, 1988. 7–19.

Woodsworth, J.S. *Strangers within Our Gates, or Coming Canadians*. 1909. Toronto: U of Toronto P, 1972.

Young, Alan R. 'Thomas H. Raddall.' *Canadian Writers and Their Works*. Fiction Series, vol. 5. Ed. Robert Lecker, Jack David, and Ellen Quigley. Toronto: ECW, 1990. 215–57.

Young, Robert J.C. 'Hybridism and the Ethnicity of the English.' *Cultural Readings of Imperialism: Edward Said and the Gravity of History*. Ed. Keith Ansell Pearson, Benita Parry, and Judith Squires. New York: St. Martin's Press, 1997. 127–50.

Žižek, Slavoj. *The Fragile Absolute – or, Why Is the Christian Legacy Worth Fighting For?* London and New York: Verso, 2000.

Illustration Credits

Index

Note: Page numbers in italics indicate an illustration.